A Guide to Eigl

A Guide to Eighteenth-Century Art

Linda Walsh

WILEY Blackwell

This edition first published 2017

Registered Office
John Wiley & Sons, Ltd, The Atrium, Southern Gate, Chichester, West Sussex, PO19 8SQ, UK

Editorial Offices
350 Main Street, Malden, MA 02148-5020, USA
9600 Garsington Road, Oxford, OX4 2DQ, UK
The Atrium, Southern Gate, Chichester, West Sussex, PO19 8SQ, UK

For details of our global editorial offices, for customer services, and for information about how to apply for permission to reuse the copyright material in this book please see our website at www.wiley.com/wiley-blackwell.

Library of Congress Cataloging-in-Publication Data

Names: Walsh, Linda, author.
Title: A guide to eighteenth-century art / By Linda Walsh.
Description: Hoboken : John Wiley & Sons, Inc., 2016. | Includes bibliographical references and index.
Identifiers: LCCN 2016006830 (print) | LCCN 2016008504 (ebook) | ISBN 9781118475577 (cloth) | ISBN 9781118475515 (pbk.) | ISBN 9781118475591 (pdf) | ISBN 9781118475553 (epub)
Subjects: LCSH: Art, European–18th century–Study and teaching. | Art, European–Historiography.
Classification: LCC N6756 .W35 2016 (print) | LCC N6756 (ebook) | DDC 709.409/033–dc23
LC record available at http://lccn.loc.gov/2016006830

A catalogue record for this book is available from the British Library.

Cover image: "The Scullery Maid" (1738) by Jean-Baptiste Simeon Chardin

Set in 10/12.5pt Galliard by SPi Global, Pondicherry, India
Printed and bound in Malaysia by Vivar Printing Sdn Bhd

1 2017

Contents

List of Figures

Acknowledgments

A survey book of this kind builds necessarily on the work of a wide network of scholars in the field, including those gallery curators who have done so much in recent years to keep eighteenth-century art in the public eye. I am grateful to all scholars who have worked so hard to deepen and extend knowledge of eighteenth-century art, including those whose work is referenced in this publication. I would like to thank in particular those anonymous reviewers who commented on early proposals and outlines of this book: their views helped to determine its shape and scope. I am greatly indebted to William Vaughan and John Bonehill for their detailed and helpful comments on early drafts. They spotted some errors and significant omissions as well as pointing me in helpful directions – any remaining errors are my own. The following were helpful in offering general support, practical help and suggestions, both for the book and for its companion website: Camilla Jordan, Catherine King, Jason Gaiger, Hannah Lavery and Clare Taylor. Librarians at the Open University, the British Library and the University of Leeds were of great assistance. I would also like to thank the team at Wiley-Blackwell for their professionalism and support, which made a difficult project seem more approachable; in particular the advice and feedback offered by Jayne Fargnoli, Mary Hall, Julia Kirk, Camille Bramall, Nivetha Udayakumar, Emily Corkhill and Caroline Hensman. Finally I would like to thank Brian, whose constant encouragement made all the difference.

Companion Website

Please visit the companion website at www.wiley.com/go/walsh/guidetoeighteenthcenturyart to view additional content for this title.

Freely available

- Links to further art resources and museums.
- Three online-only chapters on eighteenth-century art in Japan, China, and India.

Available to instructors only

- Quizzes and topics for discussion for Chapters 1–5 with suggested answers.
- Quizzes and topics for discussion for the three online-only chapters with suggested answers.

Introduction

Style, Society, Modernity

The Question of Style

This book offers guidance on how to study eighteenth-century art, rather than a survey of the prominent artists of that time. Approaches to this subject have changed radically since the 1970s. Since the Renaissance, favored methods of studying art included biographical surveys of the "complete works" of a recognized canon of artists; a tendency to discuss art-historical periods in terms of stylistic trends and developments; or connoisseurial analysis of the styles of different artists, partially with a view to accurate attribution. Scholarly texts, such as Michael Levey's 1966 work *From Rococo to Revolution: Major Trends in Eighteenth-Century Painting* (Levey, 1966), or Mary Webster's 1978 *Hogarth* (Webster, 1978), remain invaluable sources of knowledge and critical discussion; are still extremely useful for beginners; and continue to inform more recent art-historical writing.

A shift in methodologies occurred, however, with the growing significance of new fields of knowledge, including sociology and psychology, that stressed the relationship of artistic production, or of an individual creative mind, to broader social and cultural developments, values and concerns. This has involved a much greater emphasis on the role of audiences and publics in determining the nature of art as well as on the issues of class, economics, institutions and politics that shaped their taste. The 1994 (fifth) edition of Ellis Waterhouse's *Painting in Britain 1530–1790* includes an Introduction by Michael Kitson (Kitson, 1994, xi–xxvii) that illuminates with great clarity this shift of focus within art history, from the study of the careers and stylistic achievements of individual artists

A Guide to Eighteenth-Century Art, First Edition. Linda Walsh.

Companion website: www.wiley.com/go/walsh/guidetoeighteenthcenturyart

(Waterhouse's book, first published in 1953, contains separate chapters on Reynolds, Hogarth, Gainsborough and Wright of Derby, among others); to methods of analysis derived from linguistics and literary theory of the visual language artists deployed; to a focus on the influence of the broader social, political, institutional, educational, cultural and ideological contexts in which they worked. The current book seeks to illuminate eighteenth-century art through the prism of these wider considerations, while remaining indebted to earlier surveys and approaches.

In earlier histories of eighteenth-century art, the most significant narrative concerning style is the rococo's early dominance giving way, from the 1760s, to a preference for neoclassicism. It is now accepted that the style labels often applied to histories of eighteenth-century art did not have currency at the time. "Rococo" (derived from *rocaille*, relating to the shell work found in fantasy grottos) was a late-eighteenth-century term implying excessively convoluted and eye-distracting forms. The tendency to view art history as a sequence of style labels embedded in unifying grand narratives about art, cohesive bodies of works or neat linear, autonomous aesthetic developments, has been exposed as a means of obscuring the more fundamental social and economic causes of cultural change (Rosenblum, 1967, vii–viii, 4; Craske, 1997, 8, 246–247). Such narratives also gloss over the uneven nature of artistic change across different nations. Centralizing powers in Britain, France and Spain (the Georgian and Bourbon monarchies) oversaw relatively unified artistic cultures. However, the more diverse governments of Central and Eastern Europe, including the Habsburg Empire, whose territories were run with varying amounts of autonomy by a range of electors and princes, were associated with more pluralistic patterns of patronage and stylistic development (Kaufman, 1995, 342–379).

The rococo was implicated in its own time in the demise or pollution of grand history painting and in creating tensions between the different orders (classes) of society who vied for the status its affluence conferred (see Chapter 2). Its style and subject matter constituted an assault on the imagination and an explicit evocation of physical sensation. The rococo style was characterized in interior décor by white panels, gilded frames and cartouches, and abundant decorative plaster work; shiny satins, brocades, silks and flocked wallpapers, some imported from China and the Far East; and sparkling mirrors decorated with C-scroll, palm and ribbon motifs. In painting it was characterized by extensive use of pastel shades, flesh tints and "S" shaped curves derived from shells, rocks and plants; and in sculpture by an emphasis on graceful flowing curves, asymmetry and decorative detail, for example, the ribbons and *putti* often embedded in pedestals (Scott, 1995, 1–5). Grander schemes might involve large-scale mural *trompe l'oeil* (literally "deceiving the eye" or powerfully illusory) representations of buildings, arches and ruins, such as those for which Italian artists were often commissioned in the first half of the century.

The influence of the style spread across the courts of Europe, and through affluent owners of private mansions. It permeated the stylistic vocabulary of all genres, embracing genre subjects, portraits and even religious paintings (Tarabra, 2006, 328–331), as well as mythological ("history") subjects. François Boucher (1703–1770) and even the allegedly xenophobic William Hogarth (1697–1764) were among its main practitioners (Simon, 2007, 56, 170). Its influence spread to those nations wishing to emulate the latest French fashions including those, like England, where anti-Gallic feelings existed alongside the desire to keep up with foreign competition (Colley, 1984, 10–17; Victoria and Albert Museum, 1984). In part its influence was so pervasive because it relied, like the fashion for neoclassicism that succeeded it, on a unity of effect throughout all aspects of a room's décor, even if that "unity" resulted from the complex diversity of a range of commercial, industrial and technological processes used in the production of rococo goods (Scott, 1995, 6). The style was above all an exemplar of the "decorative" defined in the 1762 Dictionary of the French Academy (cited by Scott, 1995, 7) as embellishment arising from the deployment of ornament on and in a building.

According to traditional art-historical narratives, negative reactions to "gallant mythologies" and the dominance of decorative art spread more widely, especially with the unfolding of the historical and cultural movement known as the Enlightenment, which placed emphasis on reason, knowledge, moral and social progress. In the art world this led by the 1750s and 1760s to a revival of interest in classical culture subsequently identified as neoclassicism. The aim in neoclassical art was to reassert the gravitas of antiquity through reference to its themes, narratives, costumes and architectural motifs. Some artists achieved this by returning to a more simplified, austere, linear style derived from ancient friezes; compositional austerity and a minimal use of ornament; and "still" figures in heroic and dignified poses and restrained draperies that hugged the body (Rosenblum, 1967, 5). These tendencies later reached their dramatic and radical conclusion in the art of Jacques-Louis David (1748–1825). The term "neoclassical" was a Victorian invention (Coltman, 2006, 1–2). It was uttered in a derogatory spirit and at time when artists and critics viewed the past with an ill-disguised condescension that served their own claims to a regenerative "modernity." The retrospective invention of the term was motivated by a critical response to what was perceived as a reactionary "re warming" of an old aesthetic based on uncritical copying of the styles and subjects of ancient Greek and Roman art. In the eighteenth century the term "true style" was more common when referring to the neoclassical style of painting later developed by David and his followers. However, neoclassicism was characterized by stylistic pluralism, ranging from the austere to the sensual and the decorative (Coltman, 2006, 7–8). It has been described recently as a "frame of mind" or "style of thought" rather than a specific combination of formal elements (Coltman, 2006, 7, 11) (see Chapter 2). In this respect, it is ill-fitted to sum up a coherent or progressive narrative of style.

Within eighteenth-century art, both "baroque" and "classic" styles gained acceptance throughout the century, the former often "corrupted" into the rococo in the early part of the century and subject to eclectic treatments in the middle decades; the latter common in the late-century, pronounced linear clarity of David's neoclassicism, the sculptor and draughtsman John Flaxman (1755–1826) and others. The terms "classic" and "baroque" derive from the broad classification of styles as outlined in the *Principles of Art History* (first published in German in 1915) by Heinrich Wölfflin (1864–1945). Each of Wölfflin's style categories may be applied across a broad chronological range. The style label "baroque" may be applied not only to many works in the "Baroque" period of the late sixteenth and seventeenth centuries, but also to works from other periods. Wölfflin characterized the baroque style as consisting of freer, loose brushwork, contrasts of light and shade, dramatic suggestions of diagonal movement and uncertain arrangements of space. The style often incorporated an exuberant abundance of detail. The art of Rubens offers a common example of such tendencies. Wölfflin characterized the "classic" as a combination of a more stable, planimetric composition (i.e. based on a grid of clearly defined horizontal and vertical planes) and an emphasis on line (e.g. clearly outlined figures and buildings) rather than mass: Raphael and Poussin might serve as examples here (Wölfflin, 1950, 14–16). In reality of course, many paintings of the eighteenth and other centuries were more complex stylistically than this duality suggests.

Modernity and the Public Sphere

Opinions vary on the compliance of eighteenth-century art with our own recent conceptions of "modernity." Social hierarchies, significant due to the continuing dominance of aristocratic patronage and taste; and hierarchies of artistic genres, which placed grand history painting at the top, landscape and still life at the bottom, are often considered to have inhibited any impulse toward modernity, since they generally engineered the stabilization, rather than evolution, of cultural life. The European Enlightenment, a cultural movement that began in the seventeenth century but peaked in the middle to late decades of the eighteenth, included a compulsion to construct taxonomies and classifications in all fields of knowledge and creativity, and to create encyclopedias and dictionaries. The latter are often credited with "fixing" culture, although in fact such initiatives were linked at the time with ambitions to disseminate and advance knowledge. The Enlightenment's preoccupation with ordering and clarifying is seen as "holding back" the dramatic breakthroughs in stylistic innovation and individual creative freedom with which, for example, the Romantics and Modernists of the nineteenth and early twentieth centuries have become associated (Wrigley, 1993, 313, 353).

Eighteenth-century artists are often seen as being closely directed by the guilds (in the case of the "mechanical," industrial or decorative arts) or (in the case of the "high" liberal arts of painting and sculpture) prestigious royal academies concerned with the glory of state or monarch. The continuation of slavery, imperialism, religious persecution, the massive movement in land enclosures, the persistence of absolutist monarchies in many countries and of aristocratic government in all, are among those eighteenth-century phenomena seen to indicate a resistance to liberty or liberation of any kind. Canonical art from the century continued to pay homage to antique Greek and Roman history and mythology, even if the stylistic treatment of these subjects varied.

Seen from other perspectives, the century is viewed as the time when progressive Enlightenment ideals such as liberty, progress and a critical attitude to authority; rapid urbanization (especially in Britain and France and, later, Germany); and cosmopolitanism allowed new markets for art to challenge the power of older hierarchies at court and artistic academies (Craske, 1997, 11). Although classical influences remained central, the Enlightenment's emphasis on scientific method or direct observation of nature ("empiricism") was increasingly important, particularly in genres other than history painting. "Modernity" is not after all a "simple, agreed upon" concept (Said, 2003 [1978], xiv). The following outlines some of the varied meanings and complexities of the term as applied to the history of eighteenth-century art.

The Enlightenment is often regarded as a progressive influence in social, educational and political terms. It was subject to national variants. In France, for example, there was a much deeper dissatisfaction with the status quo in institutions of government (the Bourbon monarchy, also powerful in Spain) and religion (the Catholic Church), and a focus on the formulation by a largely aristocratic class of writers of new, abstract ideals relating to liberty and justice. In Britain, where a more tolerant church and a constitutional (Georgian) monarchy facilitated more open discussion of issues by writers from a broader range of social backgrounds, there was often a marked concern with more practical issues of reform. The term "the Enlightenment" has, nevertheless, a broad currency. It is sometimes defined as a chronological period, but is also used to describe a widespread reaction, in many European countries, against prejudice and ignorance (Porter, 2000, 48), and a belief in progress. Thinkers such as John Locke (1632–1704) and Isaac Newton (1643–1727) stressed the importance of knowledge gained through independent reasoning and direct experience:

> ...God had surely given men powers sufficient to discharge their earthly offices. Herein lay the enormous appeal of Locke's image of the philosopher as "an Under-Labourer in clearing Ground a little, and in removing some of the Rubbish, that lies in the way to Knowledge", so as to beat a path for the true "master-builders".... (Porter, 2000, 60)

The Enlightenment opened up new ways of seeing and thinking, with many of its faithful consciously seeking their own version of "modernity," forms of knowledge and creativity that relied less on past models and sources of authority and patronage such as royal courts and the Catholic Church, and sought to emulate rather than copy the art of classical antiquity (Porter, 2000, 3–4, 32–33, 47, 52). Nevertheless, certain ingrained hierarchies of value persisted, with classical civilization in particular providing a constant touchstone of value and achievement.

Another familiar narrative concerning eighteenth-century cultural change is that it represented a shift from Enlightenment rationalism, scientific method, objectivity and classicism to Romanticism, with its greater emphasis on subjectivity, feeling, originality, rule-breaking and fantasy. There is some truth in this (Pagden, 2013, 1–18). By the early nineteenth century "Romantic" values were in the ascendant in much European culture. As with style labels, however, these cultural dualities often disintegrate when faced with actual examples of artistic production. Many "Enlightenment" artists sought to be original, exercise their imagination and express the feelings of those they represented or arouse those of their viewers, while many "Romantics" adhered to the Enlightenment values of empirical research, first-hand observation of nature and classicism (Walsh and Lentin, 2004a and 2004b). There was no style of painting unique to or distinctive of either the Enlightenment (Kaufman, 1995, 455) or of Romanticism; nor any consistent differentiation of the stylistic trends of each movement, even if certain "family resemblances" may be discerned. Arguably, however, both movements contributed to our own understanding of modernity: the first through its dedication to intellectual critique and reasoned principle; the second in its attention to the less controllable workings of the individual mind.

Much art-historical debate on eighteenth-century art in Europe has focused on British and French art, and this is often the case in the present study. In defense of such a bias it is common to cite the pervasive influence of French language, manners and culture in "cultivated" European courts such as those in Berlin, Madrid, St Petersburg and Sweden (Brewer, 1997, 84; Craske, 1997, 19–21; Tite, 2013a, 5; Tite, 2013b, 36–45; Weichsel, 2013, 70–71). Such developments did not go unchallenged, however. Johann Gottfried Herder (1744–1803), advocate of a distinctively German Gothic tradition, as opposed to the cosmopolitan classicism that held sway, was among those thinkers who felt that distinctive national languages and cultures were necessary, since they represented a *Zeitgeist* that resisted easy translation (Gaiger, 2002, 4–5; Barnard, 2003, 6, 38–40). Royally sponsored academies of art in Paris (founded in 1648) and London (1768) served as models for academies established in many other European cities, the French Académie royale de peinture et de sculpture (Royal Academy of Painting and Sculpture, referred to henceforth as Académie royale) spreading its influence to Rome through its annexe at the French Academy there. Rome also served as a meeting point for artists from all over Europe, thus emphasizing the cosmopolitan nature of many developments in eighteenth-century art, especially neoclassicism. In Italy more broadly, French manners and culture served as a model for those wishing to stake a claim to "modern" sophistication (Pasta, 2005, 209).

Royal courts such as those in Madrid, London and Vienna welcomed artists from other countries, thus helping to disperse trends and influences (Tite, 2013a, 6). The Georgian court in Britain initially favored portrait artists from northern Europe and decorative artists from Italy; the court and Royal Academy in Madrid favored French and Italian artists in the early part of the century. The art of Francisco Goya y Lucientes (1746–1828) was, for example, influenced by the work of other nations' artists whose work he had seen and by cosmopolitan Enlightenment ideals, to which his art is not, however, reducible (Pérez-Sanchez, 1989, xvii–xxv; Luxenberg, 1997, 39–64). In all European courts open to the influence of Enlightenment writers and thinkers, there was a competitive attitude toward keeping up with the vanguard of knowledge. Joshua Reynolds (1723–1792) was a member of societies that brought him into contact with major writers such as Samuel Johnson (1709–84), and Goya frequented circles where he met leading financiers, lawyers, collectors and enlightened social and political reformists. At the same time, in the second half of the century, European nations began to aspire to France's achievements by establishing or encouraging their own national schools of artists.

Scholarly assessments of the relative "modernity" of eighteenth-century art have proceeded beyond ill-defined notions of openness to change or the progressive, to consider more historically specific factors. Central to any progression toward modernity in this period was the development of a new bourgeois "public" as theorized and described by Jürgen Habermas (born 1929) in his 1962 work *The Structural Transformation of the Public Sphere: An Inquiry into a Category of Bourgeois Society* (*Strukturwandel der Öffenlicheit*). This new social grouping gained in numbers and confidence throughout the eighteenth century so that it generated a corpus of critical opinion in cultural affairs located between previously dominant autocratic royal courts, and the realm of private life, as evident, for example, in family life, sociable discussion and private property ownership. An expanding class of professional people merged with or aspired to the lifestyle of the feudal nobility. Encouraged by greater freedom of the press, increasingly popular urban forms of sociability such as the coffee house, tea drinking, the salon (an informal club or private gathering for the educated and culturally aware), learned societies and art markets that offered alternatives to traditional forms of patronage, this section of society was able to assert its taste and opinions in the name of a new form of "civil," "elegant," "polite" or "good" society (Habermas, 1992 [1962], xi–40). Having rehearsed its cultural expertise in the private domain of the family, it achieved the status of a self-empowered audience:

> The bourgeois public sphere may be conceived above all as the sphere of private people come together as a public; they soon claimed the public sphere regulated from above against the public authorities themselves, to engage them in a debate over the general rules governing relations in the basically privatized but publicly relevant sphere of commodity exchange and social labour. (Habermas, 1992, 27)

The role of this new public in facilitating cultural and artistic change has been extensively analyzed in recent decades (Crow, 1985, 1–6; Solkin, 1992, 187, 214; Brewer, 1997, 94–95). It exerted its influence through commerce and trade, helping to create an art market in which culture was consciously transformed into a commodity (Solkin, 1993, 1–2, 30; Bindman, 2008, 16). As an audience it was often self-consciously critical; for example, in requiring (especially from the 1760s) as a "commodity" representations in art of a more sentimental, affective and essentially moralizing view of the ("private") family and, through portraiture, new forms of social identity (Pointon, 2001, 105–106; Ogée and Meslay, 2006, 25–26). Material acquisitiveness united this expanding art-buying public with the aspirations of traditional aristocratic patrons. At times, the strong moral and reformist imperatives of enlightened professional classes united with a more conservative, aristocratic elitism to contest the (potentially vulgar) modern taste for "luxury" in, for example, decorative art (Brewer, 1997, xxi; Terjanian, 2013, 32).

This new public enjoyed wider opportunities to encounter art, as exhibitions multiplied in formal academies, less formal street displays, private collections and dealers' shop windows. The central importance of display and the act of viewing to developments in eighteenth-century art and its reception has recently generated a cluster of art-historical studies that stress the role of exhibition visits in "refining" the sensibilities of eighteenth-century viewers in a way that encouraged further development of the civic humanism inherited from the previous century (Bonehill, 2011, 461–470; Solkin, 1993, 2, 30). As forms of social practice, exhibition visits complemented other forms of sociability, such as conversation, in the formation of "polite" taste. The latter was also nourished by an expanding art press, freely expressing its opinions in those nations, such as Britain, largely unaffected by censorship; and expressing them more covertly but effectively elsewhere (Porter, 2000, 28–31; Selwyn, 2000, 181–184). By such means, there arose discourses of art that validated the opinion of the informed layman and disrupted old continuities of thought. The eighteenth century is often identified with the birth of art criticism as a separate and increasingly professionalized genre of writing (Wrigley, 1993, 1–2).

The concept of "discourse" as theorized by Michel Foucault (1926–1984) may be used to cut across the history of art often conceived in terms of a coherent period, movement or theme, or of the *oeuvre* of an individual artist, in order to highlight the specific historical conditions, rules and strategic options that enabled cultural developments (Foucault, 1969, 317–333; Foucault, 1972 [1969], 3–31). A "discourse" is a signaling system (clusters and repetitions of words or types of vocabulary) in language and communication implicitly encoding power structures in contemporary society and culture. Although Foucault was more concerned with its operations in literature and journalism, in art it may be seen to work through the relations established between the viewer, the objects viewed (visual artifacts, motifs and conventions) and any statements or critical judgments made about them. The systems necessary to disperse discourses (known as "discursive formations") would have included in the eighteenth century the functioning of institutional teaching models and regulations, techniques of analysis and interpretation, such as those to be found in the academies and the art press, and the correlations between all of these (Foucault, 1972 [1969], 3–42). Discourses of art and taste, and the ways in which people spoke, wrote about or represented themselves and others, were generated by the newly established viewing public discussed earlier. Habermas also has much to say on the subject, describing the gradual liberation of artists from the religious institutions, guilds and royal courts as proceeding hand in hand with widespread critique of the arts and the democratization of taste, no longer the exclusive domain of elite *amateurs* and increasingly the concern of lay and professional critics (Habermas, 1992, 40).

"Modernity" in art may also be defined on a simpler level as an impulse toward new styles; for example, the rococo, which was sometimes seen as a sweetened form of the baroque, and was referred to in the eighteenth century as "the modern taste." The rococo style popular in the early part of the century suited the newly rich and their Parisian mansions, while presenting a "modern" alternative to classical austerity (Scott, 1995, 233). German courts acquired a lively taste for this French style, as did the Georgian court in Britain, which was heavily influenced through its Hanoverian origins by German taste (Tite, 2013b, 36; Weichsel, 2013, 55–65). The adoption of new subjects in art, especially where modern or contemporary life is included in these, is also interpreted as the result of a modernizing impulse. The *fêtes galantes* or outdoor party scenes created by Jean-Antoine Watteau (1684–1721) offered new, informal and delicate representations of aristocratic leisure that offered an alternative to more formal royal courtly scenes (Berger, 1999, 206). Closer perhaps to our own more recent conceptions of "modernity" lie Hogarth's satirical prints and painted narrative series, which referred to figures drawn from less elite groups within society and were consciously defined in his own time as "modern moral subjects," openly conceived to provide a new source of income for the artist:

> … a new way of proceeding, viz painting and Engraving *moder[]n moral subject[s]* a Field unbroke up in any Country or any age. (From Hogarth's *Analysis of Beauty*, 1753; cited in Riding, 2006b, 73)

Inspired by empirical observation of modern metropolitan life, series such as *The Rake's Progress* (1733–1735), a visual account of profligacy and ruin, contrasted with grand Catholic paintings from the continent in their reference to the visually familiar. It is perhaps unsurprising that satirical art should be regarded as topical or "modern." But "modern life" also became more prominent through the burgeoning taste for genre painting. Toward the end of the century many history painters tackled more recent or contemporary events and employed more naturalistic, less grandiloquent styles (Solkin, 1993, 223–229). In his portraits Hogarth appealed more directly to an actively engaged public for art by producing more naturalistic representations of sitters than had been common before then and, in his conversation pieces, "natural" family gatherings celebrating their more private relationships (Hallett, 2006a, 16–17, 160, 198; Riding, 2006a, 33; 2006b, 73–75). In a marked inversion of the normal hierarchical order placing the grand classical above the naturalistic, he also applied the moral gravity of history paintings to scenes from everyday life (Webster, 1979, 42–46; Craske, 2000, 30–31).

The work of Hogarth and other innovators might be used to argue that it was only by subverting traditional hierarchies (such as those of genre or class) that modernity could be achieved. In adopting market-responsive practices that undermined from the outside the standards of the Royal Academy of Arts in London (referred to henceforth as the Royal Academy), Hogarth is often cited as an emblem of eighteenth-century modernity. However, much innovation (e.g. relating to genre) occurred within the traditional hierarchies and structures of the artistic establishment:

> Art-historical accounts of eighteenth and nineteenth-century European art have been overwhelmingly disposed to seek out and celebrate innovation. In such progressive narratives, longer-term continuities of art practice and their associated habits of thought are included only as necessary but *retardataire* evil. In the history of French art, this is nowhere more the case than in relation to the hierarchy of genres.... In a purely chronological sense, the hierarchy of genres might seem to provide reliable witness to academic conservatism because it survived the institutions [the academies] which put it into practice. Yet it only endured because it was an extremely flexible framework which was capable of diverse applications. (Wrigley, 1993, 285)

For Foucault, one of the problems with the idea of "modernity" lies in its being defined in opposition to "tradition," since such debates seem to insist on the measuring of innovation against that of continuities, matters of "influence," "development," "evolution" or some other ongoing cultural "spirit" (Foucault, 1972 [1969], 23–24). In fact, the narratives of art history contained even within a single century cover much messier ground. Developments in western art from the 1760s onwards, within the history genre, have been seen as so diverse and transformative that they have been described as "hydra-headed": irreducible to any simple frameworks such as those provided by style labels or unifying narratives of change (Rosenblum, 1967, viii).

It is the intention to highlight in the following chapters, often through sections headed *Questions of modernity*, both the traditional hierarchies (institutional, social and cultural) within which eighteenth-century art was produced and any innovations that took place within and outside them. It is hoped that this will allow the reader to form a critical response to claims concerning the century's (proto) modernity, while at the same time remaining wary of any neat chronological narratives.

Tradition and Modernity in Art Outside Europe

Due to issues of space the main focus in this book is on western art and artists, including the work they produced in relation to colonial contexts, particularly India, North America and the South Pacific. Reference to the art of other cultures is brief. Those interested in more detailed discussion of the work of native artists in eighteenth-century China, Japan and India will however find more on this rapidly evolving area of scholarship in the website accompanying the book, at www.wiley.com/go/walsh/guidetoeighteenthcenturyart.

Eighteenth-century art produced outside Europe is often regarded as clinging to old traditions in a way that did not happen in Europe itself, where challenges to "authority" of all kinds (cultural, moral, social and political) created the first steps toward a proto-modern art world. "Non-western" nations are often seen as resistant to cultural evolution due to perceived essentialist characteristics of race and nation, or to environmental or historical conditions (Mitchell, 1989, 409). Increasingly, however, trade routes and colonialism brought with them cultural interactions with the wider world that benefited "east" and "west" equally. Sometimes, as with western imports of Chinese porcelain or tea-wares, and of Indian textiles, the material objects imported into and eventually copied by European countries rose to a highly fashionable status and were considered the epitome of modern taste. It has been argued that the British "Chinese taste" in tea-drinking, established since the seventeenth century, and in interior décor, influenced broader social practices and gender roles in eighteenth-century Britain (see Chapter 3).

China, Japan and India were among those countries that introduced innovations in the paintings, porcelain and other objects they produced for their own internal markets (Krahl, 2005, 214; Fahr-Becker, 2006, 231–233; Krahl and Harrison-Hall, 2009, 16–17, 80–87). Japanese *ukiyo-e* or "floating world" (a metaphor for "carefree life") prints representing modern life in Tokyo's pleasure district appealed to the expanding urban markets in the country (Tinios, 2010, 8–9). The visual cultures of each of these countries accommodated, if to varying degrees, some artistic autonomy (Stanley-Baker, 2000, 173–178; Murck, 2005, 342; Fahr-Becker, 2006, 213–225; Hongxing, 2013, 45–46). In China scholar-artists well versed in traditional native styles and subjects valued studies of the humanities and were committed to individual creativity. "Eccentric" and "Individualist" artists working at some distance from court-based academies produced highly unconventional works. Western artistic styles and techniques such as one-point perspective became more familiar to each of these nations, if not widely practiced (Mitter, 2001, 123–124; Chongzheng, 2005, 81; Waley-Cohen, 2005, 180–182; Losty and Roy, 2012, 15–18, 155, 187–195; Hongxing, 2013, 49, 310–313). This was particularly so in China where the Jesuit missionary artist Giuseppe Castiglione (1688–1766) rose to the position of Chief Minister of Imperial Parks and worked collaboratively with Chinese artists. Hybrid east–west styles such as the "western brush mode" in China brought together western techniques in suggesting depth and recession with Chinese brushwork (McCausland, 2013, 49–50).

Scholars have challenged crude polarizations of artistic and cultural "progress" (or lack of it) within and outside Europe. Edward Said, Timothy Mitchell, Dipesh Chakrabarty, Partha Mitter and David Porter are among those who see the association of "non-western" nations with backwardness or static tradition as a distorting, retrospective projection of the west's recent political dominance onto an earlier age (Porter, 2010, 4). The common phrase "non-western art" itself may be seen to indicate a tendency to measure all achievement against that of the west and to downplay more positive differences between individual cultures. In such characterizations of the world beyond Europe, all the markers of liberalism and modernity began in the west and spread to other lands: industrialization, capitalism, free-thinking and free-acting citizens, an influential public sphere and the rational, scientific and progressive ways of thinking associated with the European Enlightenment (Mitchell, 1989, 409; Clunas, 1999, 134; Porter, 2010, 4–11). Asian art of the eighteenth century is characterized as "archaic" when it refers back explicitly to its own ancient traditions, or in response to its own cultural and political context (Mitter, 2001, 1), while late-eighteenth-century European neoclassicism, though based on the art of ancient Greece and Rome, is often seen as a force for modernity, political and cultural regeneration (Clunas, 1999, 134–135). The west's incorporation of elements of Chinese and Japanese visual culture has been seen as innovative, whereas the borrowings those Asian countries made from western art have been located in a narrative of belated progress (Clunas, 1999, 136–137).

Some of those who acknowledge differences in the rates of change in artistic cultures within and outside the west point to the inevitability of this given the very different social, political and economic structures involved: conditions were not ripe for industrialization in eighteenth-century China, for example, but this did not constitute a principled objection to modernity (Rawski, 2005, 39–40). China was unifying as a nation after its recent submission to the Manchurians, thus making cultural and political integration a higher priority than the kind of scientific advances, democratic, social and religious reforms prioritized in the western Enlightenment. Others emphasize that western countries had not always set the pace of change. China had developed a sophisticated tradition of painting during the Song dynasty (960–1279 CE), at a time when the "west" was involved in the violence of the crusades. Well ahead of similar (nineteenth-century) developments in Europe, China produced inventive landscape paintings stimulated and validated by its Buddhist traditions of retreat and contemplation, as well as by Daoist and Confucian ideas of nature as an embodiment of human attributes and affairs. Such insights disrupt conventional narratives of a sluggish culture struggling to keep up with the west. Equally, it might be pointed out that prior to the eighteenth century, Chinese trade and interaction with the rest of the world was prolific, in spite of its failure to modernize its political and economic systems. It was unlikely to measure its "progress" in cultural matters by comparison with Britain, which was on the periphery of its trading empire.

It is not possible, of course, to generalize about these west versus "non-west" perspectives, since much depends on individual nations and the ways in which they were governed during the eighteenth century. China is an interesting example because it was never colonized. Those in the west associated it with Orientalist fantasies and actual experience of the country was rare. Many eighteenth-century writers saw it as an example of a society in which philosophy, poetry and all the arts had thrived; it was therefore, at least until the later eighteenth century, a source of envy as much as an emblem of western superiority. Diderot wrote in the article *China* (*Chine*) in the *Encyclopédie* that it was "the most populous and cultivated country in the world." The perceived reasons for China's prosperity included its own positive contributions to traditions of thought and creativity (Porter, 2010, 6).

Eurocentric narratives of art history are challenged increasingly by alternative viewpoints that see the west, and not the east, as different or "other." For example, the tensions arising from the western distinction between fine and mechanical arts (see Chapter 1), have never been of great concern in China. Calligraphy is considered the most important art form there, with painting a close second, in part because the former is seen to share many of the attributes (fine brush work, the study of specific traditions) relevant to the latter. Ceramics, textiles, metalwork, lacquerwork, sculpture, painting and calligraphy are regarded as almost equal in status (Clunas, 1999, 121–122). In western scholarship the discipline of material culture studies has done much to stress the importance of all kinds of artifacts, and not just the fine arts, as agents of social practice and value.

If it remains common in scholarship to judge non-colonized lands on the basis of the relative modernity of their cultures, the main preoccupation with regard to colonized lands and peoples has been with the ways in which the land, peoples and lifestyles of the colonized were represented in western art and (principally) by western artists. It has been stated that the notion of empire (both as political construct and as an ideological framework) is central to any study of art from the middle of the eighteenth century to the middle of the twentieth (Barringer, Quilley and Fordham, 2007, 3, 7). Much post-colonial scholarship has also focused on what colonial art reveals about the anxieties, tensions and evolving identities of the colonizers, since many works of art seem to assume a viewer well acquainted with imperial circumstances and (speculatively) with attitudes shaped by these. There are also increasing attempts to study the indigenous cultures of colonized peoples, as the disciplines of anthropology and art history form creative alliances. There is a greater willingness to consider the artifacts made by native peoples as "art" rather than as "crafts," something more than specimens of archaeological or anthropological investigation. Nevertheless, our post-colonial era continues to focus on black, American Indian, Pacific and Asian peoples as objects of representation, partly as a means of understanding previous constructions of racial identity and the "western" lens through which they were viewed.

France and Britain were the dominant colonial powers in the eighteenth century, with the latter gaining the leading role throughout the century as France became more absorbed by power struggles within Europe. These two countries, along with the Netherlands, had established many colonies, dominions, protectorates and mandate territories throughout the seventeenth century, in addition to trading posts that focused (initially at least) on commerce rather than conquest or rule. The Dutch presence in South Africa fueled the print production and trade in most of Africa (Bindman,

Ford and Weston, 2011, 213). Portugal and Spain already had well-established colonial territories in South America. Struggles among European nations over political or commercial dominance occurred in North America, the Caribbean, Africa, India and the East Indies, with a view to securing lucrative trade in sugar, coffee and tobacco (the Caribbean), furs (Canada), spices (the East Indies) and, most controversially, through trading posts on the west coast of Africa, the acquisition of slave labor exported to the Caribbean to work the sugar and tobacco plantations. The main struggles occurred between France and Britain, and between France and the Netherlands: the accession to the British throne of the Dutch monarch William of Orange (who reigned in Britain 1689–1702) had put an end to previous Anglo-Dutch conflict. Hostilities and the fight for territories resumed as the Netherlands fell to France in 1795 and Britain took over most Dutch colonies.

The race to establish colonial power was linked with conflicts in Europe seeking to assert economic and political dominance through changing alliances. A series of major wars, the War of the Austrian Succession (1740–1748), the Seven Years War (1756–1763) and the American Revolutionary War (1775–1783) and their ensuing treaties, led to a series of changes to the governorship of many colonized lands. Britain became the dominant power in India and, until the American Revolution, which established American independence, in North America, the Caribbean and Canada. As America receded from its grasp, Britain focused on its colonial presence in India, the Pacific and Africa. In 1788, after the discovery by James Cook (1728–1779) in 1770 of the east coast of Australia, Britain also established a penal colony at Botany Bay, where wool and gold were valuable commodities. Trading companies were set up to regulate and effectively abolish domestic commercial competition in overseas trade. The English East India Company (from 1707, following the union with Scotland, the British East India Company) had been established in 1600 by Queen Elizabeth I (reigned 1558–1603) and granted a British monopoly in trade with the east, woolen and silk textiles and spices being the main imported commodities. The Company also became involved in the slave trade. This was followed in 1602 by the establishment of the Dutch East India Company; in 1621 by the Dutch West India Company; and in 1664 by the French East India Company. In the same year the French West India Company was founded and granted the French monopoly on the slave trade between Africa (mainly Senegal) and the West Indies.

These trading companies were massive organizations, often incorporating military forces and complex, hierarchical and administrative structures, that financed the shipment of goods from established trading posts in the colonies. Britain's East India Company established in India, due to aggressive competition from rival colonial powers, military forts and a private army dependent on the recruitment of local troops (sepoys). Naval convoys accompanied its shipments. It gained political influence over an increasing number of Indian provinces, and many Company officers returned to Britain with sufficient wealth to purchase parliamentary seats and prestigious country estates. These "nabobs" were often accused of nepotism, greed and corruption (Quilley, 2011, 148–151). During the nineteenth century inhuman treatment of Indian peoples and heavy financial losses led to the downfall of the Company, and the British government began to rule the subcontinent directly (Robins, 2006, 1–6).

The main source of African slaves shipped across the Atlantic was the west coast of Africa, from the Senegal River to Angola. The British, French, Dutch, Danish and Prussians were all involved in this trade, each having their own trading posts and using middlemen to capture and deliver to European merchants native inhabitants of local villages. The resulting transportation across the Atlantic of slave labor made possible imports to Europe from the Caribbean and other places of coffee, tobacco and sugar. European governments either issued policies supporting the use of slave labor, or encouraged private investors to deal in chattel slavery, in which slaves became the personal property of their owners and were treated as commodities. The growth of urban culture in wealthier European countries encouraged the purchase of slaves from the colonies for domestic service, as more members of the upper middle (professional and commercial) classes sought to copy this aristocratic practice. The laws surrounding this practice were often unclear in Britain and France, where some slaves might be deported back to the colonies against their will, while, in other households, they acquired the same rights and status as white servants. Some took to the streets, becoming entertainers, musicians or beggars. Both plantation-owning and other families sought to purchase black slave-servants. All of these issues inflected eighteenth-century art.

Scope and Structure

The chronological span of the book (1700–1800) may in itself raise questions, since it has become common to speak in terms of a "long" eighteenth century, from the Glorious Revolution of 1688 to 1830, the date of another important Revolution in France and a watershed in Britain with the "Victorian" age. A more modest chronology, covering the actual eighteenth century, was decided on the basis of space and the difficulties of doing justice here to the rich post-Revolutionary and early "Romantic" developments that came later. There are, however, frequent references to art of the seventeenth century, and of earlier periods, where essential to the discussion. As is the nature of basic introductions, the reader will find many artists omitted. It is hoped nevertheless that this book will present analytical concepts and frameworks that may be applied to a range of eighteenth-century artists, institutions and works of art. In-text references are provided to facilitate the search for further information on specific points.

Chapter 1 focuses on issues relating to artistic institutions and the discourses of hierarchy relating to different types of art object. Chapter 2 investigates the complex and shifting allocations of status within the hierarchies of genre or subject matter of art. Chapter 3 focuses on the evolution of a new public for art and the expression of its developing tastes, with reference to the art market, exhibitions, practices of viewing and imperialism. Chapter 4 examines the new critical discourses of taste and art journalism that helped inform this public. Chapter 5 examines ethical issues relating to the production and reception of art, including the debates surrounding luxury, consumerism, Orientalism and the practices of "moral looking."

Further Reading

Blanning, Timothy C.W. 2000. *Eighteenth-Century Europe 1688–1815.* Oxford: Oxford University Press. This book helps to locate the eighteenth century between the "old" world and "modernity." It introduces key aspects of eighteenth-century European history: demographics, politics, economics, the social order, religion, war and empire.

Rudé, George. 1972. *Europe in the Eighteenth Century: Aristocracy and the Bourgeois Challenge.* London: Weidenfeld and Nicolson. An accessible introduction to eighteenth-century European history.

Waterhouse, Ellis. 1994 (fifth edition; first published 1953). *Painting in Britain 1530–1790, with an Introduction by Michael Kitson.* New Haven, CT, and London: Yale University Press.

1

Institutional Hierarchies

Art and Craft

Establishing a Fine Art Tradition: The Spread of Academies

The French *Encyclopedia or Philosophical Dictionary of the Sciences, Arts and Crafts* (*Encyclopédie, ou dictionnaire raisonné des sciences, des arts et des métiers*, hereafter the *Encyclopédie*), published between 1751 and 1772 in 17 volumes of text and 11 of plates, contained articles spanning the full range of human knowledge and activity. The article "Art" was careful to distinguish between on the one hand the liberal arts (also referred to in this period as the "fine" or "beautiful" arts), and on the other the "mechanical" arts such as the manual crafts of glassmaking, weaving or ceramics. From late antiquity, the "liberal arts" had included grammar, rhetoric, dialectic (the debating of different points of view to find reasoned truth), arithmetic, geometry, astronomy and music. In 1746 the Abbé Charles Batteux (1713–1780) had established in his book *The Fine Arts Reduced to a Common Principle* (*Les Beaux-Arts réduits à un même principe*) a tradition of defining as "fine" the arts of poetry, music, painting, sculpture and architecture. Dance, engraving and landscape gardening were also often included in this category, but anything produced primarily for functional, ornamental or decorative purposes; for example, over-door, carriage or fire-screen paintings, was excluded.

Journeyman artists catered for a large market in decorative paintings, textiles and sacred images for homes and churches, and objects of domestic folk art were popular. Many of these have not survived for us to study, but they are valued increasingly highly: the Metropolitan Museum of Art

A Guide to Eighteenth-Century Art, First Edition. Linda Walsh.

Companion website: www.wiley.com/go/walsh/guidetoeighteenthcenturyart

in New York has, for example, some good samples of eighteenth-century needlework. These "jobbing" artists created most of the visual culture known to those living outside cities, museums and palaces. The liberal arts were regarded principally as a product of the mind, the "mechanical" of the hand. An association with laborious physical effort (dirty hands), commerce and mass production had tainted for the intelligentsia the reputation of the mechanical arts. The liberal arts had, by contrast, benefited from their association with the dignity of human intellect. The *Encyclopédie* was in the vanguard of those calling for a change of attitude, and Denis Diderot (1713–1784), author of the article "Art" as well as one of the co-editors of the *Encyclopédie* proclaimed:

> Craftsmen have thought of themselves as contemptible because we have held them in contempt; let us teach them to think better of themselves. (Diderot and d'Alembert, 2013; I:717, my translation)

This heartfelt challenge to prejudice reflects eighteenth-century European concerns with status and hierarchy. These pitted the claims of the intellect and of knowledge (of history, literature, classical and Christian art and culture) against those of manual dexterity; study of the humanities against the messy materials of art; the disinterested artist against the "sordid" seeker of financial gain; and the unique products of genius and the imagination against the mass-produced. Such prejudices were often based on false assumptions and oppositions. "Craft" products could demonstrate originality; fine or liberal artists were often concerned with copying past art and with financial gain. In eighteenth-century Europe, however, theoretical statements crystallized into powerful discourse as they were institutionally strengthened and disseminated. By the end of the century the term "artist" was most closely associated with the liberal or fine arts. Prestigious academies of art, especially those conferred with "royal" status, defined their interests primarily in opposition to those of craftsmen. They were dedicated to the gentrification and professionalization of artists (Hoock, 2003, 2–7).

The physical craft of painting (mixing colors, preparing canvases, basic painting and drawing techniques) and sculpture (carving and casting) were taught traditionally through studio and workshop apprenticeships (Hallett, 2014, 41–42). The artist Henri Testelin (1616–1695), Secretary and Professor at the Académie royale, decried the fact that before the foundation of this Academy, painters and sculptors had sunk to the level of mere church decorators (Duro, 1997, 10–11). In 1685 the writer William Aglionby (*c.*1642–1705) lamented the fact that the British showed so little serious interest in art and treated their artists as "little nobler than Joyners or Carpenters" (cited in Bindman, 2008, 195). In the *Biographical History* (1769) by the biographer, clergyman and print collector James Granger (1723–1776), consisting of engraved portrait heads of famous Englishmen up to and including the Glorious Revolution of 1688, "Painters" are ranked alongside "Artificers" and "Mechanics," and below "Physicians, Poets, and other ingenious Persons" (cited in Pointon, 1993, 56). Artists in England were often ranked socially alongside carpenters, farriers and pin-makers (Brewer, 1997, 290). In Germany Johann Wolfgang von Goethe (1749–1832) admired the neoclassical designs of Flaxman, while deprecating their use in the ceramics produced by Josiah Wedgwood (1730–1795):

> ...the English, with their modern "antique" pottery and wares made of paste, their gaudy black and red art, gather piles of money from all over the globe: but if one is truthful one gets no more out of [this] antiquity than from a porcelain bowl, pretty wallpaper or a pair of shoe buckles. (*Italian Journey* (1786–1788), cited in Brewer, 1997, xxiii)

The massive increase in academies of art throughout the eighteenth century responded to the desire for respectability in occupations that had previously enjoyed a more ambiguous status. In this respect, art underwent a similar process to that of other professionalized activities such as medicine.

The term "academy" had first been applied to informal gatherings of philosophers and scholars held by the ancient Greek philosopher Plato. It was later applied in the early Renaissance to informal gatherings of artists and *amateurs* (those with a serious, scholarly interest in art) held in artists' studios or collectors' homes, sometimes supported by influential patrons such as members of the Medici family. The first official academy established on more formal lines, to include training, informed discussion, exhibiting opportunities and the representation of artists' interests with a wider public, was the Academy of the Arts of Drawing or Accademia del Disegno in Florence, later known as the Accademia di Belle Arti, when it merged with other drawing academies in the city. Giorgio Vasari (1511–1574) assisted with the inauguration of this academy in 1563, in an attempt to raise the status of artists above that of craft guild members. However the academy incorporated a guild for the benefit of all (not just exclusively the best) artists and continued to offer some training in craft skills. Some recent accounts have played down its success in establishing a higher status for fine artists (Hughes, 1986, 50–61). This was followed in 1593 by the establishment of the Academy of Saint Luke (Accademia di San Luca) in

Rome, which implemented more successfully a methodical art education embracing the study of anatomy, geometry, perspective, life drawing, mathematics, proportion, architecture and debates on theory (Percy, 2000, 462–463). The Accademia di San Luca remained the only site of life-drawing classes in Rome until the foundation in 1754 of the city's Life Drawing Academy (Accademia del Nudo) set up by Pope Benedict XIV (in office 1740–1758) as an affiliated institution and as a means of bolstering such provision (MacDonald, 1989, 77–91; Percy, 2000, 461). Papal support for these and other Roman academies led to their dominance in public commissions and they received many visiting foreign students, especially those who lacked such facilities in their own countries (Barroero and Susinno, 2000, 49). An academy was established in Milan in 1620.

The Académie royale in Paris (established in 1648) was greatly influenced by its Italian forebears. It benefited from the active support, including funding for salaried posts, of Jean-Baptiste Colbert (1619–1683), the minister of Louis XIV (reigned 1643–1715) in charge of Fine Arts policy. It enjoyed a virtual monopoly in France over the teaching of "elevated" art, as well as the most prestigious royal commissions. It offered artists the opportunity to exhibit in regular Salons or public exhibitions, and established the paradigm for all subsequent European institutions in the "academic tradition" that aspired to teach and support the visual liberal arts. Its influence spread further through the establishment in 1666 of a partner institution, the Académie de France à Rome (the French Academy in Rome), where its best students were awarded scholarships in order to study at first hand ancient, Renaissance and seventeenth-century works recommended as models of excellence. A number of art schools and wealthy patrons in other European countries such as the Netherlands and Poland sponsored artists to study at the Académie royale.

The influence of the Académie royale in Paris and of its British equivalent, the Royal Academy of Arts founded in 1768, was extensive throughout the eighteenth century. Both of these institutions, however, were preceded by other groups and societies established to protect the interests and extend the expertise of artists. In France the Académie royale had originated in power struggles in the 1660s between the *Maîtrise* (a guild representing since the Middle Ages craftsmen of all kinds, including painters) and *brevétaires*, artists privileged and protected by the court and allowed to operate outside guild restrictions. The foundation of the Académie royale eventually established some clear distinctions; for example, academicians were not allowed to keep shops, "tainted" by association with commerce (Crow, 1985, 23–25). The ground had already been prepared for the craft–fine art distinction through the formation, in early seventeenth-century France, of a number of private academies, salons and learned societies encouraging intellectual debates about the content and form of the arts. Generous patronage from the royal court and the Catholic Church had rewarded the talents of history painters versed in antique art and educated partly through visits to Italy.

Prior to the foundation of the Royal Academy in London, informal societies and academies had offered artists support with their work. From the late seventeenth century gatherings in London taverns and coffee houses had brought artists into regular contact with collectors, connoisseurs and antiquarians with the wealth, knowledge and social status necessary to support and promote artistic careers (Hallett, 2014, 25–32). This was the case with the Society of the Virtuosi of Saint Luke, a forerunner of the Royal Academy in London with an emphasis on connoisseurship and studying old masters (Hargraves, 2005, 8). Founded in 1689 (and active until 1743) its members included practicing artists and lovers of art. It held meetings in taverns, where portraits and architectural drawings were discussed and some works of art raffled (Bignamini, 1991, 21–44; Figure 1.1). The Rose and Crown Club (*c.*1704–1745) was a "conversations

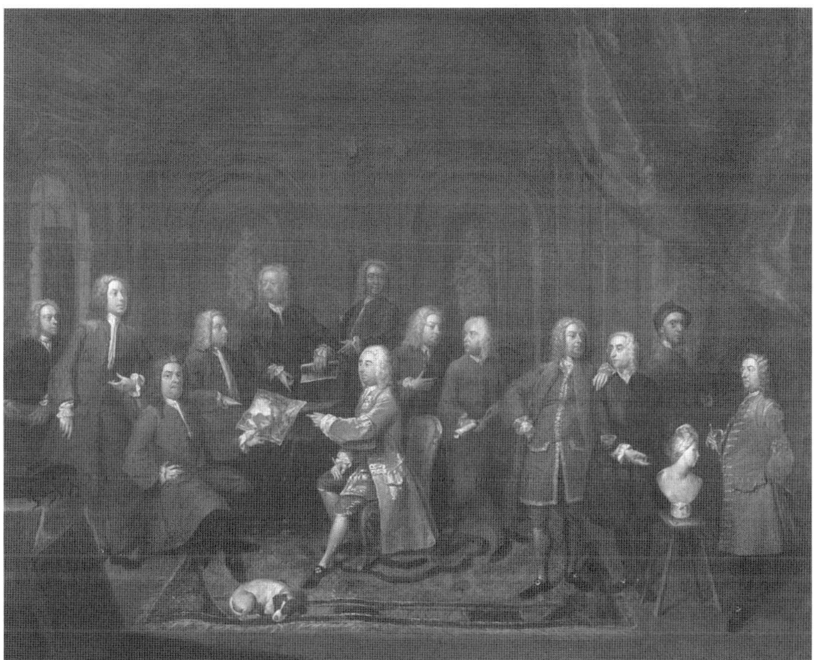

Figure 1.1 Gawen Hamilton (1698–1737): *A Conversation of Virtuosis … at the Kings Arms*, oil on canvas, 87.6 × 111.5 cm, 1735. National Portrait Gallery, London. Source: © National Portrait Gallery, London.

Clubb [sic]" and almost a parody of the Virtuosis that was active in promoting the genre of the conversation piece or informal group portrait (Bignamini, 1991, 44–61; Hargraves, 2005, 9). A private academy (or fee-paying art school) in Great Queen Street was set up in 1711–1720 by a group of artists, its first Governor being Sir Godfrey Kneller (1646–1723). This included a life class (Bignamini, 1991, 61–82). Between 1720 and 1768, private academies were set up in Britain not only in London but also in other cities including Dublin, Edinburgh, Glasgow and Birmingham (Bignamini, 1989, 443–444). In Edinburgh, the Cape Club was established in 1764 in order to bring together actors, painters, poets and musicians. Some of its members later joined the Society of Antiquaries of Scotland, founded in 1781.

Such societies were "social formations" in the Marxian sense that contemporary historical, social and market conditions played a key role in their development. They were often founded on and helped to disseminate a discourse of sociability, politeness, gentility and refinement (Myrone, 2008, 196), and prepared the ground for artistic markets, practices and audiences that continued throughout the eighteenth century to provide a wider context for artistic production than that offered by academies of high art. This issue will be discussed further in Chapter 3, but it is perhaps worth mentioning here that communities such as the Society of Dilettanti founded in the early 1730s as a society of art patrons, connoisseurs and Grand Tourists, continued throughout the eighteenth century to bring together over the fine wines and dining tables of gentlemen's clubs artists, connoisseurs and other arbiters of taste. This particular society sponsored research into antiquities and granted practical support to artists in the form, for example, of travel grants to Greece and Rome.

An important early institution in London was the Saint Martin's Lane Academy, which brought together members of these early groups and remained active until the Royal Academy was established. This was set up in 1720 by the artists John Vanderbank (1694–1739) and Louis Chéron (1660–1725), and formally re-established in 1735 by Hogarth (Bignaminim 1991, 83–124). It offered training in anatomy and drawing, including the copying of abstract shapes, parts of the body and of the whole body. Unlike the later Royal Academy it did not give precedence to an Italianate idealizing style, but placed emphasis on the close observation of nature. Under Hogarth's leadership it offered an alternative to continental academic approaches: the artist disliked intensely the reverence for antiquity, hierarchical structures and "foreign" values of continental academies. Hogarth found these to be over-bureaucratic and undemocratic and challenged, in his *Analysis of Beauty*, what he saw as a pretentious continental aesthetic. He instituted an egalitarian constitution at Saint

Martin's (Hargraves, 2005, 10–15). Unlike the Académie royale in France, Saint Martin's Lane was a privately, not publicly, regulated institution; it was financially self-supporting (through uniform subscription rates) and did not include court-sponsored, salaried, hierarchical posts. Hogarth was more involved in day-to-day teaching there than Reynolds would later be at the Royal Academy in London. He set up at the Saint Martin's Lane Academy a life-drawing class that was run on democratic lines, with those attending able to take it in turns to "set [pose] the Figure," and was large enough to accommodate a substantial number of artists at any one time rather than being exclusive. Hogarth was keen, however, for artists to seek other ways of working from observation.

As well as offering teaching, Saint Martin's Lane functioned as a gentleman's club, but one in which students might rub shoulders with their teachers, connoisseurs and patrons (Hallett, 2006b, 56). Like many of his contemporaries, Hogarth valued more informal kinds of social intercourse between artists, their students and assistants. He disliked the "high art" practice of copying old masters without necessarily understanding the visual "grammar" or underlying principles that unified the separate parts of a work (Fenton, 2006, 59–62). Toward the end of his life, he was critical of the view that it was necessary to travel abroad or to learn from continental masters working in the antique tradition even though he himself had continued to draw inspiration from French art and artists in particular (Simon, 2007, 1–68):

> Everything requisite to compleat [sic] the consummate painter or sculptor may be had with the utmost ease without going out of London at this time. Going to study abroad is an errant farce and more likely to confound a true genius than to improve him. Do skyes look more like skies, trees more like trees? Are not all living objects as visible as to light or shade or colour? Do mens bodys [sic] act and move as freely as in Rome? If so, all their limbs must be the same. (Hogarth, 1968 [1760–1761], 85; some original spelling and punctuation corrected)

Hogarth was among those artists who took part in exhibitions hosted by the Society of Artists, which grew out of the Society of Arts. The Society for the Encouragement of Arts, Manufactures, and Commerce (subsequently often known as the Society of Arts) was founded in 1754, with a view to improving the nation's commercial successes in trade and manufacturing (Craske, 1997, 25; Green, 2015). It offered the first significant opportunity for many British artists to exhibit their works in public. The Society focused mainly on the "lesser" genres of conversation pieces, genre paintings and novel treatments of, for example, fashionable subjects and northern-style light effects. It particularly encouraged less experienced and amateur artists. It was later subject to internal division, with breakaway groups focusing on the competing aims of practical (including monetary) support for artists and a role in public education (see Chapter 3).

Many official academies or proto-academies were set up in eighteenth-century Europe, although not all survived. They varied in the degree to which they tried to emulate a liberal arts culture, some moving on to do so some years after their foundation, but all provided artists with a more secure professional base. Those specializing in the fine arts were in a minority (Hoock, 2003, 27). Many (such as those at Berlin, Stockholm and Dresden) reorganized in order to serve better the needs of national manufacturing and commerce. Eighteenth-century academies or art schools included those in Antwerp (1663), Perugia (1673), Vienna (1692, transformed in the 1720s in line with the more exclusive fine art, French Académie royale model), Berlin (1696, reorganized 1786), Dresden (1705, reorganized in 1762), Edinburgh (where the short-lived Saint Luke's Academy was formed in 1729 in order to protect the interests of Scottish artists and culture, following the union with Britain in 1707; Macmillan, 1986, 12), Madrid (1744), Brussels (1711), Glasgow (1753), Copenhagen (1754), Naples (1752), Venice (1750), Mainz and St Petersburg (1757), Kassel (1760), Düsseldorf (1762), Leipzig and Meissen (1764), London (1768), Stockholm (1768, reorganized 1779) and Mannheim (1769).

The Académie royale in Paris went on to influence branch schools in the French provinces as well as academies in other countries, which sometimes appointed French academicians and artists as directors or teachers. At the Kongelige Danske Kunstakademi (Danish Royal Academy) the French artist Jean-François-Joseph Saly (1717–1776) supervised drawing classes and competitions and generally "transplanted" French academic traditions until 1771 when Danish artists took over leadership roles and helped to establish a national tradition of painting that drew on both French and German examples (Saabye, 1989, 525–529). The internationalization of academic training is also evident in the fact that the German diplomat and arts administrator Christian Ludwig von Hagedorn (1712–1780) was among the directors of this academy (Craske, 1997, 132–133). By such means, academic art attained in the eighteenth century an unprecedented international consensus on the values and education relevant to high art.

By 1790 there were over 100 art academies, some of which extended beyond Europe to, for example, Mexico (1785) and, later, the first North American academy at Pennsylvania (1805). The rise of the academy has been linked with a move away from court and church patronage as the growth of industry, commerce and a wider art-buying public facilitated fresh thinking on the forms and purposes of art. The growth of cities as centers of cultural excellence and consumerism was also influential. The burgeoning of academies undermined extensively, from the eighteenth century, the role of the guilds as social and economic communities for artists. Although "royal" or fine arts academies such as those in Paris and London tended to distance themselves from tuition in the "messy" or practical aspects of painting (mixing and applying paint, priming canvases), and left these to the realm of studio apprenticeships, other academies taught the technical skills traditionally required for the physical making of objects, and were thus commensurate with the power of the guilds. Academies varied with respect to the amount of control exercised over them by political leaders. The French monarchy gave a grant to cover all costs of the Académie royale and often intervened in matters of policy, regarding public culture as an arm of government, to be controlled through court-appointed Directors of Public Buildings.

The Royal Academy in London used royal support mainly as a temporary form of sponsorship until its income from exhibitions allowed a self-funded approach. This did not, however, prevent its members from feeling they were servants to the king, forced to seek his favor. This led to tensions at times, particularly from the 1790s, when advocates of political "liberty" (e.g. supporters of the French Revolution) objected to the Academy's apparent submission to royal propagandist agendas (Hoock, 2003, 9–12, 20–22, 25–26, 50–51, 130–135); while loyalty to the monarchy was welcomed by some as an alternative to dissent (Hargraves, 2005, 146–147). There were ongoing ideological conflicts between its patriotism and its commitment to a more cosmopolitan cultural agenda, as it sought to establish a British School of painting (Hoock, 2003, 52, 67–70, 109–123, 222). Commissions, financial security and cultural prestige were to be gained from royal patronage. George III (reigned 1760–1820) lent the royal apartments at Somerset House to the Academy. He was a keen practitioner of architectural drawings and an important patron to the architect William Chambers (1723–1796); he collected Italian paintings and drawings and commissioned paintings from Nathaniel Dance-Holland (1735–1811), Benjamin West (1738–1820) and Thomas Gainsborough (1727–1788). A royal yet artist-led academy such as that in Britain, hosting its own exhibitions, also meant potentially that artists could extend their skills, promote their work and establish their status with less dependence on individual aristocratic patrons, although in practice many struggled to achieve this.

In those academies where state control or intervention occurred, such as that in St Petersburg, this was often for reasons of improving national skills, prospects and reputations in design, trade and manufacture. Precise motivations varied. In Spain, for example, the establishment of the Real Academia de Bellas Artes de San Fernando (the Royal Academy of Fine Arts of San Fernando) in Madrid allowed artists to avoid taxes and military service. There were also local variations in the precise instruction on offer. The French Académie royale's curriculum did not include architecture, which was taught in a separate school, whereas the British Academy's did.

Academic Hierarchies: Institutions, Theory and Gender

Academies of art established and perpetuated hierarchies of many kinds; these were "discursive formations" (see Introduction; Duro, 1997, 117) disseminating a particular set of cultural values and terminologies from a position of power and influence. In those aspiring to fine art status (such as those in Paris, London and Madrid), this was seen as part of their attempt to restore dignity and order to the less stable values of craft guilds (often known in the eighteenth century as "corporations"), whose outputs were related much more closely to the values of technical skill, commerce and fashion. Chapter 2 will look closely at the hierarchies of subject matter or kinds of art (genres) practiced by members of elite academies, the chief categories being (in descending order) those of history, portraiture, genre, landscape and still life. The focus here is on institutional hierarchies, the status attached to different artistic skills and the importance of theory in establishing the status of those forms of art considered the very highest or "grand."

As academies formed, and in spite of their anti-guild prejudices, they often assumed a hierarchy for artist members that mirrored that of the guild. The latter's categories of apprentice, journeyman and master became in academies those of student, provisional or associate member and academician. The submission and approval of a suitable piece of work or "reception piece" (the guild equivalent being a journeyman's masterpiece) ensured progression from provisional or associate membership to the rank of fully fledged academician. In the French Académie royale, membership was linked with a particular genre, history painting (large-scale, complex compositions representing religious, historical, antique or mythological subjects) being considered the most severe test for a liberal artist. Acceptance as a history painter was a prerequisite for access to the higher salaried ranks of Professor and then, in ascending order of importance, Rector, Assistant Rector, Treasurer, Secretary, Counsellor, Director or Chancellor. Such hierarchies were underpinned by bureaucratic systems of governance devised to distinguish academies from the more informal proceedings of gatherings of *amateurs*, society artists, *connoisseurs* (scholarly experts in art) and craft guilds (Hoock, 2003, 27–32). The career prospects of artists were related to the institutional frameworks in which they trained and developed.

It was often relatively easy for artists to gain admission to academy schools; for example, on the basis of the presentation of a piece of recent work such as a drawing of a sculptural cast or through the sponsorship of an existing academician who could confirm the student had already received some basic training. However, financial support for students varied considerably. Students at the Royal Academy in London complained that their peers in France did much better in terms of grants, as well as having easier access to apprenticeships in the workshops of eminent artists. This meant that, even though their education at the Academy was free, artists in Britain had to find independent means of supporting themselves; for example, as teachers and illustrators, and often resorted to self-taught access to the profession (Hoock, 2003, 54, 59–61). Travel abroad was often possible only through aristocratic patronage, but the Academy did offer some three-year Rome scholarships (Hoock, 2003, 59, 111–113). For artists enrolled at prestigious academies, tests, competitions and prizes on a range of topics from figure drawing to expression, perspective, osteology, anatomy, head and hand studies, were used to distinguish those who might succeed as fine artists in the highest genres.

The Académie royale supported its best students by preparing them to enter its Prix de Rome (Rome Prize) competition, which involved submitting oil sketches (done in the presence of a Professor) and, if successful, full-scale works. Winners received a medal and were granted three years advanced study (in drawing, history, literature, geography, costume, geography, geometry, perspective, anatomy and life classes) in the École des Élèves Protégés (School for Sponsored Students) founded in 1748, and, following the closure in 1775 of this School, royal pensions in preparation for studies in Rome (Crow, 1985, 178; Schoneveld-Van Stoltz, 1989, 221). They then proceeded to funded study (normally for three years but it could be as many as five) in individual studios in the French Academy in Rome, the city still regarded as the home of canonical art. There was in fact, from 1676, a close amalgamation of the French and San Luca academies that united and strengthened two of the most powerful artistic institutions in the city, even though they retained their separate titles.

Students who went to Rome found themselves at the heart of lively international networks, both artistic and diplomatic (Hallett, 2014, 73–81). They studied the works of antique and more recent (especially seventeenth-century) masters and were frequently asked to send any work they completed back to France, for the benefit of the monarch or of the Academy. If they continued to produce good work on their return to France, they attained associate and then (on successful completion of a reception piece) full academician status. Some artists, for example, François Boucher, Hubert Robert (1733–1808) and Claude-Joseph Vernet (1714–89), went to Rome at their own expense: they no doubt felt that the experiences and networks gained there would ultimately benefit their commercial fortunes. Other academies such as that in Madrid followed the French example by offering bursaries for study in Rome to its best students. It was common for German artists to serve their apprenticeships with artists based in Rome.

The main way in which academies of art attempted to assert their power and influence was through the use of theoretical debate to facilitate the formulation or application of rules governing artistic practice. The French Académie royale had established this way of working in the seventeenth century, through the *Conférences* ("Lectures") inaugurated in 1667 by its Director, the history painter Charles Le Brun (1619–1690). Le Brun's lecture notes were edited and published from 1680 onwards by colleagues at the Academy including Henri Testelin, Secretary to the Academy. The lectures focused on the works of revered masters such as Raphael (Raffaelo Sanzio da Urbino) (1483–1520) and Nicolas Poussin (1594–1665) in order to highlight the ways in which artists might emulate the best work of Renaissance and classically inspired art. Le Brun was also keen to offer instruction in general pictorial issues such as the representation in painting of the facial expression of emotions. Paul Duro has suggested (1997, 122) that, although the ambition was to generate in this way the "rules" of art (especially history painting) that would serve contemporary artists, in fact there were practical difficulties in applying to one artist's work the principles deduced from another's. As the French Academy moved into the later seventeenth, then eighteenth centuries, the emphasis was much more on trying to emulate the general approach taken by earlier, esteemed artists rather than on any prescriptive following of rules. By this time the concept of the formal lecture series had also degenerated into the repetition or the delivery of eulogies of deceased artists, with little critical content. There were some exceptions: at the end of the seventeenth century, the writer Roger de Piles (1635–1709), appointed as "honorary amateur" in the Academy, stimulated fresh critical debate there (Crow, 1985, 36). Critical commentary was offered increasingly in France and throughout the rest of the eighteenth century by a growing number of journalists, amateurs and critics working outside the Academy (see Chapter 4).

In England the *Discourses on Art* written and delivered every one or two years between 1769 and 1790 to academicians and students in London by the President of the Royal Academy, Joshua Reynolds, covered many topics: the need for a disciplined approach to art; the essence of the grand style; the nature of beauty, invention, expression, color, drapery; consistency of style, taste, imitation, ideal beauty, novelty, contrast, variety and simplicity; sculpture and modern dress; genius and the need to study old masters; poetry, painting and nature; and the significance of Gainsborough's looser style of applying paint. Though infrequent by comparison with the lectures and seminars offered to twenty-first-century fine art students, Reynolds' lectures offered, like their French antecedents, important judgments on issues that permeated all aspects of the academic curriculum, from drawing classes to the choice of masterpieces for copying. They assumed great authority in critical and aesthetic debates across Europe. The Academy in London also offered public lectures. Reynolds expresses a perceptibly looser mid-eighteenth-century approach to the "rules" of art than that expressed by the French Académie royale, especially in the latter's earlier days of establishing power and authority over artistic production. Even at that time, those who recorded or articulated academic doctrine, such as Henri Testelin and the writer on art, André Félibien (1619–1695), knew that it would be applied to practice with a pragmatic moderation.

For Reynolds imitation and originality were not incompatible. He felt it was indispensable to study old masters in order to gain understanding of the principles guiding their work, the general workings of taste, but also as a means to achieving individual creativity:

> Invention, strictly speaking, is little more than a new combination of those images which have been previously gathered and deposited in memory: nothing can come of nothing: he who has laid up no materials, can produce no combinations. (Reynolds, 1975 [1797], 27)

To Reynolds, the artist of "genius" was well educated in the liberal arts of poetry and history, conversant with the formal techniques and aesthetic principles derived from close study of masters such as Raphael and Tiziano Vecellio, known as Titian (*c.*1485/90–1576) and able to create a general effect (rather than a minute imitation) likely to please the informed viewer (Reynolds, 1959, 198–199). Reynolds himself drew generously on the compositional formats and details of past masters such as Anthony Van Dyck (1599–1641), in the creation of his own works (Hallett, 2014, 4–6, 38–39, 59–60, 81–88, 105–108). He introduced professorships in ancient literature, history and antiquarianism alongside those already established in painting, sculpture, anatomy, perspective and geometry. Kauffman's portrait of him reveals his attachment to learning, including books and a bust of Homer (Figure 1.2, see color plate section). Reynolds considered that the cultivation of genius, with its judicious yet creative use of erudition, was an essentially male pursuit of which female artists could offer at most a pale imitation: they were perceived as having little capacity for independent thought or creativity (Perry, 2007, 50–51).

For women artists, training outside the academies was often a necessity, since decorum barred them from attendance at life-drawing classes and observation of the male nude model. From 1770 the display of "women's art" such as embroidery was banished from Royal Academy exhibitions. Angelica Kauffman (1741–1807) was one of only two women founder members of the Royal Academy in London, but could not attend life classes (Wassyng Roworth, 1992, 23). This was a disadvantage with regard to history painting, which made extensive reference to the heroic male body. However, as with many women artists, this did not prevent her from securing important commissions. She traveled to study in Rome and Florence. She studied literature, history and languages, and this allowed her to produce work in the "masculine" genre of history in spite of the later charge that her work was that of a "sentimental woman" (William Shaw Sparrow, 1905, cited in Wassyng Roworth, 1992, 12; Hyde and Milam, 2003, 9). This may have been due to the fact that she often feminized male bodies in her history paintings. Kauffman also took advantage of exhibiting opportunities at the Society of Artists (Chapter 3) and the Royal Academy. In her decorative roundels for the ceiling at Burlington House, site of the present-day Royal Academy, she emphasized both the intellectual skills (invention, composition) and practical skills (color and drawing) valued by contemporary male artists, and represented these attributes through a series of allegorical female figures (Wassyng Roworth, 1992, 68–72).

Mary Moser (1744–1819) was the other woman founder of the Royal Academy, her work being less controversial in that it focused on the traditionally feminine skill of flower painting. Anne Seymour Damer (1749–1828) tackled the more traditionally masculine medium of sculpture. She worked in a neoclassical style and was an honorary exhibitor at Royal Academy exhibitions. Like Kauffman she was often taunted on the basis of her forays into masculine artistic concerns. It was not until the 1860s that women students were fully admitted to the Royal Academy's schools and the first female academician was appointed in the early twentieth century (Hoock, 2003, 32, 55).

The Venetian artist, Rosalba Carriera (1675–1757), a miniaturist and painter of pastel portraits, was admitted in 1705 as a member of the Roman Accademia di San Luca. Her celebrity, the popularity of the works she produced and her willingness to include more "elevated" allegorical references in her work contributed to her success in acquiring full, rather than honorary membership (Johns, 2003, 20–45).

In France in 1770 a resolution was passed limiting the number of women members of the Academy there to four. The portrait painter, Élisabeth Louise Vigée Le Brun (1755–1842), one of the fortunate few, was admitted in 1783, but not as a history painter (Goodden, 1997, 49). She was among those women artists who learned their trade mainly in the studios of relatives or local artists. She was taught a great deal by her fellow artists Gabriel-François Doyen (1726–1806), Claude-Joseph Vernet and Jean-Baptiste Greuze (1725–1805), and was a favorite of the royal family prior to the Revolution. The latter brought little advantage to women artists, as the Institut de France, a temporary replacement for the Académie royale established by revolutionaries critical of the Académie, banned all female members.

A Hierarchy of Skills

What then were the "rules" or values fine art academies identified, if only as rough guides to practice? A hierarchy of skills persisted in eighteenth-century academic theory, although it was at times subject to challenge. From the seventeenth century, the most important skill was that of composition, often known as "design" (or the Italian *disegno*, which could also mean simply 'drawing'). This involved the total intellectual, narrative and formal conception of a painting: decisions about which figures, accessories, backgrounds, areas of light and shade to include in a work, and how to place them in relation to one another. The term "invention" was also used in relation to this nexus of conceptual skills. Next came expression – the codified configurations of facial features, gestures and bodily poses that expressed the emotions of figures in a way that would be legible to the viewer. This skill was seen as equal to that of the epic poet, legitimized by the dictum *ut pictura poesis*, "as is poetry, so is painting," formulated by the ancient Roman poet Horace (65–8 BCE), which suggested an equivalence of the arts of poetry and painting. Then came skill in perspectival effects (founded on the liberal art of geometry), considered important for general pictorial organization, which would help viewers to orientate themselves imaginatively and spatially in a scene.

Very close to the former skills in importance were drawing and proportion, both of which involved a close understanding of anatomy, mathematics and antique conventions in the representation of the human form. Illustrated drawing books helped to disseminate these skills in those countries that had not yet formed their own national academies, and these were often composed of copies of engravings from (mostly) French, Italian and Dutch seventeenth-century art. By the middle of the eighteenth century, such manuals made reference to formal academy studies and expressions; that is, those derived from poses and expressions prescribed for models in the life class (Hsieh, 2013, 395–397). Color was often demoted, as it was felt to offer a trivial, sensuous or decorative distraction from these more intellectual aspects of art. There was also an understanding that the texture of brushwork should not draw attention to itself. A smooth finish, in which brushstrokes merged seamlessly into one another, was necessary in order to prevent the pleasure of the eye taking precedence over that of the mind, the latter provided by a painting's intellectual and philosophical meanings.

There was a hierarchy of media regulated by major academies. Oil paintings enjoyed a higher status than watercolors, which were for much of the century considered unsuitable for public exhibition, as their practitioners battled against an association with amateurism, "feminine pursuits" and quick landscape sketches (see Chapter 2). However, the medium of gouache (an opaque form of watercolor), was chosen increasingly as the century progressed, as some artists used it to suggest the gravity and surface textures of oils. Portraits in the "quick" medium of pastel were often derided by academic or professional artists until the technique matched the weightiness and sophistication of oil painting (Jeffares, 2015). Painting was generally viewed as more important than sculpture, the production of which was more closely associated with dirt and physical labor. At the same time, sculpture was often associated closely with the material remains of antiquity (see Chapter 2). Sculptures in bronze and marble enjoyed a much higher status than wood; plaster and terracotta were reserved for preliminary models. Prints were often considered inferior to paintings due to their mass production and their status as copies. Engravers were sometimes excluded from or marginalized by academies with a liberal arts focus, though some were so skillful and original in their methods that they enjoyed a healthy reputation (see Chapter 3). Drawings were not generally appreciated as works of art in their own right, or worthy of exhibition, but rather as stages in the evolution of finished works. Handicrafts, "curiosities" and needlework were favored by institutions specializing in the applied arts rather than by liberal arts academies (Hargraves, 2005, 28–8, 56). Architecture inhabited an ambiguous space between the "practical arts" and the cultivation of knowledge of antiquity.

Drawing was often taught by encouraging students to progress from the copying of drawings or engravings of antique sculptures (a stage omitted in the Royal Academy in London; Hoock, 2003, 55), to drawing from casts of these: students often copied specific body parts such as hands and feet before progressing to whole figures. Life drawing followed; nude models (normally male) sometimes posing in pairs (Figure 1.3). The Royal Academy in London used female models, however, and paid them more than the males it employed. The study of plaster casts of antique sculptures allowed students to form a storehouse of "memories" of bodily form that they might then apply selectively to drawings done from observation of the live model, so that they were seeing through the eyes of past masters or what Reynolds would describe as "material" (Macsotay, 2010, 183–191). Live models held poses taken from a repertory of antique sculptures, and managed to maintain them for the required length of time only with the help of blocks, pulleys and ropes. The provision of life classes was a feature that often distinguished fine art academies from other forms of art

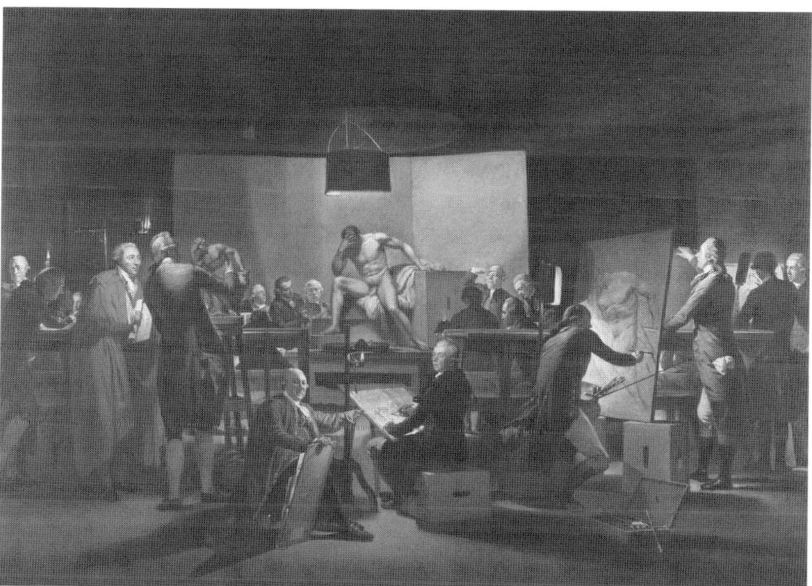

Figure 1.3 Martin Ferdinand Quadal (1736–1811): *The Life Class of the Vienna Academy in the St Anne Building*, oil on canvas, 144 × 207 cm, 1787. Academy of Fine Arts, Vienna. Source: Gemäldegalerie der Akademie der biidenden Künste Wien.

education. The French Académie royale won at its inception exclusive rights (that lasted until 1705) to run a life-drawing class. Most academic life drawings were done in red and black chalk with white highlights, on white or tinted paper. The emphasis was on the contour or outline of a figure, but some cross-hatching and parallel strokes were used to suggest muscle masses. Lessons in anatomy involved close study of wax, plaster or bronze flayed figures: *écorchés* or bodies stripped of their skin to reveal the muscles beneath. These ensured that students produced plausible representations of the human form. Competitions such as the half figure drawing competition introduced at the Académie royale in 1784 reinforced the standard to which they should aspire.

By proceeding from the study of antique sculptures to that of live models inspired by these sculptures, eighteenth-century artists did not necessarily think of themselves as deserting the "natural" in art. They believed that ancient Greek and Roman sculptors had developed their representations of the human form as a result of frequent observation of real bodies in action. From these frequent observations the ancients had developed a mental image based on those elements of the human form most consonant with their conception of beauty. The resulting intellectual constructions, "ideal beauty" or, more broadly, "ideal nature" (the essence of a particular human type or natural phenomenon), existed in no single model but derived from many models observed at first hand. They allowed artists to create a vision of the human form that transcended that of any individual mortal. In 1755, in his widely translated *Reflections on the Imitation of Greek Works in Painting and Sculpture* (*Gedanken über die nachahmung der Griechischen Werke in der Malerei und Bildhauerkunst*), the scholar and art historian Johann Joachim Winckelmann (1717–1768), who placed developments in art in their historical contexts, popularized the view that for the ancient Greeks the process of deriving beauty from natural forms was much easier than for his own contemporaries: the Greeks had enjoyed a climate, a conception of physical beauty and an exercise regime that brought them much closer to the transcendent ideal to which all art should aspire. Faith in the existence of such an ideal derived from the notion expressed by Plato (428/427–348/347 BCE) that all individual earthly forms were but imperfect copies of perfect originals:

> In the masterpieces of Greek art, connoisseurs and imitators find not only nature at its most beautiful, but also something beyond nature, namely certain ideal forms of its beauty, which, as an ancient interpreter of Plato [Proclus] teaches us, come from images created by the mind alone. (Winckelmann, 1987 [1755], 7)

In practice, for the students of eighteenth-century academies, this meant that any drawings from life they did were subject to correction by their masters, who might suggest that a profile be made more graceful or the configurations of facial features altered to give greater nobility. The canonical antique sculptures or prototypes on which such advice was based included the Apollo Belvedere, the Antinous, the Medici Venus, the Gladiator and the Farnese Hercules. The antique models used were normally available to academies in the form of plaster casts taken from ancient Roman copies of Greek originals.

Over-reliance on such models carried the risk that artists would prioritize a conventional representation of the human form over naturalism or authenticity. As the eighteenth century progressed, more radical critics such as Diderot and Hogarth pointed out the potentially detrimental effects, in figure studies for paintings, caused by insufficient direct observation of the real human body. Diderot wrote in his Salon of 1765:

> Anyone who scorns nature in favour of the antique risks never producing anything that's not trivial, weak, and paltry in its drawing, character, drapery, and expression. Anyone who's neglected nature in favour of the antique will risk being cold, lifeless, devoid of the hidden, secret truths which can only be perceived in nature itself. It seems to me one must study the antique to learn how to look at nature. (Diderot, 1995a, 157)

In other words, those too much in thrall to the antique had forgotten that the ancients themselves learned from nature. In his 1792 address to the Royal Academy of Fine Arts of San Fernando in Madrid, Goya exclaimed:

> What a scandal to hear nature deprecated in comparison to Greek statues by one who knows neither the one, nor the other, without acknowledging that the smallest part of Nature confounds and amazes those who know most! What statue, or cast of it might there be, that is not copied from Divine Nature? As excellent as the artist may be who copied it, can he not but proclaim that placed at its side, one is the work of God, the other of our miserable hands? (Goya, "Address to the Royal Academy of San Fernando regarding the Method of Teaching the Visual Arts," cited in Tomlinson, 1994, 306)

The fact that such protests were still necessary so late in the century testifies to the enduring influence of academic idealism; that is, the search for a form of ideal beauty sanctioned by antique precedent. This dominant aesthetic value was reinforced by the existence, in most academies, of a collection of sculpture casts (often plaster) of antique sculptures, engravings and drawings of works by old masters. It was difficult for students to travel to see the originals unless they secured a travel scholarship or patronage of some kind. In terms of more recent exemplars, works by Raphael, Leonardo da Vinci (1452–1519) and the seventeenth-century masters Nicolas Poussin and Charles Le Brun were often at the center of the canon of art respected by academies, although this canon could vary with time and place: in Britain, for example, Reynolds was less keen than his continental counterparts on Poussin. There was a certain irony in the selection of Poussin and Raphael as exemplars of an academic style, since neither had been members of academies or subject to their rules. Italian art was often privileged over northern European models because it promoted an idealized nature over the more direct copying from nature thought to characterize Dutch or "northern" art. Furthermore, Raphael (as archetypal "Roman" artist) and Poussin were often singled out as appropriate examples since their art was felt to focus on drawing and clearly ordered design rather than on more sensuous or spectacular effects. However, academies and their artists remained open in practice to a wide range of classical styles in painting inherited from the Renaissance and seventeenth century (see Chapter 2).

Academies varied considerably in the size and richness of the teaching collections used to supply students with material for copying. At the Royal Academy in London a number of artists, such as the sculptors John Flaxman, Thomas Banks (1735–1805), Jean-Baptiste Pigalle (1714–1785) and Jean-Antoine Houdon (1741–1828), and collectors such as Charles Townley (1737–1805; see Figure 4.1) contributed copies and casts (Fenton, 2006, 23). There was also a rich collection of books and prints (Hoock, 2003, 55–56).The Royal Academy of Fine Arts of San Fernando in Madrid fared less well and did not acquire a substantial collection until the Spanish seized as a prize of war the cargo of the merchant ship the *Westmorland*, which was carrying home the Italian purchases of a number of British Grand Tourists, from books of prints to architectural plans, drawings and copies of canonical sculptures (Sánchez-Jáuregui Alpañes and Wilcox, 2012). Teaching collections were often a vital part of students' education, especially where there were few local opportunities to see the originals of works of art they were expected to study. At the Danish Royal Academy a library of books and prints of canonical works and a collection of casts from antique sculptures provided a vital supplement to the Royal collection of paintings at the Christiansborg Palace (Saabye, 1989, 520; Thygesen, 1989, 516). Teaching collections could also enable one nation's artists to influence another's. As the Imperial Academy of Fine Arts in Saint Petersburg was establishing itself, it benefited in 1769 from Greuze's gift of over 200 expressive head sketches and figure studies (Bailey, 2003, 10).

Such collections promoted visual styles derived from antiquity and the Renaissance, and provided students with a repertory of compositional arrangements, figure groupings, poses, gestures and expressions that constituted the vocabulary of academic classicism. Representations of facial expression could be particularly formulaic. Illustrative prints from pattern books such as Charles Le Brun's *Lecture on Expression* (*Conférence sur l'expression*, first published in 1698) and the expressive types in *Various faces for use by the young and others* (*Diversae Facies in usum iuvenum et aliorum delineatae*, 1656) by the artist Michael Sweerts (1618–1664) continued to be influential throughout the eighteenth century, particularly in its early decades (Percival, 2012, 60). Both Le Brun and Sweerts drew their facial prototypes for the expression of emotions such as fear and astonishment from the old masters they had studied. Academic tradition thus ensured the transmission of a legible code of expressive types, and the measure of a great artist within this system derived in part from his ability to deploy this code while adjusting it to observation of the live model. Because academies attached the greatest status to narrative art, it was very important that the viewer of a work of art should be able to understand clearly the emotions being represented, as these were among the primary means of revealing a figure's role and character in the particular story being told. So great was the importance attached to expression that the Académie royale in Paris launched in 1760 a competition dedicated to it. This was the only context in which it employed female models. In their finished works, however, artists often softened or modified the rigidity of expressive prototypes, following the principle of honoring the spirit, rather than the letter, of their mentors in this aspect of art (Walsh, 1999, 117).

Although color was often regarded in the seventeenth century as inferior to drawing, it became more highly valued later in that century and into the eighteenth. From the 1680s, younger French artists such as Charles de la Fosse (1636–1716), Jean Jouvenet (1644–1717) and Antoine Coypel (1661–1722) produced art that celebrated color effects. This development had been facilitated by what has come to be known as the "quarrel" between line and color, captured in lectures offered at the Académie royale from the 1670s. Whereas line (or drawing) was closely associated with the intellectual interpretation of a painting, clarity of line or form being seen as essential to the successful communication of meaning or ideas, color was regarded as a more purely pictorial element, appealing to the eye and the senses in general in much the same way as superficial decoration. For some the battle-lines were drawn around the duality of mind and body, which had recently been postulated by the philosopher René Descartes (1596–1650). Factional politics were also involved, not only between artists within the Académie royale, but also in opposition to guild members, often described as mere "color grinders," the physical process of grinding pigments being associated with the material aspects of painting. Those who championed line were characterized as supporters of Poussin; that is, of disciplined composition and intellectual appeal; those who championed color as supporters of Peter Paul Rubens (1577–1640), whose art was regarded as an exemplar of high-colored, baroque drama. This was of course a huge over-simplification of the facts, Poussin himself being an accomplished colorist in many of his works. Poussin's biographer, André Félibien, acknowledged this in his remarks on the artist's talent in the handling of light and color:

> So noting that the difference between sounds causes the soul to be moved in different ways, according to whether it is moved by low or high sounds, he [Poussin] was confident that the way in which objects are displayed in a particular sequence or arrangement, expressions of varying degrees of vehemence are represented, and in colors placed next to one another in different combinations, could offer the eye diverse sensations which could make the soul susceptible to as many different passions. (Félibien, 1967 [1725], 323; my translation)

Félibien was not alone, in seventeenth-century academic circles, in offering such a defence of color.

At the turn of the century, Roger de Piles gradually persuaded academicians of the value of color through his lectures. He argued in his 1708 work *Lessons in the Principles of Painting* (*Cours de peinture par principes*) that color was just as intellectual a part of art as line, as it was just as important in the process of imitating nature. Furthermore, color was the distinctive quality of painting – that which helped it stand apart from other arts such as poetry that were addressed principally to the mind. Both line and color were essential components of great art. As de Piles's message was assimilated by subsequent generations of artists, there was greater respect for colorists such as Rubens, Titian and other artists of the Venetian school renowned for its skill in color. By 1765 the writer on art Michel-François Dandré-Bardon (1700–1783) identified color as an important element of artistic creativity:

> It is only with the aid of delicate sentiment that one can capture, following Nature, the diverse nuances of the warmth or paleness of color; of the lightness or vigor in light and shade; and of the delicacy or assertiveness in brushstrokes inspired by passion. (Dandré-Bardon, 1972 [1765], 66; my translation)

The role of color, chiaroscuro and brushwork grew in importance as eighteenth-century artistic culture and criticism acknowledged more openly, particularly from the 1760s, the importance of emotion in both the creation and the viewing of art. In the context of the "grand style," Reynolds advised, however, an appropriate restraint with regard to color and light, consonant with the classical principles of simplicity, unity in variety and harmony:

> With respect to Colouring, though it may appear at first a part of painting merely mechanical, yet it still has its rules.... To give a general air of grandeur at first view, all trifling or artful play of little lights, or an attention to a variety of tints is to be avoided; a quietness and simplicity must reign over the whole work; to which a breadth of uniform, and simple colour, will very much contribute. (Reynolds, 1975 [1797], 61)

For Reynolds, the use of color, light and shade was welcomed as long as they were contained within a framework of unity and grandeur. The popularity in the early part of the century of the rococo style, with its use of strong color effects, could, however, test the limits of critical tolerance. Harmonizing color effects involved a careful consideration of the tonal values (degrees of light and darkness) in each color used, and of the ways adjacent colors reflected one another. The still life and genre artist Jean-Baptiste-Siméon Chardin's (1699–1779) expertise in this was much praised by Diderot (Bukdahl, 1980, 409). The art critic Étienne La Font de Saint Yenne (1688–1771) was among those who called for restful, unifying effects on the eye rather than the butterfly-like dazzle that some artists produced in their use of light and color (La Font de Saint Yenne, 1747, 47–48, 59).

Art schools and academies in Paris did not teach the practical skills of painting until 1863. Artists studied at the Académie royale in order to extend their learning in the humanities and their drawing skills, following or during their studio training in practical painting techniques. Most eighteenth-century academies similarly avoided teaching the physical aspects of sculpture such as cutting and carving marble or making bronze casts, although some encouraged the production of clay models, regarded as the equivalent of a painter's preliminary sketches (Lock, 2010, 256). Sculptors were educated at the academies in a very similar way to painters, with an emphasis on drawing, especially expressive heads and compositional sketches for reliefs. For the practical skills of their trade they had to access workshops or foundries, where they might be taken on as apprentices or assistants.

For painters brushwork was an important practical skill learned in the studio. The academic ideal was associated with a smooth finish. To wary academicians, visible or "loose" brushstrokes might, like intrusive attention to color and light, enhance the surface effects and visual appeal of a painting at the expense of its intellectual content. While preparatory, rough sketches were an acceptable part of the evolution of a work, and indeed were felt increasingly to express the workings of "genius," sketchiness in a finished work implied a kind of "libertine" approach incompatible with the moral aspirations of those working in the higher genres (Wrigley, 1993, 276–277). "Painterly" surface-textural effects might also undermine the emphasis on a well-ordered composition or clearly defined lines central to the ethos of *disegno*, thus undermining any desired clarity of meaning or interpretation. A painterly style became more acceptable in practice, however, if not in theory, as the eighteenth century progressed. Artists such as Watteau, Jean-Honoré Fragonard (1732–1806) and Gainsborough became well known for their looser, expressive brushwork. When Reynolds spoke of Gainsborough he expressed somewhat begrudgingly his admiration of the latter's painterly approach:

> ...it is certain, that all those odd scratches and marks, which, on close examination, are so observable in Gainsborough's pictures, and which even to experienced painters appear rather the effect of accident than design; this chaos, this uncouth and shapeless appearance, by a kind of magick, at a certain distance assumes form, and all parts seem to drop into their proper places; so that we can hardly refuse acknowledging the full effect of diligence, under the appearance of chance and hasty negligence. (Reynolds, 1975 [1797], 257–258)

The Art–Craft Divide: Unifying and Divisive Developments

There was a growing realization that in order to meet the needs of industry and trade, there should be some interaction between academic training and craft skills. In 1767 the Royal Free School of Drawing (*École royale gratuite de dessin*, later the National School of Decorative Arts or *École nationale supérieure des arts décoratifs*) was set up in Paris to improve the drawing skills of craftsmen, thus extending to the "lower" sphere of artistic practice the teaching of a skill highly valued in academies. Led initially by the flower painter Jean-Jacques Bachelier (1724–1806), pupils copied drawings and prints of figures, animals, flowers and ornaments as well as learning geometry and architecture. Many academicians set up or ran free drawing schools for artisans, or taught at these (Schoneveld-Van Stoltz, 1989, 223). Drawing schools opened across Europe (Guillomet, 1989, 255; Schoneveld-Van Stoltz, 1989, 223; Kaufman, 1995, 395). These included, in London, Shipley's Drawing School (established *c.*1750) attached to the Society for the Encouragement of Arts, Manufactures and Commerce (Brewer, 1997, 296); in Vienna, the Craft School (*Manufakturschule*) (1758); and, in Edinburgh, the Trustees' Academy of Design (1760). Drawing manuals were widely available. By the middle of the century they covered not just figure drawing but also landscape and still life, and were useful to those engaged in a wide range of crafts and manufacture (Hsieh, 2013, 402–406). Academy sculptors such as Claude Michel (also known as Clodion; 1738–1814) and Étienne-Maurice Falconet (1716–1791), shared their skills in drawing and modeling by helping to train those who designed ceramic objects at the established royal Sèvres porcelain factory. In Britain, Flaxman contributed designs for Wedgwood pottery. The state-sponsored Nymphenburg Porcelain Manufactory in Munich employed the sculptor Franz Anton Bustelli (1723–1763) as model master. He specialized in rococo designs for ornamental figurines; for example, of stock *Commedia dell'Arte* (Italian travelling theatre) characters, made familiar early in the century through Watteau's paintings, validated by the Académie royale (Figure 1.4, see color plate section) and generally at the Venice Carnival.

This crossing of art and craft followed the tradition established by the seventeenth-century history painter Charles Le Brun, who, in addition to serving as Director of the Académie royale, had overseen the decoration of Louis XIV's Hall of Mirrors at Versailles. He had also run the royal Gobelins tapestry factory in Paris, thus establishing an enduring collaboration of academic and "mechanical" artists. This factory continued to offer into the eighteenth century court-sponsored accommodation for artists invited and willing to train the Gobelins' craftsmen. The eighteenth-century manufacturer and aspiring artist Jean de Jullienne (1686–1766) received such training and subsequently used his expertise as an art collector and related artistic networks to attain in 1739 the status of "honorary academician and *amateur*" at the Académie royale in Paris (Plax, 2007, 51). A ministerial statement of 1795 stressed that the Gobelins factory (closely associated with the "craft" of weaving) was still supported by the government because it produced art "beautiful in itself," independently of any profit motive (Archives Nationales, Paris, cited in Scott, 1995, 105): it aligned closely with the fine or liberal arts. Jean-Baptiste Oudry (1686–1755), painter of still lifes and hunting scenes, was among those academicians who assumed leading roles at the Beauvais and Gobelins tapestry works, his "royal" patronage also extending to carriage door and over-door decoration (Bailey, 2007, 2, 5). The medium of tapestry occupied an ambiguous space in the art–craft spectrum. Its subjects could be light-hearted (like those produced by Goya earlier in his career) or serious, but its high cost and the amount of wall space it required meant that it was associated with elite royal or noble buyers. Tapestries had been included in the 1699 Salon in Paris, though were not in later ones (Crow, 1985, 36).

Giovanni Antonio Canal (known as Canaletto; 1697–1768), whose landscapes and urban views later became so popular and who was received into the Academy in Venice in 1763, had designed theatre sets in his early career. Such cross-influences between the high and decorative arts were easier to achieve when decorative styles such as the rococo, with its sinuous curves and bright colors, were in play: the style thrived naturally inside and outside academic institutions. It was also quite common to reproduce high-art portrait busts of well-known sitters and religious subjects in a broad range of styles for domestic display, and academic artists could assist with this process. Many of the founder members of the Royal Academy in London were "jobbing" artists, such as drapery painters, scene painters and coach painters (Saumarez Smith, 2012, 86) and their counterparts in France regularly carried out commissions for decorative work such as over-door, fire-screen and wall panel paintings (Scott, 1995, 27–28). Some interior wall paintings were quite elaborate and provided in Paris a good income for Italian artists and their assistants (Scott, 1995, 24). Some painters of the signboards so prevalent in Parisian streets also painted "high art" (Plax, 2000, 167).

Similar synergies between the fine and applied arts were evident elsewhere. In Scotland Alexander Runciman (1736–1785), who was master at the college set up by the Trustees for the Board of Commerce that encouraged Scottish industry) trained as an ornamental painter specializing in house decoration that incorporated both landscapes and subject paintings. His work included increasingly references to historical and literary subjects that aligned his interests with those of history painters at the Royal Academy in London, on whom he exerted a growing influence (Macmillan, 1986, 44–58). The Scottish portrait and landscape artist Alexander Naysmith (1758–1840) followed a similar trajectory to that of Canaletto and Runciman, progressing from decorative to "heroic" or poetic painting, following a trip to Rome in 1782–1785 (Macmillan, 1986, 140–146). The successful portrait artist Henry Raeburn (1756–1823) had trained initially in gold-smithing and miniatures (Macmillan, 1986, 74).

Angelica Kauffman practiced through to the later part of the century the "noble" and "heroic" pursuit of history painting while adapting her designs to fashionable domestic items such as porcelain, tea trays, fans, ceiling and wall decoration, and watch cases (Forbes Adam, Malise and Mauchline, 1992, 113–140).

In spite of the discourses of high art, the fact that London was a hub of artists' associations made isolationist policies difficult to achieve in practice. Hierarchical divisions between, on the one hand, the "mechanical" and "decorative" and, on the other, the "liberal," were highly problematic. The advent of more formal fine arts academies created divisions where previously a creative fluidity had existed. Saint Martin' s Lane Academy had provided until the mid-century forms of training and tuition that were useful to furniture designers, illustrators, engravers and painters of theatre scenery, as well as to those producing portraits and other genres of painting and sculpture later recognized by the Royal Academy. Once the latter had been established, Saint Martin's lost many of its formal membership to the new institution, as members of the Royal Academy were allowed simultaneous membership only of general literary or cultural societies. Saint Martin's became less active as an institution, but its members continued to influence fine art practitioners and did not necessarily see these interests as contradictory.

The painter and illustrator Francis Hayman (1708–1776), one of the Directors of Saint Martin's Lane, later became one of the founding members of the Royal Academy. Hayman also belonged, like Hogarth, to the Society of Artists, the first formal exhibiting society in England. This society collaborated with and grew out of the Society for the Encouragement of Arts, Manufacture and Commerce, an institution that awarded prizes encouraging designers for industry as well as novice artists (see Chapter 3; Bindman, 2008, 198; Saumarez Smith, 2012, 173–176). Gainsborough, who is thought to have frequented Saint Martin's, did not travel abroad but later exhibited with the Society of Artists before becoming a founder member of the Royal Academy. The latter institution was built on the shoulders of artists whose work had previously, and necessarily, evolved in associations and institutions that had treated craftwork seriously. On the other hand, members of Saint Martin's had included, in spite of Hogarth's misgivings, those interested in developments in continental high art. George Knapton (1698–1778), a painter, draughtsman and connoisseur at Saint Martin's, went on the Grand Tour and was keen to study art in Rome. Knapton was a member of the Roman Club (for artists and literary men aspiring to connoisseurship) founded in 1723; he was also a member of the aristocratic Society of Dilettanti. Also at Saint Martin's, the designer, engraver and illustrator Hubert-François Gravelot (1699–1773) and the "high art" sculptor Louis-François Roubiliac (1702–1762) taught students there. They helped to establish in Britain the French rococo style, even influencing Hogarth, demonstrating that first-hand interaction with continental high-art traditions could be productive in manufacture, publishing, trade and commerce (Colley, 1984, 10–17).

Some academies tried to accommodate in significant ways the needs of industry and design. The Academy of Fine Arts in St Petersburg, founded in 1757 and directed initially by French masters, trained craftsmen alongside fine artists. The two groups shared the early stages of their training; those who failed tests in classical drawing at the end of the first year either returning home or transferring to workshops inside the Academy. The Academy trained craftsmen in ornamental engraving, gilding, mosaic, lacquer work and ironwork. Students studying these skills boarded at the Academy alongside their fine arts colleagues and could compete for similar (if slightly less prestigious) prizes. Their masters had fewer privileges than their fine arts peers and no pensions. This institution formed part of Russia's ambition to share in the modernity and high culture of academies further west, while developing the skills necessary for industry. There were at this stage no commercial workshops in Russia for applied arts such as textiles, tapestry or porcelain, although there were some state-run enterprises. Craft students at the Academy were often ex-soldiers or slaves, their education seen as a sign of the country's potential for progress. Many artists however had "serf" status, in spite of the social pretensions of the Academy (Craske, 1997, 77). The higher cultural ambitions of the Academy became clearer when there were enough fine arts students to fill its places, at which point it became exclusively dedicated to these. Other academies such as those at Berlin, Dresden, Stockholm and Vienna also made efforts to educate craftsmen alongside fine artists, during the early stages of their training, with a particular focus on improving the drawing skills of the former. All of these academies were reorganized during the eighteenth century in a way that made them more relevant to the interests of crafts and industry.

The Decline of the Guilds: Defining the "Artist"

Craft guilds in many parts of Europe, with their regulated structures of advancement and trade, survived for much of the eighteenth century but weakened toward the end of it, as liberal or free trade economics and industrialization took hold. Germany was among those nations where such a shift was produced by mass consumerism (McGregor, 2014, 344–345). James Farr (2000, 276–282) has drawn attention to the fact that the guilds had created for both journeymen and their masters an accessible means of establishing social identity and rank, and this had no doubt allowed them to persist for a while as institutions parallel to those of high culture. With the French Revolution came a distrust of trade organizations, which were perceived as holding ideals of solidarity that competed with those of the state, as well as with notions of individual rights. The guilds were officially abolished in France in 1791, following the Terror. Revolutionaries were suspicious of the vested interests and power structures they represented. Similar developments unfolded throughout the nineteenth century in other European countries. In Britain, Livery Companies emerged to replace guilds and their apprenticeship system. These were charitable associations very loosely connected with particular trades. Reynolds bought himself out of his own apprenticeship early in his career and in 1784 was "made free" of the Painters and Trainers Company, which acquired honorary rather than regulatory status. The Company had in any case been unable to sustain its monopoly over art as more and more artists moved beyond London (Simon, 1987, 131–132; Hargraves, 2005, 6).

In France relationships between the fine and mechanical arts came to a head in the period 1766–1776. After the failure of the *Maîtrise* or craft guild to consolidate an amalgamation in 1676 with the Académie royale, the guild continued into the eighteenth century as the Paris Corporation of Master Painters and Sculptors. Prior to the Revolution artists were still expected to be guild members unless excused from this requirement by their royal employment. In 1705 the Corporation obtained permission to establish a life-drawing class for the benefit of apprentices and journeymen and this class, along with others in architecture, anatomy, perspective and geometry, formed the basis of the later-named Academy of Saint Luke (Académie de Saint Luc), the latest in a long line of academies dating from the fourteenth century dedicated to the patron saint of painting. Those most closely associated with this school included fine artists who had been unsuccessful in gaining admittance to the Académie royale in Paris. They adopted the institutional practices of high art by classifying themselves according to the ranks of professor, assistant professor and a range of officers. Artists contributing to the exhibitions of the Académie de Saint Luc in the early eighteenth century included Oudry and the sculptor Jacques Caffiéri (1678–1755) (Guiffrey, 1872). Both of these artists had been successful in gaining royal and aristocratic patronage and commissions. Oudry became a professor; Caffiéri became famous for designing gilt furniture, thus demonstrating the practical and decorative applications of the work of artists at the Académie de Saint Luc. The animal painter Jean-Baptiste Huet (1745–1811) was among those who studied there before being accepted as a member of the Académie royale.

In 1766 artists of "higher" status (i.e. who perceived themselves as fine artists) at the Paris Corporation mounted a legal challenge to the Directors in charge of the Académie de Saint Luc, demanding greater representation on its governing body. Katie Scott has related the ensuing legal proceedings (Scott, 1989). Essentially painters and sculptors associating themselves with the liberal arts (often specialists in figurative or representational art) claimed that the practitioners of other, "lesser" trades and crafts such as gilders, carriage decorators, monumental masons, varnishers, house painters and color merchants, were unfit to represent the interests of those whose work required genius and intellectual effort, even though the protesters included in their number practitioners of these very same crafts. They claimed that the influence of craft practitioners through the current Directorate was too great in admissions processes, competitions and exhibitions at the Académie de Saint Luc.

The ensuing power struggle was bound up with ideas on political and cultural liberty and the distinctions between, on the one hand, guild solidarity and, on the other, the notion of the solitary genius; between tradition and progress, the fine artists aligning themselves with the latter. Directors defending their established power argued that "art" could be defined in broad terms as a rational, ordered practice that embraced both mechanical and fine arts, and that any differences (e.g.between the use of the hand and the mind) were of degree rather than kind. Ironically, the legal challenge by "higher" artists at Saint Luc backfired as members of the Académie royale interpreted the protestors' motives as a challenge to the exclusivity of their own institution and managed to intervene in order to ensure that the Académie de Saint Luc, its school and exhibition venue were closed in 1776, a royal edict of 1777 attributing exclusive liberal arts and "gentleman" status to artists of the Académie royale (Schoneveld-Van Stoltz, 1989, 225). All the protest had achieved was a clearer distinction between the two academies in Paris, and between the fine and mechanical arts, which had for much of the century crossed naturally into each other's territories through a range of visual arts: the internal decoration of domestic and public buildings, the designs on objects such as snuff boxes, theatrical scene painting, carriage decoration, fire-screens and ceramics. Such cross-fertilizations continued in practice.

The struggle in France demonstrated that it was not just the objects produced by artists and craftsmen, but also their functions, that aroused

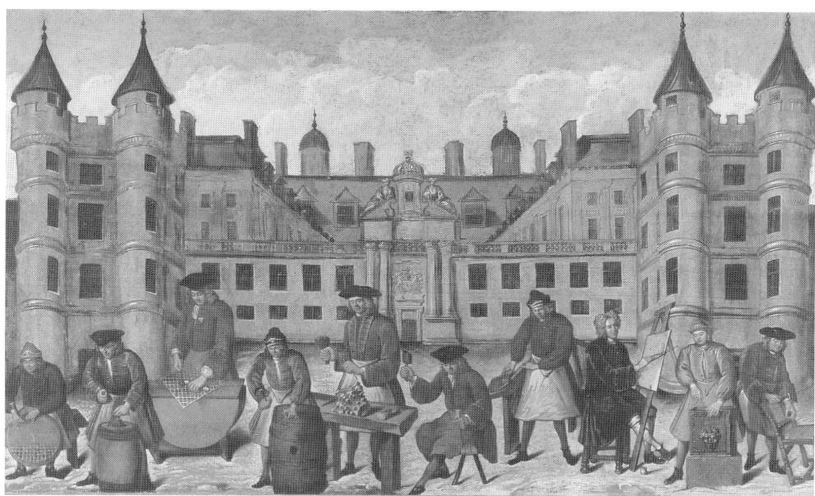

Figure 1.5 Roderick Chalmers: *The Incorporation of Wrights and Masons in Front of the Palace of Holyrood House*, oil on canvas, 104.4 × 182.1 cm, 1720. Trade Incorporation of Wrights and Masons of Edinburgh. Source: Trade Incorporation of Wrights and Masons of Edinburgh.

the need to draw boundaries of status. A 1720 image of tradesmen in Edinburgh shows a similar segregation of practitioners, the genteel fine artist and his easel standing out from the workmanlike artisans (Figure 1.5). There was in the 1760s, as there had been earlier in eighteenth-century France, a distrust among many fine artists of art produced for decorative purposes. Protesting fine artists at Saint Luc characterized their own work as much more than "ornament," "gilding and varnish" (Scott, 1989, 65). As we shall see in Chapter 2, rococo interior design, with its ceiling-high mirrors, chandeliers and gilt decorative flourishes (Duro, 1997, 244), was often perceived as a threat to the production of "serious" fine art (Duro, 1997, 244). Cabinet-makers and clock-makers often saw themselves in a class apart from other craftsmen, but in France at least those associated with the creation of luxury items were regarded with suspicion during the Revolution. As the decorative invaded the spaces of high art, critics and scholars worked harder at theoretical distinctions promoting the fine arts.

In 1762 the *Dictionary of the French Academy* (*Nouveau Dictionnaire de l'Académie*) pointed out in its formal definition of the term "artist," which had previously been used to refer also to scientists, that genius, as well as the manual skill associated more closely with crafts and the decorative arts, were both essential qualifications. It asserted that the term "artist" should be used of "he who works in an art in which genius and a skilled hand must coexist" (my translation) (Académie française, 1762, I, 107). Furthermore, its definition of "genius" (*génie*) referred to qualities of "Talent, inclination, or natural disposition for something estimable and belonging to the mind" (my translation). It went on to associate this term with "doing something of one's own invention" (my translation) (Académie française, 1762, I, 814), thus differentiating "art" from more repetitive or functional forms of visual culture. Meanwhile, the term "artisan" was still defined as "A worker in a mechanical art" and was associated with the term *métier* ("trade" or "craft") as well as with the running of a shop (Académie française, 1762, I, 107). In Britain, Reynolds reinforced such prejudices through the statement in his 1770 *Discourse*: "However the mechanic and ornamental arts may sacrifice to fashion, she [fashion] must be entirely excluded from the Art of Painting" (cited in Saumarez Smith, 2012, 160). Such distinctions continued to cause tensions. French *coiffeurs* were among those who sought to call themselves "artists," both for reasons of status and in order to be free of the trade restrictions imposed by the guilds. They wanted to distance themselves from more "mechanical" tradesmen (such as barbers) by stressing their "genius"; and aspiring (ultimately without success) to run academies (Falaky, 2013). It is perhaps ironic that by the end of the eighteenth century the Académie royale in Paris itself came to be regarded as a bastion of the closet favoritism, protectionism and the rule-bound work of "trade" previously associated with the guilds, thus inspiring rebellion among some of its members, including David, whose interventions led to its temporary closure (Crow, 1985, 230–232).

Questions of Modernity

In many ways the persistence of academic artistic education throughout eighteenth-century Europe suggests powerful continuities with the priorities set by French and Italian academies in the preceding centuries. Life drawing and composition remained the most important skills for artists aspiring to produce the highest forms of art. Italian masters of the High Renaissance and their idealizing style retained their powerful influence as models to be followed by history painters, the realist traditions of northern European art being considered as a form of servile copying more appropriate to the lower genres. Such observations have led in the past to the teleological assertion that more radical (or more truly "modern") developments in art in the late nineteenth and early twentieth centuries were essentially a reaction against the conservatism generated by academic culture. Modernity in an eighteenth-century context is more often associated with the responsiveness of artists to trade and to a varied market for art rather than to court- or church-dominated commissions. This subject will be examined further in Chapter 3. It is clear that the eighteenth century witnessed, in the writings of Enlightenment thinkers and in some academies, more progressive attitudes towards manufacturing and the "mechanical arts." Political, discursive and institutional pressures in more exclusive academies often countered such progress, and "trade" was often respected only if confined to state-sponsored manufacture or to commerce aimed at a social elite. Another potential barrier to change was a marked desire in critical texts to delineate and protect the main values of the "fine arts."

However, revisionist accounts of even the more "conservative" academic art have placed emphasis on more progressive aspects of these fine art academies. Carl Goldstein's 1996 work *Teaching Art: Academies and Schools from Vasari to Albers* addresses the prevailing anti-academicism in our contemporary art education and turns to an earlier (1967) source, Thomas B. Hess (in his "Some Academic Questions." In *The Academy: Five Centuries of Grandeur and Misery, from the Caracci to Mao Tse-tung*), in order to challenge any simple polarization of academic and modernizing impulses. Such challenges relate to the academic practice of copying or taking inspiration from the work of canonical "great" artists of the past. Since the Romantic movement of the early nineteenth century many commentators on art have valued imaginative invention or originality above tradition (Barker, 2012a, 299). Goldstein argues (1996, 7), however, that for those working within academies of art "originality" simply meant something different and was judged according to the degree of independent interpretation and discrimination demonstrated by an artist when "copying" or drawing inspiration from a canonical work.

This is to restate in different terms the idea of the philosopher Roland Barthes (1915–1980) that all "texts" (whether written or visual) are in fact *inter*textual in that they usually incorporate elements of previous texts (in this case paintings) that bring together past influences in a way that "destabilizes" or reinterprets them. The Enlightenment ideal of progress incorporated critical study of classical culture. To influential academic artists such as Reynolds and West, who witnessed at first hand the works of antiquity and of Renaissance masters, and who copied these works as part of their education, copying and looser forms of "imitation" were a formal but necessary prelude to invention (Schiff, 2003, 236–239). Furthermore, the academic practice of critical debate, which had been such a significant feature of the Académie royale in the seventeenth century, persisted in

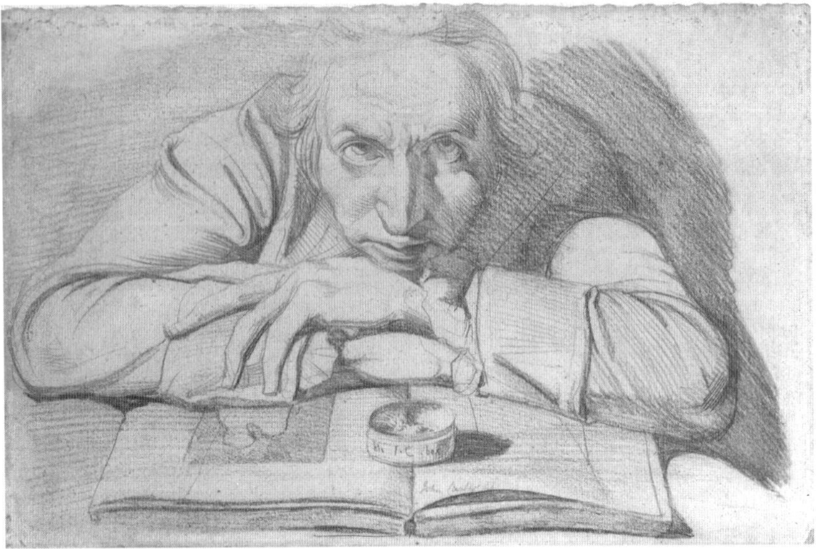

Figure 1.6 Henry Fuseli: *Probably John Cartwright*, black chalk, 32.4 × 50.2 cm, *c*.1779. National Portrait Gallery, London. Source: © National Portrait Gallery, London.

some eighteenth-century academies (e.g. in London) or was re-embodied in some cases (e.g. in France) in the critical writing of those who saw the works of academicians exhibited (Walsh, 1999, 117). This constant scrutiny of the art created by academicians made conservative or doctrinaire approaches less viable.

Eighteenth-century art practice also had its dissidents and innovators, particularly as the century drew to a close, who helped to reinvigorate and broaden the concerns of academic artists. In Britain, Henry Fuseli (1741–1825) and Benjamin West, both of whom occupied positions of responsibility at the Royal Academy, were innovators in terms of the subjects and styles they used, which included (in the former case) eroticism and fantasy, and (in the latter) the natural, romantic and "exotic." A portrait thought to represent the artist John Cartwright (Figure 1.6) shows the sitter in an intense mental state often associated with the Fuseli's own creativity. James Barry (1741–1806) was ferociously independent of the Royal Academy, from which he was expelled in 1799, as well as being critical of the British political establishment (Hoock, 2003, 190–191). His attempts to work in his own manner were very much a part of early trends in Romantic attitudes to art but also came at great expense as his work, like Fuseli's, secured little financial support. He died in poverty. What this seems to show with regard to London academic artistic culture is that more discreet forms of "originality" (e.g. Reynolds' blending of portraiture and mythological references, see Chapter 2) were more easily achieved within the confines of the Royal Academy than were more radical innovations.

Artistic autonomy is now considered to be one of the markers of modernity. There was certainly scope in the eighteenth century for artists to flourish outside the safety net provided by academies, although there were risks. Artists' studios provided spaces in which they could create works independently and free from academic strictures of any kind. These spaces could also be used in order to exploit through patronage rather than the shop window the commercial opportunities presented by expanding markets for art. Fragonard had not studied at the Académie royale in Paris when he won the coveted Rome Prize in 1752. Although he subsequently developed a position of respect at the Académie, his relations with the institution later cooled so that his career focused increasingly on works produced in his lodgings at the Louvre, free from the conventions of the Académie itself (Percival, 2012, 3). This allowed him to devote time to subjects and styles such as his "fantasy figures," half portrait and half imaginative improvisations. His distinctive style, with its loose brushwork, facilitated swift production and a timely response to high public demand, especially in the 1760s, for paintings in this genre. In similar vein, Gainsborough was a member of the Royal Academy in London but fell out with the institution following a row in 1783 over the ways in which his paintings should be hung at the Academy's 1784 exhibition (Fenton, 2006, 122–123; Solkin, 2001, 16). He then exhibited works at his own home, exploiting, like Fragonard, the market for paintings produced with the looser brushwork that stood against academic preferences for a precise finish. The fashionable nature of his work was demonstrated by the fact that his career also continued to benefit from royal patronage. The careers of both of these artists demonstrate the relatively autonomous creativity possible for artists who had already established a name for themselves: they perpetuated in this respect the relative independence of prestigious masters from the Renaissance onwards working in socially popular genres such as portraiture. Artists' studios remained the main locations in which eighteenth-century artists and apprentices learned the practical skills of painting, thus allowing some degree of originality or personal style to develop.

Earlier in the century it had been left to exceptional artists working outside the academic fine art tradition, for example, Hogarth, to introduce innovations in British visual culture. Many of the boldest departures from tradition occurred toward the end of the century, as Romantic conceptions of the artist began to take hold. The spirit of rebellion characteristic of many innovators is captured in the famous pronouncement by William Blake (1757–1827) on Reynolds: "This Man was Hired to

Depress Art" ("Annotations to Sir Joshua Reynolds' *Discourses*," 1808). Blake's visionary works had little connection with the Royal Academy, of which he was not a member. Late-century imaginative innovations in Goya's art were largely achieved outside the Real Academia in Madrid and, as we have seen, this artist was among those who rebelled against the strictures of academic classicism.

In Germany, Goethe was among those writers who championed the cause of the autonomous genius. He objected to the stifling effects of an over-rational or over-prescriptive approach to art. This kind of objection to the ideology of control underlying much academic discourse was expressed with increasing frequency. While the practice of academic artists themselves had often demonstrated that "rules" were to be interpreted quite loosely, the establishment of professional art criticism kept a vigilant eye on the dangers of conservatism and a doctrinaire approach. The concept of "genius" played a key role in such defenses. In a marked reversal of Reynolds' prescription of learning the rules in order to attain some inventiveness, later commentators such as Alexander Gerard (1728–1795) in his 1774 *Essay on Genius* recognized clearly the primary dependence of "genius" on a unique creative personality (Quilley, 2011, 16–18). Here too are the words of the art critic Diderot, in his Salon of 1765, on the oil sketches of Saint Gregory produced by the history painter Carle Van Loo (1705–1765). As Diderot ponders the relationship between Van Loo's moving art and the artist's social awkwardness, the critic offers a poetic evocation of the creative genius:

> Beware those people whose pockets overflow with intelligence and who scatter it about on the slightest pretext. They don't have the demon; they're not sad, melancholy, and taciturn; they're never awkward or stupid. The finch, the lark, the linnet, and the canary chatter and babble all day long; when the sun sets they poke their heads under their wings and go right to sleep. But this is when the genius takes up his lamp and lights it, when the solitary bird, wild, untameable, his plumage dull and brown, opens his throat, begins his song, making the wood resound, melodiously piercing the silence and gloom of the night. (Diderot, 1995a, 18)

Or note his comments on the most effective way of using color, which he opposes to a well-planned and ordered palette:

> Someone with a vivid sense of colour fixes his eyes on the canvas; his mouth hangs open, he pants; his palette is the very image of chaos. It's into this chaos that he dips his brush, pulling from it the very stuff of creation.... (Diderot, 1995a, 197)

Diderot was in the vanguard of such opinions on the artist as free spirit, but notions of "genius" were beginning to circulate extensively and to legitimize rule-breaking (Crow, 1985, 183; Wrigley, 1993, 317). The Enlightenment "genius" typified by Reynolds, was driven by rational reflection and a wise summation of the "great" qualities of previous artists. But toward the end of the century, the genius was conceived more often as an extraordinary individual who could afford to disregard all norms and canons. Matthew Craske (1997, 35, 42–43, 244) has suggested that such theoretical statements on genius were motivated in part by market conditions: as the number of artists and artworks flooded the market, it became more important to declare one's originality. Whatever the cause, this was an important step toward what we now consider a "modern" attitude toward creativity.

Further Reading

Bindman, David (ed). 2008. *The History of British Art 1600–1870.* London: Tate Publishing. A useful general survey including some case studies.

Goldstein, Carl. 1996. *Teaching Art: Academies and Schools from Vasari to Albers.* Cambridge: Cambridge University Press. An excellent introduction to the teaching methods used in fine arts academies.

Hoock, Holger. 2003. *The King's Artists: The Royal Academy of Arts and the Politics of British Culture 1760–1840.* Oxford: Clarendon Press. A useful introduction to the politicized relationship between Royal Academy Artists and the Georgian monarchy.

Kaufman, Thomas da Costa. 1995. *Court, Cloister and City: The Art and Culture of Central Europe 1450–1800.* Chicago, IL: University of Chicago Press.

Levey, Michael. 1993. *Painting and Sculpture in France 1700–1789.* New Haven, CT, and London: Yale University Press. A useful survey of eighteenth-century French art, unusual in its equal attention to painting and sculpture, and helpful in its coverage of all genres.

Milam, Jennifer D. 2011. *Historical Dictionary of Rococo Art.* Lanham, MD: The Scarecrow Press. This is pan-European in its coverage and includes a detailed bibliography.

Miller, Elizabeth and Hilary Young, eds. 2016. *The Arts of Living in Europe 1600–1815.* London: V and A Publishing. An excellent introduction to design and manufactured goods in the period.

Perry, Gill and Colin Cunningham, eds. 1999. *Academies, Museums and Canons of Art.* New Haven, CT, and London: Yale University Press. Part 2, chapters 3–5, offer useful discussion of fine art academies and their hierarchical values.

Scott, Katie. 1995. *The Rococo Interior: Decoration and Spaces in Early Eighteenth-Century Paris.* New Haven, CT, and London: Yale University Press. A comprehensive, in-depth study of the rococo, in its social, cultural and commercial contexts.

2

Genres and Contested Hierarchies

From the Renaissance onwards there was an understanding among the scholars and institutions of art that certain kinds of paintings and sculptures, those representing edifying historical, religious or allegorical themes and narratives, should enjoy the highest status. The hierarchy of genres (or subject types) became an integral part of artistic culture right through to the nineteenth century and provided a fundamental structure for most writing on art (Wrigley, 1993, 289–290). The varying subject matter of art was awarded status in relation to the presence, role and importance of the human figures represented; the grandeur and rhetorical power of the chosen subject (as opposed to the everyday or "common"); the amount of erudition – in history, literature, the classics or religion – required; the degree of idealization or imaginative transformation evident in the style of representation (as opposed to "mechanical" copying of directly observed objects, sitters and locations); and the degree of "genius" or invention displayed in the way a particular narrative or subject was conceived.

The genres of art were codified in 1669 by André Félibien, who was at the time an honorary *amateur* (a kind of consultant scholar) to the Académie royale in Paris. In his Preface to the *Lectures of the Royal Academy of Painting and Sculpture* (*Conférences de l'Académie royale de peinture et de sculpture*) he expressed the basis of academic hierarchies of genre as a preference for "…a particular kind of art quite separate from the artisan's manual skill and physical materials, involving the prior creation of pictures in the mind, without which a painter and his brush

A Guide to Eighteenth-Century Art, First Edition. Linda Walsh.

Companion website: www.wiley.com/go/walsh/guidetoeighteenthcenturyart

cannot create a perfect work. This art is not like those in which hard work and manual skill alone can create beauty." Félibien went on to specify that those works including the human figure ("God's most perfect work on earth") must stand above the rest; artists must represent "historical and legendary subjects and … the great actions recounted by historians or the pleasing subjects treated by poets," which must be ranked above portraiture. As far as other subjects were concerned, he felt that it was more difficult to paint animals than inanimate objects ("fruit, flowers or shells") and more difficult to paint landscapes than either of these (Félibien, 1669, 35; my translations).

This hierarchy of genres codified academic values and served to protect the status of history painting. It remained influential throughout the eighteenth century within European academies of art and in art criticism. By the middle of the century, drawing manuals included sets of prints on a wide range of subjects that reinforced such hierarchies, proceeding (in order of importance) from the human figure to landscape, still life and other motifs (Hsieh, 2013, 409–411). At the same time, however, changing conditions in the art market and evolving social, political and moral imperatives (which will be discussed in Chapters 3 and 5) led in practice to a blurring of Félibien's categories and values: academies were forced to respond to such changes by adopting a more inclusive approach to artists and subjects of all kinds. Notions of "quality" also began to challenge the pre-eminence of subject matter. In France the 1750s and 1760s witnessed a resurgence of interest in still life, landscape and genre subjects (the latter in the more restricted sense of representations of scenes from everyday life) that had already been so popular elsewhere, especially in seventeenth-century Holland. Patrons and buyers began to tire of "history" subjects, especially when poorly executed, and to prefer the high quality, naturalistic paintings by still life and landscape artists such as Oudry, Chardin and Vernet (Levey, 1993, 162; Wrigley, 1993, 299).

This tendency later played a part in a major uprising against the Académie royale just after the start of the French Revolution, in 1790, when David and other dissident artists, who had formed a group known as the Commune des arts, rebelled because of perceived prejudices against those practicing the "minor" genres: they were generally barred from taking up the higher offices of the institution, which remained exclusive to history painters. As a result of such pressures the minor genres featured more prominently than in the past in Salon exhibitions held in 1791 and 1793 (Conisbee, 1981, 193, 199–200). The crisis led to the closure in 1793 of the Académie, which nonetheless reopened in 1795 as part of the National

Institute of Sciences and Arts (Institut National des Sciences et des Arts) and was reinstated as a separate Arts institution in 1816 as the School of Fine Arts (École des Beaux-Arts). By the time the Salon or Academy's exhibition of 1799 occurred, exhibited works were displayed in numerical order rather than being grouped by genre, demonstrating the great shift that had taken place in French eighteenth-century attitudes to generic hierarchies.

For some artists, specialization in one genre was impractical. This was particularly true of landscape artists, who found it difficult, certainly until the 1760s, to generate enough business from their own specialism. Oudry, renowned for most of his career for still lifes, hunting scenes and exotic animal portraits, was accepted initially into the Académie royale as a history painter, a fact that influenced his career-long emphasis on careful preparatory drawings (Bailey, 2007, 1–3; Giviskos, 2007, 75–89). Joseph Wright of Derby (1734–1797) was, however, exceptional in the degree to which he continued, well into the century, to paint a range of subjects, from portraits to landscapes, scenes from contemporary life and mythological subjects. In practice some degree of specialization remained necessary, especially from the 1760s, from which time the landscape genre acquired greater respect in its own right and public demand for it increased.

The descriptive terms for generic categories with which we are now so familiar (history painting, portraiture, genre painting, landscape and still life) were not used so extensively or exclusively in the eighteenth century. Hence the history genre might be referred to in the eighteenth century as the "high style" or the "grand genre" (Wrigley, 1993, 292–293), and still life painters might be distinguished more precisely as "flower painters" or as "painters of flowers and fruit." Commercial imperatives and social fashions could also cut across traditional or crude hierarchies; for example, in Bath, where the need to create likenesses quickly for tourists could undermine the generally higher status of portraiture (Pointon, 1993, 2–3). The precise status of a portrait might also be determined by the way in which it was painted; for example, whether in a decorative or grand classical manner (Myrone, 2008, 201). For much of the century portraits continued to dominate many academy exhibitions, where they were great crowd-pullers, thus undermining the officially higher status of history paintings. Félibien's theoretical hierarchy was challenged increasingly by a pragmatic pluralism. In practice, academies protected and supported a wide range of artists, styles and genres throughout the century (Schoneveld-Van Stoltz, 1989, 224), and those who operated outside academies enjoyed even greater freedoms when choosing the subject matter of their art.

History painting

> Of all the genres of painting, history is without question the most important. The history painter alone is the painter of the soul, the others only paint for the eye. He alone can bring into play that enthusiasm, that divine spark which makes him conceive his subjects in a powerful, sublime manner; he alone can create heroes for posterity, through the great actions and the virtues of the famous men he presents; so the public does not coldly read about but actually sees the performers and their deeds. Who does not know the advantage the faculty of sight has over all the others, and the power it has over our soul to bring about the deepest, most sudden impression? (Étienne La Font de Saint Yenne, *Reflections on some Causes of the Present State of Painting in France* (1747) (*Réflexions sur quelques causes de l'état present de la peinture en France*) in Harrison, Wood and Gaiger, 2000, 556)

The term "history painting" derives from the Italian term *istoria* meaning story, history or chronicle. Leon Battista Alberti (1404–1472) used it in his 1435 treatise *On Painting* (*De Pictura*), as he tried to attribute to this kind of painting the same high cultural status as that of the ancient liberal arts of Grammar and Rhetoric, exemplified in the writings of Cicero (106–43 BCE) and Quintilian (35–*c*.96 CE). When applied to painting *istoria* designated a (generally) large-scale work most often representing a number of figures mutually engaged in a significant incident derived from a canonical written source such as those produced by the writers of ancient Greece or Rome (often Ovid, b.43 BCE; Virgil, 70–19 BCE; Livy, *c*.59 BCE–17 CE), the Bible, or Renaissance works such as the poetry of Dante (1265–1321). Key narrative moments from such sources provided moral and intellectual exemplars with universal relevance: such were, for example, moments drawn from the exemplary lives of Christ, the apostles or saints, which were intended to inspire in the viewer theologically based contemplation and meditation. These and other "history" subjects were represented in styles often described as "grand," "noble," or "sublime." "Grand machines," as such paintings were often known, were characterized by dramatic action, emotionally intense, expressive figures and poses, and styles of representation that owed a great deal to the low reliefs, murals and figurative vase designs of antiquity, or to the "ideal" bodies, classical dress and expressive features carved by ancient Greek and Roman sculptors, many of which were familiar to an eighteenth-century audience through the medium of line engravings.

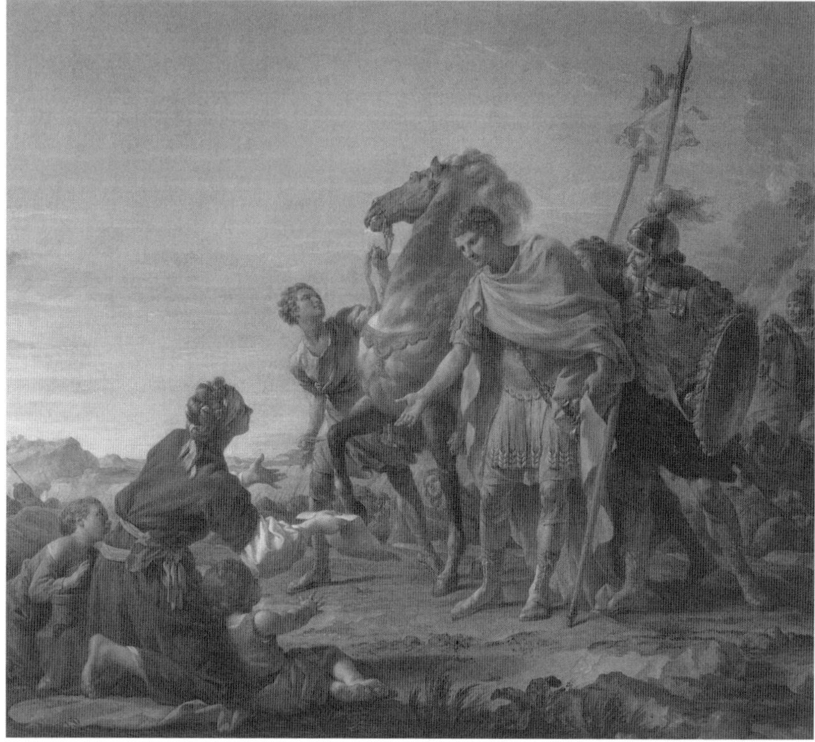

Figure 2.1 Noël Hallé: *Trajan Showing Mercy*, oil on canvas, 265 × 302 cm, 1765. Musée des Beaux Arts, Marseille. Source: Musée des Beaux-Arts, Marseille, France/Bridgeman Images.

In grand history painting heroes appeared centre-stage and a unified composition, including an appropriate distribution of light and shade, subsidiary actions and figures, appeared around them (Figure 2.1). Such subjects and styles were felt to embody the degree of liberal education and imaginative transformation appropriate to the highest and most "heroic" kinds of art. Eighteenth-century history painting was highly literary in nature, deeply influenced by hagiography, legend and myth (Scott, 1995, 177). In order to fend off occasional charges regarding the esoteric nature of such subjects, a tradition of written explanations had developed from the Renaissance onwards and was continued into the eighteenth century in, for example, exhibition catalogues, pamphlets, letters and learned articles. On the whole, however, the chosen subjects were familiar to an educated audience.

History painters were expected to engage in a suitably elevated and elaborate form of creativity that involved erudition (the study of history, literature, geography), drawings from antique prototypes (especially sculptures), initial figure sketches from the live model and compositional sketches, as preparation for their highly complex works (Percy, 2000, 462–463). Although their inspiration can be traced back to the forms and subjects of antiquity, these sources had been mediated and codified in the seventeenth century by artists such as Poussin and Charles Le Brun; the work of the latter providing a paradigmatic academic approach. In sculpture, the example of the ancients was again paramount, in, for example, funerary monuments, allegorical and mythological subjects. The baroque idiom of Gian Lorenzo Bernini (1598–1680) was commonly emulated and was felt to provide the "grandeur" required for large public or funerary commissions. Due to its association with liberal education, reason and abstract thought, the history genre and those who produced it were often seen as embodying masculine virtues and tastes that also assumed in many cases a male viewer keen to see the idealized bodies of female goddesses (Kriz, 2001, 56). Such tendencies were, however, challenged in the history paintings produced by Angelica Kauffman, whose representations of male and female bodies were often felt to transgress such stereotypes, placing women in more traditionally male heroic roles and representing male figures with less conventionally masculine physiques and expressions (Rosenthal, 2008, 82–83). This development was facilitated by the fact that not all of her history paintings were multi-figure compositions. Some were single-figure works representing, for example, saints, allegorical figures or the heroines of antiquity, in which Kauffman could explore in depth the characteristics of female subjects often relegated elsewhere to more subordinate roles.

History paintings were more complex and expensive to produce – a large painting taking several months to complete. They required more display space and were normally restricted to grand public commissions from royalty, corporations and the church, or to the patronage of aristocrats or financiers with sufficient status to own large mansions. This meant that for many artists history subjects, while representing the pinnacle of artistic accomplishment, were not a very good commercial proposition, with the possible exception (in Catholic countries) of images of the Virgin Mary, Christ and the Saints, often mass-produced for more modest domestic contexts. Paintings, tapestries and prints on historical and mythological subjects remained popular with the wealthy and the highly educated. This group included artisans and merchants able to buy, for example, prints of Nicolas Poussin's series *Seven Sacraments* or of other popular seventeenth-century masters such as Le Sueur and Charles Le Brun (Crow, 1985, 42). Grand Tourists were keen to buy copies or prints of Italian history paintings. But the tastes of the wealthy were by no means restricted to these forms of high art and, increasingly, throughout the eighteenth century, the popularity of the "lower" genres grew among all sections of the art-buying public.

For much of the eighteenth century the history genre was felt to be at risk due to a growing taste for the decorative, including the vogue for the rococo, which risked undermining its customary gravitas. It was also subject to competition in the growing art market from the "lower" genres. Félibien's endorsement of the history genre reverberated not only through much of the critical and theoretical discourse of the eighteenth century (as in the words of La Font de Saint Yenne, cited above) but also through the pronouncements and actions of academies made in response to such threats. There was a strong connection between academic rank and generic hierarchies. It was necessary to be a history painter (or sculptor) in order to become a professor, and professorial status was necessary in order to assume the higher offices of academies. Those in high office could then close ranks in order to perpetuate the status quo. In France a succession of royally-appointed Directors of Public Buildings looked to preserve this hierarchy, from the 1736–1745 term of office of Philibert Orry, Comte de Vignory; that of Charles-François de Tournehem between 1745 and 1751; of Abel-François Poisson de Vandières, Marquis de Marigny from 1751 to 1773; of Joseph-Marie Terray from 1773 to 1774; and finally that of Charles-Claude Flahaut de la Billarderie, Comte d'Angiviller from 1774 to 1789. They were supported in this by a number of Directors of the Académie royale (including, from 1770 Jean-Baptiste-Marie Pierre, 1714–1789) and First Painters to the King (*Premiers peintres du roi*). They took fright at signs that a growing public taste for "lesser" genres as well as for the decorative rococo style were placing "high art" at risk (Schoneveld-Van Stoltz, 1989, 217–219). D'Angiviller was among those responsible for commissions of "high art" that sought explicitly to renew the commitment of art to historical and national subjects.

In a move typical of academies elsewhere, the library stock of literature and history books at the Académie royale was increased in order to nurture the erudition required by practitioners of the history genre and a new membership category of "free associate" (*associé libre*) was created in order to arouse further public interest in historical subjects. In London, Paris and Rome a series of academy competitions (e.g. invention, expression and composition) and prizes (often involving money) was developed with a view to encouraging the production of "high" art when public taste seemed resistant to it (Goldstein, 1996, 56; Conisbee, 1981, 75–7, 80), and there were frequent attempts to enhance opportunities for life-drawing classes. The École des élèves protégées (see Chapter 1) in Paris, whose Directors included Carle Van Loo, Nicolas-Bernard Lépicié (1735–1784) and Dandré-Bardon, provided a rich liberal arts education.

Part of the threat to the pre-eminence of the history genre was the paucity of commissions. Churches and other religious institutions continued to need religious paintings and sculptures harmonizing with their specific tastes, beliefs and values (Conisbee, 1981, 45–46). However, the best commissions for secular history paintings came increasingly from the decorative arts, in particular tapestry designs and spectacular ceiling paintings, rather than from those specifically seeking morally serious art. Some easel paintings were commissioned, and regular Salon exhibitions encouraged this, but in many ways the market for history paintings remained tenuous in France throughout the century. Royal commissions increased in the second half of the century, thanks in part to the patronage of art lovers such as the Duc d'Orléans (1747–1793), but even these tended to produce "pleasing" rather than grand subjects.

In London Reynolds installed his two friends, Oliver Goldsmith (1730–1774) and Samuel Johnson, as professors, respectively, of ancient literature and ancient history at the Royal Academy (Hutchison, 1989, 453). As a devotee of Michelangelo di Lodovico Buonarroti Simoni (1475–1564), known as Michelangelo, Reynolds wanted the Academy to prioritize history painting in its teaching, as did most subsequent presidents and teachers there. Even artists such as Hogarth, who disliked continental trends in history painting, principally its perceived obsession with the antique, aspired to prove their credentials on this important testing ground. In 1736, Hogarth produced his *Pool of Bethesda*, a well-known biblical subject. It is noticeable, however, that although he was successful in gaining some of the few public commissions available to history painters in early eighteenth-century London, his efforts in this genre were later derided by Reynolds, who doubted that an artist so used to dealing with "low" subjects could be of sufficient caliber to tackle the intellectual demands of history (Hallett, 2006e, 197). In spite of its dwindling popularity with the public, history painting remained a major determinant of artistic status.

In general, the eighteenth-century critical establishment measured contemporary history painting against the high standards set in the golden age of the genre, the seventeenth century. There was a tendency to look backwards to the work of French, Flemish and Italian artists. As well as Poussin and Le Brun, Bon and Louis de Boullogne (1649–1717 and

1654–1733), Eustache Le Sueur (1616–1655) and Rubens provided suitable models for emulation. Other models included even older works such as those of the Roman and Bolognese schools by Raphael and the Carracci brothers: Ludovico (1555–1619), Agostino (1557–1602) and Annibale (1560–1609). Le Brun's prototypes of facial expression remained influential in history painting throughout the century and well into the Romantic period. A great deal of early eighteenth-century French history painting was heavily influenced by the Italian tradition, suitably translated into a more "correct" and finished style; and in both France and Britain it was rare to see any significant progression in style or subject matter until later decades. England lacked its own tradition of history painting prior to the establishment of the Royal Academy, since there had been so much reliance on visiting foreign artists to produce such works.

In France, artists such as Carle Van Loo established their presence through Salon exhibitions and enhanced their popularity through their willingness to tackle a wide range of subjects from the historical to the mythological and religious. Like other French history painters of the early eighteenth century, Van Loo shared with other artists such as Pierre Subleyras (1699–1749), Boucher and Charles-Joseph Natoire (1700–1777) the absorption of Italian influences gained when resident in Italy. But for Natoire and Boucher in particular, the influence of Venetian artists such as Paolo Caliari Veronese (*c.*1528–1588), known for their attachment to visual spectacle and color effects, meant that the conventional moralizing grandeur of history painting was not a central concern. Natoire completed in around 1736, for the then-Director of Public Buildings Orry, a serious work of national history relating to the legendary rule of the founding king of France, Clovis I (reigned *c.*481–511), *The Siege of Bordeaux* (*Le Siège de Bordeaux*). However, he was generally more attracted to a picturesque rather than rhetorical treatment of historical themes, and his works on the theme of Sancho Panza fell into the category of "gallant mythologies."

In the Netherlands, the great popularity of history painting evident in the seventeenth century, in, for example, the work of Rembrandt (1606–1669), had generated many manuals on emblems and mythological subjects with a view to increasing public understanding. As elsewhere, the popularity of the genre subsided there in the eighteenth century as there was greater demand for other genres such as portraiture. Genre painting became less prevalent in the Netherlands than it had been in the seventeenth century. The popularity of paintings of "everyday life" combined with the lucrative genre of portraiture, in many European countries, to undermine demand for history subjects. By the end of the century, history painting had absorbed many of the conventions of genre painting: modern rather than classical dress and greater naturalism. It also turned increasingly to more recent national or literary topics.

The increased taste in the early eighteenth century, and particularly in continental Europe, for "gallant" mythological subjects, led to widespread unease, in official circles, regarding history painting's loss of dignity and moral purpose. Mythological subjects were treated with much less gravitas and more rococo "playfulness" than their seventeenth-century precedents. They revealed the influence of the Italian artist Giovanni Battista Tiepolo (1696–1770) and his sons Giovanni Domenico (1727–1804) and Lorenzo Baldissera (1736–1776), whose services, like those of their predecessor Sebastiano Ricci (1659–1734), were in great demand across the most prestigious courts, churches and palaces of Europe, particularly for frescoes (Figure 2.2, see color plate section). Although many of G.B. Tiepolo's works were on a large scale, his style was often applied to smaller-scale decorative works. Larger royal commissions, such as Coypel's Aeneid scenes for the Palais Royal in Paris, or the work by François Lemoyne (1688–1737) at the Salon d'Hercule, Versailles, were exceptional.

In France, the Salons (exhibitions held by the Académie royale) and a number of official initiatives by a succession of Directors of Public Buildings aimed to reinvigorate the moral powers of the history genre, but this was not straightforward at a time when the monarchy's own tastes often veered toward the pleasures of the senses. Nevertheless the Directors regulated the prices of history paintings in an attempt to make them compare more favorably with the cheaper, more popular genre of portraiture (Conisbee, 1981, 75). Marigny and d'Angiviller, Coypel (First Painter to the King from 1746 and Director of the Académie royale from 1747), Charles-Nicolas Cochin (1715–1790; Secretary to the Académie royale from 1755) and Jean-Baptiste-Marie Pierre (Director of the Académie royale and First Painter to the King from 1770) all made attempts to restore the original spiritual and moral ideals of the Académie, which had been founded to express the nation's "glory" (Crow, 1985, 154–161; Schoneveld-Van Stoltz, 1989, 216–225). Royal commissions for the Château de Choisy in 1765 included military subjects, with an emphasis on clemency, generosity and humanity. These paintings (which included the *Trajan* by Noël Hallé, 1711–1781; Figure 2.1) were intended to represent symbolically the sovereign's virtues through reference to successful and benevolent leaders from ancient Rome such as Trajan (53–117 CE), Titus (39–81 CE) and Marcus Aurelius (121–80 CE). In the end, the paintings were considered, ironically, too serious and perhaps even too small to make the larger decorative impact desired for the hunting lodge for which they were intended (Crow, 1985, 12–13). In 1771, Pierre commissioned a series of paintings for the École militaire in Paris, which was equally unsuccessful, due to its use of archaic, medieval scenes (Crow, 1985, 188–189).

D'Angiviller, a member of the hereditary ("sword") nobility, aspired to reconcile the interests of royal power with Enlightenment ideology, which included a respect for social utility. In 1777, he instituted a series of commissions of historical subjects designed to reinvigorate the genre. These were based on the following broad subject areas: (i) Act of Religious Piety among the Greeks; (ii) Act of Religious Piety among the Romans; (iii) Act of Unselfishness among the Greeks; (iv) Act of Unselfishness among the Romans; (v) Act of Incentive to work among the Romans; (vi) Act of Heroic Resolve among the Romans; and two subjects from French national history: (i) Act of Respect for Virtue; (ii) Act of Respect for Morality (Crow, 1985, 189). While these subjects focused on themes of public-spiritedness, it has also been pointed out that they represent the urban public sphere, and the crowds that formed part of it, as a hostile and unstable environment in which heroes (and, by extension, public servants, the Académie or even artists) might be expected to function (Crow,1985, 189–208).

In spite of its uncertainties and inconsistencies, the taste of the French court enjoyed pan-European influence. Between 1746 and 1764 Mme de Pompadour (1721–1764), the mistress of Louis XV (reigned 1715–1774), did much through her direct patronage and with the assistance of her uncle, Le Normand de Tournehem, then-Director of Public Buildings, to stimulate renewed public interest in art: her taste was largely for Boucher's decorative rococo mythologies. The most popular literary source for such paintings was Ovid's *Metamorphoses*, from which tales of fantastical human–divine transformations were drawn. These subjects suited an era and an elite interested in disguise, masquerade, "flirting" with nature and theatrical entertainments, an emphasis on intimacy replacing the "grand manner" of painting better suited to the cultural and political prestige statements favored by earlier monarchs (Figure 2.3; Schoneveld-Van Stoltz, 1989, 217–218). Other popular rococo subjects included allegorical representations of the elements, senses, seasons, times of day, the arts and muses.

The radical nature of La Font de Saint Yenne's reaction against such trends, expressed in his review of the 1746 Salon arose from the fact that he spoke as an amateur critic representing men of feeling and taste, rather than as someone of professional or academic standing. He saw the growing preoccupation with decorative painting as a serious threat to public welfare (Harrison, Wood and Gaiger, 2000, 554–557), and linked this very clearly with the declining importance of serious history painting.

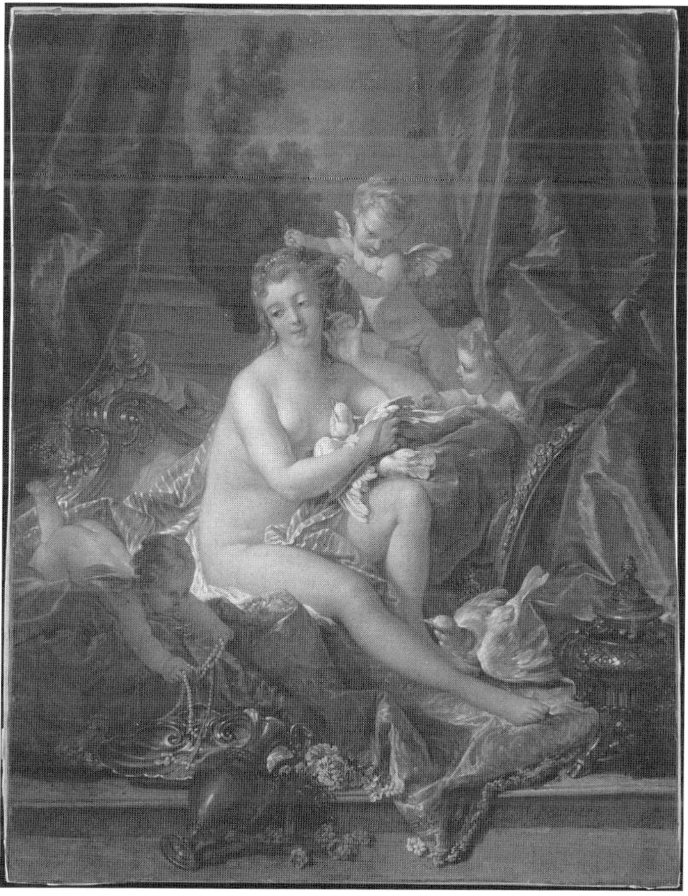

Figure 2.3 François Boucher: *The Toilette of Venus*, oil on canvas, 108.3 × 85.1 cm, 1751. The Metropolitan Museum of Art, bequest of William K. Vanderbilt, 1920, Acc. No: 20.155.9. Source: The Metropolitan Museum of Art, www.metmuseum.org

Repeating familiar regrets for the loss of the golden age of this genre he blamed an obsession with "ornamentation" and contemporary fashions in interior décor for the physical lack of space remaining for history paintings, which were now forced into small, narrow spaces above doors or mirrors, within the gilded frames of wall panels or painted on fire-screens. He bemoaned the lack of erudition possessed by contemporary history painters and their limited repertoire of (often trivial) subjects: their work represented "the triumph of the plagiarist journeyman painter, requiring neither genius nor imagination" (Harrison, Wood and Gaiger, 2000, 558). Such work provided "eye candy"-flattering portraits and silk tapestries, both of which he associated with selfishness and vanity. Women in particular were often blamed for this profusion of *boudoir* taste, a charge which more recent feminist histories have attributed to a dominant masculine discourse of art (Casid, 2003, 97–98).

A building boom in Paris in the 1740s, when the French court moved there from Versailles, led to the construction of many private mansions for aristocrats and wealthy financiers. They needed works of art that would fit the spaces in or between their lavish rococo panels, mirror frames and decorative moldings. Smaller cabinet paintings (smaller-scale works intended for small, private rooms) were also popular in Paris in this early part of the century: these trends did not favor history painting.The Beauvais tapestry factory became adept at producing smaller tapestries in the "lower" pastoral and genre scenes (Scott, 1995, 36). It was particularly successful from 1726, when under the direction of Oudry; and from 1739 tapestries could be exhibited at the Salon, which enhanced their popularity and marketability. Tapestry designs of "gallant" subjects by Boucher and landscapes by Vernet were of a suitable size for the domestic interiors of the elite and set the right tone of light entertainment. Wealthy collectors such as Pierre Crozat (1665–1740) welcomed into their homes artists such as Watteau, who was then able to mix with other artists, amateurs and writers on art. Prints of "gallant" subjects by Watteau and his imitators, including Jean-Baptiste Pater (1695–1736) and Jean-François de Troy (1679–1752), were very popular with this circle. An interest in "lower" or less "grand" genres existed, for this class of buyers, alongside an ever-weakening interest in courtly, classical art.

As indicated by previous references in the Introduction to the rococo, the issue of generic status was often bound up with artistic style which has in the past served as a focal point in histories of the period. Katie Scott has argued that in eighteenth-century France the heroic ideal embedded in conventional history paintings no longer served the purposes of members of an aristocracy who had enjoyed but lost positions of authority and influence in the final years of the reign of Louis XIV. The adoption of "gallant" rococo subjects and styles of decoration, aiming to entertain the eye with their profusion of graceful curves, gold and white, pastel shades, gleaming mirrors and reflected candle light, served as a means of establishing moral and social authority independently of court favor and appointments, and as a means of negotiating one's cultural status within evolving social groups or "classes" of the wealthy. Distancing themselves from mythic visions of public military or political power (traditional themes in grand history painting), the concerns of aristocrats with new, social forms of influence became displaced to the realms of gallantry and the "conquests" of love, in which they sought more private forms of cultural validation (Scott, 1995, 177).

Representations of "heroic" mythological subjects such as those in Coypel's Aeneas series became valued by the elite more for their picturesque appeal, their relevance to society at large or their emotive power, than for any association with exclusive or effective power (Scott, 1995, 182, 200). On a political level, the rococo might be seen as an indictment of absolute monarchy, defined by its general reluctance to share power, and as a new way of negotiating social status. This led however to further tensions. Its relatively "low-brow" classical references were accessible not only to the disempowered nobility, but also to "new money" (financiers, art collectors, connoisseurs) aspiring to noble status and to notions of *honnêteté* (politeness, a cultivated sociability) inherited from the seventeenth century. This broadening of social and cultural aspiration weakened the power of rococo mansions to endow a more exclusive social status. When Louis XV assumed the throne, the continuing taste for the rococo could be seen as a symbol of his regime's "slack moral will" (Scott, 1995, 7, 10, 81–99, 101–117, 133–136, 177–211, 213–239). The rococo was regarded as an even greater threat when it was accepted outside the domain of decorative art; for example, in the work of academicians or in Salon exhibitions, where it was increasingly displayed without reference to any original or intended decorative context (Scott, 1995, 222–260). Writers such as Jean-Bernard, abbé Le Blanc (1707–1781), Cochin and François-Marie Arouet (known as Voltaire; 1694–1778) echoed La Font de Saint Yenne's anti-rococo sentiments. The very success of the rococo served as a metaphor for a morally bankrupt state. By the end of the 1740s it was however in serious decline in France (Scott, 1995, 262–264).

Burgeoning sub-genres of rococo decoration sprang up in order to cater for its widening audience and took the style well beyond the bounds of history painting. There were different trends across Europe. In southern Germany, for example, the rococo often co-existed with the Italian baroque, its precise character adapting to the differing characters of church and palace interiors and to local traditions (Kaufman, 1995, 367–371). The style drew on a range of motifs including the *grotesque*, derived from ancient Roman and Renaissance decorative schemes. This was an entertaining, apparently improvised and provocative form of decoration that mixed antique motifs with more plebeian allusions to fairground and theatrical spectacle, sometimes featuring, for example, performing monkeys and musicians. It allowed the social elite to flirt with a transgressive street culture, yet in a safe, picturesque way (Scott, 1995, 123–136). The *arabesque*, a curvilinear form of decorative pattern derived from the Renaissance and based on foliage, urns, horns and other similar motifs, was also popular, as was use of figural motifs familiar from the *fêtes galantes* devised by Watteau or the pastoral subjects of Boucher, each of which represented a kind of safe, at-a-distance dalliance with nature, hence alluding (indirectly and hypothetically) to a social paradise (Scott, 1995, 152–161). Boucher's painted lovers, shepherds and shepherdesses often drew attention to their own artificial dress and forms of behavior rather than claiming to serve any serious moral purpose.

The adoption of the rococo by a broader range of non-aristocratic clients sparked its decline. If the nobility could no longer distinguish themselves through their rococo possessions and environments, they could at least reassert older cultural ideologies of antiquity and tradition: their knowledge of the classics singled them out. A more austere classicism regained its position as a signifier of social distinction. In the eighteenth century, what we now describe as the fashion for neoclassicism (discussed in the Introduction) was often justified as a means of elevating art to its previous aesthetic and intellectual grandeur, and was supported by an increasingly strong, international artistic community in Rome that catered for elite cultural tourists from Europe and beyond (see Introduction; Johns, 2000, 17–40; Barroero and Susinno, 2000, 48–49, 53–58). When the École des Élèves Protégés closed in 1775 (see Chapter 1) its Director, Joseph-Marie Vien (1716–1809), became Director of the French Academy in Rome, which acted as an international hub of neoclassicism. Neoclassical artists included painters such as Anton Raffael Mengs (1728–1779), Gavin Hamilton (1723–1798), François-Guillaume Ménageot (1744–1816), François-André Vincent (1746–1816), Jean-François Peyron (1744–1814), Joseph-Benoît Suvée (Figure 2.5), David (Figure 2.12), Jean-Baptiste Regnault (1754–1829) and Angelica Kauffmann; and the sculptors Houdon, Étienne-Maurice Falconet (1716–1791), Jean-Pierre-Antoine Tassaert (1727–1788), Flaxman, Antonio Canova (1757–1822) and Bertel Thorvaldsen (1770–1844), some of whom had produced earlier works in a rococo style. Neoclassical art could be inflected at times by rococo elements of eroticism or "charm" as in Vien's *Cupid Seller* (1763), or by elements of Gothic horror (Rosenblum, 1967, 7, 19–20, 11–19), while in other contexts, and particularly in David's paintings, its austere linearity and elevated themes set it apart more clearly from preceding styles.

Viccy Coltman has redefined neoclassicism as an attitude of mind, prevalent in the cultural elite, derived from more scholarly study of ancient

Greece and Rome. In the second half of the eighteenth century, Roman ideas of liberty and civic virtue were disseminated and reformulated for a modern audience through public education and the arts (Coltman, 2006. 7–8, 11, 195–196). The movement took many forms, with national variations, the decorative neoclassical schemes of Robert Adam (1728–1792) and Wedgwood in Britain contrasting with Winckelmann's Greek-inspired taste for ideal forms in Germany or David's need for a visual analogue of republican zeal (Coltman, 2006, 7–9). Neoclassical art attracted generous critical support. However, this classical revival could not in itself rescue the history genre, especially as royal commissions were so sparse. The popularity of genres other than history continued to grow. In the second half of the eighteenth century the prevailing taste was for portraits or smaller "cabinet" pictures in the more naturalistic Dutch and Flemish tradition inspired by scenes from contemporary life.

In other respects, and within its diminishing field of influence, eighteenth-century history painting embraced stylistic pluralism. A common duality in play in discussions of style was that between the "Roman" school, which corresponded largely with Wölfflin's "classic" (see Introduction) and the "Venetian" associated with a vivid use of color and looser brushwork in, for example, the work of Veronese and Titian. The influence of Veronese was still very much alive in eighteenth-century Venice, where Sebastiano Ricci tried to emulate in his history paintings the colorist effects of the master (Levey, 1959, 19–24). In historical sculpture (figure groups based on ancient mythology, religion and history, with some narrative content), the sublime and baroque effects of Michelangelo (swirling drapery, dramatic gestures and poses) were as well esteemed in the eighteenth century as more "restrained" styles, although the purer, more austere forms of neoclassical sculpture, derived from early classical Greek sculptural traditions of the fifth century BCE, became prominent in its later decades. Stylistic flexibility, hybridity and flux in academic history painting and sculpture illustrate the artificiality of any neat dualism in such matters. An eclectic range of stylistic models reduced the hazard of conventionality, even within academic practice.

Many of the social elite would have seen at first hand works by the masters from a range of schools or traditions, as part of their Grand Tour of Europe – and would have learned to use canonical artists' names as ciphers for specific styles or "manners." Thus, Raphael's name was often evoked in references to the work of High Renaissance and seventeenth-century Roman, Bolognese and French artists such as Poussin, Carlo Maratta (1625–1713), Andrea Sacchi (1599–1661), Louis de Boullogne, the

Carraccis, Guido Reni (1575–1642) and Le Sueur; while a Venetian emphasis on color, movement and loose brushwork was evoked by the names of Titian, Jacopo Tintoretto (*c.*1518–1594) and the Tiepolos; Rubens' name was shorthand for a Flemish baroque tradition of color, dramatic composition and fleshy, non-idealized bodies; and Michelangelo Merisi da Caravaggio (1573–1610), known as Caravaggio, evoked baroque realism, dramatic compositions and effects of light and shadow. Taking France as an example, Subleyras was heavily influenced by Maratta and Sacchi, while the mid-century work of Doyen and Louis-Jean-Jacques Durameau (1733–1796) emulated the Italian baroque tradition. The austerity of the Roman school best suited those artists who wished to distinguish their work from the "merely decorative," since it was felt to appeal primarily to the mind rather than the eye. History painters were judged by academicians and critics less on their choice of style than on their ability to live up to the example of their illustrious predecessors, but all were expected to produce well composed, legible narrative scenes based on a well-chosen "moment" with significant expressive potential and historically convincing costumes.

In the last three decades of the eighteenth century, French history painters, including David and his pupil Jean-Germain Drouais (1763–1788) were significantly influenced by Caravaggio, whose style was encountered by many of the students at the French Academy in Rome (Conisbee, 1981, 59–68). Caravaggio's emphasis on realism and dramatic effects of light and shade was often combined, in late-century neoclassical paintings, with the influence of Poussin's dignified, "classic" figures and compositions. Jean-Charles-Nicaise Perrin (1754–1831) and Suvée were among the artists influenced by Poussin; Regnault was also influenced considerably by the more disciplined, restrained classicism of Reni. These few examples demonstrate that academies encouraged or condoned a wide range of stylistic influences within the history genre.

The pattern in France was copied elsewhere. Neoclassical art popular internationally in the late eighteenth century was influenced by the more austere classicism of the Roman, Bolognese or Poussinesque traditions, and acquired a moral "edge" through its greater distance from decorative visual effects. Neoclassical artists based in other countries included Nathaniel Dance-Holland, Gavin Hamilton, Angelica Kauffman, Benjamin West, James Barry, Christian Gottlieb Schick (1761–1812), Eberhard Georg Friedrich von Wächter (1762–1852) and Philipp Friedrich von Hetsch (1758–1838). The work of these artists reflects varying degrees of drama and spectacle, as well as stylistic variation: neoclassicism was not monolithic. For example, the historical compositions of Gavin Hamilton were more crowded than those of Poussin, the hero of many neoclassicists; his figures more massive, Michelangelesque, closer to the picture plane and less correct than their academic antique prototypes (Macmillan, 1986, 32–43). There were differences in emphasis: Hamilton was among those who championed Greek, Homeric subjects rather than Roman subjects (Macmillan, 1986, 33–58) as he built on the lead given by the writer and philosopher George Turnbull (1698–1748) and instigated an international taste for such subjects through strong commercial and cultural networks in Rome.

The growing dominance of neoclassicism might be linked more broadly with the Enlightenment's emphasis on moral, social and political reform, discussed further in Chapter 5. Paintings such as David's *The Oath of the Horatii* (*Le Serment des Horaces*, 1785) (Crow, 1985, 212–217) and West's *The Death of General Wolfe* (1770) (Figure 2.4, see color plate section; Abrams, 1985, 161–164) were often read in their own time as vehicles for political allegory; in the first of these through a representation of young soldiers whose vigor might be seen as emblematic of radicalized, revolutionary youth. David's neoclassicism or reforming "true style" constituted a sober alternative to the earlier, playful mythologies of the neoclassicist Vien (Rosenblum, 1967, 55–86; Conisbee, 1981, 95, 98, 100, 106). West's painting offered a similarly uplifting, heroic and patriotic interpretation of British colonial ambitions in what is now French Canada.

Portraiture

Portraiture was the dominant genre of eighteenth-century art, particularly in Britain and America. From the 1780s, portraits dominated public exhibitions in Britain (Pointon, 1993, 39; Simon, 1987, 6; Solkin, 2001, 43). They often provided a more secure form of income for artists than history painting (Retford, 2011, 101) or landscapes, pastel portraits being particularly quick to produce and requiring less expensive materials. In the second half of the century, and in the more highly regulated art world of Paris, various Directors of Public Buildings stepped in to regulate the market in portraiture, which was perceived as one of the causes of the decline of interest in the history genre. In his *Reflections on Some Causes of the Present State of Painting in France*, La Font de Saint Yenne complained that many history painters were driven for financial reasons to portraiture. The critic's views show more than a little snobbery in response to people of "middling" social status joining their social superiors in acquiring portraits of themselves:

> What resource will be left to the history painter if he is not in a position to feed his family on more solid fare than glory? He will sacrifice his personal tastes and natural talents to his needs, in order not to see his fortunes waning, despite his skill and efforts, in contrast to the rapid financial gains made by his colleagues the portrait painters, especially those working in pastel. He will suppress his inner callings and divert his brush from the path of glory to follow that of material well-being. He will, in all honesty, suffer for a time to see himself forced to flatter a simpering, often misshapen or aged face, which almost always, lacks physiognomy; reproducing obscure, characterless people, without name, without position, without merit.... (cited in Harrison, Wood and Gaiger, 2000, 559; see also Wrigley, 1993, 304–305)

In the same year, 1747, the Director of Public Buildings, Le Normand de Tournehem, reduced the prices to be paid for portraits and regulated those of history paintings on a sliding scale determined by their size. This initiative proved unpopular with portrait painters (Conisbee, 1981, 77).

As La Font de Saint Yenne's comment suggests, the status of a portrait was affected in part by that of its sitter, ranging from royal subjects (whose portraits often "starred" in public exhibitions) to wealthy financiers and more modest subjects from the worlds of commerce and the professions. It became more common for writers, actors, politicians and artists themselves to have their portraits painted (Retford, 2006, 7). The association of portraiture with vanity often led to claims that it was a feminine vice and that its influence spread particularly effectively through a sordidly mercantile (i.e.non-aristocratic, market-based) culture, especially in Britain (Kriz, 2001, 61). The formats or portraits helped to determine their status, with those reproduced on broadsheets, snuff boxes or trade cards regarded as utilitarian or decorative rather than examples of fine art (Pointon, 1993, 84). Portraits could be turned into prints (those of Kauffman and Reynolds were very popular in this form; Hallett, 2014, 120–123) or applied to ceramic jugs, paste plaques, signs and even wallpaper designs (Pointon, 2001, 98). The status of portraiture was generally considered lower than that of history painting because there was a popular perception that it involved "mere copying" rather than erudition or imaginative transformation, although as we shall see, there are problems with this view of any work of art.

The term *portrait* derived from the French phrase "trait pour trait" (literally "line for line"), which placed emphasis on copying or producing an accurate physical likeness. This aspect of portraiture had legendary force due to the description of Pliny the Elder (23–79 CE), in his *Natural History* of the origin of painting and sculpted portrait reliefs. He identified this as the occasion (in around 600 BCE) on which the daughter of the ancient Greek artisan and tile-maker Butades of Sicyon traced on a wall the shadow of her young lover, who was about to set out on a journey. Her father subsequently pressed clay into the outlined shape so that he could make a portrait relief. The story is captured in Suvée's *The Invention of Drawing* (*L'Invention du dessin*) (1791) (Figure 2.5, see color plate section). It is widely acknowledged today, however, that in the great periods of portrait production, including the eighteenth century, both artists and sitters were motivated by concerns extending well beyond the pragmatic requirement of a physical likeness.

The eighteenth-century fashion for portraiture is now often associated with an increased emphasis on a sitter's subjectivity, or individual identity, that took hold as a "modern" market economy allowed a broader public to commission and buy portraits. This contrasts both with previous, more aristocratic conceptions of portraiture that had much more to do with recording the ancestry, land and property rights of a social elite, and with patterns of cultural patronage exercised by the state, absolutist monarchies and (in Catholic countries) the Church. Such interpretations have sometimes drawn loosely on Marxist-derived explanations of the ways in which cultural production is influenced by a substratum of political, economic and social structures, the eighteenth century being seen as the time at which a more independent *bourgeois* and manufacturing class emerged in order to alter in radical ways the markets and key "products" of art. As such classes established their authority and legitimacy within the social hierarchy, so the concept of the self-determined, active, self-conscious or self-aware subject (rather than the passive servant of autocracy or feudalism) gained in currency. In the case of portraiture this resulted in a growing interest, especially from the 1740s, in the "pyschological" portrait, that went beyond a physical likeness to embrace aspects of an individual's character and personality.

This is not to suggest that such changes occurred in any neat or universal way. Indeed, those members of an emerging middle class could (as we have already seen, in the adoption by "new wealth" of aristocratic rococo interiors) assert their new status by aping previous aristocratic practices. Some commissioned family portraits in order to establish their newly found social credentials and to compensate for their prior lack of ancestral portrait displays or galleries. In America, sober, upright portraits of professionals (doctors, magistrates, merchants, lawyers, judges, churchmen, politicians and diplomats) helped to establish the status of those anxious to record in a colonial context their familial (or "dynasty") and national status (Miles, 1995, vii), while American portrait artists studying in Europe returned home to practice the most sophisticated styles they had discovered on their travels (Miles, 1995, 3–10, 21).

Recent investigations into eighteenth-century portraiture and, in particular, Marcia Pointon's *Hanging the Head: Portraiture and Social Formation in Eighteenth-Century England* (1993) have stressed the central role of portraiture in "constructing" rather than simply reflecting new forms of social identity. According to this view, the genre of portraiture in particular should be regarded as a social practice or activity, associated with contemporary discourses derived from relationships of hierarchy and power defining society more broadly. Such a view emphasizes the sitter's "self" as an actively constructed entity, determined by the cultural and interpretative conventions of a society and by an individual's specific way of engaging with such conventions (through, for example, the commissioning of a portrait) (Pointon, 1993, 1–8). A significant part of the entertainment offered by exhibitions was the opportunity to speculate about the gestures, expressions, costumes and characters of sitters (Conisbee, 1981, 113; Pointon, 1993, 62–63). The different ways of constructing a portrait (e.g. degrees of formality; compositional formats and choice of settings and accessories; forms of dress and pose) carried symbolic significance concerning social roles, rank and gender. Portraits were also used and displayed, for example, as miniatures displayed in homes, as collections of prints or book illustrations or as part of an ancestral country house display, in ways that suggested particular symbolic meanings. Country houses in particular provided semi-public spaces opened up to many beyond a family's intimate circle thus making ostensibly private identities and virtues a kind of public property (Retford, 2006, 10–11). Pointon suggests (1993, 6–7, 56) that representations of sitters' heads were the principal means of suggesting meanings and values: the head often stood in a metonymic relationship to the body, social identity and character of an individual.

One decision relating to the head was whether a sitter should be represented wearing a wig. Particularly in the early decades of the century, gentlemanly decorum required the wearing of a wig, which also functioned as a symbol of masculinity. Those who appeared wigless risked being seen as barbaric, insufficiently masculine or a threat to the social order. Later in the century, when fashions relaxed and revolutionary fervor became more familiar, it became more acceptable to appear in public with one's own (powdered) hair, although many men chose to wear their own hair greased and powdered so that it resembled a wig, in order to avoid appearing as a republican sympathizer. Decisions about a sitter's appearance in portraits could in such ways actively regulate discourses of social and political status in the interests of (or as a challenge to) political influence, ideologies, nationalist or propagandist messages (Pointon, 1993, 107–136). They could also facilitate forms of self-enactment, self-fashioning or role-playing (Hallett, 2014, 7–10, 114–120, 193–194) that belied any notion of an essential, "natural" self. Sitters could play with varying identities; for example, by wearing clothing provided as studio props and associated with another, possibly "exotic" nation or period. Turkish and ancient Roman dress were particularly popular and, toward the end of the century, ancient Greek costume was in vogue. Social rank could also be the subject of disguise, masters dressing as servants, and vice versa. This was the great age of the masquerade in which people enjoyed flirting with new identities very different from those assumed in their own day-to-day lives, but choice of costume could also signify deeper social and even international relations, Turkish dress potentially representing colonial or western perceptions of the east, the objectification of women or, in cases where women patrons played a more active role in a commission, a means by which they might control their public image (Pointon, 1993, 143–157). Such costumes also answered a need for fantasy (Williams, 2014, 62–87).

Poses drawn from classical statuary (e.g. the Apollo Belvedere) or from Renaissance masterpieces might also be used to boost, or occasionally pass witty comment on, sitters' social pretensions. Those drawn from contemporary conduct books; for example, a correctly arched back, correct hand gestures or feet positioned at elegant right angles to each other, conveyed a suitable air of gentility (Simon, 1987, 36–96). Such symbolic systems of representation were often marred, however, by artists' uneven skills or on occasion by their tendency to rely too much on earlier visual formulae. Some artists used dolls or jointed wooden lay figures to try out various poses or costumes, which could result in stiff representations. Many artists used sets of prints from which sitters could select poses or expressions, which must then be made to look spontaneous or "natural." Non-standard poses or accessories often triggered an additional charge to the sitter. Manipulating such sets of conventions, both artists and sitters rose beyond mere copying or realism in order to create a more dynamic interplay of the real and the imaginary: there was no essential "self" for them to copy. It was still assumed however that portraiture made much more reference to "real" physical appearances and character than, say, history painting (Wrigley, 1993, 301; Vaughan, 2008, 65).

The art of portraiture involved an integration of social and business skills. It has been suggested (Pointon, 1993, 41, 47) that sitting for one's portrait was primarily, in the eighteenth century, an opportunity for social interaction. It satisfied a need to be recorded and flattered, and required sophisticated social skills from an artist, especially when dealing with high-status clients, who often enjoyed the privilege of sittings arranged in their own homes. In general, for the actual completion of a work, there was a workshop system in which it was common for the portrait painter to focus on the sitter's face and hands while other elements such as background landscapes, accessories, animals, flowers or clothing were delegated to artists who specialized in one of these areas, or to former apprentices now employed as studio assistants (Simon, 1987, 9–13, 97–130; Hallett, 2014, 42). Even "great" portrait painters such as Reynolds and Allan Ramsay (1713–1784) had up to 80% of their canvases completed by someone else (Simon, 1987, 97, 103; Macmillan, 1986, 21). Not all artists worked in this way. It was quite common, for example, for Gainsborough to execute a portrait in its entirety, including landscape settings, drapery and flesh painting; and Hogarth's were all his own work. Reynolds often used the services of assistants for the painting of drapery, landscape and accessories, and for the production of replicas. Gainsborough commented that assistants often enjoyed more lucrative careers than those who painted portrait heads:

> There is a branch of Painting next in profit to portrait, and quite in your power without any more drawing than I'll answer for your having, which is Drapery and Landskip backgrounds. Perhaps you don't know that whilst a face painter is harassed to death the drapery painter sits and earns five or six hundred a year, and laughs all the while. (Quoted by Whitley, 1915, 389)

This is slightly disingenuous in view of the fact that the most celebrated portrait artists could charge higher prices. Many worked with several sitters over the same period of time; for example, when they made themselves available to well-to-do clients staying in the fashionable spa resort of Bath, for the "season." Reynolds often saw several sitters each day (Simon, 1987, 130; Reynolds, 1968, 115–140). In order to make their businesses economic they also worked to a fixed scale of sizes and prices, from what was termed a "three-quarter format" (which could be just head and shoulders) to the larger "kit-cats" (near half-length, with one or both hands), half-lengths, "bishop half-lengths" (wide enough to accommodate a pair of lawn sleeves) and full-length. The use of a "store" of poses (from previous works), accessories and costumes was common. Gainsborough made extensive use of candlelight in his sittings, particularly the earlier ones, and often detached large canvases from their frames so that he could move them temporarily closer to a sitter in order to achieve a better likeness.

Reynolds used a mirror in which sitters could see the current state of their portrait reflected. Artists varied a great deal in the extent to which they used under-drawings as a basis for their paintings. Reynolds was among those who avoided use of draughtsmanship, painting heads directly onto canvas. In spite of such efficiencies portraiture became less popular toward the end of the century when the growing fashion for wallpapers in domestic interiors meant that there were fewer spaces in which to place such works. In the nineteenth century, other, more "minor" categories of art such as genre or subject paintings challenged increasingly the eighteenth-century dominance of portraiture.

"Grand manner" portraits

The eighteenth century is often seen as a period in which grand, public-facing art was mitigated increasingly by the production of works with a less formal, at most semi-public or private function. This is certainly true of portraiture. Grand portraiture remained important, however, particularly with patrons and institutions concerned to assert their "high" status. As the "old regime" of dominant royal courts and aristocracies persisted throughout the century, interrupted only temporarily in France by the Revolution, so did the conventions of grand portraiture characteristic of the golden age of Louis XIV. Corporations and other institutions wishing to celebrate their grandeur and prestige helped to perpetuate it. The large-scale baroque configurations of artists such as Hyacinthe Rigaud (1659–1743) and Nicolas de Largillière (1656–1746) had set the pattern for what came to be known as "historical," "great" or "grand style" portraits. Formal, "correct," ceremonial, genteel or commanding poses (some derived from antique statuary) and styles of dress, classical allusions and allegorical references to social and political power, backgrounds of sweeping drapes, country estates or antique columns, set the tone for grand public statements emulated in the eighteenth century by artists such as Reynolds (Wrigley, 1993, 301; Simon, 1987, 18–19, 54, 76–86, 112; Conisbee, 1981, 4, 113–115, 125, 137). Reynolds also added bitumen to his black paint in order to cultivate an "old master" look. This technique has led unfortunately to surface cracking in many of his works. Grand portraits often carried important messages regarding ancestral rights to land, wealth and title in which large extended families featured significantly (Pointon, 1993, 16–33). They also laid claim to an association with the "highest" form of art, history painting.

In both painting and sculpture, commissions for grand portraiture provided a means of asserting the high status of the "historical style." In

1774 in France, the Comte d'Angiviller, recently appointed Director of Public Buildings in France, set up a series of commissions of "grand style" paintings and sculptures intended to celebrate the "great men" of France. The choice of subjects was determined by the royal household and conveyed to Pierre, at the time First Painter to the King. The plan (ultimately uncompleted) was to create works that might decorate the Grande Galérie at the Louvre, as there was already an intention to open up the royal collections there to the public. The focus, intended as an appeal to national sentiment, was on the great military figures, writers and magistrates of French history, and it was hoped that such subjects would appeal to all France's social "states" from the aristocracy and clergy to the broader "third estate," many of whom expressed an increasing interest in art.

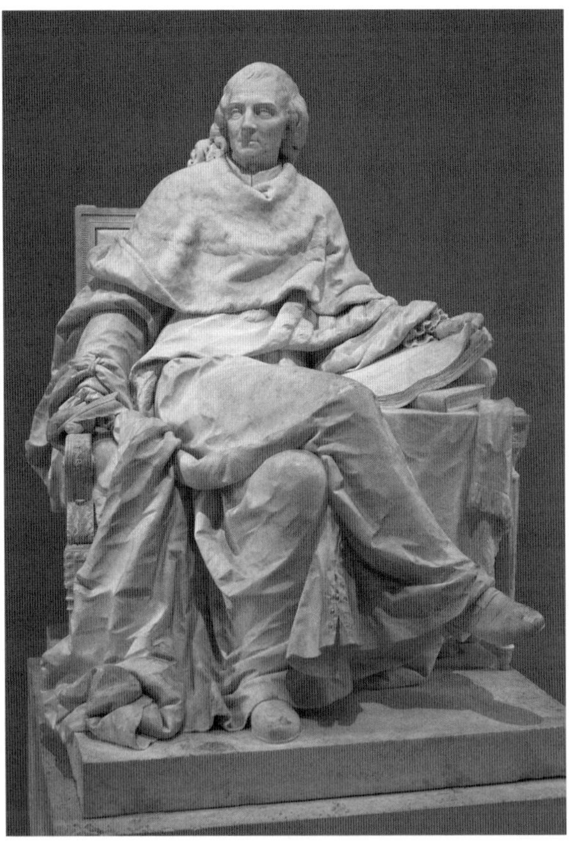

Figure 2.6 Claude Michel, known as Clodion: *Charles de Secondat, Baron de Montesquieu* (1689–1755), marble, h. 164 cm. Paris, Musée du Louvre. Source: © 2015. White Images/Scala, Florence.

These commissions for historical portrait sculpture focused on both ancient and more recent history. Clodion's *Montesquieu* (1783) (Figure 2.6) celebrates, for example, a recent philosopher and writer who had been at the heart of the French Enlightenment. The Sèvres factory eventually used the models produced for this series, in order to produce porcelain reproductions, demonstrating an interplay of "high" and artisanal visual cultures.

In the case of actress portraits, historical, classical and allegorical references could elevate sitters who might otherwise be seen as objects of a desiring, male gaze: the stage performance trappings of tragedies, including the costumes and attributes of significant figures form ancient history and mythology, gave these women added cultural and social status, especially when their portraits were exhibited alongside those of women from the higher echelons of society (Perry, 2007, 62–6, 76). It was, however, more difficult to elevate by such means the status of comic actresses, singers and dancers (Perry, 2007, 81, 137–167).

In the early part of the century the portrait painter, collector and writer, Jonathan Richardson (1667–1745), wrote several works with the intention of developing a livelier British interest in "historical" painting, dominated at the time by continental artists. In the first of these, *Essay on the Theory of Painting* (first edition 1715), Richardson celebrates not only the cerebral and idealizing tendencies of history painting, which raise it above the merely entertaining, "decorative," "ornamental" or mimetic (Pointon, 1993, 6), but also the fact that such qualities could and should be captured in "lesser" genres such as portraiture (Hallett, 2014, 33–36):

> A Portrait-Painter must understand Mankind, and enter into their Characters, and express their Minds as well as their Faces: And as his Business is chiefly with People of Condition, he must Think as a Gentleman, and a Man of Sense, or "twill be impossible to give Such their True, and Proper Resemblances." (Richardson, 1725 [1715], 330)

Hogarth's 1740 portrait of Captain Coram (1668–1751), a naval officer who created the Foundling Hospital in London, drew on the influence of Rigaud, demonstrating that British artists were capable of producing the same grandeur as their continental predecessors (Simon, 1987, 14). The fusion of classicism and gentility in such portraits was influenced in part by conduct books such as François Nivelon's *Rudiments of Genteel Behaviour* (1737), which proclaimed, among other things, that when standing "the left Leg must be foremost, and only bear its own weight, and both feet must be turned outwards..." (Nivelon, 1737, section on "Standing").

The pose suggested here was highly reminiscent of the elegant Roman sculpture of the Apollo Belvedere. Such fusions "naturalized" (represented as natural or justifiable) the superior station of the ruling ranks of society. Portrait painters took this trend one step further when they dressed their sitters in the costumes and attributes of the ancient gods, in classical garb like that worn by Poussin's figures, or in a fashionable "Van Dyck" costume evocative of the seventeenth-century Caroline court and of dynastic nobility: these costumes were also popular at eighteenth-century masquerades (Simon, 1987, 64; Retford, 2006, 7, 218–221; Retford, Perry and Vibert, 2013, 9).

Grand portraiture acquired a new impetus in the 1760s, with the ascendancy of Reynolds. The aim, in the artist's words, was to produce a "general air" of the sitter in question rather than a precise likeness. Capturing a "likeness" depended in part on viewers' ability to recognize such "general airs" and relate them to social peer groups, such recognition often being mediated further by gendered stereotypes (Pointon, 1993, 81). However, as an astute businessman Reynolds also recognized the appeal to contemporary genteel audiences of portraits combining traditional formal settings with more informal poses and expressions: a kind of public–private hybrid type. He was adept at combining grandeur with more fashionable concerns of dress and feminine gracefulness. A recent research project by the Wallace Collection, London, has discovered through the use of X-rays and infra-red images the ways in which Reynolds often altered an original hairstyle in a painting, to reflect a more modern trend. Reynolds often gave his female sitters fantasy roles in grand mythological narratives or portrayed male sitters in grand dress indicative of their public roles, while also representing at times more private capacities for introspection and a refined sensibility (Hallett, 2014, 18–19, 108–113, 226–239). He also introduced less formal settings, such as the "natural" yet stormy backdrop in his *Anne Dashwood (1743–1830), Later Countess of Galloway* (1764) (Figure 2.7). In Gainsborough's portraits, such settings assumed a larger role, reflecting a growing interest not just in naturalism but also in spending time *in* "nature."

Grand manner portraits were executed with varying degrees of formality, Élisabeth Vigée Le Brun, for example, treating some of her female sitters in a gentler way that focused on their capacity for feeling, if not "character," the latter often being stereotyped as a masculine virtue. Male sitters were often represented in more grandiloquent style, and with greater reference to public office, in order to reflect the contemporary view of a "natural" gendered order of society (West, 2008, 144–145).

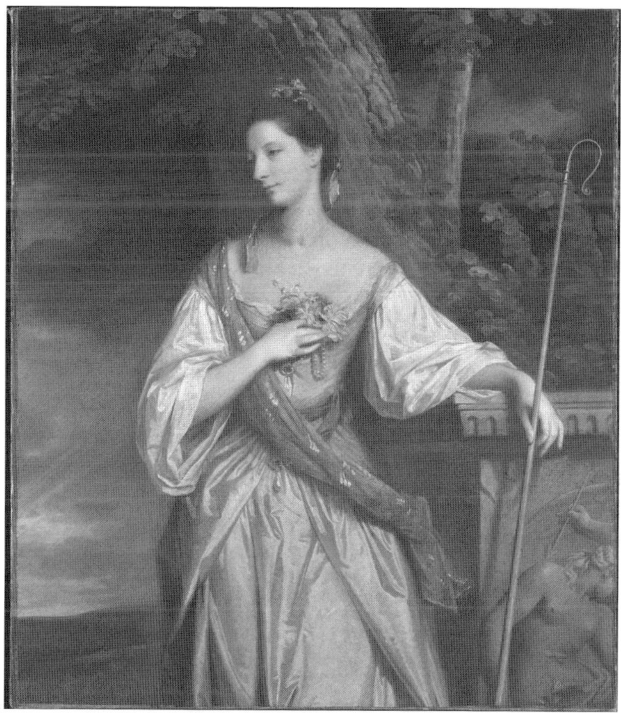

Figure 2.7 Sir Joshua Reynolds: *Anne Dashwood (1743–1830), Later Countess of Galloway*, oil on canvas, 133.4 × 118.7 cm, with strip of 18.1 cm folded over the top of the stretcher, 1764. The Metropolitan Museum of Art, Gift of Lillian S. Timken, 1950. Acc. No: 50.238.2. Source: The Metropolitan Museum of Art, www.metmuseum.org

However, Angelica Kauffman was among those artists who challenged such values by blurring the boundaries of "feeling" women and "rational" men (Rosenthal, 1992, 105; 2008, 82–83). The "grandeur" of portraits of sitters from both sexes could also be undermined or reduced to a fussy prettiness when the rococo style was used; for example, in Boucher's 1756 portrait of Louis XV's mistress, Mme de Pompadour. When applied to portraiture this style emphasized decorative detail (frills, ruffs, ribbons) and delighted the eye through the representation of dazzling surface textures; for example, the suggested sheen of satin or the use of pleasing pastel shades. Strong eighteenth-century traditions of satire, the mock-heroic and the salacious could also undermine the pretentions of grand portraiture.

Private portraiture

Growing demand for portraits in a more informal style appropriate to private or semi-private display was evident from the 1740s. In works such as these more relaxed, everyday poses, occupations and dress were common. Marcia Pointon (1993, 54) has described "privacy" as an eighteenth-century invention. As stated earlier, the representation in portraiture of private individuals (sitters) through the use of concrete and symbolic objects helped to construct the notion of the self-regulating subject who might strive for and express identities beyond those dictated by more formal visual discourses. Relations of power or social standing were defined in part through a series of opposing concepts, in this case the less powerful "private" and the more powerful "public". However, contemporary discourse on the social passions, popularized through works such as *The Wealth of Nations* (1776) by Adam Smith (1723–1790) and the *Enquiry Concerning the Principles of Morals* (1751) by David Hume (1711–1776), along with a growing interest in personal biographies and autobiographies, also led to an interest in the personal or private feelings that lay behind public social intercourse, from self-love to empathy (Retford, 2006, 8).

Conventionally, a rise in interest in the naturalistic representation of sitters involved in daily occupations such as walking, reading and relaxing with their families, is linked to the influence on European art of Dutch portrait and genre painting (Conisbee, 1981, 113–131). This issue has been related on occasion to national cultural identities, the Dutch manner (and those with a close affinity to it) sometimes defined in opposition to the "affectation" associated with a dominant Francophile culture. Duncan Macmillan has explained the emphasis on close observation of nature in Scottish portraiture (including that of Ramsay) by reference to the Scottish Enlightenment's emphasis on practical reform. He interprets this, however, as a desire to mediate, rather than deny, the influence of continental classicism, idealism or the rococo (Macmillan, 1986, 19–30). Naturalistic portraits varied in style and approach. Some, such as those by the pastellist Maurice Quentin de La Tour (1704–1788), or the more detailed representations of sitters by Ramsay, implied an emphasis on the individual character of the sitter, whereas others conformed to looser human types such as the daydreamer, the lover, the mother or father, the upstanding professional, writer, musician and so on. Greater formality crept into the genre later in the century as the neoclassical style came into vogue and restored the popularity of ordered classical interiors or neutral backgrounds. In such works, however, the emphasis on more private, familiar, everyday poses and activities, "interiority," subjectivity and personal relationships often remains, as in David's *Monsieur et Madame Lavoisier* (1788).

Kate Retford, in *The Art of Domestic Life: Family Portraiture in Eighteenth-Century England* (2006) has explored in the context of family portraiture this growing emphasis on informality, a private inner life and inward, "absorbed" expressions in portrait representations that seem much less explicitly to address or impress the viewer than their antecedents in grand public portraiture. She stresses that the emphasis in such portraiture on private, personal feeling or, as it was increasingly known, "sensibility," was in fact a fiction constructed by artists in order to counter what they saw as the even greater artifice of the codes of gentility that had hitherto dominated the genre of portraiture. This fiction resonated from the 1760s onwards with developments in literature and philosophy that associated the experience or outpouring of emotion with personal virtue. Bonds of feeling and empathy made particularly good subject matter in this context and often lay at the heart of what is now termed "sentimental(ist)" art; that is, art referring to feeling or sentiment (Retford, 2006, 1–4). The broader ancestral relationships central to much earlier formal portraiture became less interesting than more intimate gatherings of immediate family (Wrigley, 2007, 258).

Children were shown in more child-like dress, playing informally with animals and toys, as opposed to earlier grand family portraits in which they had appeared to be as stiff and formally dressed as adults were. Notions of childhood and adulthood are culturally and historically specific, and the eighteenth century is often considered to mark a watershed in this respect. The "special" nature of children – their fragility, unstable identities, uncertain morality ranging from innocence to cruelty, growing self-consciousness, changing physical form and emerging sexuality, were increasingly acknowledged, particularly in the sphere of artistic representation (Kayser, 2003, 10, 14, 29, 119, 149–152; Scott, 2003, 97). This change generated a range of adult responses to children, from the relatively libertarian ideas on education of John Locke, whose views were reinterpreted in the mid-eighteenth century by thinkers such as Jean-Jacques Rousseau (1712–1778), to sterner, disciplinarian views characteristic, for example, of the Weslyan Church.

Portraits of children became popular with both the aristocracy and with patrons from the middling to wealthy ranks of society. They were exhibited in public a great deal from the 1770s. Even artists like Reynolds, who constructed fairly formal classical family portraits, included in them playful, chubby, *putti*-like children who were meant to pull on viewers' heartstrings. It has been suggested that such representations could sometimes serve as a vehicle for the expression of cross-generational desire (Pointon, 1993, 5, 177–193), especially as child portraits were painted mainly for the delight of adults. There is also some evidence that many "pretty" representations of children in other genres, such as the rosy-cheeked figures featuring in cottage scenes by Gainsborough, hinted at notions of victimhood and poverty that were more explicit when embedded in satirical images (Crown, 1984, 163–7). Some "stiffer" representations of children persisted, for example, in the society portraits of Arthur Devis (1712–1787), who used wooden lay figures as his models. His work declined in popularity from the 1760s, due to a growing taste for the "natural" (Figure 2.8).

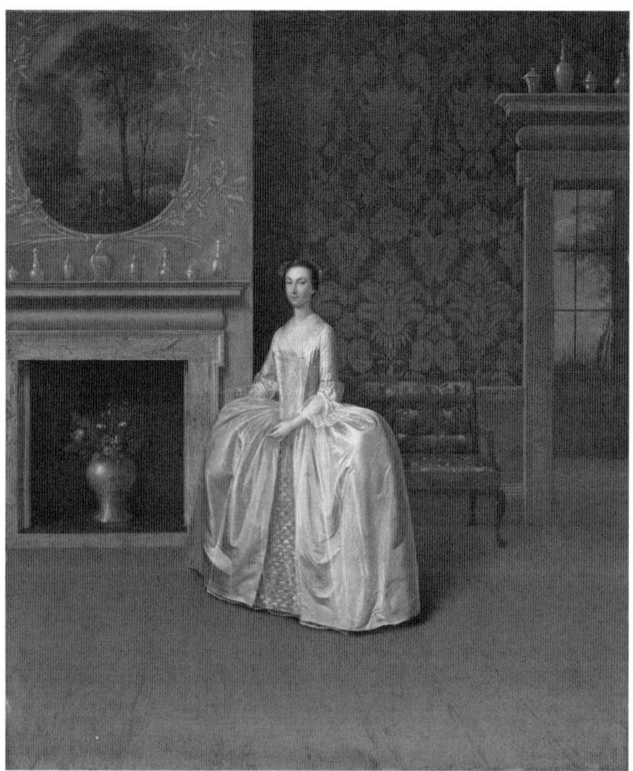

Figure 2.8 Arthur Devis: *Portrait of Lady Juliana Penn*, oil on canvas, 91.8 × 79.1 cm, 1752, Philadelphia Museum of Art. Source: Philadelphia Museum of Art, Pennsylvania, PA, USA. 125th Anniversary Acquisition. Gift of Susanne Strassburger Anderson, Valerie Anderson Story, and Veronica Anderson Macdonald from the estate of Mae Bourne and Ralph Beaver Strassburger, 2004/Bridgeman Images.

Kate Retford's analysis of "private" art foregrounds the view that art presents mediated representations of historical reality. According to this view, informal family portraits representing "feeling" subjects and exemplifying mid-century virtues of "sensibility" constructed a fiction of "naturalness" or candor, through facial and bodily expression, composition and the interaction between figures, that often concealed complex tensions among their actual sitters. A proliferation of conduct books informed the social and the artistic expression of more private, intimate family life. However, an underlying concern with patriarchy, ancestral rights and lineage persisted throughout the century, alongside prevalent representations of caring mothers and fathers and innocent children yet to be molded by considerations of rank and society. Portraits representing the higher echelons of society often appropriated the visual fiction of candor, whose origins lay in a discourse of bourgeois or middle-class disinterest, in order to conceal other more self-regarding messages about their rights to power and prestige (Retford, 2006, 16–17, 232–233). While portraits of feeling, virtuous yet modest families became popular, as did genre paintings referring to people of a similarly modest background, there also remained in many portraits an emphasis on precise identities and family ties. In country house displays of portraits in particular, there remained an emphasis on issues of lineage, dynasty, political and national allegiances. Such messages could be conveyed simply through the ways in which works were arranged or juxtaposed on the wall, or their sitters juxtaposed in a group portrait, and would be decipherable by those attuned to such issues in their own family lives.

Demand for portrait busts with commemorative, market or ancestral value grew as the century progressed, among the middle or professional sections of society. These showed a similar trend towards the "natural" as in painting, particularly in informal, expressive busts of children. There was some resistance, however, to abandoning the "severity" of sculpted portraits since sculpture as a medium was particularly associated with the gravitas of the antique. While eighteenth-century connoisseurs had relatively few examples of ancient painting to study until, at least, the discovery of Pompeii and Herculaneum, plaster casts, prints and copies of ancient Greek and Greco-Roman sculptures were more readily available as models. Diderot was among those who described a particularly close affinity between the medium of sculpture and antique gravitas:

> ...it [sculpture] is serious, even when striking a light note.... The painter and the sculptor are both poets, but the latter never makes jokes. (Diderot, 1995a, 159)

For similar reasons, sculpture was considered to be better suited to the representation of ideal nature than to naturalism. However, the medium became both more realistic and more expressive in the hands of sculptors such as Houdon, who used various techniques such as incised pupils (to suggest "living" eyes), wrinkles, open mouths, tilted heads and necks, trailing strands of hair and informal poses to suggest a living, breathing and feeling subject appropriate to the new emphasis on "sensibility" (Walsh, 2008, 460–461). Houdon represented his sitters dressed in loose antique robes or in formal contemporary costume. As was the case with painting, the degree of formality increased as the neoclassical style took hold later in the century, but even when this was the case his method of sculpting faces could introduce a note of informality, feeling or individual character (Figure 2.9). Other sculptors, such as Falconet and Augustin Pajou (1730–1809), aspired to bring a similar lifelikeness and less formally rigid classicism to sculpted subjects. This "naturalism" was often acknowledged as an artifice, due to the fact that living flesh was represented in hard marble, but one that required great skill on the part of the sculptor. Wax busts were also renowned for their realism, which often attained the level of *trompe l'oeil*. They were often used in funerals or, in the Revolution, to record the severed heads of guillotine victims: they conveyed associations of an eternal alertness that upset conventional distinctions of the real and the represented (Goudie, 2013, 57–74).

As the eighteenth century was a time of emphasis on genteel and affectionate social intercourse, it is perhaps unsurprising that this was the time when the sub-genre of the "conversation piece" flourished. This consisted of group portraits of family members, corporations, professionals or formally constituted societies at leisure and were distinctive in their emphasis on the ways in which such groups appeared unified by lively interactions of conversation (of word, expression or gesture), or feelings of affection, entertainment or some convivial activity (Retford, 2011, 120–122). They often focused on setting and narrative detail. Originating mainly in Dutch and Flemish art (Solkin, 1993, 51; Fenton, 2006, 52; Vaughan, 2008, 50) and lying originally outside the domain of academic art, the type became most popular in Britain, especially among the aristocracy and gentry, particularly in the 1730s and 1740s. Some of its most successful practitioners included Hogarth, Philippe Mercier (1689–1760), a French artist whose work was popular with the Georgian court (Hallett, 2006c; Weichsel, 2013, 57) and Devis. Later in the century artists such as Johan Zoffany (1733–1810) received commissions for conversation pieces from the wealthier ranks of society; for example, his *The Gore Family* (*c.*1775) (Figure 2.10, see color plate section). Even royal subjects were represented

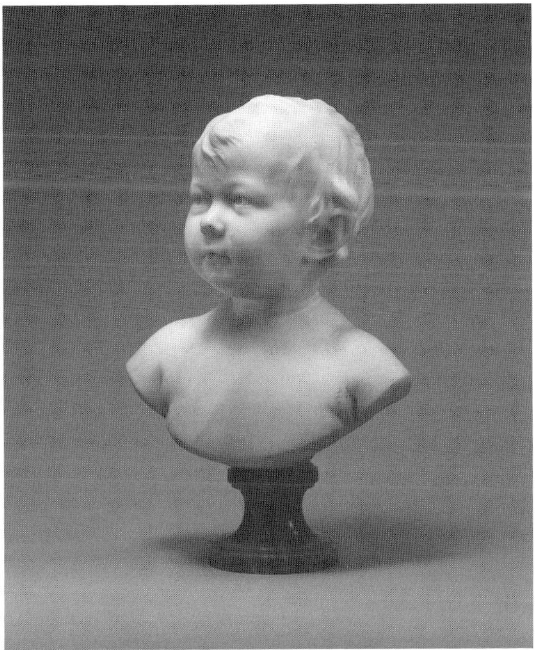

Figure 2.9 Jean-Antoine Houdon: *Sabine Houdon (1787–1836)*, white marble on gray marble socle, overall, without base (confirmed): H. 27.3 × W. 22.5 × D. 14.9 cm, 9.0719 kg; H. with base (confirmed): 34.3 cm, 1788. The Metropolitan Museum of Art, Bequest of Mary Stillman Harkness, 1950, Acc. No: 50.145.66. Source: The Metropolitan Museum of Art, www.metmuseum.org

more often in their private roles as fathers, mothers and other family members within a relatively private setting (Campbell Orr, 2011, 89–90). The strong accent in conversation pieces on "everyday" activity was more typical of genre scenes, but in the case of higher status patrons the use of compositional complexity and grandiose settings could lend the genre the dignity of history. The critical establishment was, however, generally opposed to the use of the ambitious techniques of history painting where artists had not undergone the proper training (Bordes, 2007, 257–273). When conveying a group portrait of sitters from polite society, the conversation piece could express a "will to refinement" and an emerging sense of public identity through the sitters' shared forms of behavior and highly regulated poses (Solkin, 1993, 106). They straddled the private (affectionate) and public (polite) domains of the family and the wider social relations it represented (Solkin, 1993, 104, 200).

Hogarth was adept at adapting the conversation piece in his satirical prints, where "gracefull and naturall easy actions" (George Vertue cited in Fenton, 2006, 52) often combined with examples of mischievous, immoral or corrupt behavior. Zoffany, like Hogarth, often approached his conversation pieces like theatrical performances in which the sitters appeared to participate in a performance (Retford, 2011, 113–117). Marcia Pointon (1993, 159–172) has decoded more serious treatments of the sub-genre, revealing how the position of each sitter is carefully chosen, as a playful yet effective means of conveying relations of gender, genealogy, inheritance and succession. The "modern" eighteenth-century conversation piece offered a more intimate and affectionate alternative to grand Baroque group portraiture of the preceding century, even though some artists, for example, Hogarth, used an "observational" approach that quoted freely from the visual conventions of Baroque classical theatre (Webster, 1978, 16).

Genre Painting

The taste for portraits of sitters in more informal, domestic settings, and for conversation pieces, coincided with a growing interest in genre paintings; that is, paintings of figures often (but not exclusively) from more modest social backgrounds engaged in everyday activities or recognizable narrative events. The term "subject painting" is normally applied to later, nineteenth-century examples of the type. While such subjects continued to be regarded as inferior to history paintings, since they did not represent actions of an exceptional, heroic or epic nature, they gained considerably in status with critics and public alike as the eighteenth century progressed, largely as a consequence of the increasing amount of attention attracted by their display in public and academic exhibitions, the vibrancy of the market in genre prints and the opening up of the art market to those whose interests and tastes extended beyond those of social elites (Schroder, 1997; Conisbee, 2007, 11, 32; Chapter 3). This fashion for paintings of more modest lifestyles has also been interpreted as arising from the vogue among collectors, from the late seventeenth century onwards, for naturalistic Dutch portraits and domestic scenes of the "middling" and servant classes represented in plainer settings and engaged in relatively humble (but usually harmless or implicitly virtuous) activities (Dejean, 2007, 39–47; Bailey, 2003, 2, 18–21). It has also been seen as signifying a growing opposition to more decadent aristocratic values. Aristocratic buyers themselves might purchase and display such paintings as a means of neutralizing or distancing themselves from the more corrupt moral values often associated with their class, particularly in France where there was a backlash, in the second half of the century, against luxury and its association with selfish hedonism (see Chapter 5). For city dwellers owning country estates, scenes of virtuous peasant life might also help to perpetuate a fiction of happy rusticity preferable to accounts of actual rural poverty (T.W. Gaehtgens, 2003, 88).

The formal establishment of the genre was not straightforward. Christian Michel (2007, 277) has pointed out that the term "genre painting" as we now use it was a late-eighteenth-century invention and when used during most of the eighteenth century was applied to a whole range of subjects, from still life to domestic family scenes, or in fact anything that fell outside the history genre, that prioritized naturalism over idealization or the grand manner (see also Wrigley, 1993, 293; Bailey, 2003, 3–5). Only three artists (including Greuze) were admitted to the eighteenth-century Académie royale specifically as genre painters, the only types of figural painting normally recognized at the time being history and portraiture (Bailey, 2003, 2). Artists painting genre subjects were described in a range of ways, such as "painter with a particular talent for animals and fruit" (with reference to Chardin); "painter in the genre of figures in modern dress" (with reference to Antoine de Favray, 1706–1798); "painter in the genre of scenes from common life" (with reference to Johann Georg Wille 1715–1808); or "painter of bambochades" (defined in 1752 as "paintings of gallant or country scenes, fairs, smoke dens and other cheerful subjects"; Bailey, 2003, 2) with reference to Nicolas Lancret (1690–1743). Genre paintings were known by a host of terms, many of which originated in northern Europe or Italy, including "scenes in the Flemish taste," "kitchen scenes," "beautiful scenes from civil life," "familiar scenes," "scenes from private life," "domestic scenes," "peasant scenes," "grotesque" subjects (which introduced an element of ugliness, disorder or horror), "peasant weddings," "guardroom scenes" ("corps de garde"), scenes from fashionable society (most evident in the French tradition of *tableaux de mode*), sporting, racing and hunting scenes (popular with the British landowning gentry; Blake, 2004, 43–63) and, in France, *fêtes galantes* (Watteau's invented genre of the early century showing the aristocracy at play) (Wrigley, 1993, 292). Many paintings of contemporary life, such as those by Hogarth or Gaspare Traversi (1722–1770), had a satirical function and conveyed an underlying moral message: this will be discussed in greater detail in Chapter 5. Hogarth and Hayman were specialists in the sub-genre of paintings of theatrical performances (Allen, 1987, 11–23).

Our modern usage of the term "genre painting" tends to be applied most frequently to domestic or family scenes conveying social and moral values such as those implicit in the works of Chardin, Greuze and their followers, which became well known not just in the print market but also in the writings of art critics, particularly from the 1760s. The term "genre painting" itself was not formally defined until 1873, when the English definition given was "a style of painting which depicts scenes and subjects of common life" (Bailey, 2003, 3). Diderot (cited in Wrigley, 1993, 293) stated that such subjects demanded mere patience and technical skill and little by way of genius or imagination: his main preoccupation remained with history painting and its improvement. However, he adopted a more flexible attitude when he encountered the bourgeois dramas of Greuze, who had been refused entry to the Académie royale as a history painter and was instead received as a "genre painter." Greuze's paintings were often seen as a special category in their own right, "paintings of morals" (Bailey, 2003, 4). One reviewer of the 1769 Salon wrote that Greuze deserved to be called a "painter of sentiment" as the scenes he created were so "philosophical, touching and novel" (*Letter on the Exhibition of Paintings and Sculptures at the Salon of the Louvre; or Lettre sur l'exposition des ouvrages de peinture et de sculpture au Sallon du Louvre*; cited in Barker, 2005, 9). The visual representation of feeling (sentiment) allowed the viewer to enter into an empathetic relationship with the figures represented, thus allowing the kind of moral understanding generated in more heroic mode in history paintings (Conisbee, 2007, 195). His paintings represented the lives and households of gentleman farmers and the middle classes (Figure 5.8). Diderot felt particular works by Greuze, such as his *The Father Reading the Bible (Le père de famille lisant la Bible*, 1755) were particularly worthy of "history" (Barker, 2007, 111).

Greuze's reception piece *Septimius Severus and Caracalla* (1769) was considered to pay too much attention to naturalistic detail and a meticulous finish, and too little to classical idealization, to allow him to be received as a history painter, in spite of the classical subject (Schieder, 2003, 60–62). There is considerable evidence, however, that throughout the eighteenth century elements of genre painting (its references to a private, common life; its naturalism) increasingly merged in a creative fashion with all the other genres (Schieder, 2003, 60–77; Scott, 2003, 94–102). Chardin's paintings of children engaged in activities often seemed to conflate the conventions of portraiture and genre and conveyed, through captions often added by those who later engraved them, significant moral messages, some hinting for example at the status of children as "liminal" or potential adults. In art institutions and theory however an over-riding allegiance to idealizing history painting remained in place to the end of the century (Bailey, 2003, 4–5).

Genre paintings by innovator-artists such as Chardin and Greuze presented edifying scenes that could, in some ways, serve the moralizing function previously ascribed to history paintings (Crow, 1985, 136–174). This effect was particularly pertinent in the larger-scale works by Greuze, which represented family scenes on tragic themes such as sin and repentance (Figure 2.11). Paintings such as Chardin's *The Scullery Maid* (1738; see cover image), offered in a more elegant, native idiom the spectacle of everyday virtues and sobriety previously admired in Dutch and Flemish genre paintings, which remained popular throughout the century. Works by these French artists were popular with all sections of the art-buying public until the end of the century, when they faded slightly from view due to renewed attempts to reinvigorate the history genre. Genre paintings suited a Parisian culture of leisure and domesticity. Buyers included those with more wealth than the modest bourgeois families these

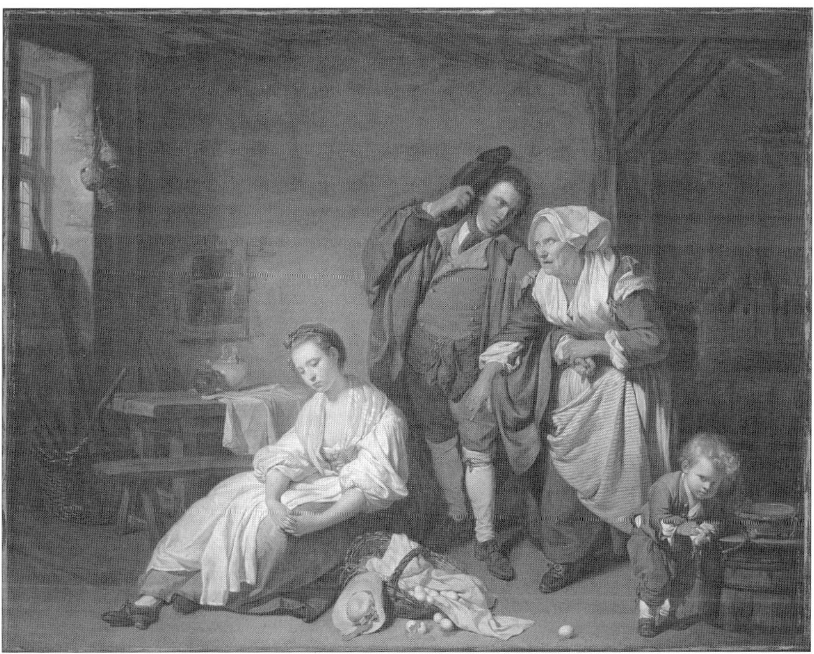

Figure 2.11 Jean-Baptiste Greuze: *Broken Eggs*, oil on canvas, 73 × 94 cm, 1756. The Metropolitan Museum of Art, Bequest of William K. Vanderbilt, 1920, Acc.No: 20.155.8. Source: The Metropolitan Museum of Art, www.metmuseum.org

paintings represented (T.W. Gaehtgens, 2003, 79–80). Between 1750 and 1790 there was an increasing number of references to them in French exhibition catalogues, a reflection of their popularity with collectors and critics (Collins, 2003, 396–398). Throughout the century royal and aristocratic patrons commissioned genre paintings as much as they did history, their lively interest demonstrated by a vogue for explanatory captions. Artists such as Watteau, Boucher, Chardin, Greuze and Louis Léopold Boilly (1761–1845), benefited from this trend and attracted buyers from an international market (Bailey, 2003, 13–18).

Genre paintings reflected, particularly from the mid-century, a new interest in the family. Mothers, fathers, children, servants and governesses feature heavily as do social rituals such as marriage. The demand for such scenes from contemporary domestic life has been linked with confidence in the values of an increasingly important middle class or "bourgeoisie" (T.W. Gaehtgens, 2003, 79–80). Greuze's genre paintings often suggest the concerns of Enlightenment writers with the value of agriculture as well as with the moral and social importance of the family. A French aristocracy increasingly aware of its own unpopularity coveted such values and could acquire them through its choice of art.

One of the most marked developments in eighteenth-century art was the fact that both buyers and critics increasingly saw narrative genre painting (sometimes known at the time as the "low" genre) as a serious rival to history painting, in its potential to move the public towards higher social and moral standards (Wrigley, 1993, 293–298). Wright of Derby was among those who chose genre subjects but treated them with the moral seriousness and grand *chiaroscuro* effects of Caravaggio and of another important predecessor in genre painting, Georges de la Tour (1593–1652). Wright's genre paintings often took the format of the conversation piece and showed the prosperous middle classes engaged in elevating activities such as the observation of scientific experiments. He painted contemporary, imaginative and Shakespearean subjects that appealed to the educated classes. In Britain, Hogarth's "modern moral subjects" (discussed further in Chapter 5) straddled the allegorical complexities of history paintings and the entertainment value of comic genre scenes (B. Gaehtgens, 2003, 48).

In a reversal of this history–genre conflation and toward the very end of the century, the art of history painters such as David strove to incorporate some of the "honesty," "truth to nature" and references to the familiar or everyday for which domestic genre scenes had become well known. His classical history painting, *The Lictors returning to Brutus the Bodies of his Sons* (*Les Licteurs rapportent à Brutus les corps de ses fils*, 1789)

(Figure 2.12, see color plate section) highlights the type of family drama imagined by Greuze (one of his early teachers), as well as a still life detail of a sewing basket, rather than the classical hero Brutus, shown brooding over his own responsibility for his sons' executions as he had denounced them for their part in a royalist conspiracy, during the first Roman republic. For David's coteries this generic hybridity constituted a means of undermining traditional old-regime power structures, hierarchies and styles of composition in history painting (Crow, 1995, 102–109). Additionally, from the 1780s (and especially in the 1790s) the Paris Salon was more open than before to significant numbers of artists from outside the Académie royale, and this meant that larger numbers of genre paintings were displayed. A growing preoccupation in art with contemporary manners and the interest in them shown by a broader public are among the qualities that often lead to the view that eighteenth-century genre paintings exerted a modernizing influence (Conisbee, 2007, 10). Genre paintings also assigned a more prominent role to women as artists, subjects and viewers (Conisbee, 2007, 29–32). Through their active involvement in the semi-public world of the Paris salons, as well as in their visits to Salon exhibitions, women became increasingly accustomed both to viewing others and to being viewed by them: social interactions of this kind facilitated a more active role for women in visual culture.

Mid- to late-eighteenth-century French genre paintings were "modern" in their sustained attention to the daily lives of the expanding bourgeoisie or "middling" ranks of society. Small-scale Dutch paintings of this nature had been common in the previous century, and popular in France, but at that time prominent French artists had focused on larger-scale works on the "simple" or peasant life, or fashionable narrative scenes, such as those produced by the brothers Antoine (*c.*1599–1648), Louis (*c.*1603–1648) and Mathieu (*c.*1607–1677) Le Nain, all of whom had become members of the Académie royale (Mérot, 1995, 157–179). *Tableaux de mode* or French paintings of fashionable society, popular in the 1720s and 1730s, focused on the lifestyles of the higher classes (Ebeling, 2007, 73–89). These paintings, by de Troy, Lancret and others, represented royalty, aristocrats and would-be aristocrats such as wealthy financiers in their leisure hours – hunting, making music, dining, drinking chocolate. These groups were united by their taste for luxury and were distinguished by their dress (e.g. red-heeled shoes, worn only by those who had attended court) and the presence of their liveried servants. Re-enacting seventeenth-century codes of gentility or *honnêteté*, these classes often viewed *tableaux de mode* as a means of validating their wealth and status or of identifying similarities, differences and tensions in class allegiances

(Bailey, 2003, 24). To the art critic Louis-Guillaume Baillet de Saint-Julien (1726?–1795) the propensity of those aspiring to an aristocratic lifestyle to acquire their own art collections served as a metaphor for the controversial materialism of their taste and, by extension, their lives:

> It seems to be a misfortune bound to the richest productions of art, to fall in the hands of people who appreciate less their value than that of the gold used to acquire them. (From his 1748 *Lettre sur la peinture, la sculpture et l'architecture à M****, cited in Ebeling, 2007, 77)

The lifestyles and aspirations of the wealthy were also represented more indirectly, in the early eighteenth century, through the dream-like fantasies of Watteau's new genre, the *fête galante*. These paintings lacked the heroic modes of representation or serious moral intent of history painting and, although they drew at times on mythological themes, they were more closely related to street theatre and masquerade. Watteau has been described (Plax, 2000, 1–2) as "toying" with generic categories and conventions. His *fêtes galantes* represented the aristocracy at leisure in elaborate garden parties, fantasy excursions, masquerades and theatrical performances influenced by popular theatre, the fairground and ballet. His powers of invention and technical accomplishments gained him in 1712 full membership of the Académie royale in Paris (B. Gaehtgens, 2003, 50) and he was allowed, unusually, to submit his reception piece some years later. This was his famous *Pilgrimage to the Island of Cythera* (*Le Pèlerinage à l'île de Cythère*, 1717) (Figure 2.13). As this work did not fit the requirements for a traditional history painting (or in this case the conventions of paintings documenting heroic court events), a special membership category, that of painter of *fête galantes*, was invented for him. *Cythera* had initially been classified as a history painting – it did after all include some references, however indirect, to Venus (represented in the painting in sculptural form), and to the morality of love and flirtation, at least as much as Boucher's erotic fantasies did – but the association with classical culture was less evident or serious than ultimately required in the history genre (Plax, 2000, 148). The case illustrates well the pragmatism of academies wishing to embrace the talented even when traditional hierarchies would seek to exclude them.

Julie Anne Plax has argued (2000, 1, 33, 75, 81–82) that Watteau often subtly subverted the conventions of history painting in a way that would have been meaningful, but not overtly political, to his aristocratic clientele. Thomas Crow has shown (1985, 54–60) how Watteau's combination of classical references with those to popular street theatre and fairground

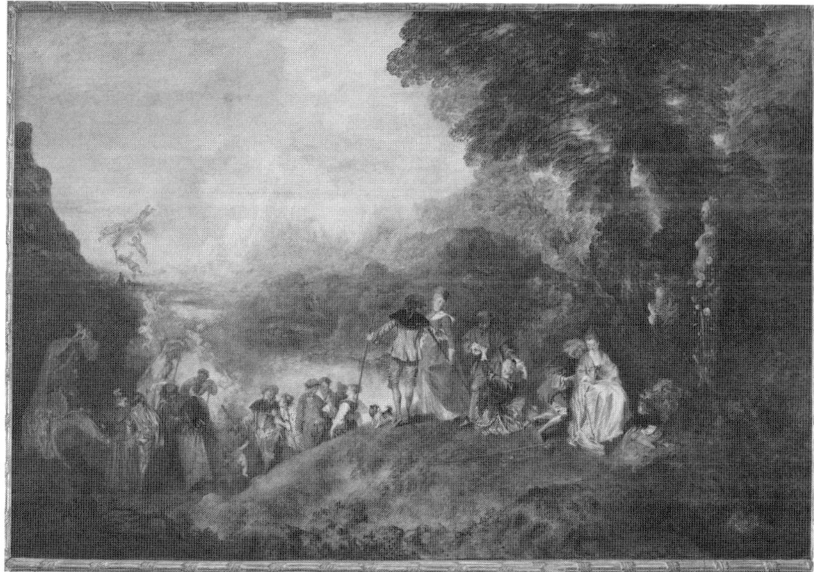

Figure 2.13 Jean-Antoine Watteau: *Pilgrimage to the Isle of Cythera*, oil on canvas, 129 × 194 cm, 1717. Paris, Musée du Louvre. Source: akg-images/Erich Lessing.

culture, made his paintings fall outside any existing generic categories. Watteau's use of decorative grotesque and arabesque motifs included witty fairground elements (such as "monkey business" or *singeries*) that enhanced the popular appeal of his works (Crow, 1985, 58–59). As discussed earlier the aristocratic or quasi-aristocratic social groups represented by Watteau were adapting, during the Regency, to a style of life that excluded them from older military roles and required that they redefine their distinctiveness through their social and cultural comportment (Crow, 1985, 66). In terms of the growing trend for "naturalness," Watteau's works drew on contemporary developments in women's fashion, reflecting the vogue for looser, more private styles such as the *manteau* (a loose-fitting gown): a proliferation of seamstresses and fashion prints popularized this style of dress, appropriate for a modern and evolving courtly lifestyle (Dejean, 2007, 32–47).

In Crozat's social circle, which welcomed Watteau, prints of subjects by the artist and his imitators, including Pater and de Troy, were very popular. An interest in "lower" genres existed, for this class of buyers, alongside an ever-weakening interest in courtly, classical art. The costumes, gestures, actions and narratives of "play" captured in Watteau's paintings showed an elite social group indulging in self-fashioning and display in a way that reassured them they still had the ability to win power over others, if only through love (Plax, 2000, 113). This play on roles and identities and the general ambiguities of action in Watteau's paintings (e.g. their lack of narrative or expressive unity) worked against the legibility of meaning necessary to the traditional functions of history painting (Crow, 1985, 63). However, his works included jokes and witticisms that could be detected by those in the know; their meanings opaque as befitted a culture that relished the improvised identities of the masquerade (Plax, 2007, 49–69).

This elusiveness suited an age in which the powers and social mores of royalty, aristocracy and newer, emerging classes were in a state of flux. New ideologies formed as older ones dissolved, creating the perfect conditions for innovation, not just in society but also in art. Watteau's visual innovations drew on the traditional type of the courtly landscape idyll, as expressed in earlier works by Rubens, Veronese and Antonio da Correggio (active 1494; *d.*1534). Like Boucher's idylls, they attempted to balance antiquity (specifically, its pastoral fictions) with "nature," their landscape settings serving as a backdrop for the exploration of transgressive personal relationships. Some of his followers (e.g.de Troy) fused the *fête galante* with bourgeois genre scenes, their figures dressed in everyday fashions and their erotic suggestiveness minimalized, thus "normalizing" the signifying mechanisms of the genre (Conisbee, 1981, 156). Watteau's *fêtes galantes* declined in popularity from the mid-century, when critics such as Anne-Claude-Philippe de Tubières-Grimoard de Pestels Levieux de Lévis, Comte de Caylus (1692–1765) fought for a return to classical values and argued that Watteau's works simply fell short of the narrative power, expressive intensity and range of history paintings (B. Gaehtgens, 2003, 50).

The chronicling of "everyday manners" of a range of social and national groups was a traditional function of genre painting that remained important, however, in the eighteenth century. Such paintings might have a documentary function, constructing a visual record of the ways people lived. In Scotland the paintings of David Allan (1744–1796) created a record of the games, dances, folk cultures and costumes of a number of nations including those of his native country. Sophisticated buyers provided a market for scenes of such "unspoiled" life (Macmillan, 1986, 65–70). The paintings of Pietro Longhi (1701–1785) of the haunts, lives and foibles of Venetian peasants and nobles found an enthusiastic market, his works often made in a satiric or comic vein similar to that of Hogarth. Scenes of rural life painted by George Morland (1763–1804), an honorary exhibitor at the Royal Academy, became more popular internationally as the century progressed and as an ideology of naturalness and simplicity took hold. These included representations of everyday activities and narratives, often based on British farm life. Morland's paintings tackled some of the moral themes (e.g. industry and idleness) represented in Hogarth's works, and included representations of the less conventional lives of marginal groups such as gypsies and pedlars. The rural subjects, animal and sporting subjects tackled by George Stubbs (1724–1806) were normally undertaken as private aristocratic commissions, as the activities represented (hunting, racing) related more to the landed gentry, but his works reached a wider audience in the later eighteenth century through the print market.

By contrast with *tableaux de mode* and *fêtes galantes*, or perhaps Stubbs' racing scenes, many genre paintings from later in the century are considered to demonstrate social and moral standards around which many groups (including the bourgeoisie and aristocracy) sought to coalesce, outside the frameworks of traditional social hierarchies. In some respects this has been read as a debasement of the genre, reduced in the work of artists such as Boilly to scenes dominated by a concern for fashion and anecdote: Diderot called for reform of the genre (Bailey, 2003, 32). However, there were attempts to redress such trends. Although the taste for *tableaux de mode* spread slightly "downwards" through the social scale, extending to others seeking the wealth, status, tastes and values of a landed aristocracy, there was also among many art buyers and collectors later in the century a desire that genre paintings should symbolize a new social order based on political, social and moral reform. Genre painting met the interests of participants in an "elite sociability" prevalent in Parisian and other urban contexts, embracing their interest in particular social activities, states of mind and feeling (Bailey, 2003, 22). The genre as a whole came into greater prominence in France in the years following the Revolution. In 1791 the Salon opened its doors to artists of all kinds, regardless of whether they were academicians. Then in 1799 the Minister of the Interior echoed the public reaction against the prevalence of history and insisted that genre paintings should embody the capacity of history paintings to convey patriotic and political (in this case republican) virtues (B. Gaehtgens, 2003, 56).

Landscape

The landscape genre flourished mainly in the nineteenth century. Unlike history painting, there was in Paris no Rome prize for landscape until 1816. This was in spite of the fact that it often featured in Salon exhibitions and gained in popularity as the eighteenth century progressed. It was sometimes seen by the authorities, along with portraiture and genre painting, as another unwelcome rival to history painting. Pierre, then-Director of the Académie royale, complained in the early 1780s that "There are two hundred French painters in Rome and all of them are landscape painters" (cited in Conisbee, 1981, 184). This was partly because word had spread of new opportunities there so that artists were tempted to work there regardless of the lack of support from the Académie. Natoire had in the 1750s encouraged other artists to join him in Rome and to paint more landscapes, as the history genre was in decline (Levey, 1993, 181). However, it was also in the 1750s that Vernet returned from Italy as Louis XV had awarded him an important commission to paint a series of works representing France's seaports. Vernet exhibited those he had completed at the Salons, between 1755 and 1765: they demonstrated a merging of topographical detail with the idealizing visual formulae established in the previous century by Claude Lorrain (1604/1605–1682). Changes to artistic culture in France during the Revolution redressed any earlier prejudices concerning the "lower" genres, and in the 1791 and 1793 Salons far more landscape paintings were exhibited in public.

Many sub-genres co-existed in eighteenth-century landscape painting, each differing in purpose, production, status and significance. These included marine paintings, country house portraits, "historical" or "poetic" landscapes, cityscapes, pastoral idylls, *capriccios* (scenes freely combining the real and the imaginary of which Giovanni Battista Piranesi (1720–1778) is now the most renowned practitioner, *grotesques* (architectural fantasies based specifically on underground classical ruins and their decorative motifs) and *vedute* (topographically accurate landscape views). It was common for artists to combine these genres and *capriccios* were inherently composite: the *capriccio Ancient Beech Tree* (1794) by Paul Sandby (1731–1809) was based on topographical elements from Windsor (an ancient beech) and the Wye valley (the general view).

The term "landscape" dates from the late sixteenth century, the related terms of "Landschaft" – German – and "paese" – Italian – from the early sixteenth century, and "scenery" from the late eighteenth (Margaret Drabble, cited in Cumming, 1985, 182). In the early part of the century it was very difficult for eighteenth-century artists to make a living from landscapes alone. As with the other "low" genres, private patronage was crucial: with the exception of decorative schemes, there were relatively few royal or state commissions. Many artists who frequently incorporated landscape into their work (such as Boucher and Gainsborough) were not primarily landscape artists, and the conflation of landscape with other genres was often a case of economic necessity. Initially limited to lesser roles such as providing backgrounds for hunt or country house scenes, the landscape genre as a whole grew in importance in France and Britain in particular. The traditional view of landscape as a form of representation emphasized its ("low") tendency to provide a close imitation of observed reality and to exemplify laborious effort rather than flights of genius (Wrigley, 1993, 299–301). Such "naturalism" was often associated with northern European (principally Dutch and Flemish) approaches to the genre.

An arcadian or idealizing tradition of landscapes in oils grew in status from the mid-century, aided by the liberal arts emphasis of many academies, and the genre's association with literary, historical and poetic themes and sensibilities, developed by artists who had visited Rome. Joseph Mallord William Turner (1775–1851) often represented both specific (topographical) sites and classicized landscapes by reference to literary or historical themes intended to provoke meditation or scholarly reflection. Picturesque and sublime landscape art incorporated increasingly "romantic" sentiment, symbolism, and literary and classical references more commonly associated with the history genre. Landscape was also commonly "elevated" by its conflation with high society portraits. By the end of the century the landscape view came to be valued in its own right and Turner's approach to the genre ensured that it became associated with imaginative creativity rather than being seen as limited by convention or the simple need to record visually an actual site. By this time developments in landscape aesthetics more broadly also ensured that painted "views" of all kinds enjoyed greater status.

Dutch and Flemish artists of the preceding century, such as Jacob van Ruisdael (1628/1629–1682), provided important models for more naturalistic styles. Grand historical, idealized or "poetic" or arcadian landscapes in the Italian tradition had been established in the seventeenth century as a European paradigm by the French artist Claude Lorrain, whose diverse influences included Agostino Tassi (*c.*1580–1644), northern artists such as Adam Elsheimer (1578–1610), Paul and Matheus Brill (1554–1626 and 1550–1583) and the idealizing style of Poussin, who had been influenced in turn by the Italian artists, Titian and Annibale Carracci. The two landscape traditions of "naturalism" and "idealism" are sometimes defined in opposition to each other and it is true that the former focused much less than the latter on fantasy or literary inspiration. However, "naturalistic" landscapes in the Dutch and Flemish tradition often relied on repetition of the representations of natural motifs (trees, skies) by previous artists, rather than on direct observation: such paintings remained imaginative constructs. A number of landscape compositional "templates" (e.g.for waterfall views, coastal scenes, farmland or woodland views) were in frequent circulation for artists working in the northern "realist" tradition as well as for those working on "poetical" compositions.

Prior to the eighteenth century, some landscape artists had taken their sketchbooks out into the countryside in order to observe nature at first hand. Most had then finished their works in the studio and it remained relatively uncommon until the mid-1740s to work more substantially outdoors, from nature, except when recording specific views for travel guides, topographical studies, tourists or specific patrons. Artists studying in Rome, such as Fragonard and Hubert Robert, were among those most likely to paint and draw directly from nature, from observation of the classical sites they observed. The situation changed toward the end of the eighteenth century as it became more fashionable for both professional and amateur artists at all levels of society to visit and sketch rural views. It was also a question of materials. While chalk and ink sketches had been practical for outdoor sketches prior to the eighteenth century, and some eighteenth-century artists, for example, Watteau, Alexandre-François Desportes (1661–1743) and Pierre-Henri de Valenciennes (1750–1819), did oil sketches, oil paint as it was at the time mixed and stored was heavy as well as slow-drying. Later in the century ready-mixed watercolor paints, more portable and quick-drying, became more accessible. One of the significant changes as the nineteenth century began was a greater public interest in and critical acceptance of finished works in watercolor, as well as a continuing interest in watercolor sketching for private viewing; for example, in bound albums.

At the beginning of the eighteenth century, landscape paintings were appreciated mainly as decoration. These were normally in the Italian tradition as assimilated by (Nicolas) Poussin and Claude, and were inspired by classical Greek and Roman myths and pastoral idylls. Such landscapes were often completed as panels for over-doors or over-windows, chimney-breasts or fire-screens, as well as free-standing easel paintings, and were, along with other furnishings, expressive of a refined and genteel classical erudition (Conisbee, 1981, 171–173). Decorative landscapes might also set a poetic mood or introduce a note of drama, some murals consisting of architectural fantasies or *trompe-l'oeil* paintings suggesting stage scenery to those parading through grand homes and mansions. One artist who carried out such commissions for the French Crown was Pierre-Salomon Domenchin de Chavannes (1673–1744), who completed some original, dramatic landscape paintings as well as more conventional Claude-inspired bucolic scenes. Boucher's pastoral landscapes, alluding to classical ruins and tumbledown cottages, and populated by highly improbable shepherds and shepherdesses, continued to be in demand through to the end of his life in 1770. Their pretty pastel shades added to an air of fantasy and made them commercially desirable as decorative pieces, especially as Boucher exhibited many of his landscapes at the Salons (Brunel, 1986, 181). Hubert Robert, an artist specializing in picturesque paintings of ruins, was among those who catered for Grand Tour clients who had visited Rome and wanted to capture the experience for visitors to their homes. He also practiced as a landscape gardener, another way of gaining earnings from a landscape specialism in this period. These decorative works had much in common with the techniques of painted stage scenery and were appropriate to a society heavily invested in masquerade, parade and self-fashioning. The fashion for decorative rococo landscapes persisted through to the end of the century in the work of Jean-Baptiste Pillement (1728–1808), Fragonard and others.

In Britain, Italian painters were often sought out for decorative landscape commissions, as wealthy British patrons became better acquainted with Italian art through the Grand Tour, the cultural journey across Europe embracing Paris, Switzerland, Rome and Florence – and often, Venice and Naples. This journey helped them to acquire social and cultural prestige and involved the purchase and shipping home of substantial numbers of prints, drawings, paintings and sculptures, including works by the celebrated Canaletto and his pupil Bernardo Bellotto (1722–1780). Artists such as Francesco Zucarelli (1702–1788), Sebastiano Ricci, Giovanni Battista Cipriani (1727–1785), who taught at the Saint Martin's Lane Academy, and Antonio Zucchi (1726–1795), Angelica Kauffman's husband, worked with architects to create appropriate landscape paintings and murals that ranged from arcadian rococo idylls, evocative Claudean scenes, *vedute* and *capriccios* of classical ruins to (in Zucchi's case) ornate but more austere neoclassical mythological and allegorical scenes.

Landscape was viewed on occasion as a form of public entertainment or spectacle for a genteel, discerning audience. Artists such as Philippe-Jacques de Loutherbourg (1740–1812) combined work on serious landscapes exhibited at the Salons with commissions for stage scenery and with performances (e.g. at exhibition rooms in the Strand) of his own Eidophusikon, a small stage on which scenes from battles, poetry and nature would be evoked through sound, lighting and moving pictures. Gainsborough devised something similar, a showbox, which sought to avoid the lurid color effects of Loutherbourg's innovation while using landscape scenes painted on glass, back-lit by candles, to provide more private entertainment in the drawing room. This entertainment aspect of landscape painting continued into the nineteenth century in the forms of the diorama and panorama.

The genre had a much more utilitarian application when it prioritized accurate topography. Artists such as the brothers Thomas (1721–1798) and Paul Sandby straddled the divide between fine and applied arts. As well as being founder members of the Royal Academy in London, they were both expert draughtsmen involved in producing topographical studies for military, map-making or survey purposes, or for privately commissioned landscape views. Thomas later became Professor of Architecture at the Royal Academy in London. They contributed significantly to the development of watercolor techniques, and stand as prominent examples of artists who could produce precise studies of specific locations as well as more aesthetically constructed compositions. Their services were sought not only by the Crown but also by the owners of country estates who wanted a visual record of their land and homes. There was a growing market from 1715 to 1755 for the topographical "prospect" view or print (Grindle, 2008, 128). Antiquarian studies of national monuments and sites also became popular (Crowley, 2011, 10–11). Accurate, "made on-the-spot" topographical studies grew in importance with the acquisition of colonial territories, particularly from the Seven Years War onwards, since there were strong practical, navigational and military reasons for "mapping" less familiar territories (Crowley, 2011, 2). Topography was often combined with creativity. The cityscapes of Canaletto rose to fame and offered technically accomplished and imaginatively reconstructed representations of spectacular and complex urban spaces, in which elements of the view were subtly rearranged or repositioned. They were particularly sought after for the country mansions of the landowning gentry.

At the other end of the hierarchy from decorative, ornamental and topographical landscapes were the "historical" or "poetic" landscapes often composed in oils and in sizes similar to those of history paintings. Smaller pastoral subjects by Watteau (inspired in turn by Giorgione, who worked in the late fifteenth and early sixteenth centuries), and larger scenes by his followers Boucher, Fragonard and Gainsborough (who had been inspired both by French rococo and Dutch traditions), raised the popularity of the genre. Classically inspired "poetic" landscapes evoked utopian scenes in which human beings existed in harmony with nature. The example set by Poussin and Claude, both of whom operated outside the Academy system, continued to inspire artists throughout the eighteenth century, and into the nineteenth, notably in the work of Richard Wilson (1714–1782) and Turner. Claude's compositional formula encouraged nostalgic and elegiac readings of his landscapes that raised the genre to levels of philosophical significance often absent from more sensuous, rococo landscape scenes such as those of Boucher. He used atmospheric or aerial perspective (the use of light and color to suggest recession into depth, with warm foreground browns giving way eventually to a paler middle ground and "distant" blues) and a clear structure of receding planes interlinked by bridges and streams, through which the eye was gently led. "Stage-wing" or framing effects were provided by clumps of trees at left-hand and right-hand edges and both the scale of and attention to detail receded with depth. Above all, he was famous for enveloping his large compositions in a unifying golden light. Narrative figures and incidents were situated in the nearest planes and represented scenes from classical myth or poetry that inspired thought on the human condition.

Vernet rose to fame in the Paris Salons of the 1760s and was inspired by Claude. It was, however, for the greater truth to nature his works represented that he achieved most critical acclaim. Diderot praised the fact that the artist's skies, seas and light effects seemed to be those of nature itself. Vernet's work often introduced theatrical or dramatic effects by including incidents such as storms and shipwrecks. These references to heroic suffering, further popularized through a range of Salon reviews that transposed his paintings into heroic narratives, raised implicitly the status of much of his work to that of history painting. By this stage of the century, works in lower genres that avoided some of the mannerism (the routine or exaggerated application of a conventional style) found in less effective history paintings, gained in status. This applied particularly when, as in Vernet's case, "historical" elements were incorporated in order to appeal to the feelings and imagination. In Britain, Richard Wilson thrived as an eighteenth-century emulator of Claude, Nicolas Poussin and Gaspard Dughet/Poussin (1615–1675). (The latter was Nicolas Poussin's brother-in-law, whose style combined elements from the work of both his close relative and from Claude: he eventually adopted his brother-in-law's surname.) Like Canaletto and other widely known landscape artists, Wilson produced works for an educated elite versed in ancient classical sites and culture, and his best known "heroic" works, such as his *The Destruction of the Children of Niobe* (1760) had their reputation further enhanced by extensive circulation in print form (Grindle, 2008, 122). He produced some works representing his native Welsh landscape, such as his Claude-inspired *Snowdon from Llyn Nantle*, but also spent several years studying and working in Italy (Figure 2.14, see color plate section). Interest in classical, "poetic" landscapes continued to the 1790s; for example, in the works of Valenciennes, inspired by Claude and Poussin (Conisbee, 1981, 193). Like Claude, Valenciennes did some excellent direct studies from nature, but it was well into the nineteenth century before such studies or sketches acquired in their own right the status of works of art that might be exhibited in public.

Many eighteenth-century landscape artists worked on idealized or fantasy scenes while developing other approaches aiming at more naturalistic effects. Fragonard's fantasy landscapes were produced alongside others in a more northern, realist style. Loutherbourg produced earthy, naturalistic scenes as well as his more fantastic pastorals or theatrical creations. Toward the end of the century, the work of landscape artists such as Georges Michel (1763–1843) was indebted to the naturalistic effects valued in the Dutch tradition. And yet it remained rare for fine artists to rely solely on first-hand observation of nature. Even Vernet, eulogized by Diderot for being so "conversant ... with natural phenomena" was reported to have a "fruitful imagination, aided by close study of nature," which helped the viewer to "see nature better." The idea of imaginative transformation was considered central to this process, Vernet being considered to have "better things to do than rigorously transcribe..." (Diderot, 1995b, 88–89).

Marine paintings featured heavily in the 1784 exhibition at the Royal Academy in London. These paintings, some of which featured naval battles, helped to establish a new sense of British national identity in a context of international wars and rapidly expanding colonialism (Hughes, 2007). Marine paintings conflated the traditions of landscape and (depending on the type of actions depicted) history or genre scenes. Geoff Quilley has explored in depth the ways in which maritime paintings constructed a national British identity through frequent reference to the imperialism that, from the second half of the eighteenth century, increasingly defined it (Quilley, 2011). The iconography of sea voyages reinforced ideas of a national community of loyalty and entrepreneurism.

The medium in which landscapes were painted could affect their status. Watercolor painting was associated in the early part of the century with a genteel refinement typical of the amateur (often female) artist or with the artisanal practice of "coloring in" maps, drawings, prints, topographical or architectural sketches, or book illustrations (Smith, 2001, 190). From the 1760s onwards, the medium acquired greater public exposure through exhibitions. Watercolor artists such as John Robert Cozens (1752–1797) aimed to create some of the aesthetic effects of high art and influenced late-century works by Thomas Girtin (1775–1802), whose progress in the medium was taken further at the beginning of the nineteenth century by Turner. Turner's larger-scale watercolors emulated the drama of grand landscape or history paintings in oils. In the later eighteenth century, however, the status of watercolor still lay in the balance. In the 1770s, watercolor paintings were still regarded principally as colored drawings, and the Royal Academy in London declared in 1772 that those who produced only drawings could not be accepted as Associates of the Academy, although this prohibition did not extend to miniatures or works in pastel or gouache, the latter being a heavier, more opaque medium than watercolor and therefore closer to oils. Large-scale works in gouache or body color, in which Chinese white was added to watercolor in order to make it opaque rather than transparent, were completed by artists such as Paul Sandby and were parallel in status to oils, although the fashion toward the end of the century swung toward more transparent watercolor effects. It was in the following century that the formation of specialist watercolor societies and the impact of Turner helped to secure greater public knowledge and critical acclaim for the medium. In the eighteenth century, watercolor painting enjoyed popularity mainly in the private domain, particularly in the vogue for sketching and painting landscapes as a tourist activity.

Imaginative representations of landscape achieved primary importance in the vogue for the picturesque and the sublime evident in Britain in the 1780s and 1790s. This arose as part of the growing attraction for viewing, sketching and painting (often in watercolor) native landscapes, including those that had previously been considered too wild and barbarous for genteel travelers (Walsh and Wilkinson, 2004, 12). High-quality views were often bound as albums of prints, or guides. At this time Revolutionary and Napoleonic wars made travel further afield too risky for many, but domestic landscapes featured increasingly on tour itineraries. "Picturesque" (from the French *pittoresque* derived from the Italian *pittoresco*) meant "like a picture" (Andrews, 1989, vii). The term had been in regular use from the seventeenth century and applied to a range of artistic genres. In the eighteenth century it acquired a particular significance in the domains of landscape art, poetics and aesthetic theory. Originally applied to scenes viewed in nature, use of the term "picturesque" became extended to pictorial representations of these and suggested use of a very specific visual vocabulary that (in the manner of Claude) transformed an observed view into a carefully framed and organized composition. As an aesthetic, the picturesque was explored and explained (with varying degrees of success) by writers such as Thomas West (1720–1779) in his *A Guide to the Lakes, in Cumberland, Westmorland and Lancashire* (1778); William Gilpin (1724–1804) in his illustrated *Observations, Relative Chiefly to Pictorial Beauty, Made in the Year 1772, on Several Parts of England; Particularly the Mountains, and Lakes of Cumberland, and Westmoreland*, published in 1786 (but in circulation in manuscript form from the mid-1770s); and

Uvedale Price (1747–1829) in his *Essays on the Picturesque, as Compared with the Sublime and the Beautiful* (1794). *A Philosophical Enquiry into the Origin of our Ideas of the Sublime and Beautiful* (1757) by Edmund Burke (1729–1797), of which an extended edition appeared in 1759, had prepared the ground by defining the aesthetic categories of the "beautiful" and the "sublime," although it had not defined or analyzed the more hybrid category of the "picturesque."

Burke theorized different experiences of nature in terms of their emotional effect on us. He drew on the common eighteenth-century notion that our sense of sight has a particularly strong effect on our physiology, nerves and emotions. His category of the "beautiful" applied to scenes from nature that evoke in us responses of love and affection, and he characterized such scenes by referring to formal attributes such as smoothness, gradual variation and delicacy (Burke, 1988 [1759], 146–150). To many eighteenth-century artists, such attributes were exemplified in the works of Claude, with their subtle tonal effects and delicately curving hills and paths leading the eye into the distance. Claude's works emphasized general effect rather than intricate detail. The "sublime," on the other hand, was associated with feelings of terror that produce "unnatural tension and certain violent emotions of the nerves" (Burke, 1988, 163). Triggers of the sublime include "obscurity," great power, vastness and elements of "privation" such as darkness, which deprives us of light (Burke, 1988, 163–177). Landscape artists could translate these ideas visually into mist and cloud (which "obscure" vision), powerful, high waterfalls, vast vistas on an apocalyptic scale that seem to spill beyond the picture frame, lightning storms, jagged rocky chasms and dark caves or shadows. The works of Salvator Rosa (1615–1673) were deemed to incorporate elements of the sublime (Andrews, 1999, 130), and those of Gaspard Dughet/Poussin to combine elements of both the sublime and the beautiful. The aesthetic of the sublime was adopted extensively by artists of the Romantic (late eighteenth to the early nineteenth centuries) era, as it suited their ambitions to transcend pictorial rationality and realism in order to appeal to the realm of the imagination. In the eighteenth century, artists such as Caspar Wolf (1735–1783), John Robert Cozens, Julius Caesar Ibbetson (1759–1817), Loutherbourg, Richard Wilson and Wright of Derby made liberal use of sublime motifs, though not always in the more dramatic and fantastic ways of their Romantic successors. Larger-scale works in oils of such subjects carried increasing status.

The picturesque as described by Gilpin, Price and others, was applied to a range of landscapes, with mountainous regions such as the Welsh mountains, the Lakes, the Peak District, the Wye Valley and the Scottish

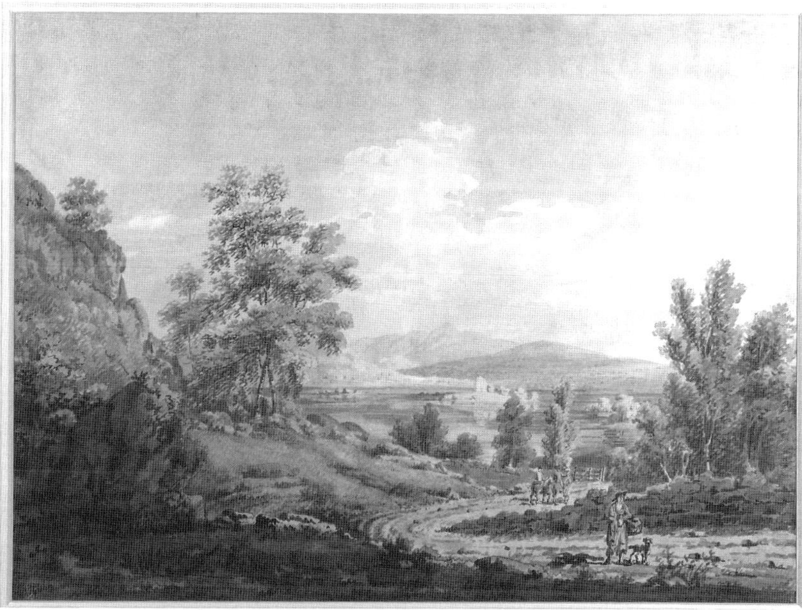

Figure 2.15 Thomas Girtin: *Lake Windermere and Belle Isle*, pencil, pen and ink and watercolor on paper, 35.3 × 48.7 cm, *c*.1792–1793. The Wordsworth Trust, Grasmere. Source: Courtesy of The Wordsworth Trust, Grasmere.

Highlands considered particularly appropriate to its requirements (Figure 2.15). West was among those who introduced tourists (and their sketchbooks) to the concept of viewing "stations" or spots from which "pictorial" views might be observed, recorded and modified. The picturesque tourist would also be equipped with a Claude glass, a mirror mounted on a tinted base that a viewer could use while standing with their back to a view, looking at its reflection as they held the mirror over their shoulder. The reflection in this "mirror" (or glass) would then color the view in a way that made it resemble the subtle gradation of warm, brownish tones typical of a Claude painting. In terms of content, an eighteenth-century picturesque composition was expected to have a kind of controlled ruggedness that combined a Claudean ideal beauty with the variety and rough edges of a landscape in the northern European landscape style. It presented an artful rearrangement of the natural world, drawn from Claudean conventions. To this was added sufficient naturalistic detail (of light, color, cottages, castles, vegetation, passing figures, animals, paths, streams, rippling waves, rough rock surfaces, bridges) to provide the visual intricacy and variety necessary to guide and entertain the eye. Foreground figures such as laborers, fishermen and beggars were often used to lead the eye into a composition or to add human interest. Watercolor works by Thomas Hearne (1744–1817), John "Warwick" Smith (1749–1831) and larger oil paintings by Gainsborough composed picturesque scenes full of dappled light and visual intrigue.

The aesthetic theories of writers such as Burke, Gilpin and others, combined with direct experience of landscape tourism, assisted the development of a richer, more discriminating taste in landscape art, particularly in Britain, as the eighteenth century progressed.

Still Life

Still life painting, or the painting of arrangements of objects, food and flowers, had flourished from antiquity onwards, reaching its "golden age" in Dutch and Spanish works of the seventeenth century. The term "still life" was not used in many contexts in the eighteenth century, when the works to which it now alludes were often described in France as "genre" paintings.

The term "still life" derives from the seventeenth-century Dutch term *still-leven* meaning "still" or "motionless" nature (Cummings, 1985, 251). The later French equivalent, *nature morte*, takes things one step further by suggesting that "dead" or inanimate objects are the main focus in such works, although in fact they often included live animals. Paintings of animals enjoyed a status similar to that of still lifes. Oudry specialized in hunting scenes on a grand scale that contained dog and horse portraits; on animal portraits based on the royal menagerie; and on luxurious buffet scenes, all of which established a "superior" type of painting within the "lower" genres (Bailey, 2007, 6, 10, 16–17). In the eighteenth century, still life remained a relatively lowly genre due to its association (as with many landscapes) with close copying of real objects and to the relatively limited scope it was felt to offer an artist's powers of invention and imagination. Norman Bryson (1990, 175) has described it as the "mechanical other" to history painting, as it draws attention to technique rather than invention and particular objects rather than general messages for humankind. As with landscapes, there were several sub-genres, from the humble to the slightly grander, and artists were often identified specifically as practitioners of these. Sub-genres included scenes of meal preparation, fruit and flowers, kitchen scenes, studies of trophies of the hunt, "attributes" (representative objects) of the arts and sciences, grand buffets and "vanitas" images in which traditional symbols of mortality such as skulls, wasting flesh and wilting flowers represent the vanity of human aspirations. Seventeenth-century artists had practiced successfully all of these sub-genres.

Still life paintings such as those representing the attributes of the arts and sciences, that conveyed serious allegorical messages or that portrayed objects from more lavish or erudite lifestyles, claimed implicitly a higher status. In the middle of the century, however, Chardin, who also made paintings of these kinds, tackled more modest assemblages of objects that were perceived by many critics to convey "nature itself," largely due to the artist's skill in harmonizing light and color as effectively as the "light of the sun" (Diderot, 1995a, 60). His work enhanced the status of "technique," which was felt capable of conferring in its own right a certain moral dignity. "Technique" is particularly emphasized in discussions of still lifes across all periods, as the genre is often seen to represent (if indirectly) the techniques used by the craftsmen who made the physical objects it depicts. This is perhaps most obvious in representations of high-end luxury goods such as chased silver, but is also apparent in, for example, the representation of porcelain.

Still life painters such as Chardin were accepted into the Académie royale as practitioners of their own (sub-)genre, although Chardin himself moved on to genre painting for a while, reportedly having been taunted by the portrait artist Jacques-André-Joseph Aved (1702–1766) by the comment that it was much easier to paint a "saveloy sausage" (which Chardin was at the time painting on a chimney-screen) than the human figure (Scott, 2003, 90). In 1757, Chardin was granted living quarters at the Louvre, a distinctive honor at the time, and he eventually took on during the period 1761–1774 the relatively prestigious role of picture hanger at the Salons. This was a position of some influence since he could determine the exact position and attention drawn to works painted by his peers.

Chardin's career was exceptional for an artist working within this genre and was boosted by critical acclaim based on an acknowledgment that the artist's work resonated so well with contemporary interest in the moral virtue of following nature as opposed to the mannerism and lack of observation of nature increasingly identified in "high" art. There was also a healthy interest, for much of his career, from buyers, who ranged from newly rich members of the middle classes to the aristocracy and to royal buyers such as Frederick the Great of Prussia (reigned 1740–1786) and Catherine the Great of Russia (reigned 1762–1796). Royal and aristocratic buyers derived some moral capital from buying his genre paintings of "everyday life," on which he focused his attention in the middle part of his career. They were also attracted to his still life paintings. In general, however, still life paintings paid much less well than history paintings or portraits, and were often commissioned, like landscapes, for decorative use (Schnapper, 2000, 58). Their status suffered further as the demand for works with explicit human interest capable of arousing moral emotion increased. In 1763, the art critic Charles-Joseph Mathon de la Cour (1738–1793), influenced by previous commentators such as Jean-Baptiste Du Bos (1670–1742) and La Font de Saint Yenne, stated:

> Men like to meet others everywhere; this propensity is the seed of sociability.... Landscape, fruit and animals are admired, but they will never be as interesting as a good head. (cited in Démoris, 2000, 106)

In the mid-eighteenth century the term "interesting" carried strong connotations of emotional human interest.

Diderot was among critics such as the engraver and art critic, Cochin, and the antiquarian, Caylus, who described Chardin's technique as "sublime" (Diderot, 1995a, 56), an accolade more normally applied to "high" art (Démoris, 2000, 108). Outstanding technical skill was felt to be essential in the still life genre, where the subjects themselves were "ordinary." Most praise was directed at Chardin's subtle compositions, use of brushwork, color and light, which provided an antithesis to more glamorous or spectacular still lifes playing on the surface brilliance of shiny objects or dramatic, theatrical arrangements of space. Not only was Chardin's technique much subtler in these respects, it drew full (and "modern") advantage from a loose focus on (rather than clear delineation of) the edges and surfaces of objects, diffuse lighting, uncertainly defined spaces and a lack of any dominant central motifs. This carefully contrived "naturalness," which had to be appreciated at some distance from the canvas, has been described as part of a constructed fiction of the "casual" glance, making his works appear "unaware of" or uninviting to the viewer (Weisberg and Talbot, 1979, 18–21; Bryson, 1990, 91; Démoris, 2000, 107). His approach does not assume in the viewer a "commanding" or "sovereign" (even perhaps "aristocratic") way of seeing, but allows a freer negotiation of the viewer's position in relation to the scene presented. Partly for this reason it is often characterized as offering a more "democratic" form of viewing. This subtler approach to still life painting shows a substantial revision of the rococo-inspired techniques Chardin had used earlier in his career (Bailey, 2000, 90). It had something in common with the "humble," non-spectacular presentation of everyday objects in the seventeenth-century still lifes of Juan Sánchez Cotán (1561–1627) and Francisco de Zurbarán (1598–1664) (Bryson, 1990, 63–65), but even they had used more dramatic effects of light and composition, and some of their objects had been represented in startlingly clear focus. Luis Egidio Meléndez (1716–1780) continued their style of still life painting into the eighteenth century.

For a very long time, and for reasons connected with its focus on "technique," still life painting was overlooked within art history and art criticism, with exceptions made for artists such as Chardin. This was largely the case in the eighteenth century, but scholarship has now closed this gap and has applied to still life painting of the eighteenth and other centuries the kind of critical enquiry more commonly applied to other genres. Norman Bryson has described still life painting as "the life of people among material things" (Bryson, 1990, 131), suggesting that the representation of objects in still life paintings can reveal a great deal about the lives, discourses and societies of those who made and viewed them. Although the range of objects represented in still lifes has remained fairly constant since antiquity, these paintings often inflect this standard repertoire with specific historical and material circumstances, including contemporary ideologies, economic developments and understandings of class and gender (Bryson, 1990, 12). On a simple level, this means that we may choose to study eighteenth-century still lifes in order to see what they reveal of contemporary lifestyles; for example, the growing eighteenth-century fashion for drinking coffee, chocolate and tea. Chardin's art has been studied with a view to tracing the increasing affluence of his own home (from which his still life objects came) as well as new middle-class fashions for Chantilly porcelain, tin-glazed earthenware, crystal glassware and ceramic designs influenced by or imported from the Far East (Rochebrune, 2000, 37–54). His assemblages of table ware illustrate the ranges of tureens, sauceboats and centerpieces typical of the fashionable contemporary "French dining service" in which large serving dishes were placed together in, and not moved from, fixed table spots.

Allegorical still lifes referred inevitably and on a different level to prevalent social and moral concerns. Although Chardin generally avoided working in the "vanitas" tradition, at least one of his works, *The White Tablecloth* (*La Nappe blanche*, *c.*1732) (Figure 2.16, see color plate section) has been identified by Thomas Crow as a possible allegory of the Catholic Communion, its rather austere arrangement of bread and wine perhaps even a tacit reference to contemporary prejudices against the Jansenist sect (Crow, 2005, 97–113). Still life technique itself, as a form of representation, has also been read as a commentary on politics, with spectacular or theatrical displays of luxury objects, for example, being read as an affirmation of the dominant power of those who owned such things. Chardin's more discreet approach to composition has sometimes been interpreted as a de-emphasizing of the individual creativity of artists, although his "finish" or brushwork might be read as expressive of his own individual style and vision (Bryson, 1990, 131; Démoris, 2000, 108). The ill-defined focus and "egalitarian" placement of the objects in his paintings have been associated with a less hierarchical or disruptive female (as opposed to male) gaze (Bryson, 1990, 161–172), evident also in the works of his female contemporary, Anne Vallayer-Coster (1744–1818). Still life as a genre was considered particularly suitable for women, well versed in the "domestic."

Questions of Modernity

Although the hierarchy of genres remained extremely influential, it was also subject to creative disruption and destabilization. Throughout the century there were multiple examples of conflation of different generic types. Some new genres (e.g. the *fête galante*) emerged. Many genres were invigorated by new trends in style and subject matter. Academies had little choice but to accommodate these developments, while maintaining publicly and in theory an allegiance to traditional hierarchies. Writers and artists demanded during the Revolution in France greater attention to more "democratic" styles (including naturalism) and subjects (the "lower" genres). The drive to celebrate the Revolution's heroes and rebel against the outwardly rigid attitudes of the Académie royale in matters of genre, created a climate favorable to the modernizing ideology expressed in works such as David's *The Dead Marat* (*La Mort de Marat*, 1793) and his drawing *The Tennis Court Oath* (*Le Serment du Jeu de paume*, 1791). Such works injected the realism associated with the "lower" genres into the representation of momentous contemporary (rather than chronologically remote) events. West and Hogarth also explored morally significant themes closely related to contemporary social and political developments (Hallett, 2006e, 198).

Neoclassical history paintings of the type created by David achieved stylistic innovation. His disciplined, linear, neoclassical style brought grand political and historical themes literally into sharp, dramatic focus in a way that was considered revolutionary at the time. Together with his politically controversial subjects, this brought fears from officialdom that his work might incite unrest, one of d'Angiviller's officials stating in 1789 that he thought David's *Lictors Returning to Brutus the Bodies of his Sons* (Figure 2.12) might "furnish more food to the fermentation [of the Revolution]" due to a possible association in the public's mind of Brutus (who hated tyranny) with the cause of revolutionaries. David's earlier *The*

Oath of the Horatii (1785) had also carried controversial connotations of the endowment of power on a rising generation (Crow, 1985, 213).

In France these forms of modernization brought high drama to a charged political environment and have been interpreted as constituting an implicit critique of academic conservatism, even though much late-eighteenth-century art criticism did not characterize the Académie royale as archaic (Crow, 1985, 214–215; Johnson,. 1993, 8–9; Wrigley, 1993, 313–314; Walsh, 1998, 182–184). History painting, the genre conventionally regarded as the most socially exclusive and erudite, was used to convey themes popularly associated at the time with republicanism. In this respect it shared the ambitions of much of the more popular imagery (such as satirical prints) created by artists during the Revolutionary period (Walczak, 2007, 247–249). In spite of rebellions against the dominance of history painters in the Académie's administration a strong institutional and theoretical bias toward the history genre remained until the end of the century. In such a context, artists achieved "modernity" by modifying, rather than obliterating, the genre (Duro, 2005, 690–694).

David's art developed further trends that had been apparent earlier in the century. The history genre, in paintings such as *The Death of du Guesclin* (*La Mort de Du Guesclin*, 1777) by Nicolas-Guy Brenet (1728–1792) absorbed increasingly, and especially from the 1770s, the rhetoric of feeling made popular by Greuze's genre paintings. Greuze had in turn revivified, and adapted to more private settings and subjects, a vocabulary of feeling previously used in the grander context of history, in works such as those of Nicolas Poussin. As is often the case, "innovation" often involved a recycling and recombination of older possibilities. Stylistic and iconographical continuities from the seventeenth century to the eighteenth were inevitable, given the hand-down of traditions through artistic dynasties, academies and master–pupil relationships (Conisbee, 1981, 53, 71–75). Even David's "revolutionary" art owed a debt to Caravaggio, Giovanni Francesco Guercino (1591–1666), Poussin and Le Brun. "Modernity" in art was at this time cyclical or fluctuating, the "new" arising from a shared visual vocabulary that lent itself to infinite recombinations. Innovations such as the rococo styles developed by Boucher and Watteau, which had challenged more conservative, erudite forms of classical inspiration, often served by the end of the century as symbols of the old regime, degenerate and morally suspect (Honour and Fleming, 1999, 615–619). Such charges failed to acknowledge its subtly allusive playfulness, which captured such prevalent contemporary preoccupations as the performative aspects of gender, or the "looser" moral codes gradually replacing in France more severe, retrogressive religious codes of behavior

(Barker, 2009, 307–308). More recent scholarship has done much to re-evaluate rococo art.

Generic categories evolved in ways consonant with broader ideological change. In Britain, West's history paintings, for example, evolved to explore Britain's contemporary colonial interests and activities in North America (Wrigley, 1993, 287). Marine paintings, hybrid landscape–history or landscape–genre paintings, grew in popularity as Britain forged a new national identity through its imperialist ventures through dramatic depictions of (largely) white heroism and sacrifice (Quilley, 2011, 3–10, 113–164).

There are marked "spots" of originality in eighteenth-century art and, for all their in-built conservative, hierarchical structures, some of these were achieved by artists working within the framework of the academies. Thomas Crow points out (1985, 134) that the "surprise outsider" to the Académie royale (artists such as Watteau, Greuze, Chardin, David) could ultimately win its favor by sheer originality and force of talent. One famous example is Fragonard's 1765 history painting, *The High Priest Coresus Sacrifices Himself to Save Callirhoë* (*Le Grand prêtre Corésus se sacrifie pour sauver Callirhoë*), unusual both for its choice of subject – a high priest who chose to defy the gods by killing himself rather than Callirhoë, the intended victim – and for its treatment, a dreamy apparition with ghost-like figures. Diderot described this painting as embodying in an unprecedented way the artist's powers of imagination. Rather than proclaiming an assertive heroism, it represented figures in a poetic, trance-like state of half-being that placed them in a different plane of existence. This work gained for Fragonard provisional membership of the Académie royale. Later in his career, he worked outside the domain of Académie's exhibitions, however, in order to exercise even greater creative freedom (Percival, 2012, 3, 10–11).

The increasing use of more naturalistic styles and motifs in history painting was more radical in some contexts than in others. Earlier in the century the bold realism and references to the everyday in the religious paintings of Giuseppe Maria Crespi (1665–1747) were regarded as highly radical, given the Catholic Church's attachment to visual tradition (Conisbee, 1981, 35–41). In secular subjects naturalism jarred less, especially later in the century when more recent historical events were often represented. The most frequently cited example of this is the use of modern dress in history paintings of this kind, and particularly in Benjamin West's *The Death of General Wolfe* (Figure 2.4), which represented a glorious military death in the context of Britain's North American colonial wars. It was unusual to represent a hero in this way, as an "ordinary" (as opposed to classicized) mortal (Abrams, 1985, 180). Reynolds objected to the idea but West replied that "the event intended to be commemorated took place … in a region of the world unknown to the Greeks and Romans, and at a time when no such nations, nor heroes in their costume, any longer existed" (John Galt's 1820 biography of West, cited in Fenton, 2006, 158–159). Eventually Reynolds conceded that West's work was not only acceptable but would also give rise to a "revolution" in art. The painting was also radical within the history genre in using a contemporary setting (rather than a classical or biblical one) to deliver universal messages about patriotism, loyalty, courage and sacrifice (John Galt's 1820 biography of West, cited in Fenton, 2006, 158–159).

Scenes from recent or national history became more common in the second half of the century but could cause concerns due to the fact that they undermined the heroic idealization evoked by the nude or draped classical body (Wrigley, 1993, 291). Battle paintings also grew in importance, a reflection of a new focus on national identity, patriotism (the need for "domestic" heroes) and artists' increasing skill in using war scenes in order to engage the sympathetic imagination of viewers (Bonehill, 2005, 155–160; Bonehill and Quilley, 2005, 1–4; Crowley, 2011, 56). The Royal Academy in London encouraged, toward the end of the century a more varied repertoire of subjects for history paintings, many of them drawn from the literary canon and including, for example, scenes from William Shakespeare (1582–1616) and John Milton (1608–1674). By these means the viewing public became accustomed to encountering elevating ethical and social ideas in less culturally or historically remote contexts (Bindman, 2008, 56, 67), going further even than those historical works by David, which cast subjects of contemporary relevance in canonical classical settings, recognizably ancient Greek or Roman in type. Innovation could occur both within and outside the use of academic classicism.

Portraiture was such an inherently flexible and omnipresent genre that it was ripe for innovation while hostage to the fluctuations of "fashion." We have already seen how "historical portraits" incorporated some of the mythological, heroic and allegorical devices of history paintings in order to achieve higher status. The work of Reynolds was central to the popularity of such conflations, aiming to merge an academic concern with antiquity with the business of capturing a likeness, the pragmatic, commercial core of the genre. Reynolds' portraits of military officers referred to the realities of war among other subjects of contemporary relevance (Hallett, 2014, 165–188). Marcia Pointon (1993, 104) has characterized eighteenth-century portraiture as "an ambiguous, controversial and disputatious genre." It constantly redefined its nature and status, as its social uses ranged from recording likenesses of high society patrons to those of infamous villains and "madwomen," from caricature and parody to propaganda (Pointon, 1993, 84, 96–99). Satirical portraits thrived in line with the Enlightenment's propensity for social critique. Portraiture, while not regarded primarily as a field of "genius" or "originality," due to its association with close imitation of a specific model, encouraged nevertheless technical innovations such as the sweeping brushstrokes of Gainsborough or the simplified contours of a neoclassical bust, as well as "higher" conceptual innovations, such as the very particular classical and modern hybrids made by Reynolds. Artists such as Hogarth developed established portrait types in new ways (Hallett, 2006d, 160). Given its commercial role and potential for endowing social prestige, however, such innovations rapidly acquired fashionable status.

It was also in the eighteenth century that portraiture focused so closely on sitters as individual personalities expressing more openly a range of emotions. So prevalent was the "feeling subject" that the type also spread to other genres such as animal portraiture. It had been common since antiquity to anthropomorphize horses and endow them with a human capacity for feeling. These tendencies intensified in the eighteenth century and are evident in, for example, the equine portrait *Whistlejacket* (*c.*1762) by George Stubbs (Warner, 2004, 9–14).

The main development within genre painting was its high profile, from the middle of the century, in the role of social and moral reform, the latter being considered traditionally as the role of history painting. In the case of Greuze, genre painting was perceived to transcend generic hierarchies because of its appeal to "sentiment." It therefore constituted a radical challenge to the hierarchy of genres, in much the same way as had occurred in the theatre, where the naturalistic French *drame* or English comedy of manners, based on bourgeois life, came to be seen as more attractive than the more high-flown rhetoric of classical tragedy. Greuze's compositions were reminiscent of stage tableaux, highly charged emotional scenes featuring stock figures such as the "Greuze girl," a type of adolescent girl figure often characterized by sweet melancholy and sensual awareness (Fort, 2007, 130). They formed a sub-genre in their own right. These paintings relocated rhetorical representations of intense feeling typical of the history genre in scenes of everyday contemporary life, connecting the private, domestic realm with more public and communal moral codes (Ledbury, 2007, 186–187, 195). These issues will be discussed further in Chapter 5.

It became more common and desirable in the second half of the century for portraits of individuals to be incorporated into genre paintings. Hybrid works of this kind resembled conversation pieces, but qualified as "genre" due to a clear emphasis on everyday activity of some kind, rather than on the identity of the model or sitter. Greuze, Chardin and Reynolds were among others who composed, respectively, images such as *The Well-Beloved Mother* (*La Mère bien aimée*, 1765), *The House of Cards* (*Le Château de cartes*, *c.*1737) and *The Age of Innocence* (1788). Such works used studies of real individuals in order to explore issues such as the moral aspects of leisure pursuits or the vulnerability, innocence and distractions of childhood (Conisbee, 1981, 138–139; Pointon, 1993, 181). In this way, plausible scenes featuring private friends and patrons could convey semi-public moral themes. Susan Siegfried (2007, 11, 15–35) has discussed the ways in which portraits within genre paintings, particularly those of female subjects, brought a suggestion of reality to a fictional (or, often play-acting) composition, while allowing the sitters involved to assert that they belonged to a particular class and its achievements. Female sitters in these works often addressed the viewer through a direct outward gaze, akin to a theatrical aside, explicitly inviting or mediating engagement in the construction of a painting's meanings in such a way as to draw attention to the act of looking itself. These figures were constructed as both viewers (of the imagined actual viewer) and as objects of the viewer's gaze. Such a device ran the risk of associating the women concerned with the behaviors of acting or artifice, but it was commonly used (see Figure 2.10).

The hierarchical classificatory system shifted to accommodate other genres that sat "in between" official categories. As emotional expressiveness became fashionable, so did works known as "expressive heads" (Kayser, 2003, 118). These were general representations of emotions (such as "Fear" or "Innocence") in portrait formats, but not based (or only very loosely so) on specific individuals. They drew on stock types such as the "pupil" or the "letter writer." The late work of Greuze included many such paintings, which appropriated some of the moral import and emotional rhetoric of history painting. This type of painting, which combined a portrait format with allusions to everyday life and a high expressive key, lay somewhere at the intersection of portraiture, history and genre.

The "fantasy figure," which drew on the tradition of the "expressive head," was another kind of work that adopted portrait formats in order to create imaginative subjects with little or no connection to identifiable sitters but presented as types such as the "cavalier" or the "artist." Fragonard was something of a trendsetter in this respect. His work evaded the legible moral codes and lessons typical of history painting, especially when he later worked independently of the Académie royale and achieved commercial success. This is evident in the free, expressive brushwork in which he executed these works (Percival, 2012, 38, 50). The very term "fantasy" was associated with rule-breaking and spontaneous modes of creativity (Percival, 2012, 12), although Fragonard drew on many precedents from earlier art; for example, Italian, Dutch and Flemish works of the seventeenth century and Renaissance such as those by Rembrandt, Frans Hals (1582/3–1666),Titian and Caravaggio (Percival, 2012, 51–63), as well as on many more recent French and British works by Watteau, Boucher, Greuze, Reynolds, Gainsborough and Wright of Derby. The ambiguous nature of Fragonard's fantasy figures, and their emphasis on activities (e.g. writing, reading, painting) has in the past led to their classification as genre paintings. However, they seem to enter more comfortably into the wide range of sub-genres in play in the eighteenth century before the term "genre painting" was in common use. British versions of the fantasy figure appeared more rooted in everyday life (Percival, 2012, 71). In general, the subjects and meanings of fantasy figures were unclear, even when sitters were named in titles. In Fragonard's fantasy figures, costumes (often overtly in the tradition of "dressing up" or masquerade), identities and expressions were ambiguous in a way that was deliberately intended to stimulate the viewer's imagination and to evoke alternative, transgressive and escapist identities and lifestyles, in a way that we would now consider to be "modern" (Barker, 2009, 309–310; Percival, 2012, 122, 133).

Generic fluidity worked very much in favor of the "lower" genres, which gained in stature. In the case of landscape painting, there was a recognition that the genre could engage the imagination in a way that reduced its distance from history painting. There was also an increasing acknowledgment of the fact that a well-painted landscape, however closely based on reality, was better than a badly conceived or executed history painting. Reynolds revealed, in his *Discourses*, a brave departure in this respect:

> I am well aware how much I lay myself open to the censure and ridicule of the academical professors of other nations, in preferring the humble attempts of Gainsborough to the works of those regular graduates in the great historical style. But we have the sanction of all mankind in preferring genius in a lower rank of art, to feebleness and insipidity in the highest. (Reynolds, 1975 [1797], 249)

British landscape painting reached new levels of invention and sophistication, with the assistance of a growing literature dedicated to aesthetic types and ideals. In France, Vernet's landscapes were recognized for their appeal to the feelings and imagination, especially when they included, however marginally, narrative scenes of human activity or elements of the sublime (Consibee, 1981, 181). They were regarded as modern adaptations of seventeenth-century historical landscapes, infused with the new vogue for *sensibilité*. Valenciennes developed further Vernet's poetic treatments of light and atmospheric effects.

Works in the still life genre were regarded as the least susceptible to innovation, due to their longstanding and ever-continuing (even into our own century) iconography. We have seen, however, how talented artists such as Chardin could revolutionize their technical execution, suggesting new ways of looking that facilitated greater subjective engagement in the viewer. If still life was regarded as inhabiting the borders of "craft," other works that had often been regarded as craft, such as engravings, miniatures and enamels, crept toward the status of "art." The paintings on enamel by the artist and writer, Jean-Étienne Liotard (1702–1789), of servants serving chocolate or figures dressed in "exotic" costume, appealed to buyers from the highest sections of society and resonated with the Enlightenment's taste for "curiosities" of all kinds. Like watercolor, this medium could transcend or bypass more formal hierarchies.

Further Reading

Andrews, Malcolm. 1989. *The Search for the Picturesque: Landscape Aesthetics and Tourism in Britain, 1760–1800*. Aldershot: Scolar Press. A useful introduction to eighteenth-century landscape aesthetics.

Chardin (exh.cat.) 2000. London: Royal Academy Publications. Includes a useful series of essays on still life in its broader social and cultural contexts.

Conisbee, Philip, ed. 2007. *French Genre Painting in the Eighteenth Century*. New Haven, CT, and London: Yale University Press. An outstanding series of essays on genre painting.

Hallett, Mark. 2014. *Reynolds: Portraiture in Action*. New Haven, CT, and London: Yale University Press.

Levey, Michael. 1993. *Painting and Sculpture in France 1700–1789*. New Haven, CT, and London: Yale University Press. See the Further Reading section in Chapter 1.

Retford, Kate. 2006. *The Art of Domestic Life: Family Portraiture in Eighteenth-Century England*. New Haven, CT, and London: Yale University Press. An excellent survey of eighteenth-century English portraiture in its broader social context.

Wrigley, Richard. 1993. *The Origins of French Art Criticism: From the Ancien Régime to the Restoration*. Oxford: Clarendon Press. Chapter 8 contains an extremely useful introduction to the hierarchy of genres.

3

Markets, Publics, Expert Opinions

An extensive market for art developed in the eighteenth century. This was not of course the first period in which art had been traded. Particularly from the Renaissance, monarchs, religious and political leaders had commissioned and purchased art on a significant scale. In the seventeenth century, and particularly in northern Europe, a growing merchant class had also played an important role in the market for art. As new and expanding social groups wished to buy art, they shaped its development. Issues of social, religious, moral, philosophical or political allegiances were often a decisive factor in such developments. However, the European market for art is considered to have reached a much wider public and to have achieved a more modern complexity in the eighteenth century, when culture became "commodified" on an unprecedented scale (Solkin, 1993, 1–2). From the middle of the century, cultural institutions in many European countries, particularly in Britain, France and Germany, but also in important Italian Grand Tour cities, acknowledged a broader "public" for art, that extended far beyond the traditional ("pre-modern") circles of court and church to artistic societies, clubs and academies, both formal and informal, whose members developed, along with many domestic buyers, self-consciously critical views and preferences.

A Guide to Eighteenth-Century Art, First Edition. Linda Walsh.

Companion website: www.wiley.com/go/walsh/guidetoeighteenthcenturyart

Markets and Patrons

Royal and aristocratic patronage remained important, particularly in those countries where a broader art market had not yet developed. Royally sponsored porcelain works in many cities (including Berlin, St Petersburg and Stockholm) boosted specialist palace collections (Touati and Flemberg, 2013). In Britain, royal households had favored since Tudor and Stuart times portraits and historical works by artists from northern Europe, such as Anthony Van Dyck (1599–1641), Hans Holbein the Younger (1497–1543) and Rubens (Vaughan, 2008, 57), but Georgian royal households also bought the work of contemporary artists such as Canaletto, Roubiliac, Liotard and Kneller. George I (reigned 1714–1727) had a relatively small budget for art but awarded major commissions for decorative art to James Thornhill (1675–1734), who completed the massive ceiling painting in the Great Hall at Greenwich Hospital, and to William Kent (1685–1748), a lover of Italian art who oversaw the redecoration of Kensington Palace. Duke Christian Ludwig II of Mecklenberg-Schwerin (in power 1747–1756), who governed a principality in what is now north-eastern Germany, was an important patron for Oudry (Bailey, 2007, 14; Frank, 2007, 31–57). The portrait artist and genre painter Johan Zoffany built his career initially through court appointments and commissions at Thurn und Taxis and Trier (both part of the Habsburg Empire), London, Florence, Parma and Vienna. Work as a court artist carried a higher status than that of court musicians and actors, and in London in particular Zoffany's work for George III (reigned 1760–1820) brought him into contact with a much wider range of clients, as the British court was linked with other potential client groups such as parliamentarians and politicians (Postle, 2011, 75–99).

While the British court dealt directly with artists it wished to commission, French royal commissions were often negotiated through the various Directors of Public Buildings, in consultation with the Director of the Académie royale or the royally appointed First Painter to the King. Court patronage remained important through to the nineteenth century in Stockholm, Copenhagen, Dresden, Berlin, Vienna, Madrid, Warsaw and St Petersburg. Stanislav August Poniatowski of Poland (reigned 1764–1795) was, until the loss in 1795 of his country's independence, among those monarchs who funded the studies of native artists abroad, so that they could learn more of painting as a liberal art and move beyond the approaches of the guilds. Even those artists from countries with a more developed art market welcomed court commissions for specific works as a welcome relief from the imperative of market trends (Craske, 1997,

71–73). In France commissions for history painters in particular were few and far between in the late seventeenth and early eighteenth centuries, and this remained the case through much of the eighteenth century, though various Directors of Public Buildings attempted to secure and award such commissions at various times (see Chapter 2).

Many eighteenth-century courts aspired to model themselves on France and welcomed French artists. In Rome, the papacy, along with cardinals, visiting princes and prestigious Grand Tourists, served for much of the century as generous patrons of art and scholarship to artists from France and across Europe (Johns, 2000, 17–40). In France itself the state was the exclusive client of the Gobelins tapestry factory (Scott, 1995, 36). Royal portraits provided a consistent source of commissions. In the early eighteenth century, Boucher received portrait commissions from Mme de Pompadour, mistress to Louis XV; Goya carried out such work for the family of Carlos IV of Spain (reigned 1788–1808) and the French artist Élisabeth Vigée-Lebrun was welcomed by the Russian court in St Petersburg after she had fled the Revolution in France, in order to continue painting the governing elites of Europe. Liotard received royal commissions both in Britain and on the continent (Hauptman 2015a and b).

In the middle of the century, German princes commonly commissioned Venetian artists to paint decorative frescoes for their palaces. In 1708, at the Dresden Court of Augustus the Strong, Elector of Saxony (1670–1733), Johann Friedrich Böttger (1682–1719) discovered how to make porcelain, although some argue that the discovery was made, if not claimed, earlier (McGregor, 2014, 322–326). It took some time to perfect the technique in Europe, which lagged behind China in this respect. Augustus was an avid collector of Chinese porcelain, often described at the time as "white gold," who wished to make it more easily available in Saxony (Fahr-Becker, 2006, 231). The collecting of porcelain was particularly popular in German courts: Frederick the Great of Prussia's *Wunderkammer* at the Charlottenburg Palace in Berlin offers a vivid example of such a collection (Tarabra, 2006, 133).

Monarchs and governments were not alone in issuing public commissions. Throughout the eighteenth century many commissions came still from churches. When we see such paintings in situ today they may look dark and forbidding, if badly lit or preserved. They were less so in the eighteenth century, when clear window glass, bordered by colored panes, was in fashion (Conisbee, 1981, 31). Religious controversies could however disrupt such commissions. In 1780 in Britain, the anti-Catholic Gordon riots, provoked by recent attempts to mitigate previous discrimination against British Catholics, stemmed commissions for large-scale religious works at a time when public money was already in demand for the American War of Independence. Dissenting religions were not inclined, for doctrinal reasons, to encourage a strong visual or decorative culture. As Clare Haynes has shown, visual culture in Britain (including that found in homes and churches) was defined by a suspicion of Catholicism as much as it was on the continent by the pre-eminence of Catholic art (Haynes, 2006, 1–13).

Commissions for more "modern" work came from a wider public than those associated with the court and church. This was especially the case with portraiture. Hogarth's sitters included those from mercantile, professional, church and scientific groups, for whom newer modes of representation were more appropriate: direct or "natural," unpretentious, polite but without "airs and graces," energetic and "sincere" (Hallett, 2006d, 160). He moved on to secure commissions from the higher echelons of society, including the aristocracy and upper gentry (Solkin, 1993, 96), and in works representing these groups he adapted his compositions to a culture of luxury. Zoffany's clients included the holders of both new and established money – merchants, explorers, surgeons, theatrical performers, musicians and artists (Postle, 2011, 13–49). In France Fragonard's fantasy figures (see Chapter 2) sold well to artists and wealthy bourgeois as well as to aristocrats (Percival, 2012, 42). From the early eighteenth century, a rising financier class in Paris sought to emulate its aristocratic superiors by vying with them in the commissioning of art. They sought decorative and cabinet paintings in particular. Chardin was among the beneficiaries of such new commercial opportunities (Conisbee, 1981, 113, 163). There was a growing sense of a newly competitive, nuanced market, with a range of prices demanded for variously ambitious and sized works of art, prices depending on the wealth and rank of those commissioning them, with royal households generally paying the highest prices. As many artists were also aware of the economic, social and political factors that could impact on such a market, they produced a sensible mix of self-chosen and customized work, always having something in hand for unexpected commercial opportunities (Siegfried, 2007, 29–30).

Wealthier Catholic and continental countries had earlier overshadowed Britain's artistic culture, with France, Italy and the Netherlands competing for the most prestige. However, Britain became in the eighteenth century Europe's most prosperous nation (Craske, 2000, 11). London hosted a cosmopolitan artistic culture. Later in the century, rapid urban growth across Europe fostered international competition and a desire to emulate the cultural achievements of ancient Rome and Greece (Craske, 1997, 28). Many artists felt that their prospects in London might be better than in already saturated markets such as that in Rome. In addition, Britain had acquired a reputation for upholding the values of liberty, Enlightenment and prosperity that were felt to favor artistic production; it had also acquired a reputation for its championing of commerce (Voltaire, 1964 [1734], 45–47; Brewer, 1997, xxv–xxvi). Paris became a major center for the display of art from the 1760s onwards (Berger, 1999, 202). However, war and revolution could easily upset the art trade. This was the case in France during the Seven Years War and the Revolution. In the years leading up to the Revolution grain shortages affected attitudes to luxuries of all kinds, from elaborate hair styles to art collecting (Falaky, 2013, 45–46). During this period even the royal family had to rein in its taste for exclusive goods and the Queen, Marie Antoinette (reigned 1774–1792), came under severe criticism for any signs of excess. Post-Revolutionary and Napoleonic wars also ensured that trade was disrupted, as naval blockades were imposed on some ports in Britain and the wealthy were prevented from traveling to the continent for the Grand Tour, which had previously encouraged the purchase and shipping back home of goods obtained directly from artists or their agents. Canaletto was among those artists affected by such difficulties. His agent in Rome, Joseph Smith (1682–1770), had been accustomed to wining and dining British patrons in particular when their Grand Tour itineraries brought them to Venice. But the War of the Austro-Hungarian succession (1740–1748) stemmed the flow of British clients to the point where Canaletto traveled to Britain to find more secure sources of patronage, particularly from the Duke of Richmond.

International rivalries affected the balance of the art trade across Europe, as did the tendency for artists to travel to countries where they felt their prospects of finding work would be best. The market reflected tastes and values that changed with time and place. For example, Dutch and Flemish genre paintings were popular throughout the eighteenth century, particularly in France, but they assumed there in the second half of the century the pre-eminence enjoyed previously by Italian painting, which was considered inadequate for the moralizing culture that gained ground in the 1760s and 1770s. Works produced by French artists also became more marketable in eighteenth-century Paris, as the dominance of Italian art waned (Percival, 2012, 98). Meanwhile, in Spain prints of Italian works (e.g. by the Tiepolos) overtook in the later eighteenth century the country's earlier taste for prints of French art (Craske, 1997, 250–251; Yarrington, 2001, 175).

There were, however, some persistent trends: classical Italian sculptures, and casts and copies of these, remained predominant in private gallery collections throughout Europe.

Issues of national and social identity affected tastes. The growing popularity in France of Dutch and Flemish works representing the "natural" and "humble" enhanced the desire for Chardin's genre paintings and still lifes: a style or genre associated with a specific national identity was appropriated by a different nation. One of Chardin's works was completed as a pendant to a similar Flemish work (T.W. Gaetghens, 2003, 80). Seventeenth-century works by Adriaen Brouwer (1606–1638) and Philips Wouwermans (1619–1668) fetched high prices across Europe. At the same time, an early eighteenth-century English aristocratic disdain for Dutch art was based on the fact that it was seen as neither "polite" nor "great." English prejudices against French decorative painting, regarded as immoral, also influenced the market (Solkin, 1993, 51). These negative perceptions of foreign art contributed to a growing dissatisfactio with the lack of a national school of art in England, made all the more obvious since auctioneers knew little about English art and buyers, and were more interested in copies of Italian paintings brought back from the Grand Tour.

Hogarth is widely recognized as the first British artist to make a conscious attempt to develop a national school of art, directly challenging the prior pre-eminence (especially at court) of foreign artists. In his portraits, such as that he produced in 1740 of Captain Thomas Coram, he competed explicitly with traditions established in Britain by Van Dyck, by using grand portraiture devices such as the classical column and drapery included in the background. In an attempt to assert his own style, he combined these with a more naturalistic pose, costume and expression. In spite of the founding in 1768 of the Royal Academy, English art was slow to acquire a truly international reputation until the nineteenth century (Pointon, 1993, 49), although the home-grown talent of its sculptors fared better from the 1760s (Craske, 1997, 262). Printmakers helped to raise the reputation of the British art works on which their prints were based (Vaughan, 2008, 68).

This brief discussion of the significance of the national origins and associations of works of art should however be set against the growing cosmopolitanism of much artistic culture, as many artists traveled across Europe to secure work and learned from one another in major urban centers such as Rome. Networking (local, national, international) was an essential skill in a profession that could lead equally to poverty or affluence. It was common to work as a drawing tutor, illustrator or salesman of art supplies in order to supplement income (Myrone, 2008, 190). Many artists turned to portraiture because it was more lucrative than other genres – few buyers having the funds or the wall space required for grand history paintings (Conisbee, 1981, 111–113). In many cases restorers, gilders, frame-makers and copyists had a more reliable income than artists, since these craftsmen were paid directly by artists, while artists themselves were often dependent on clients who varied in their readiness to pay bills (Pointon, 1993, 50). As previously mentioned in Chapter 2, sharp business practices were a key part of successful commercial outcomes for portrait painters.

Artists such as the sculptors Francis Leggatt Chantrey (1781–1841) and Joseph Nollekens (1737–1823), and Goya (at least in the early part of his career), courted patrons through their refined social manners. Hogarth was a consummate artist-businessman, and artists such as Reynolds moved graciously through the highest echelons of society (Craske, 1997, 62–5; Hallett, 2014, 19, 45–48). As an alternative to social conformity, artists might also adopt, particularly later in the century, the persona of the non-conformist, radical or "genius," in order to enhance their reputations and improve business. While artists in Stuttgart and St Petersburg wore a type of civil service uniform emphasizing their service to the state, society artists elsewhere courted patrons by appealing to an established sense of social hierarchy. There were some dissidents rising above the need to conform to such behaviors. In Britain, Barry fought against the conventions of the Royal Academy in an (ultimately unsuccessful) attempt to establish a career on the basis of a unique creative vision (Craske, 1997, 46–59; Fenton, 2006, 162–163). In Rome, Grand Tour portraits by Pompeo Girolano Batoni (1708–1787) were in great demand as status symbols produced by an international celebrity (Figure 3.1), while other members of the growing circle of neoclassical artists there, such as Mengs, also acquired superstar status.

The art market worked in a variety of ways, and financial support for artists was complex. At the top end of the market, aristocratic patrons could support artists financially and lend more general support by inviting them to stay and create art in their country mansions, as Lord Egremont did for Turner at Petworth, where the degree of creative freedom afforded the artist was exceptional. They might also allow artists to view and learn from their private collections or introduce them to other potential patrons through their dinner party networks. The Duke of Richmond was, for example, highly instrumental in enabling Stubbs, among others, to establish his career, by introducing him to a range of social contacts. In return, a patron might bask in reflected glory. A broader, astute approach to sales by an artist might involve painting subjects taken from popular broadsides

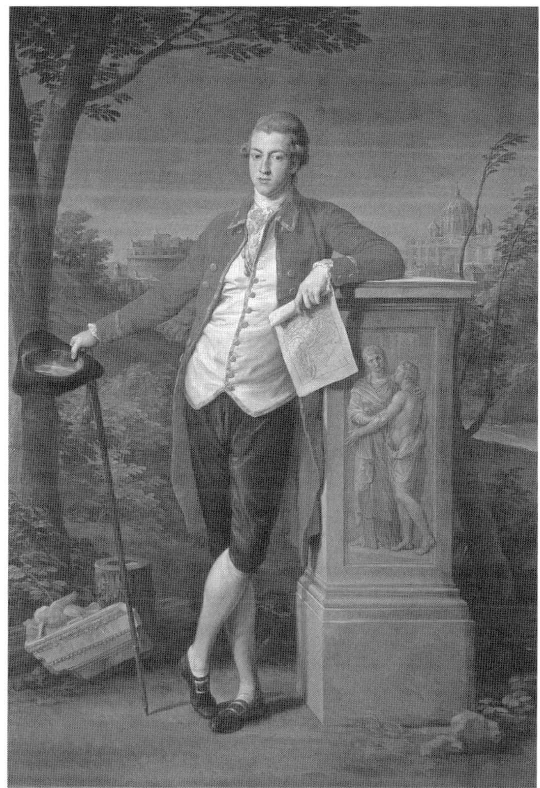

Figure 3.1 Pompeo Batoni: *Francis Basset, 1st Baron of Dunstanville*, oil on canvas, 221 × 157 cm, 1778. Madrid, Museo del Prado. Source: akg-images/Album/Joseph Martin.

or theatrical productions, as did Hogarth and Zoffany (Simon, 2011). Artists might also sell works through the shops of picture dealers, or exhibit works in locations that drew the crowds, such as (in Paris) the St German Fair or the Pont Notre Dame and nearby riverside spots, where works would be displayed outdoors (Wrigley, 1993, 20–24).

Guild members could set up shops at Parisian fairs, as could Flemish artists in Paris, who were free from trade restrictions. Visitors came from a wide social spectrum – servants, merchants and nobles. The St Germain fair included a street where painters' wares could be sold alongside those of ironmongers (Crow, 1985, 46). Such outdoor locations often acquired a reputation for selling poor quality works or "mere" copies of Salon exhibits, while the shops of more established picture dealers (such as that of Edme-François Gersaint, 1694–1750) (Figure 3.2, see color plate section) often sold paintings and sculptures alongside other luxury goods intended for domestic interiors. Dealers advertised paintings and prints through newspapers, sales catalogues and shop windows. They were part of a large commercial network that, in developed markets such as Britain and France, and later in other parts of western Europe, also included a significant role for auction houses (which attracted connoisseurs, amateurs, collectors, artists and members of the general public), commercial galleries, printers, publishers, engravers and printsellers (Brewer, 1997, xvii; Schoneveld Van-Stoltz, 1989, 218). Meanwhile, the Académie royale in Paris tried to distance itself from such crude commercialization: in the 1780s, when anxious to implement moral reform, it refused to carry out monetary valuations of artworks (Wrigley, 1993, 26–27). Exhibitions held by the main academies themselves, and the critical reviews they prompted, were essential for securing sales and commissions, though some exhibits were commissioned in advance by the state, the church, corporate or private patrons (Conisbee, 1981, 26). Some Académie royale artists, for example, Maurice Quentin de la Tour, were skilled in courting the press (Craskem 1997, 30–31). Artists sometimes issued prints of their paintings in advance of academy exhibitions, as an effective publicity stunt: this was the case in London with Zoffany's *Plundering the King's Cellar at Paris* (1794).

Successful artists often aimed to please more than one section of the market. Watteau's *fêtes galantes* appealed to French aristocrats and wealthy financiers because they made implicit reference to noble codes of politeness and leisure pursuits, and were appropriate to the growing number of private hotels built or purchased by this class in the early eighteenth century. Because Watteau's native elite clientele was somewhat limited, however, many of his works were sold through the international art trade and fetched high prices by the 1770s (Crow, 1985, 72–74). In Britain, ceramics designed by Wedgwood appealed to the "middling orders," but exports to America were also popular from the 1760s. Increasingly, art became a valued commodity for anyone who could afford to buy prints, small paintings or sculptures to decorate their homes. As buyers, merchants, artisans, shopkeepers, farmers and traders formed the next tier down in status from the monarchy, aristocrats, wealthy officials and financiers. They benefited from an art trade that operated increasingly freely within and across national boundaries. As early as 1696 a ban was lifted in England on imports of old master and classical works, including copies and prints. It had been imposed originally in order to protect the trade interests of guild members, specifically, those of the Company of Painter-Stainers. Social and cultural one-upmanship fueled a thriving trade in imports from Rome ordered by collectors and dealers in search of superior copies, in a variety of media, of canonical ancient sculptures (Coltman, 2006, 123–164; Coltman, 2009, 117–158).

Auctions became a more common location for the purchase of art, dealers often trading there (Brewer, 1997, 202–204). One of the problems for British artists was that many auctioneers had a deeper knowledge of continental than of British art. Nevertheless, dealers did a great deal to encourage those from the middle ranks of society to join with their social superiors in the activity of collecting art. Where the commercial interests of native artists failed to thrive, they might use their own studios as salesrooms – an unfortunate circumstance for some, given the popular association of the studio, in the minds of the genteel, with "improper" nude models. Connections between artists and dealers were often crucial, as the latter frequently facilitated shop-front display in commercial galleries such as (in London) the Shakespeare gallery run by John Boydell (1720–1804), or the Poets' Gallery of Thomas Macklin (*c.*1752–1800), which, during their relatively brief lives, employed Royal Academy artists to produce work on literary themes (Brewer, 1997, 247–248). Some dealers responded very actively to demand. From Paris, Gersaint travelled regularly to the Netherlands, between 1733 and 1740, to buy northern genre works for clients (Conisbee,1981, 29). Beyond retail outlets, other opportunities for artists arose from attending established social occasions such as those connected with the "season" at Bath, a popular spa resort for the genteel that provided respite from the winter season spent in London, and could be particularly lucrative for portrait painters. By the end of the century, the art market grew livelier in the provinces, as self-made clients there aspired to wealthier lifestyles and provincial academies of art became more common. Wright of Derby found patrons in Derby, Liverpool and other places outside the capital; even though he continued to measure his success by reviews of the work he exhibited in London.

The eighteenth-century art market had to adapt to national, regional and global "publics." British, French and German art reached global markets, if eastern European and Scandinavian art often restricted itself more to court demand. As art commerce grew, the types of artifact on offer diversified. Global markets developed through increased trade, exploration and colonization outside Europe (Craske, 1997, 19). Johan Zoffany and William Hodges (1744–1797) traveled outside Europe to make and sell art that appealed to those interested in the growth of empire or the expansion of scientific knowledge. Chinese paintings (especially on glass or mirrors), wall hangings, prints, enamels, porcelain (from the court-sponsored factory at Jingdezhen), lacquer-work, textiles (silks, brocades and damasks from the court-sponsored factory at Suzhou) and "curiosities" (small models of Chinese features made of jade, ivory, mother-of-pearl, sandalwood, tortoiseshell, horn and soapstone) were exported to Europe from Canton, where the British East India Company had set up a factory in 1715. Diplomatic relations between China and Britain remained strained, however, and it was difficult for Britain to sell goods to China or to negotiate more favorable trading conditions (Williams, 2015, 277). Chinese *co-hong* merchants regulated trade in Canton (Jourdain and Jenyns, 1950, 11–62; Murck, 2005, 310). As the taste for *chinoiserie* (luxury goods in the Chinese taste) spread, many European clients sent their own designs to manufacturers in China; and many European manufacturers imitated or adapted Chinese designs to western tastes (Jourdain and Jenyns, 1950, 23, 51–52; Ray, 2007, 212).

The scale of this fashion for *chinoiserie* has raised interesting questions regarding cultural translation and hierarchy. There was initially resistance to the lack in Chinese art of western traditions of representing light, color gradations, depth and human figures – Chinese representations of the latter being described in a 1755 issue of *The World* as "either hideous or ludicrous" – and their general handling of chiaroscuro as "…every incoherent combination of forms of nature" (cited in Jourdain and Jenyns, 1950, 15). However, the new taste for Chinese-inspired buildings and gardens did much to reverse this kind of judgment, Chinese designs meeting fashionable demand for the "curious" and "novel." Chinese culture stimulated a range of responses, from wonder and fantasy to repudiation; for example, in response to the reputation of the "barbaric" custom of foot-binding, as well as sheer ignorance about some of its ethnic symbolism, in motifs and artifacts such as twisted rocks and scholars' stones (Porter, 2010, 98–114).

Hybrid Sino-rococo styles facilitated stylistic assimilation and it has been suggested that they may have prompted a rethinking or recalibration of traditional western aesthetic values, such as Reynolds' emphasis on a classicizing ideal beauty or the rectilinear forms of Palladian architecture (Porter, 2013, 78–83). Frederick the Great was among several monarchs to build a Chinese Pavilion on a royal estate, his own (at Sans Souci) encapsulating the waving lines and Chinese figures typical of the new taste. This served a western preoccupation with "possessing" specimens of other cultures as a means of demonstrating one's own enlightened modernity. Chinese goods also led to a reassessment of the role of women in establishing aesthetic value systems. Women were now able, through the extended social discourses associated with Chinese-style drawing rooms and tea drinking, to become agents in reformulating taste and in the consumption of luxury objects. It has been suggested that Hogarth's suspicions concerning the vogue for *chinoiserie* had much to do with his distrust of this enhanced, yet potentially corrupting role for women in the aesthetic domain (Ray, 2007, 208–210, 213–217; Porter, 2013, 4–8, 83–91). The Chinese taste may be seen as a catalyst for transforming social, and even national identities, given the central role subsequently attributed in British culture to the social practice of tea drinking (Porter, 2013, 133–134, 149). Material objects may acquire new meanings and agency as they move to "other" functions and contexts (Porter, 2013, 95–96).

Japan's trade with Europe was greatly restricted. Contact with the rest of the world was strictly regulated and the nation had limited contact with China. Christianity was outlawed and western books were frequently banned. Trade was restricted to the island of Deshima at Nagasaki and limited to China and the Netherlands, the latter through the Dutch East India Company, which had a trading base at Nagasaki. Japanese porcelain, for example, Arita ware, made using several layers of enamel glazes, was in demand from western buyers, although peaks in the production and sale of Chinese porcelain affected the market adversely. All but the most discriminating western buyers often failed to distinguish between Japanese and Chinese goods, so strong was the influence of the latter on Japanese art. Due to restricted trading conditions, however, the west did not really discover until the nineteenth century one of Japan's most innovative eighteenth-century art forms, *ukiyo-e* or "floating world" colored woodblock prints depicting the pleasure district, courtesans, Kabuki theatre and actors of contemporary Edo (present-day Tokyo) (Tinios, 2010, 12–21).

The British East India Company exported many goods to Europe from its "capital," Calcutta. Indian chintz and calico became very fashionable in Europe (Mitter, 2001, 165). It was, however, common for Europeans to confuse goods from India with those from China or Japan, as goods from these countries were often shipped through the same, intermediate ports (Jourdain and Jenyns, 1950, 22–23).

Zoffany and Hodges traveled to India due to the presence of the East India Company there, mainly to Calcutta and to Lucknow, capital of the Mughal province of Awadh, where the local ruler or *Nawab*, Inawab Asaf-ud-Daula (in power 1775–1797) asserted his status through his commissioning of works of art (Eaton, 2007, 190–202). The Company's own officers commissioned commemorative portraits of themselves, "exotic" mementoes for their return home, images of their current lives (intended perhaps to reassure them in a context of unpredictable power-play), portraits for use in diplomatic exchanges of gifts, scenes featuring Mughal architecture and, increasingly, scenes representing local events and customs, flora, fauna and ethnographic representations of local peoples

(Eaton, 2007). The commercial and cultural power of East India Company officers had been garnered initially through the transactions of "nabobs," a term referring both to Provincial governors in the Mughal Empire but also to servants of the Company who gained great wealth, often through corrupt trade practices. Trade was particularly lively in opium and attar of roses, the latter essential to the perfume trade. "Nabobery" itself acquired an association with a morally corrupt and effete Asiatic lifestyle seen as a threat to the masculine "virtues" of Britain (Solkin, 2007). Corruption was indeed rife in the Company until 1784, when it was regularized through the India Act. The ruling elite of Calcutta and other Company bases such as Sumatra represented a transposition of the London ruling elite, keen to preserve their cultural prestige (Greig, 2011, 141–166). They desired the same kinds of individual portraits, group portraits or conversation pieces as Zoffany had been accustomed to produce in Britain. Group or family portraits increasingly represented an inter-ethnic sociability, in which British and Indian elites mingled, especially in Lucknow where the British presence was more recent and the races could meet on more even terms. Zoffany's *Colonel Mordaunt's Cock Match* (*c.*1784–1788) (Figure 3.3) is a good example of this (Jasanoff, 2011, 134). However, many group

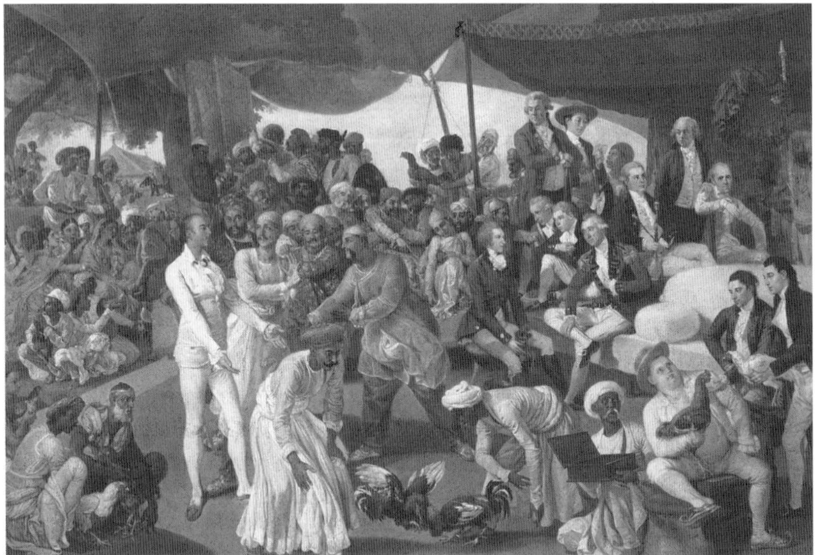

Figure 3.3 Johan Zoffany: *Colonel Mordaunt's Cock Match*, oil on canvas, 104 × 150 cm, *c.*1784–1786. Tate Gallery, London. Source: Universal Images Group/Getty Images.

portraits, such as *The Impey Family* (1783) continued to show local Indians in subordinate positions, serving and entertaining British subjects (Greig, 2011, 158). The Company's staff and presence in India also brought indigenous artists more commissions, normally for works in Mughal styles.

In the spirit of the European Enlightenment, and particularly in the aftermath of the East India Company's territorial conquest of Bengal during the Seven Years War, many Orientalist scholars and artists traveled from Europe to India to record local customs, culture, locations and natural phenomena (Crowley, 2011, 169–177). Warren Hastings (1732–1818) was an Orientalist scholar who engaged in local commercial and political intrigue, and was part of the Asiatic Society of Bengal formed in 1784. The artists William Hodges, Ozias Humphry (1742–1810), William Daniell (1769–1837) and Thomas Daniell (1749–1840) traveled to Lucknow and upper India in order to represent artistically the landscapes, monuments and other sights they saw there, often in western styles such as the picturesque. These and other artists also sought to record local sights and customs in a documentary manner appropriate to the west's quest to understand new cultures and proclaim its serious interest in colonized peoples, and hoped to discover new commercial opportunities (Craske, 1997, 116–119; Crowley, 2011, 169–203). Many prints and maps were produced for practical reasons, East India Company officer-artists and surveyors producing them as a means of giving visual expression to colonial "ownership" of new territories. Ethnographic subjects sold well to the local Company market as well as back in Britain, where they were sometimes produced in luxury editions or exhibited in London. The local customs and sights captured by Zoffany included tiger hunts, a Hindu widow's suicide at her husband's funeral pyre (the practice of *sati*), public washing in rivers, temples and monuments. Although artists from west and east had a shared interest in many subjects, stylistic cross-fertilization remained relatively rare, each set of artists remaining faithful to their own cultural traditions. Empire, with its hierarchies of ruling and subject peoples, did not provide the conditions necessary for the kind of cross-cultural assimilations we now associate with modernity.

The Print Market

The production and purchasing of prints contributed greatly to the growth of the art market in the eighteenth century. Tim Clayton has traced this development in detail (Clayton, 1997). He has shown how English printmakers and sellers competed throughout the eighteenth century with

France, which had led in this field. The sale of foreign-produced prints largely of antique, Renaissance or seventeenth-century and eighteenth-century canonical French and Italian paintings (e.g. by Poussin, Le Brun, Mignard, Coypel and Canaletto) remained common in Britain (Clayton, 1997, 123–125). There was, however, an increasing demand for English subjects and designs, especially as the Royal Academy established an "English School" of art (Clayton, 1997, xi–xiv, 261–282). The American colonies, India and many parts of continental Europe developed, by the end of the century, a taste for English prints. Prints formed part of the growing luxury trade, both as objects in their own right and as illustrations (e.g. in catalogues) of luxury goods.

Prints of works by celebrated artists such as Hogarth were successful on an international scale. He helped to make the sale of prints more lucrative for engravers, by working to achieve the 1735 engravers' copyright act. This ensured that no unauthorized persons were allowed to make copies of prints for 14 years after the publication of the original, thus reducing widespread piracy in the trade (Webster, 1979, 11). The act was strengthened in 1767 (Clayton, 1997, xiv). Some piracy continued in practice, however, and affected designs by James Gillray (1757–1815) at the end of the century (Donald, 1996, 4). Hogarth sometimes found it difficult to sell the original paintings on which many of his prints were based, but many of his other prints were designed exclusively as prints. Sales of his print series, for example, his *Rake's Progress*, *Harlot's Progress* and his *The Four Times of Day*, made him a great deal of money (Figure 5.3).

Many buyers across Europe saw prints as a much cheaper alternative to paintings or sculptures (Smentek, 2007, 221). There were, however, limits to the accessibility of prints for the majority of London's working population. Masters might purchase prints, such as those from the series *Industry and Idleness*, for the edification of their apprentices: there are records that they bought prints from the series as Christmas gifts for them (Riding, 2006e, 181), and some established artisans could afford to buy prints for their own homes. However, many from the laboring classes could view prints only in shop windows, barbershops, workshops or public houses; or they might occasionally purchase low-cost copies, including woodcuts, which involved a cheaper mode of production (Donald, 1996, 7, 31; Riding, 2006e, 181). The French dealer François-Charles Joullain *fils* (died 1790) stated in 1786 that "Prints level the inequality of fortunes by satisfying amateurs of all ranks" (from *Reflexions on Painting and Engraving Accompanied by a Short Essay on Trade in Curiosities and Sales in general*, 1786, cited in and translated by Smentek, 2007, 221). Prior to the Revolution, print shops in Paris attracted a very mixed clientele, from nobles (who bought the most expensive wares), to members of the third estate, who formed the majority of customers: artists, printmakers, lay clergy, tax inspectors, lawyers, notaries' clerks, actors, wigmakers, stationers, dyers, miniaturists, bakers and others. The availability of credit broadened the market (Smentek, 2007, 223–224).

The print market was aided by a lively culture of collecting. The trade in England flourished as the subscription system, which invited prospective buyers to pledge money before printing took place, appealed to a growing number of virtuosi and connoisseurs (Clayton, 1997, 49–74). Marcia Pointon has examined the significance of portrait print collections, a means of classifying well-known historical portrait subjects according to a respectable social order. The pastime was driven by a personal commitment to developing as complete a collection as possible (Pointon, 1993, 57–67). Such collections were often bound in volumes of mounted prints in which spaces were left for buyers' own purchases, a fashion established by James Granger. As well as being highly saleable, these satisfied a need for an ordered history of the British nation and catered for collectors' desires to place themselves imaginatively in such a context. Print collections represented a distinctive epistemology or approach to the acquisition of knowledge appropriate to the classificatory mentality of Enlightenment scholarly and scientific investigation. Like other specialist collections, they presented a modern equivalent of the cabinets of curiosities popular from the previous century in which virtuosi included a wide diversity of artifacts and natural history specimens, but their objects were less randomly and more purposefully assembled (Scott, 1995, 166–167; Brewer, 1997, 253–256).

Many artists benefited from the production of original print designs, or from the sale of prints based on their paintings. Reynolds was among many who displayed prints in order to advertise their work in other media (Hallett, 2014, 20). Print auctions, often advertised in the press, were held in coffee houses and print shops, and spread increasingly to the provinces (Clayton, 1997, 222). Large public dealerships in prints, such as those run by Joseph Ryland, John Boydell and Robert Sayer (1725–1794), all of whom sold prints of works by Angelica Kauffman as well as other celebrated eighteenth-century British artists, became more important than smaller independent dealers (Alexander, 1992, 142). Engravers normally worked directly for print-sellers rather than for artists, while having regular contact with the latter. Some engravers, such as Johann Georg Wille, Jacques-Philippe Le Bas (1707–1783), various generations of the Audran family, Robert Strange (1721–1792) and William Woollett (1735–1785), became so skilful, that their technical expertise tested the boundaries with "fine" art (Clayton, 1997, xi, 105). Excluded from full membership of the Royal Academy in London, engravers were given there the status of "associate engraver." Gillray's prints reveal a familiarity with the conventions of the "higher" genre of history learned through study at the Royal Academy's schools. Artists such as Piranesi became keen to design their own prints so that their individual styles became prominent (Clayton, 1997, 225–229; Campbell, 2000, 561). At the French Académie royale, engravers and graphic artists were officially excluded from academic areas of study but could exhibit at the Salons and were taken seriously by critics.

Artists were often commissioned by particular dealers to produce designs, and the print run of the most popular might amount to hundreds or thousands of copies, many being reissued at a later date, sometimes as part of a portfolio or album collection that could be sold or hired out. Print-sellers could also make a living through importing or exporting prints or through buying and selling on a wholesale basis (Donald, 1996, 4). They often specialized in products for a particular market, fashion or section of society. By the middle of the century, print-sellers might specialize in any of the following types or subjects: old master prints, literary subjects, views, antiquities, book illustration, battle scenes, marine or coastal views, landscapes, picturesque scenes, historical figures and events, architecture and book illustration (Clayton, 1997, 105–128). Caricature prints popular in the last few decades of the century were a specialist commercial genre, some focusing on bawdy, anti-clerical (and often anti-Catholic) subjects, while others chose to focus on more sophisticated topics. In London, comic prints and caricatures were sold mainly in the east end, to tradesmen and artisans, before spreading westwards as they became more fashionable with the upper echelons of society. Boydell was a market leader in the sale of prints of old master works and contemporary history painters, while the print shops of Matthew and Mary Darly (highly successful in the 1750s and early 1760s) specialized in political caricatures and, later, social satire. Vallée's print shop in Paris specialized in the 1780s in novelty prints, contemporary fashion plates and fashionable English stipple prints. It attracted a wide clientele though the middle or professional ranks were accountable for most of the purchases made. The print market embraced a wide range of products: narrative or satirical print series popular for private entertainment, designs for book illustrations, transfers for ceramics, handkerchiefs, fans, screens or trade cards all presented good commercial opportunities.

The print market stimulated other commercial and artistic ventures. In Paris, as in Britain, increasing print sales in the second half of the century also led to an increased trade in drawing manuals, which presented prints of paintings as subjects for study and copying (Wrigley, 1993, 20–24). Those unable to afford the services of a drawing master, or of a drawing school, could use these manuals. Artists also kept prints of their previous works in their studios, to assist portrait clients with a choice of pose, costume, accessories and so on. Books or albums of prints showing architectural and interior designs were popular with those having new homes built and were used from the early part of the century by builders and architects such as Colen Campbell (1676–1729) to impress potential clients. Pattern books of prints showed rococo decorative motifs for home décor (Scott, 1995, 251–252), which have since acquired an aesthetic value in their own right. Along with fashion plates, such prints played a central, publicity-generating role in an expanding commodity culture. Prints also served as advertisements for the work of a particular artist and Angelica Kauffman was among those who relied greatly on them. Some prints were published to coincide with the public exhibition of the paintings on which they were based.

Prints reproducing paintings spread international influences in styles and subjects. For example, the thriving market in Spain for Italian prints meant that etchings by the Tiepolos influenced Goya's style of painting. Artists also executed prints of canonical old master works for a more elite market. Goya made prints of works by Diego Velázquez (1599–1660) such as his *The Infante Don Fernando as a Hunter* (*El Cardinal infante don Fernando de Austria, cazador*, 1632–1633) and *The Drunkards* (*Los Barrachos*, 1628 1629). Carlos IV of Spain approved the production of such old master prints in order to promote the reputation of Spanish paintings in the royal collections.

The print market became increasingly sophisticated, and many buyers and collectors sought works of technical quality. Mezzotints (very popular in England and easily reworked for later editions) could serve as decorative prints, although they were sometimes considered less appropriate for the fine detail required for historical narratives where legibility was important, since the technique of producing them was based on creating tonal contrasts rather than clear lines. In the 1730s, line engravings of old master subjects made in England were popular abroad and were often captioned in both English and French for an international market. This fashion gave way in the 1770s to an international taste for English stipple engravings. The technique of stipple engraving involved printing from a plate with minute, raised dots (Alexander, 1992, 142, 169; Smentek, 2007, 225).

Angelica Kauffman catered for this market by making some drawings specifically as the basis for quality prints. Those of classical subjects were given Latin titles.

Color prints available in France earlier in the century became more widely available in England during Kauffman's career, and experimentation with techniques was common. Unlike French color prints, which used a separate plate for each color, English versions often placed all colors together on the same printing plate, *à la poupée* (the term refers to the cotton daubs or "dollies" used to apply color to the plate). There was also a medium known as a "mechanical painting" that mimicked the appearance of a painting by using recently developed aquatint prints, a form of etching that applied porous and non-porous resins to a plate to "stop out" or dim the ink on it, so that tonal variations or masses of light and shade were emphasized, as in paintings. These plates were used to make transfers onto coated paper and then onto a canvas. Vitreous colors were used and the whole was finished and varnished like a painting (Alexander, 1992, 150–160). *Avant la lettre* or first impression prints (made before the plate became worn or any text was added) became regarded as rare, collectable objects (Smentek, 2007, 226).

It became more common to buy prints as an investment, especially those in the "fine art print" category. Collectors of prints became expert in classifying them according to artist, printmaker, subject, technique or genre. Prints of Chardin's genre subjects became particularly popular, inviting the viewer to enter into a fictional world imbued with moral and emblematic significance (Scott, 2000, 61–76). Topicality could also influence trade. Some of the military scenes painted by Watteau, and his *fêtes galantes*, played on a contemporary vogue for fashion prints and prints on military and theatrical subjects (Plax, 2000, 118). Some prints capitalized on the public's desire to see images of notorious criminals (Pointon, 1993, 91).

Political, social and intellectual concerns affected the market, as did systems of censorship. Satirical prints from Britain were popular in more autocratic states, where they were appreciated by the liberal-minded as emblems of free speech (Donald, 1996, 20). In Germany, where there was relatively little knowledge of the British events or people represented, this gave rise to the need for printed commentaries, as in the journal *London und Paris* in 1798, where there were copies of and commentaries on Gillray's prints (Banerji and Donald, 1999, xiii–xiv). Conversely, in Spain Goya's satirical print series, *Los Caprichos*, (1799) was accompanied by "elusive" captions unlikely to rouse the suspicions of the Spanish authorities. His prints satirized through the use of caricature contemporary clergy, monks, religious superstition, the Inquisition and the pretentions of the nobility (Figure 5.2). In spite of the fact that Goya's previous work had won the favor of the Royal Family, the Inquisition stopped further sales of the prints soon after their release (Hofer, 1969, 1–6). In France and Italy, the print trade was often forced to operate beneath the radar of censorship. In Italy libels and lampoons were considered capital offences: the satirical works of Pietro Longhi offer mild social critique rather than any radical challenge to the (Catholic) church or state (Craske, 1997, 84–86).

Caricature prints, popular from the 1770s, targeted a range of victims, from general social types to specific individuals, and became increasingly political in nature. The mezzotint "droll" lampooned contemporary social types (such as the *nouveau riche*) in a largely apolitical way. It became more common to issue prints intended to blacken the social reputations of well-known individuals. These included in the 1780s the infamous Prince Regent (later George IV) and his circle, who led lives of unadulterated pleasure and luxury. The firm of Carington Bowles was dominant in the field of comic mezzotints. Political satire became widespread as politics itself became a national preoccupation. Throughout the century, satirical prints of all kinds used a complex language of symbols inherited from earlier Renaissance and seventeenth-century emblem books and adapted to the needs of different audiences – for example, the use of symbols in shop signs, coins and broadsheets was a "code" accessible to the "lower" orders (Donald, 1996, 47–57). Although Hogarth was not primarily interested in political topics, and claimed to prefer "natural" modes of representation to the use of caricature, he established a tradition of densely packed print images full of complex, allusive meanings. This prepared the territory for later satirists such as James Gillray and Thomas Rowlandson (1756–1827).

Political factions often sponsored Gillray, Rowlandson and other artists, sometimes secretly. It is difficult to determine, however, the extent to which their choices of subject or style were dictated by actual political allegiances or financial need. While Gillray's early career as a satirist embraced subjects from both radical oppositional and "loyalist" or conservative politics, he later focused on attacks on radical and oppositional activists such as Charles James Fox (1749–1806), Richard Brinsley Sheridan (1751–1816) and Thomas Paine (1737–1809), who saw the French Revolution as an opportunity to canvas for more widespread voting and economic rights in Britain (Donald, 1996, 26, 163–183). One possible explanation is that as wealthier landowners began to abandon oppositional politics, there was less financial support for radical causes. On the other hand, the Association for the Preservation of Liberty and Property against Republicans and Levellers, founded in 1792 by the conservative judge John Reeves

(1752–1829), enjoyed strong government support and actively used the production and dissemination of prints as a propaganda tool (Donald, 1996, 146–157). Gillray and Rowlandson were among those artists who benefited from the Society's commissions and used them to express fears of the possible dire consequences of allowing any "infectious" revolutionary fervor to undermine the social and political order, or the power of monarchs and the church, in Britain (Donald, 1996, 149–150). Such powerful forces easily defeated the faltering efforts of workers and artisans to form their own political organizations. Gillray's continuing success lay largely in his flexibility within a changing market and his ability to derive subjects from the dreams (or illusions) of all sides of a conflict (Paulson, 1983, 183–211). As the demand for more sophisticated political satire grew, he was able to adapt the learned rhetoric of classical history painting to more complex allegories relating to systems of government rather than lampooning individual politicians, and aimed at a more cultivated consumer (Donald, 1996, 60–74).

Political satirical prints were normally etchings done quickly in order to respond rapidly to contemporary events. Political crises prompted peaks in the market, such as the attempts in the 1760s, by the radical politician John Wilkes (1725–1797), to arouse popular support in favor of voting reform (and, later, the American War of Independence) in opposition to the government (Hallett, 2006f, 234–235). The market in Britain for satirical political prints, followed smartly by that for social satire, peaked in the 1780s to the 1820s, when contemporary events provided plenty of rich material and a wider public engaged with political events and issues. In the 1780s, the political opposition of Fox to the Prime Minister William Pitt the Younger (in office for most of the period 1783–1806), the French Revolution and revolutionary wars, provided fertile subject matter. From the 1760s caricature was often used in such prints in order to ridicule Britain's "enemies," both within and beyond its national borders. George Townshend (1724–1807) established a high reputation in the genre. Gillray and Rowlandson responded with equal vigor to later events, although Gillray was, of the two, the more focused on political events and figures. In spite of the fact that Rowlandson concentrated, like many of his contemporaries, on the Fox versus Pitt disputes, incidentally changing sides as his and his patrons' fortunes dictated, many of his several thousand prints were dedicated to a comedy of contemporary manners, in which the themes were often driven by humorous observation of social life at venues such as racecourses, Vauxhall Gardens, theatres and pubs. Satirical prints were often regarded as unseemly by more high-minded members of society and were not considered suitable for ladies.

There was less censure, toward the end of the century, of gently humorous social satires (Alexander, 1998, 10–13). Even British political prints were normally sold openly, legal "warnings" being the main deterrent to the sale of any subject considered subversive. The situation changed somewhat in the 1790s, following the King's 1787 proclamation against "loose and licentious prints, Books and Publications." There was more proactive censorship, and even the occasional imprisonment of print-sellers, although such prosecutions were often justified through charges against indecency, easier to prove in relation to semantically complex prints than political subversion.

Print distributors in France often relied on clandestine sales and circulation for controversial subjects. In the pre-Revolutionary period, celebrity portraits, allegories relating to contemporary social and political crises, sentimental scenes and licentious prints were particularly popular (Smentek, 2007, 222). Pre-Revolutionary and Revolutionary propagandists used the circulation of prints to intensify opposition to the royal family. There was a particularly aggressive campaign against Marie Antoinette, with defamatory pamphlets and prints representing her as the devil, a witch, a vampire, "Austria's creature," a hydra-headed monster and, generally, as a personification of vanity, sexual perversion and profligacy (Hunt, 1991, 122–126; Thomas, 2001, 105–135; Weber, 2006, 209–212). More rarely, positive representations of the queen featured in prints and print series and were exported to royalist supporters elsewhere in Europe (Wettlaufer, 1999, 1–37). In Italy, politically suspect prints could be circulated through coffee shops (Pasta, 2005, 210).

Exhibitions, Collectors, Museums and their Visitors

In addition to an expanding and increasingly complex market for art, the eighteenth century witnessed substantial improvements in the opportunities for artists to exhibit in public (and hence advertise) their work. This exhibition culture later became dominated by fine art academies, as they established themselves as centers of the highest forms of art. Earlier public exhibitions had been smaller, less formal, sometimes serendipitous and generally brief. The display of art objects had taken place in the sites of everyday life such as cemeteries (where funerary monuments were important), festivals (for which decorative artworks were made) and religious ceremonies. Churches had, for centuries, afforded natural opportunities to display religious works, particularly on the continent where Catholicism thrived. The best and most famous of these, for example, Notre-Dame-des-Victoires in Paris, which housed Carle Van Loo's painted series on the life of Saint Augustine (Wrigley, 1993, 15), were often accompanied by viewers' guides. In terms of cultural status, visiting works such as these was regarded as the equivalent of viewing the private collections of the social elite, to which access could be gained through introductions and invitations. Both ways of viewing art had been popular in Rome through the Renaissance and seventeenth century.

While the viewing of celebrated or monumental public art represented a "high" cultural pursuit, there was more suspicion from the establishment concerning more popular exhibition culture, connected traditionally with street processions and displays. Exhibitions held at the Place Dauphine in Paris, for one day a year on the Feast of Saint Bartholomew, concurrently with an open exhibition of tapestries at the Gobelins factory, had been established in 1644 through the Corpus Christi processions. This custom followed a long-established Italian tradition of linking public exhibitions with religious sites and occasions, often through one-day events. In the Place Dauphine, works were literally mounted on railings and on textile awnings covering buildings. These exhibitions focused initially on the display of high-status works from the Académie royale (Oudry was among exhibitors there) and of famous old master works, but later included works by younger, less established artists and by women. The Académie royale established its own exhibitions, which grew in stature, and from 1737 its artist members were forbidden to exhibit at the Place Dauphine, which became a byword among many critics for works of poor quality (Wrigley, 1993, 315). This judgment arose partly from the fact that the Place Dauphine exhibitions generally ignored the official hierarchy of genres, as they mixed serious art with "parade" or "festive" art and displayed works of all genres with apparent equality. After a break the shows resumed from 1759 to 1788, but in a reduced form, and became known as "exhibitions of work by young artists" (Berger, 1999, 149–155). The exhibitions were banned completely in 1788 after popular uprisings at the Pont Neuf, an adjacent site used to supplement the exhibition space at the Place Dauphine itself, amid general suspicion of the power of popular taste and protest. Yet in the early part of the century the Place Dauphine had provided an additional exhibiting opportunity for history artists such as Jean II Restout (1692–1768), Carle Van Loo and Jouvenet, as well as for Boucher's mythologies and for the still life painters Chardin, Oudry and Desportes.

The Académie de Saint Luc (see Chapter 1) provided further opportunities for the exhibition of a broad range of works of art. It held seven exhibitions between 1751 and 1774, at various venues and on different dates, in years when formal Salon exhibitions were not being held by the

Académie royale. Its exhibits consisted mainly of genre paintings, portraits, pastels, gem engravings and drawings. It struggled financially until its abolition in 1776 and for the following five years artists in Paris who were not members of the Académie royale had few venues for the display of their work. The exhibitions at Saint Luc were taken seriously outside the confines of the Académie royale, which disliked the institution's commercialism. They generated exhibition catalogues and some serious critical reviews. Although many of the latter were condescending, a review of the 1774 exhibition (in the *Mercure* of October that year) praised some of the portrait busts on display as well as works in a higher genre including Élisabeth Vigée Le Brun's allegorical representations of Painting, Poetry and Music (Berger, 1999, 229–232).

There had been some limited access to royal collections in France from the seventeenth century. The crown owned hundreds of old master works, including some by Raphael, Van Dyck, Poussin, Le Brun and Rubens (Berger, 1999, 85–87). Following an appeal in 1747 (in La Font de Saint Yenne's *Reflexions*) for wider public access, the Director of Public Buildings, Lenormand de Tournehem, put the royal collection at the Luxembourg Palace on public display. Mentioned in several eighteenth-century guidebooks, the collection included Rubens' *Marie de' Medici* cycle (1622–1625). There was also a room dedicated exclusively to French art, which encouraged critical thinking on the national school of art. Following a royal decree the gallery was opened in 1750 for roughly two days per week to the wider public, then closed to them in 1779, when the building in which it was housed passed into the possession of the younger brother of Louis XVI (reigned 1774–1793), the Comte de Provence. At this time the bulk of the royal collection remained at Versailles, where it was mainly exclusive to the court and its visiting diplomats (Berger, 1999, 210–219). Today the collection at the Luxembourg Palace has been dispersed across several museums. In 1776 another Director of Public Buildings, d'Angiviller, had begun work on boosting the royal collection (and thus the reputation of the monarch) and preparing it for public exhibition at the Louvre, but his efforts were interrupted by the Revolution. Collections such as those built by the Duc d'Orléans (Philippe II, Regent of France 1674–1723), the Duc de Choiseul (1719–1785) and Jean de Jullienne provided opportunities for "polite" visitors and artists to view art prior to the Revolution.

There were several pre-Revolutionary attempts in Paris to achieve a fuller public engagement with art, but with varying success. Following the demise of the Académie de Saint Luc and its exhibitions, an exhibition at the Colisée was organized in Paris. A site of popular entertainment, this building brought together members from a wide range of classes, and the 1776 exhibition included curios, luxury objects and paintings by foreign (especially German) artists. Many former members of the Académie de St Luc exhibited there. The exhibition was seen as a threat to the exclusivity of the Académie royale and not permitted the following year (Wrigley, 1993, 33–36). The same official distrust greeted the launch in 1778 of the Salon de la Correspondance established by Mammès Claude-Catherine Pahin-Champlain de la Blancherie (1752–1811) in order to bring together for the purposes of exhibitions and discussions artists, scientists and amateurs excluded from the Académie royale. This ran intermittently until 1787 when all salons and clubs were shut down in response to fears of political activism. Pahin de la Blancherie also organized in 1793 an exhibition dedicated to a survey of the French School, which served to intensify interest in national culture.

It is clear that a number of artists who had previously exhibited at the Académie royale, Académie de St Luc, Place Dauphine, Colisée and other sites were seeking by the late 1780s alternative exhibition opportunities and, in fact, the Académie itself was forced in 1791, after the onset of the Revolution and under pressure from its own artists, to run an "open" exhibition that welcomed a wider range of artists and downplayed genre hierarchies. "Exclusivity" was increasingly under threat. After the Revolution, efforts to show works of art beyond the narrow confines of the royal court intensified and in 1796 a catalogue of national monuments was used as the basis of the newly opened Musée des Monuments Français, which included works seized during the Revolution including funerary and tomb sculptures. Before the Revolution the main display area for sculptures in Paris had been the Tuileries Gardens. During the Revolution these were used as a display area for confiscated sculptures and for festivals; they were then converted into an open-air museum of replicas of Greco-Roman statuary (Berger, 1999, 259–279).

The Louvre did not become a public museum until 1793, when the Revolution had brought about a reappraisal of the need to provide fuller public access to works in the royal collection that had previously remained in storage or accessible mainly to those at court. As a public museum the Louvre was free and open to the public on three days a week, with artists and foreign tourists able to visit on other days, the former free (unusually) to choose themselves which works they wished to copy (McClellan, 2008, 18–20, 159, 197–198). The display of paintings, in the splendor of the Grande Galérie, was composed of works confiscated during the Revolution from the church and royal court, and paintings were arranged in chronological order, to show how the French school had built on the work of illustrious predecessors. The gallery drew in members of all social classes and established a template for subsequent "high art" museums. The Musée Spécial de l'École Française (Specialist Museum of the French School) was created at Versailles in 1797, an acknowledgment of the growing importance of the French School.

By the end of the century there were approximately 500 *amateurs* who had significant collections in France (T.W.Gaehtgens, 2003, 87). Their collections changed with fashion, French genre paintings finally overtaking the popularity previously enjoyed by Netherlandish works. Oil sketches, cabinet paintings and copies allowed those with lesser resources to begin collecting (Conisbee, 1981, 27–30). The Académie royale built up its own collection of works, consisting of reception pieces by its members, submissions for the Rome prize, gifts and replicas of antique sculptures. In 1712 this collection was given better display space at the Louvre where the Academy had moved in 1692, and a catalogue to the collection was written and published in 1715. Guidebooks included plans of the collection, which could be seen occasionally, by prior arrangement, by *amateurs*. At the end of the century, Watteau's *Pilgrimage to the Island of Cythera* played a starring role in the collection of the Académie and, subsequently, the Louvre museum.

Collections of art were an important means of acquiring status. Those who undertook the Grand Tour brought back works by celebrity artists such as Batoni (whose portraits were much cheaper than those produced by Reynolds) and Piranesi, as well as watercolors and prints of ancient sites and antiquities. Some famous collections were established, including Charles Townley's ancient marbles, subsequently donated to the British Museum (Coltman, 2006, 165–193) and the Etruscan, Greek and Roman vases of William Hamilton (1731–1803), sold to the same institution (Coltman, 2006, 16). The burgeoning taste for antiquarian publications helped to inform and validate such collections. Some patrons even ordered works from home and waited for them to be shipped back. Shipping could be risky, however. As mentioned in Chapter 1, much of the foundation collection of the Real Academia in Madrid consisted of works seized from a ship, The Westmorland, which had been looted while carrying such goods from Italy to their English owners (Coltman, 2009, 133–140).

Royal households acquired prestigious collections of art in order to impress both their own subjects and foreign visitors. In Britain, Queen Charlotte (consort to George III) asked Zoffany to carry out some of her commissions in Italy so that she might acquire by association a reputation for knowledge of Italian art. Rulers in Hungary, Habsburg and German courts saw art collections as an effective means of self-presentation and of vying with the latest artistic trends (e.g. the rococo, *chinoiserie*, the gothic and the neoclassical) in France, Italy and elsewhere (Kaufman, 1995, 307–330, 368–438). Frederick the Great acquired many French works, including genre paintings and works by Watteau and his followers, that would suit the monarch's decorative schemes. As the century progressed, it became more common, however, particularly outside Prussia, for native German, Swiss and Austrian artists to receive commissions and for their works to be collected.

Louis XV of France commissioned many genre paintings for the wooden panels at Versailles, as well as hunt and outdoor feast scenes for his private apartments. Catherine the Great of Russia acquired a significant collection from all over Europe, including the collection at Houghton Hall of Sir Robert Walpole (in office 1721–1742), Britain's first Prime Minister, in office from 1721 to 1742. Walpole's family sold this collection after his death, when they met a debt crisis. The collection comprised mainly European sixteenth- and seventeenth-century old master works in a range of genres. These paintings went eventually to the Hermitage Museum in St Petersburg, which by 1770 contained 2080 paintings. Catherine also collected old master drawings, and commissioned porcelain and furniture from the finest manufacturers in Europe. She wanted her collections to be the best in Europe.

There were lavish courtly collections in Munich and Vienna. The collection at the latter of the Habsburg ruler Charles VI (Holy Roman Emperor 1711–1740) was particularly grand, and was "opened up" to a wide public through the creation of an illustrated catalogue which presented a canonical set of "masterpieces" tracing a traditional narrative of the progress of western art (Link, 2013, 101–116). In the 1780s the gallery at the Belvedere Palace of Joseph II of Austria (Holy Roman Emperor 1765–1790) was opened free of charge to the public (Kaufman, 1995, 444). German courtly artists such as Johann Heinrich Tischbein the elder (1722–1789) created at court (in his case at Kassel) art that united the cultural interests of the court with those of a broader social elite. His *Masquerade with Personalities from Kassel Playing Cards* (*Maskenszene mit Kasseler Persoenlich-keit*, *c*.1780–1785) included references to Watteau-inspired masquerade (Tite, 2013b, 36–45). The Fridericianum Museum in Kassel, built in 1779, became the first free-standing museum in Germany. Courts across Europe, including those at Stockholm, Düsseldorf, Florence and Dresden, hired curators to organize their collections or opened these up to viewing by an increasingly broad range of the public.

The provision of catalogues and guidebooks became much more common throughout the century and encouraged wider public engagement

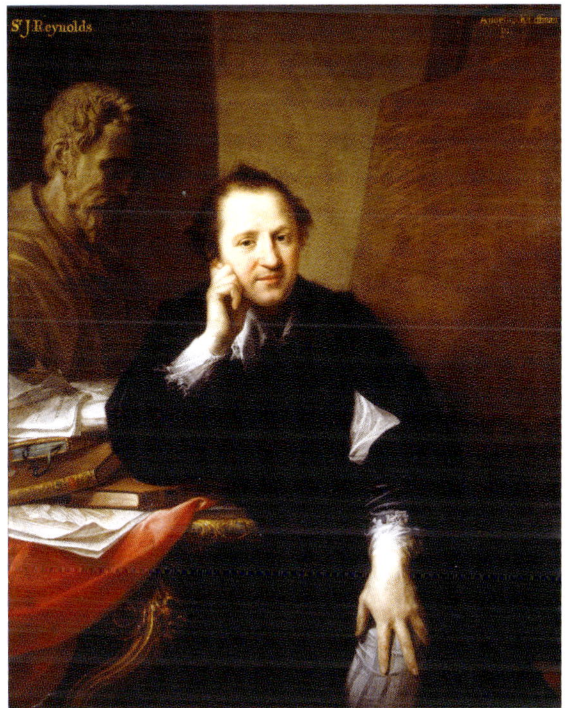

Figure 1.2 Angelica Kauffman: *Sir Joshua Reynolds*, oil on canvas, 127 × 101.5 cm, 1767, National Trust Collection, Saltram, Devon. Source: © National Trust Images/Alamy Stock Photo.

A Guide to Eighteenth-Century Art, First Edition. Linda Walsh.

Companion website: www.wiley.com/go/walsh/guidetoeighteenthcenturyart

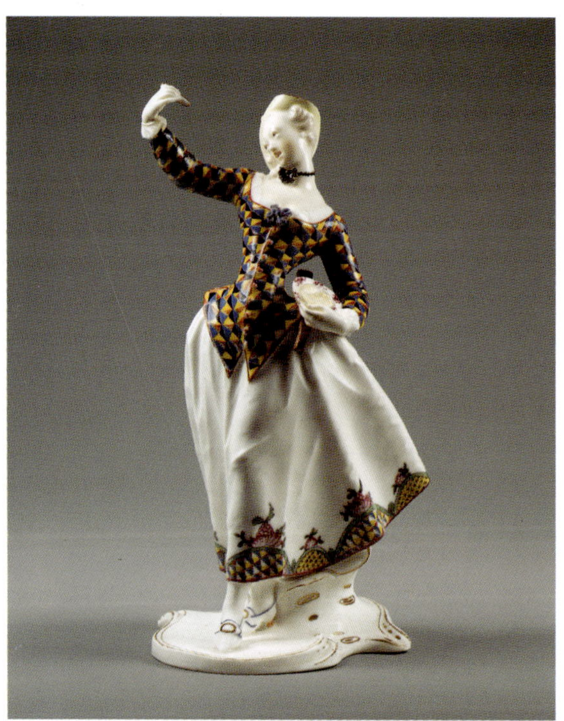

Figure 1.4 Franz Anton Bustelli: *Harlequina*, hard-paste porcelain, h. 20.3 cm, c. 1763, German, Nymphenburg Porcelain Manufactory. The Metropolitan Museum of Art, The Lesley and Emma Sheafer Collection, Bequest of Emma A. Sheafer, 1973, Acc. no: 1974.356.524. Source: The Metropolitan Museum of Art, www.metmuseum.org

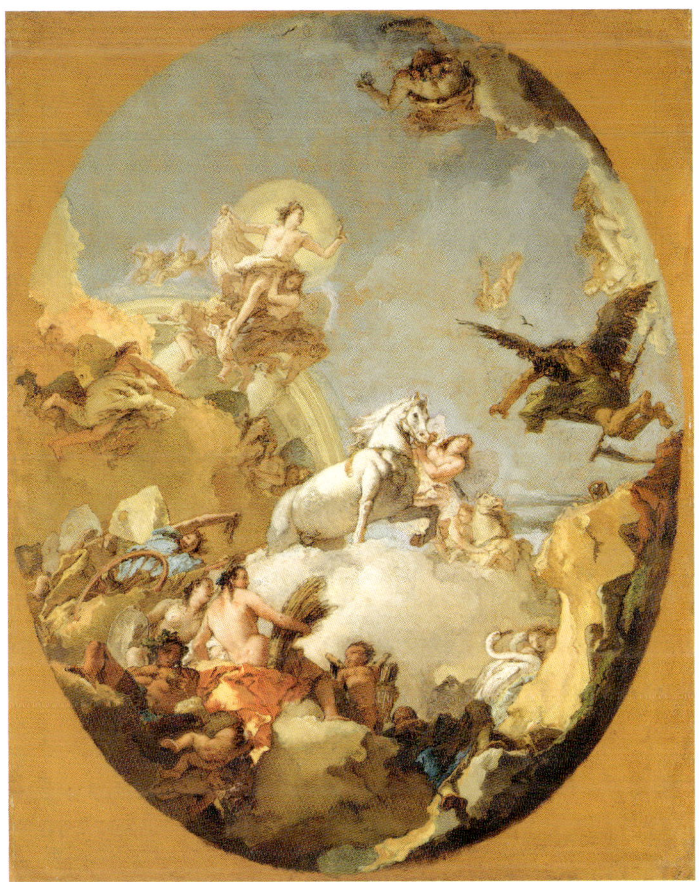

Figure 2.2 Giovanni Battista Tiepolo: *The Chariot of Aurora*, oil on canvas, 90.2 × 72.7 cm, c.1734. The Metropolitan Museum of Art, Bequest of Lore Heinemann, in memory of her husband, Dr Rudolf J. Heinemann, 1996. Acc. No: 1997.117.7. Source: The Metropolitan Museum of Art, www.metmuseum.org

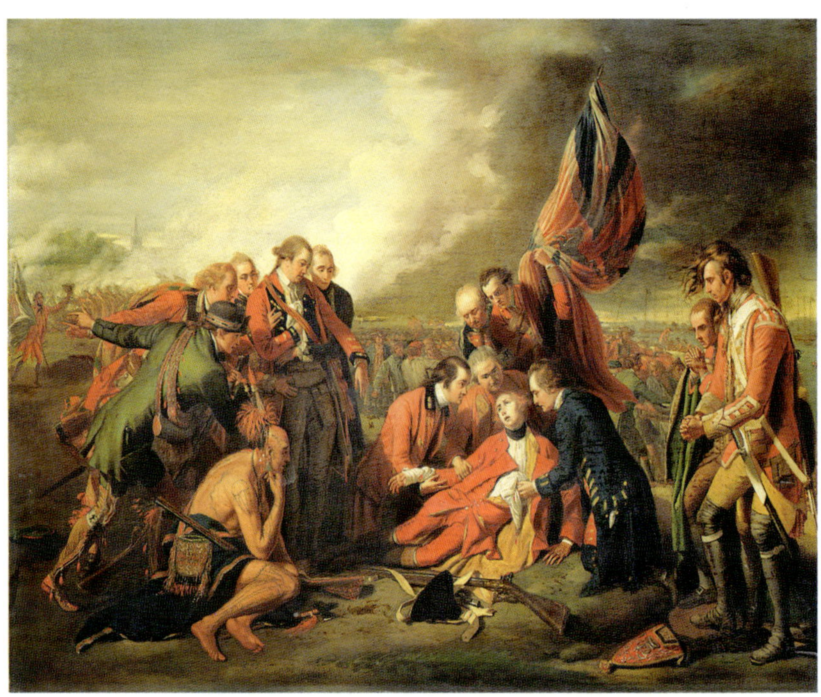

Figure 2.4 Benjamin West: *The Death of General Wolfe* (1727–1759), oil on panel, replica c. 1771, Private collection (original, 152 × 214 cm, in National Gallery of Canada, Ottawa). Source: Phillips, Fine Art Auctioneers, New York, USA/Bridgeman Images.

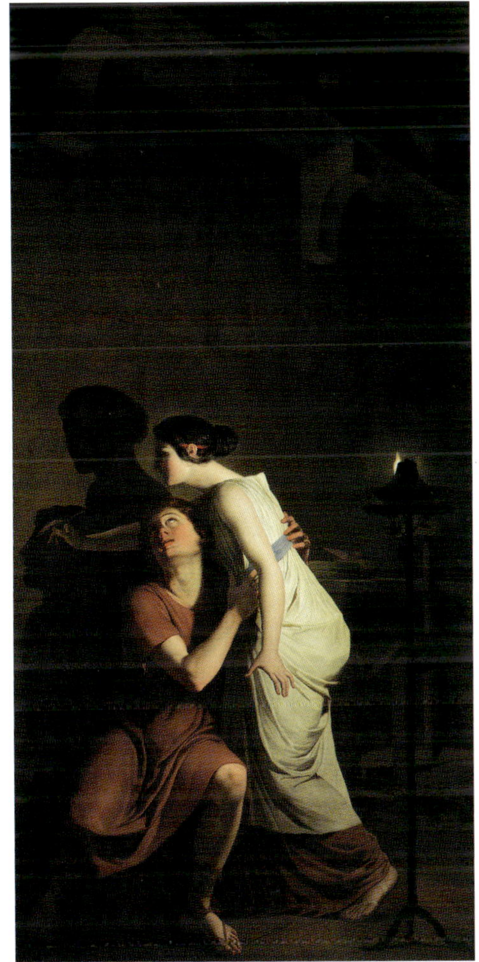

Figure 2.5 Joseph-Benoît Suvée: *The Invention of the Art of Drawing*, oil on canvas, 267 × 131.5 cm, 1791, Groeningemuseum, Bruges, Belgium. Source: © Lukas Art in Flanders VZW/Bridgeman Images.

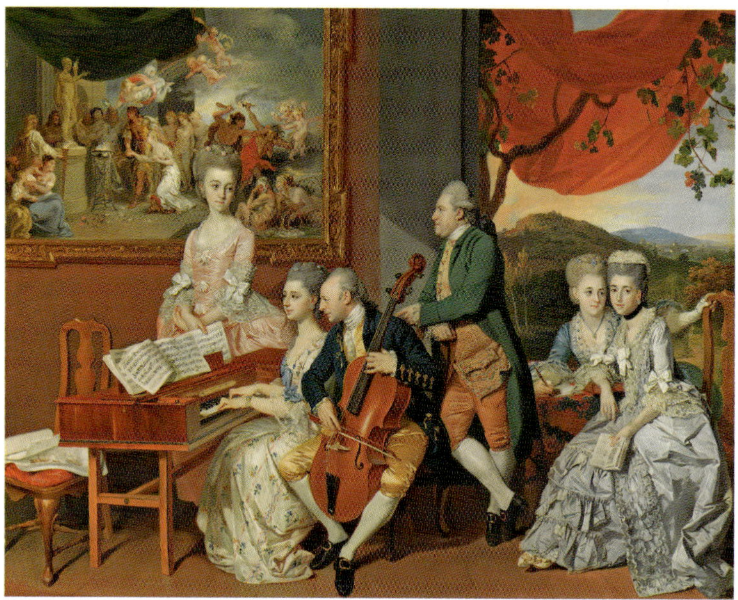

Figure 2.10 Johan Zoffany RA: *The Gore Family with George, 3rd Earl Cowper*, oil on canvas, 78.7 × 97.8 cm, c. 1775. Yale Center for British Art, Paul Mellon Collection. Source: Yale Center for British Art, Paul Mellon Collection.

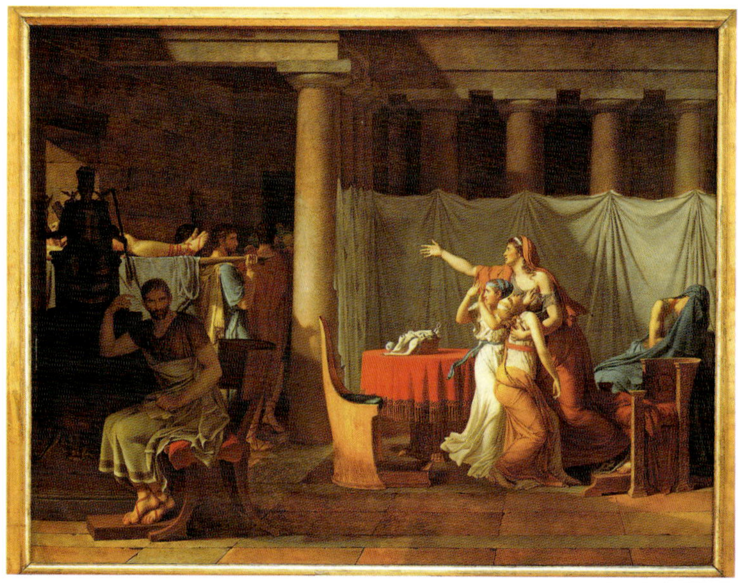

Figure 2.12 Jacques-Louis David: *The Lictors Bring to Brutus the Bodies of his Sons*, oil on canvas, 323 × 422 cm, 1789, Paris, Musée du Louvre. Source: E. Lessing/De Agostini/Getty Images.

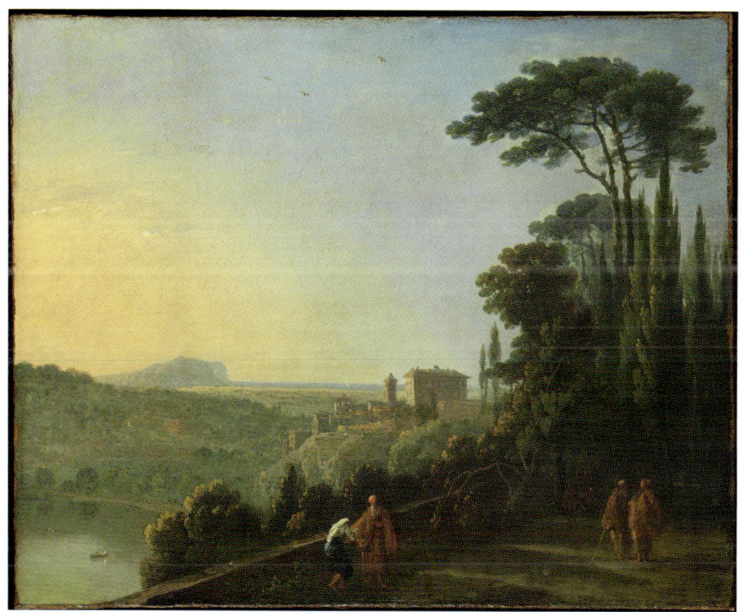

Figure 2.14 Richard Wilson: *Lake Nemi and Genzano from the Terrace of the Capuchin Monastery*, oil on canvas, 42.9 × 53.7 cm, c. 1756–1757. The Metropolitan Museum of Art, Gift of George A. Hearn, 1905, Acc. No.: 05.32.3. Source: The Metropolitan Museum of Art, www.metmuseum.org

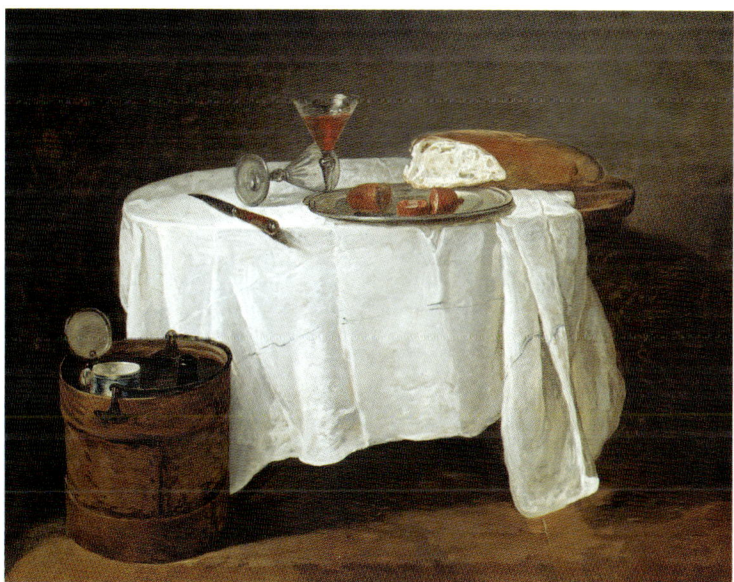

Figure 2.16 Jean-Baptiste-Siméon Chardin: *The White Tablecloth*, oil on canvas, 96.8 × 123.5 cm, 1731/32. The Art Institute of Chicago, Mr. and Mrs. Lewis Larned Coburn Memorial Collection, 1944, 699. Source: Photography © The Art Institute of Chicago.

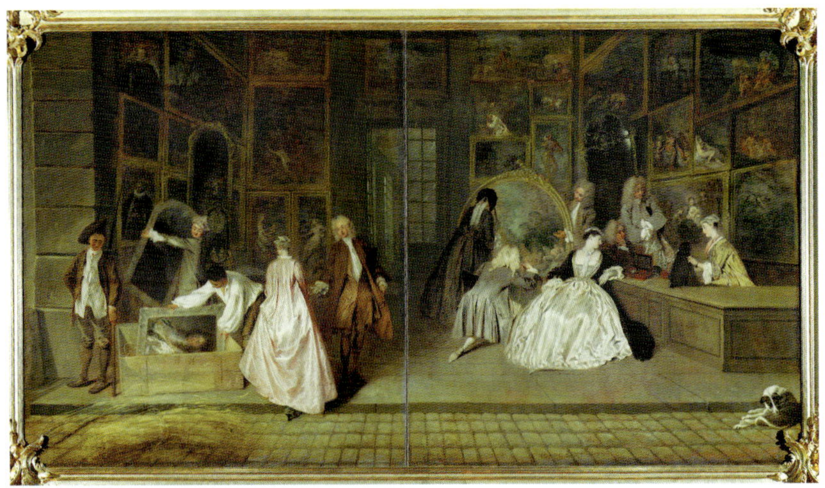

Figure 3.2 Jean-Antoine Watteau: *Shop Sign of the Art Dealer Gersaint*, oil on canvas, 163 × 308cm, 1720. Berlin, Schloß Charlottenburg. Source: akg-images/ Erich Lessing.

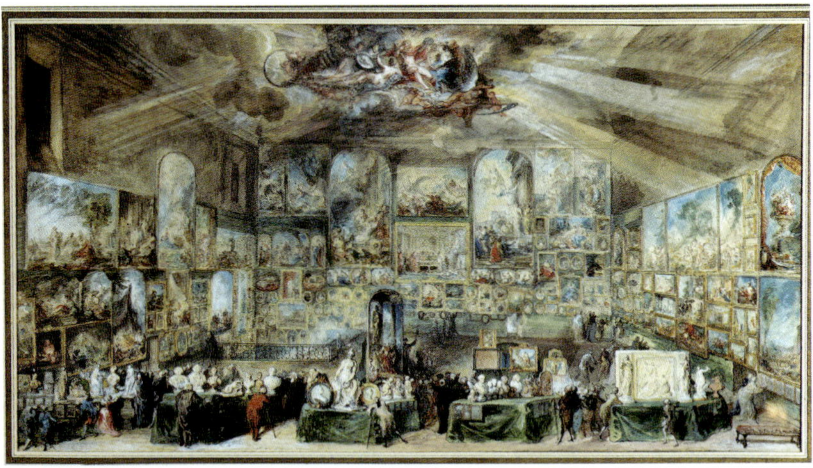

Figure 3.4 Gabriel-Jacques de Saint Aubin (1724–1780): *View of the Salon of 1767*, ink drawing, color wash and gouache highlights, 24.9 × 46.9 cm, 1767. Rouen, Musée des Beaux-Arts. Source: © 2015. © Photo Josse/Scala, Florence.

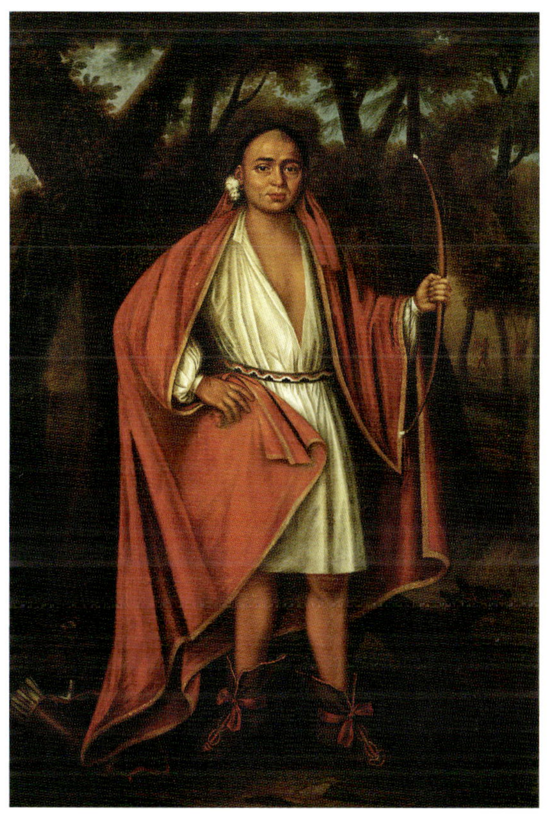

Figure 3.10 Johannes or Jan Verelst: *No Nee Yeath Tan no Ton, King of the Generath*, oil on canvas, 1710. Library and Archives of Canada. Source: Private collection/Bridgeman Images.

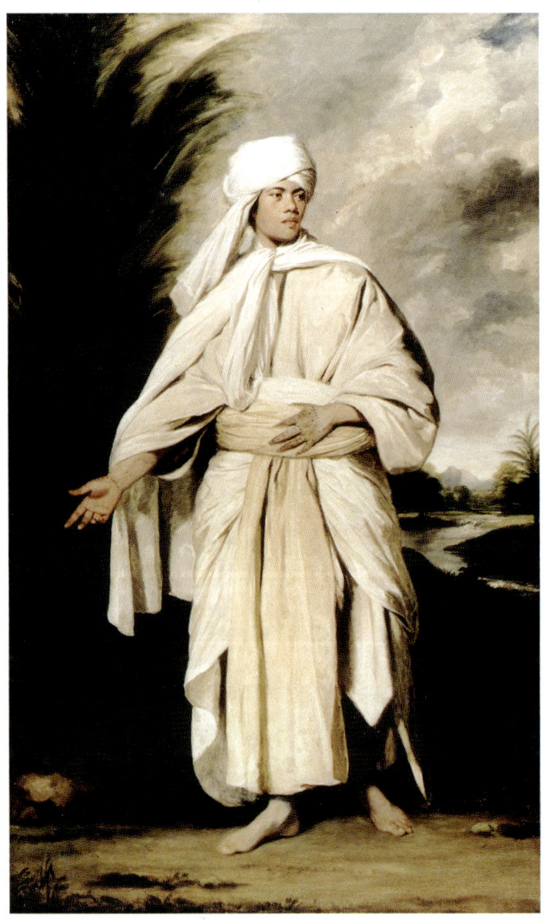

Figure 3.11 Sir Joshua Reynolds: *Portrait of Omai*, oil on canvas, 236 × 145.5 cm, c. 1776. Private collection. Source: Courtesy of Sotheby's Picture Library.

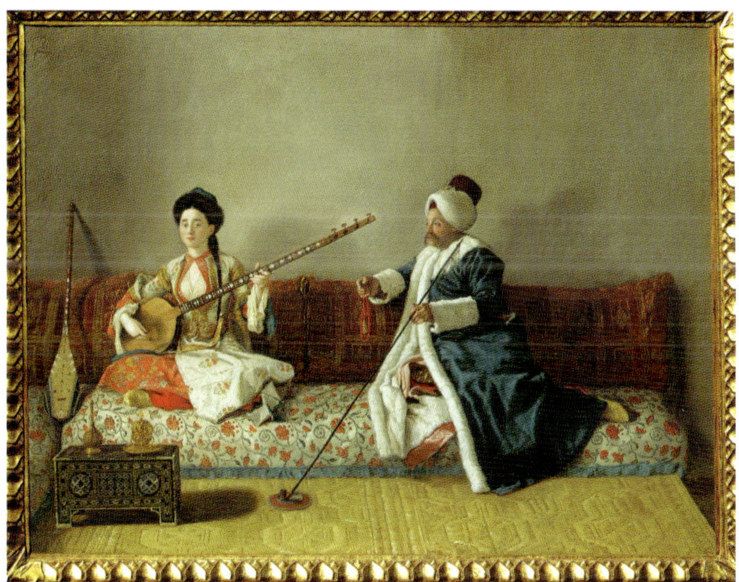

Figure 5.7 Jean-Étienne Liotard: *Monsieur Levett and Mademoiselle Helene Glavany in Turkish Costume*, oil on card, 24.6 × 36.4 cm, c. 1740. Paris, Musée du Louvre. Source: akg-images/Erich Lessing.

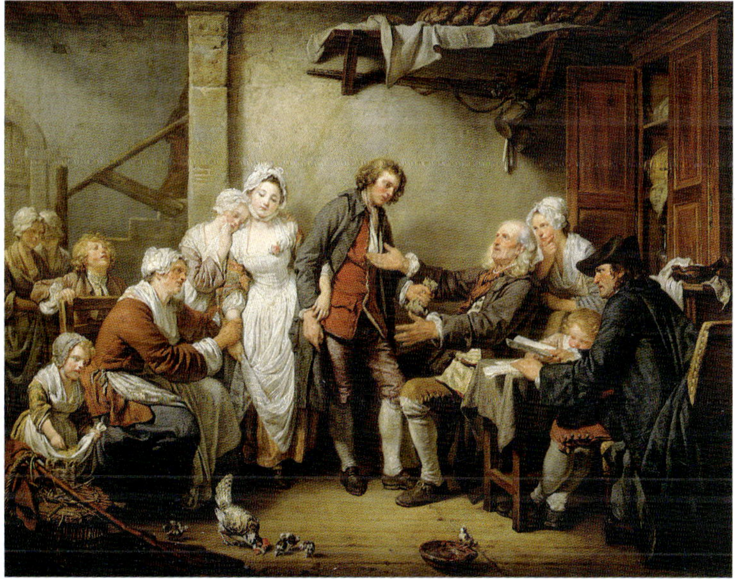

Figure 5.8 Jean-Baptiste Greuze: *The Village Bride or The Village Agreement*, oil on canvas, 92 × 117 cm, 1761. Paris, Musée du Louvre. Source: DeAgostini/G. Dagli Orti/Getty Images.

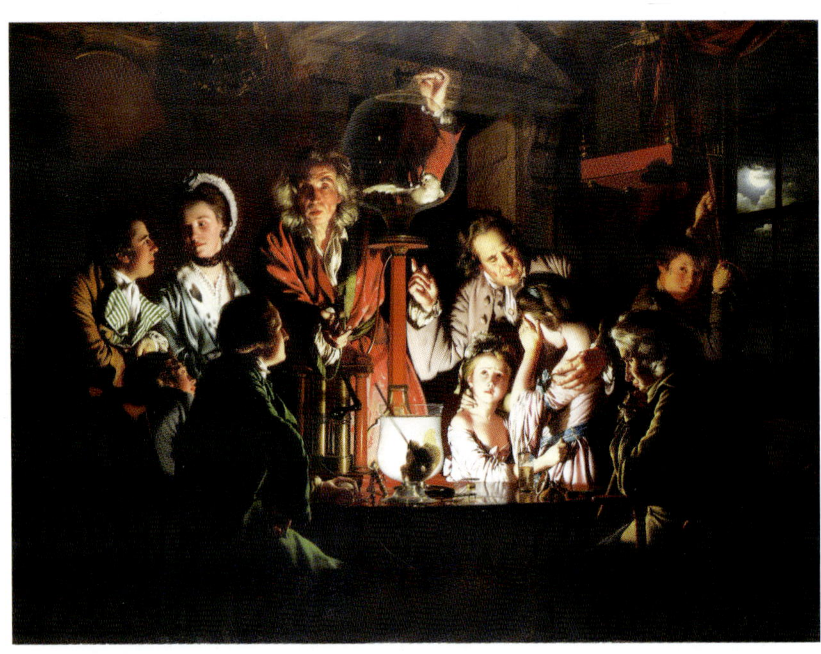

Figure 5.9 Joseph Wright of Derby: *An Experiment on a Bird in the Air Pump*, oil on canvas, 183 × 244 cm, 1768. The National Gallery, London. Source: Universal Images Group/Getty Images.

both with public and with privately owned art. In 1781 the first guidebook to the Mays of the Cathedral of Notre-Dame de Paris was issued. The "mays" were large history paintings offered to the cathedral on the first of May every year between 1630 and 1707 by the guild of goldsmiths and silversmiths. The paintings were on the theme of Acts of the Apostles and were displayed on pillars in the nave. They included works by seventeenth-century French artists still much revered in the eighteenth; for example, Le Brun, Le Sueur and Sébastien Bourdon (1616–1671). The Grand Tour also encouraged the production of pocket-sized guidebooks, to the Italian monuments, cities and works of art popular with visitors.

The Paris Salons, which exhibited work by full and associate members of the Académie royale, provided for much of the eighteenth century the most consistent opportunity for artists to exhibit their work to an informed audience (Figure 3.4, see color plate section). Their name derives from the *salon carré* at the Louvre, where they were held from 1737. They displayed many kinds of works, including paintings, sculptures, drawings and prints. In the late seventeenth and early eighteenth centuries the Salons had been sporadic and often mounted in response to special royal occasions; for example, the marriage in 1725 between Louis XV and Maria Leszczyńska (Queen Consort 1725–1768). Initiated in 1667, the Salons took place every few years until 1704 when they stopped for a while due to concerns over the expense of mounting them, followed by another in 1725. After a further break, the exhibitions were revived in 1737 in order to counter what was seen as increasing competition from street culture. They were then held annually every year (except 1744) until 1748. The 1749 Salon was canceled in response to virulent criticism (provoked by La Font de Saint Yenne) of works displayed the previous year. In an attempt to improve the general standard of entries the exhibitions became biennial, from 1751 to 1791: artists would have more time to work on their submissions. Lenormand de Tournehem established in 1748 a selection committee, with a similar view to improving quality. There was a tradition in France (unlike other countries such as Italy) of active royal control of academy exhibitions. From the 1770s d'Angiviller (then-Director of Public Buildings) made special efforts to regulate the moral standards of works exhibited and tried to distance the Salons further from the taint of commerce by forbidding the display of copies of former works, a practice regarded up to that point as perfectly respectable. Artists' self-portraits were increasingly frowned upon, as they were seen as devices of self-promotion. Paintings with explicit or implicit political themes were regarded with increasing suspicion, as prompts to popular unrest.

Catalogue sales provide a rough guide to the numbers visiting the Salons. From 1755 to 1787 between 7690 and 21,940 *livrets* (guides) were sold each year, with an estimated average figure of just over 10% of the population visiting the exhibitions (Berger, 1999, 168). In this period portraits and works on sentimental themes attracted the crowds. Occasionally members of the royal family and other esteemed guests (or those with the right connections, such as the art critic Denis Diderot) secured a private view. While the Salons were the main means by which artists could show their works in public, relatively few of these works, in the first few decades of the eighteenth century, were made specifically with the Salon in mind, and many visitors were unable to decode history paintings without the explanations of subjects offered in the *livrets.* Learned patrons used the exhibitions as an opportunity to reflect upon and consolidate their own elevated tastes. Some of the best French works exhibited were for the Royal Collection at Versailles. The Salons were not, however, the only occasions on which the public could view works by its contemporary artists. The works produced by those aspiring to the Rome prize, for example, were available to view, if briefly and just once a year, and a competition for the Académie's history painters in 1727 sought the views of the (educated) public as well as generating important sales to the royal court.

Due to pressure from the radical artistic faction the Commune des arts, and a National Assembly edict, the 1791 Salon and others held in the 1790s were open to any artists who wished to exhibit: critics complained that the standard had dropped (Wrigley, 1993, 67, 141–142). While an entrance fee had been charged in pre-Revolutionary Salons, those of the 1790s were free and this led to claims that the "high" domain of art was descending again to the level of popular spectacle, even though Revolutionary authorities promoted the exhibitions as an expression of the new patriotism. Issues of hierarchy remained controversial. For most of the century the Salon *livrets* listed works according to their rank in the hierarchy of genres – history paintings first- and to the Academic rank of the artists who had produced them. The 1791 Salon challenged the status quo by placing less emphasis on these hierarchies and more on public taste. Twelve commissioners were appointed from among artists and amateurs as judges; entries were divided into three "qualities" or grades, with members of the public consulted as to whether works should be upgraded or downgraded. In 1789 and 1791 the art dealer Jean-Baptiste-Pierre Le Brun (1748–1813) held *expositions de la jeunesse* ("young artist exhibitions") also intended to be less exclusive than the Salons.

The exposure of works of art in France to a broader public was in part a consequence of the perception that the nation was beginning to lag behind some of its neighbors in the creation of public museums, including in 1753 the British Museum, the first national public museum in the world, which was set up to display "world" culture (Crow, 1985, 9). Other museums or collections had been opened to the public in Grand Tour venues such as Rome, Florence and Venice, and in other locations including Potsdam (1764) and Haarlem (1784). In sixteenth-century Rome, papal collections of antiquities, at the time regarded as distinctively "pagan" artifacts rather than "art," had been made available to the public at the Conservators' Palace (Palazzo dei Conservatori) on the Capitol, the public Capitoline Museum opening in 1734. Papal collections grew significantly throughout the eighteenth century, although they were later plundered in the Napoleonic era. Fine art objects, for example, the famous sculptures *Laocoön*, *Antinous* and the *Apollo Belvedere* could be viewed relatively easily by arrangement;for example, at the Belvedere Sculpture Courtyard at the Vatican (Clark, 1966–1967, 141–142; Coltman, 2006, 123). The Borghese Collections were also open to Grand Tourists in Rome (Paul, 2008). The Public Sculpture Gallery (Statuario Pubblico) in Venice was open in the eighteenth century to the public at large. The Uffizi in Florence was among other institutions that welcomed Grand Tour visitors and, throughout the eighteenth century, many public Italian museums and galleries (including those at the Capitol) were redeveloped or opened in order to meet demand. The Academy of San Luca (Rome) also occasionally opened its doors to the public in order to allow them to see its permanent collection. Germany followed the example of Italy and France in the later eighteenth century, by beginning to open more art to public access.

There were motives internal to France for the expansion of public opportunities to view art there. These included prior to the Revolution the desire to add to the glory of the French monarchy and the need to advertise its commissions, an expanding critical art press and rising levels of public literacy and interest in the arts. Although, in Britain, the art establishment tended to operate more independently of the monarchy, the other factors mentioned here did apply and a similar range of causes affected the growing public accessibility of art in most European countries.

The situation in Britain provided a similar mix of formal Royal Academy exhibitions (the first being held in 1769) and less official or hierarchic public displays of art. Churches and civic buildings accommodated the display of some paintings and sculptures. Popular leisure sites incorporating the exhibition of artworks included Vauxhall Gardens, which had been recently improved by the art patron Jonathan Tyers (1702–1767), and public rooms at the Foundling Hospital, founded by Captain Thomas Coram as a charitable institution for abandoned children that attracted the patronage of the great and the good (Hallett, 2014, 61–65). Westminster Abbey and Saint Bartholomew's hospital also provided opportunities for public display, the former for sculpture (Hargraves, 2005, 6). Apart from these venues, there were relatively few public exhibitions held prior to the establishment of the Society of Arts and the Royal Academy, but even in the early years of the century, coffee houses, artists' studios, shop windows and auction rooms provided viewing opportunities, as did personal invitations to view private collections. The latter often celebrated their old master paintings, also promoted by dealers until the Royal Academy brought greater status to the "British School" (Hargraves, 2005, 7). It was rare to exhibit contemporary British works alongside old masters until the early nineteenth century: before that, they were normally relegated to staircases, dining rooms and parlors (Solkin, 1993, 221–222). Specifically British collections of paintings were rare until the 1790s. As in France, an expanding artistic culture became more diverse and fostered educated commentary or, for more populist venues, advertisements or reviews in the popular or fashionable press. Dealers, print-sellers and art fairs had existed in Britain from the Renaissance (Brewer, 1997, xviii), but rapid urbanization in the eighteenth century increased the number of exhibitions held. The success of exhibitions held by the Society of Arts and the Royal Academy encouraged later in the century the growth of commercial galleries such as those focusing on prints (Brewer, 1997, 64).

Vauxhall Gardens, where music and art were the "pleasurable" pastimes on offer, enjoyed a reputation as a den of illicit assignations. They became more respectable and began to attract a wide range of social classes to their concerts, firework displays and exhibitions. Hogarth initiated a custom there of exhibiting paintings in sheltered outdoor supper boxes and in the rotunda. These included more frivolous rococo works as well as serious history paintings; the latter were also exhibited at the Foundling Hospital, and Hogarth's early works formed part of the display. The display of history paintings at Vauxhall Gardens brought them to the attention of a wider public and the opportunity was taken to exhibit there paintings on themes of common national interest such as scenes from Shakespeare and some emotionally rousing patriotic works by Francis Hayman on the Seven Years War, colonial battles and other national events (Solkin, 1993, 190–195; Crowley, 2011, 6–7). Hayman's works ranged from the historical to the decorative, the contemporary and the anecdotal (Allen, 1987, 48–73).

There were other large public exhibitions of art in Britain outside those launched by the Royal Academy. These included those held at Glasgow (1761), Dublin (the Society of Artists set up there in 1765 exhibited until 1780 and again after 1800) and exhibitions held in Liverpool in 1774, 1784 and 1787. Additionally, it was common for private collectors to open up their homes, by arrangement, to an educated, polite public. Country houses provided semi-public display spaces; their collections established and publicized their credentials of power and lineage through, for example, the display of family portraits (Retford, Perry and Vibert, 2013, 3–8, 12).

In 1760 the Society of Arts (see Chapter 1) was asked by a group of contemporary British artists calling themselves the "present Artists," many from outside its own ranks, to host at its premises in the Strand an exhibition with the aims of raising funds for ailing artists unable to support themselves and of advancing the reputation of the arts in Britain, in the face of foreign criticism (Hargraves, 2005, 16–26; Hallett, 2014, 145–156). The exhibits included paintings, sculptures, models, handicrafts, needlework and engravings. Visitor entry was free, leading to subsequent complaints about the unrefined spectators who had attended. Money was raised through the sale of catalogues that were optional for those attending. By 1762 many of the artists involved in the 1760 exhibition had abandoned the Society of Arts, due to its efforts to impose tight control over the selection and display of works and to prioritize the display of its own premium-winning works mainly by amateur artists (Brewer, 1997, 232; Hargraves, 2005)

This generated two opposing factions ultimately forming new societies, the first being the Free Society of Artists associated for the Relief of Distressed Brethren, their Widows and Orphans, a charitable organization supporting artists in need, which continued to emphasize practical support for artists, especially those beginning their careers, and to focus on applied and amateur arts (Hargraves, 2005, 159–160). The second was the Society of Artists of Great Britain (Myrone, 2008, 189). This saw its main mission as the advancement of art rather than practical support for artists (Solkin, 1992, 176–177), and wished to prioritize the liberal arts, even if this meant charging an entrance fee to its exhibitions in order to restrict attendance to the wealthy and educated (Hargraves, 2005, 28–38). The Society of Artists of Great Britain later acquired a royal charter and called itself the Incorporated Society of Artists of Great Britain (Hargraves, 2005, 51–55). It saw itself as fulfilling an important function in increasing public knowledge of art, and held strictly managed aesthetic debates that extended beyond mechanical or craft-based skills. It increased its standing as a professionalizing force. It also set up life classes (Hargraves, 2005, 44–45, 51–53; 102–103). These higher ideals often masked commercial motives; regular auctions were held in order to help members make a living. Joseph Wright of Derby exhibited 34 paintings with the Society of Artists between 1765 and 1773. Zoffany and the painter of horse portraits, George Stubbs, also exhibited regularly with them before exhibiting at and becoming members of the Royal Academy.

Matthew Hargraves has recounted in detail how the Society of Artists (of Great Britain) became riven by internal conflict, as the "old guard" there refused, in the face of considerable protest, to reform its electoral procedures for the Directorate (Hargraves, 2005, 63–92). When George III later approved the foundation of and monarchical support for the Royal Academy, the "old guard" of the Society abandoned it to become the ruling oligarchy of the new institution. Those artists remaining with the Society of Artists promoted their organization as more libertarian than the Royal Academy, which had been established under royal protection. This strategy later caused problems, however, as "liberty" evoked in the minds of the public the trauma of the French Revolution or the American War of Independence (Hargraves, 2005, 63–88, 113–114, 145–147, 170). Society of Artists exhibitions continued but included handicrafts and "curiosities," and struggled to match the higher ideals of the new Royal Academy. The Society focused on its role as a trade association and held public lectures on craft-related topics such as pigments and chemistry (Brewer, 1997, 235). The last Society exhibition was held in 1791 (Hargraves, 2005, 92–163).

Another method of exhibiting works was the mounting of one-man shows, which often charged an entry fee and provided welcome publicity for artists. Gainsborough held exhibitions in his own home, especially after falling out with the organizers of Royal Academy exhibitions, who did not display his works to his satisfaction. Joseph Wright of Derby also had a serious disagreement with the Academy, which had granted him associate, but not full membership, and subsequently set up in 1785 a one-man exhibition at Covent Garden that included his sensational *The Widow of an Indian Chief Watching the Arms of her Deceased Husband* (1785), although this particular work remained unsold (Egerton, 1990, 261). John Singleton Copley (1738–1815) exhibited his *The Siege of Gibraltar* (1783–1791) at an Oriental pavilion on the edge of Green Park, London, charging a one-shilling entrance fee and capitalizing on patriotic pride in a recent military victory (Bonehill, 2005, 139–140).

In France, Greuze held private exhibitions of his works to coincide with the Salons. Works banned from the Salons might also be exhibited privately.

One-man shows could generate generous income. In 1799, David held a private exhibition of his *The Intervention of the Sabine Women* (*L'Intervention des Sabines*) (1799) later joined by his *Bonaparte Crossing the Alps* (*Napoléon franchissant le Grand Saint-Bernard*) (1800–1801) for which the entry fees earned him an impressive sum as well as enhanced celebrity. The paintings attracted at least 44,444 visitors (Wrigley, 1993, 79). Many artists held exhibitions of their own works in their studios. There were some who criticized such exhibitions on the grounds that an artist's studio should be a site of creativity rather than of commercial transactions or displays of vanity but during the Revolution artists' studio self-portraits helped to associate studios with more positive values. They were regarded as more legitimate signs of independence from the Academy and afterwards, as Romanticism took hold, the studio was represented as a refuge from worldliness (Wrigley, 1993, 127–136).

The most prestigious exhibition venue in Britain was the Royal Academy, where the exhibitions held from 1769 were intended to form an integral part of contemporary polite culture. They were held initially at the Academy's rooms at Pall Mall; in 1780 the Academy moved to new premises at New Somerset House. Once the Academy's exhibitions were established the King went only to those, and no longer to those of the Society of Artists of Great Britain, hence sealing with royal approval a hierarchy of exhibition (and teaching) cultures. The Academy has been described as a "patriciate" under royal patronage (Brewer, 1997, 236). Initially it depended on royal finance, but eventually funds acquired through exhibitions and sales made it financially independent. It took some time for the "higher" genre of history painting to become more important in the Academy's exhibitions as portraits and topographical landscapes dominated initially (Hargraves, 2005, 97). Many academicians saw their exhibitions as a means of making contemporary art accessible, moving beyond the usual confines of the old-master displays of private collectors. The decision to charge an admission fee was however as much a matter of social engineering as of finance. In his Preface to the first (1769) exhibition, Reynolds stated:

> As the present Exhibition is a part of the Institution of an Academy supported by Royal Munificence, the Public may naturally expect the liberty of being admitted without any Expence.
>
> The Academicians therefore think it necessary to declare that this was very much their desire but that they have not been able to suggest any other means than that of receiving Money for Admittance to prevent the Room

> from being filled by improper Persons, to the intire [sic] exclusion of those for whom the Exhibition is apparently intended. (cited in Saumaurez-Smith, 2012, 130–131)

No doubt recent memories of the unseemly crowd that had attended the 1760 Society of Arts exhibition were still very much alive. It was also common for print shops at this time to charge entry to their exhibitions, even where the "popular" genre of caricatures was displayed (Donald, 1996, 3).

Reynolds' lectures helped to raise the cultural tone by asserting the hierarchy of genres and initiating learned debate on aesthetic issues. But in reality the only way in which artists could make a living was by focusing on the "lower" genres of portraiture and landscape, which more people wanted to hang on their walls. Between 1781 and 1785 approximately 70% of Royal Academy exhibits were from these genres (Brewer, 1997, 246; Hoock, 2003, 71), with portraiture itself accounting for the highest proportion of exhibits overall. Although the Academy tried to distance itself from any "sordid" commercialism, it provided welcome publicity and many of its artists continued to exhibit at commercial galleries as well as at the Academy (Pointon, 2001, 94). Portrait sitters, sometimes named in the press, always attracted a great deal of interest among those keen to participate in high society gossip. Before 1796, sitters were listed in catalogues for the Royal Academy exhibitions only according to their rank (e.g. " a nobleman"), which added to the entertainment by generating lively speculation about identities, as sitters were often not known at first hand (Matheson, 2001, 43). The reference to rank was perhaps inevitable in such a hierarchical social structure. By the late century, there were in Britain scores of different ranks for men and women, important information taken into account in, for example, dinner table seating arrangements. The display of portraits could fuel both scandal and celebrity. The subjects of actress portraits in particular might give rise to scurrilous gossip as actresses were often regarded as possessing a "dangerous" form of female sexuality at odds with the Royal Academy's claims to moral gravity (Perry, 2007, 2–5, 59–61). Royal subjects were displayed by name.

The size of Royal Academy exhibitions increased dramatically, from 489 works in 1780 to 1195 in 1797 (Sunderland and Solkin, 2001, 23–24). In 1780, 61,000 visitors attended (Sunderland and Solkin, 2001, 37); 55,357 attended in 1783 (Matheson, 2001, 43); and in the 1790s numbers rose again, leading to good profits. A jury selected for exhibition works submitted by artists from both inside and (unlike at its sister institution in France) outside the Academy. All academicians had an automatic right to exhibit and their works were often placed in the best spots.

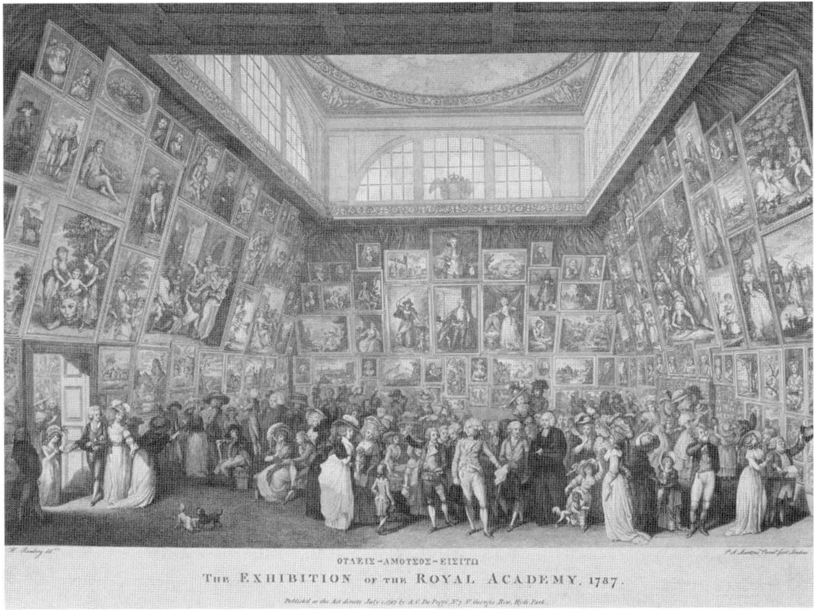

Figure 3.5 Pietro Antonio Martini (1738–1797): *The Exhibition of the Royal Academy, 1787*, engraving on paper, 36.1 × 49.9 cm, 1787. Guildhall Library and Art Gallery. Source: Guildhall Library and Art Gallery/Heritage Images/Getty Images.

The display of works in both the Salons and the Royal Academy exhibitions was characterized by a policy of "massing" works so that they spread through the full width of wall space in all rooms used and from roughly eye level to the ceiling (Figure 3.5). Artists often took this into account as they produced works. For example, portrait painters might use brighter colors and tones in order to make their works stand out. Where appropriate, some works were also shown below eye level so that it was necessary to stoop to see them: at the Royal Academy in London this often applied to smaller works that needed to be viewed from close up. Such arrangements of works in close proximity to one another made for chaotic viewing, especially when works were displayed at some distance from the viewer, who was often jostled by the crowd. More successful or famous artists often requested that their works be displayed at an appropriate height and in a prominent position. At the Royal Academy many artists wanted their work to be displayed above the "line," which was a narrow molding eight feet from the ground. Paintings just above this were displayed to full advantage and at an incline, which cut down the amount of shadow. Gainsborough distanced himself from the Royal Academy after a dispute concerning the height at which one of his works should be displayed: he had wanted it to cross this "line" in a way that the institution found unacceptable.

Watercolors were often relegated to subsidiary display spots for much of the eighteenth century, as watercolor painting wasn't really recognized as art in its own right until the early nineteenth century (see Chapter 2). It was treated, rather, as a form of colored draftsmanship. Many watercolor artists were able to take full advantage of the Academy's facilities, however, as they also painted in oils. From 1795 some watercolor paintings were offered better ("upstairs") display spots. By the early nineteenth century, when societies specifically dedicated to watercolor artists had sprung up; for example, the Society for Painters in Watercolour (1804), a more competitive display culture meant that the Academy offered better display facilities on an on-going basis to watercolor artists (Smith, 2001, 189–197). The medium of watercolor required less spectacular display than oils, since it was largely regarded still as a private medium for close up viewing, many works often destined for display in portfolios and albums. This situation was later modified by Turner's early nineteenth-century large-scale watercolors, which vied with oils in their intended impact.

At the Salons in Paris, paintings were hung from 1746 onwards against a green cloth, with larger ones hung at some height. Sometimes history paintings were lowered, however, in order to make it easier to view their narrative details. Excess works in the lower genres (e.g. portraits and genre paintings) were sometimes banished to stairwells. Drawings and engravings were often grouped together and hung to the sides of windows rather than in more prominent positions. Preparatory sketches were sometimes displayed alongside finished works. Royal portraits were mounted in elaborate frames and sometimes set on a dais with a canopy. This set them apart from the thinner frames chosen for most works due in part to considerations of space. The juxtaposition of works was a very sensitive issue. If a work was placed next to another much worse or better than it, there could be significant implications for its critical reception. The job of picture-hanger (carried out for some years by Chardin) therefore carried some status and could attract requests for favors.

Sculptures at Royal Academy exhibitions were at times displayed in a dark basement, perhaps alongside architectural drawings, or in a relatively dark life-drawing room (Yarrington, 2001, 173–175). At Somerset House, some small waxes and medallions were displayed around the fireplace in the Great Room, almost to add a decorative flourish to the more significant works on display. The spot above the fireplace itself was reserved for works by senior academicians (Sunderland and Solkin, 2001, 25). At the

Salons, smaller sculptures were sometimes displayed on tables in the main exhibition spaces but the larger ones were displayed in courtyards or in artists' own studios.

Those who hung eighteenth-century exhibitions also aspired to specific aesthetic effects. Paintings were often hung in symmetrical arrangements, with, for example, sitters' poses mirroring one another. There was often a central "triptych" of important works. Another consideration was the display of decorative works. Many rococo paintings had been devised for specific settings; for example, to sit within a decorative over-door panel or a gilded wall frame. From the 1740s and 1750s, these works were removed from any decorative framing or context for display at exhibitions (Scott, 1995, 253). Such considerations are very important in museology in our own times, as are the over-riding principles driving the ordering and categorization of exhibits. The Grande Galérie was the principal exhibition space used at the Louvre when it became a public museum. Works on display included old master works from the sixteenth to the eighteenth centuries and some antique sculptures (bronzes and busts). Works from different schools of painting were often mixed together in contemporary exhibitions, in order to facilitate connoisseurial comparisons and debate. In 1794, a conscious decision was taken at the Louvre to rehang works chronologically and according to national schools. A similar and probably influential hanging principle had been used at the Imperial Gallery in Vienna in the 1770s and 1780s. The Louvre was popular with people from all ranks of society and was renamed in 1797, after a period of closure for repairs, the Muséum Central des Arts. It then mounted specialist exhibitions, for example, of old master drawings, or of the works looted by Napoleon Bonaparte (Consul 1802–1804; Emperor of France 1804–1814/15) in Italy. The principle of grouping and displaying works according to chronology and national schools remained dominant for some considerable time after that and was seriously challenged only in the later twentieth century. In late eighteenth-century museum displays opportunities were often seized, in a context of international political conflicts, to express national pride and achievements.

The burgeoning exhibition culture of the eighteenth century brought a new emphasis to the interaction of art with its public. Spectators themselves became part of the "spectacle" of plays and exhibitions, as part of a discourse of fashion and sociability that accompanied one's presence at such events (Craske, 1997, 190). In other exhibition settings, such as the Foundling Hospital in London, some of the historical works on display invited viewers to express the kinds of moral or charitable feeling valued from the 1760s onwards (Solkin, 1993, 173). Exhibition culture brought with it an increasing awareness of the role of subjective and shared values

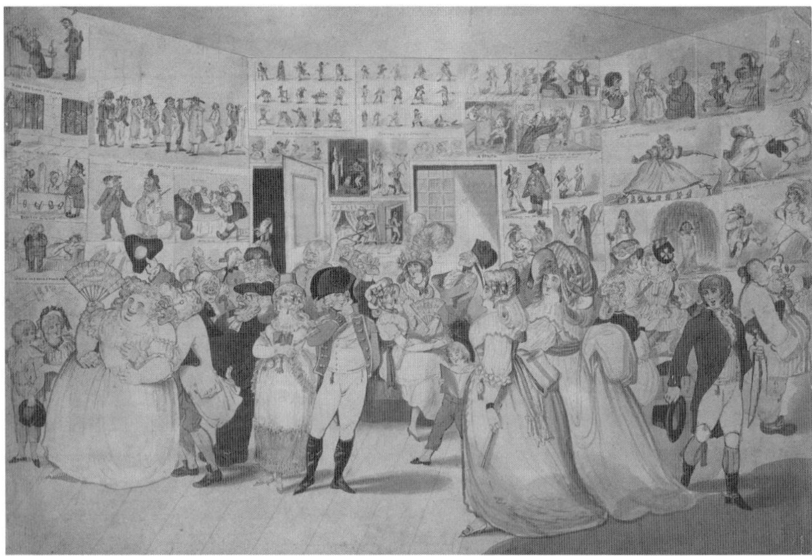

Figure 3.6 Richard Newton: *Holland's Caricature Exhibition*, watercolor drawing on paper, 1794, British Museum, London. Source: © The Trustees of the British Museum.

in the interpretation and reception of works of art. It was also highly regulated, as the "personal" act of viewing was constantly mediated by a range of devices, from exhibition catalogues to the publication in the press and elsewhere of prints representing exhibition crowds. Prints of exhibitions and their visitors provided a kind of social index of viewers, suggesting (or often lampooning) their ways of behaving (Matheson, 2001, 39–42). Richard Newton (1777–1798) was among the printmakers who parodied such representations of Academy crowds; for example, by creating a caricature image of crowds attending a 1790s exhibition of caricature prints (Donald, 1996, 8) (Figure 3.6). In France, journals and newspapers reported freely on the fashions, social rank (from nobleman to pickpocket, thief or the unemployed), overheard comments and even smells of visitors to the Salons (Crow, 1985, 89–90; Wrigley, 1993, 78–91).

A Public for Art

One of the greatest claims to the "modernity" of eighteenth-century artistic culture is the recognition that in this period there was growing awareness of an art "public" that extended well beyond the old-regime contexts of court and church. This public became more self-consciously critical of the art it viewed and more educated in matters of taste and aesthetics, which influenced, in turn, the kind of art artists produced. As art was subjected to broader scrutiny and analysis, it embraced new styles, subjects and genres. Many scholars have focused recently on these developments.

Thomas Crow has related developments in eighteenth-century French art to the changing characteristics of public life, in his seminal 1985 work *Painters and Public Life in Eighteenth-Century Paris.* In this work Crow states (1985, 31) that prior to 1747, and in relation to cultural events or products, the term "public" meant merely the "habitual audience" (or actual group of people) experiencing them. With the publication in 1747 of La Font de Saint Yenne's *Reflexions* (see Chapter 2) the role of the public as active arbiter in matters of taste became much more important. In the seventeenth century, the writer on the arts, Roland Fréart, sieur de Chambray (1606–1676), had expressed in his *Idea of the Perfection of Painting* (*Idée de la perfection de la peinture*, 1662) the idea that a constituency extending beyond "men of letters and those of noble condition" (cited in Crow, 1985, 31) to the "common man" might contribute valid opinions on art, although, still bound by the conventions of his time, he associated this broader constituency with those who valued classical artists such as Raphael and Poussin.

Crow defines eighteenth-century conceptions of the "public" as a discursive formation; that is, as a cluster of ideas shaped by new tendencies in the use of language arising from a redirection of power structures away from the religious to the secular and toward a broader merging of social ranks. Proliferating use of the term "public" related, in turn, to popular social practices that included participation in the clubs, salons, societies, exhibitions, salesrooms and publishing industry that facilitated in the eighteenth century a lively culture of social and economic exchange (Brewer, 1997, x). The term began to reflect the new ideologies or values of an expanded commercial and educated class (Crow, 1985, 4, 103–104). More recently, scholars have drawn more attention to the active role of women in this "public," particularly as patrons, consumers and subjects in art (Hyde and Milam, 2003).

The notion of the "public sphere" is one now commonly applied in eighteenth-century studies. This phrase reflects the fact that after centuries in which the power to formulate values and opinions was dictated by a small elite, in countries in which a less exclusive culture had evolved, artists, writers and composers could create works with a freer, wide-ranging "public" in mind: they could engage with, and even help to shape, new kinds of communal values (Craske, 2000, 14–15). In a country such as France, which witnessed severe political upheaval, notions of the "public" often implied the ideal of a unified Nation. The artist Coypel identified however the heterogeneity of tastes expressed in reality by this "public":

> ...twenty publics of different tone and character in the course of a single day: a simple public at certain times, a prejudiced public, a flighty public, an envious public, a public slavish to fashion.... A final accounting of these publics would lead to infinity. (*Mercure de France*, 1751, cited in Crow, 1985, 10)

The ideal of a cohesive public remained unrealized in France until the Revolution, when many saw reforming ministers and radical pamphleteers as its spokesmen. Such unity dissolved again, however, as events generated by the Revolution itself – the Terror, an emerging entrepreneurial culture – undermined previous unifying ideologies (Wrigley, 1993, 10, 91–111). And yet the idea of a "public" remained influential. Although the Académie royale had responded defensively to the disruptive 1747 attacks on its standards by La Font de Saint Yenne, there was later in the century a growing body of commentators on art, for example, Du Bos and Diderot, who welcomed the role of an educated (and ideally consensual) public taste in mitigating the effects of an arid or mannered academicism. Visitors to the Salons could play an important role in this. Reasonable public voices on art were deemed qualified to pronounce, for example, on the naturalness or plausibility of contemporary representations of people, places and stories in art. From 1747, the French "public" (salon viewers, critics, theorists) voiced increasing concerns about what it perceived as the dire state of history painting. It spoke ostensibly out of concern for the "Nation" and through suspicion of a culture still largely dictated by a government seeking to shore up its own power. In debates about history painting, the growing boldness of an art "public" began to acquire real agency in cultural politics, especially where powerful factions were involved.

Habermas (see Introduction) conceived of the "bourgeois [or middle class] sphere" as arising from eighteenth-century social practices such as the salons: informal gatherings held in private drawing rooms, of educated and refined individuals. It was manifest through groupings of private individuals who came together for the purposes of social intercourse, ultimately drawing their values and ideas from smaller units such as the family. In order for such people and their values to coalesce, the right political conditions must prevail. In Britain, the Glorious Revolution of 1688, the establishment of a free press and the newly public role of the Bank of England facilitated the formation of communities grounded in independence of thought, active commercial lives and freer expressions of taste (Brewer, 1997, xx–xiv). David Solkin (1993, 27–28) has argued that such values expressed how the British middle and upper classes wished to see themselves. The discourses of art shaped such values, even if some of these were difficult to apply in practice (Link, 2013, 108, 115). The vogue for prints representing exhibition crowds was indicative of a public conscious of its own image (Matheson, 2001, 39; T.W. Gaehtgens, 2003, 88).

The cultural interests of this public could thrive in Britain where the monarchy interfered far less in matters of artistic taste and production. Closely identified at the time with the ideals of the Whig party, the eighteenth-century British public sphere saw itself as a force of reasoned consensus, increasingly reconciling itself to lively market forces and the growing professionalization of occupations. The development of a public sphere was also linked in Britain with significant urbanization, which facilitated economic and social exchange allowing it to compete with the generous royal sponsorship of art that had allowed Catholic countries such as France and Spain to shine in the preceding century. By the middle of the century, London was the largest city in western Europe, followed closely by Paris, then Naples. Britain was regarded by Voltaire as the center of civilization as his own country, France, was in his view weakened by religious superstition, the arbitrary rule of an absolutist monarch and a lack of respect for liberty and commerce (Brewer, 1997, xxiv). The Enlightenment was, however, an international movement, its ideals of education and progress adapting to a variety of political regimes. As the cultural practices and standards of a broader, urbanized public became more influential, the role of court, church and state in such matters became less important across Europe (Brewer, 1993, 94–95).

Cosmopolitan standards of social behavior developed. We have already encountered the British notion of "politeness," *honnêteté* being the nearest equivalent in relation to seventeenth- and eighteenth-century France. In France this social virtue involved a dispersal of traditional aristocratic values through the middle ranks of society, including non-hereditary nobles, writers and members of the *haute bourgeoisie* or professions who had made their fortunes during the Regency (Ebeling, 2007, 73–76). Both "politeness" and *honnêteté* involved good breeding or refined manners that eased social intercourse. In Britain the *Characteristics of Men, Manners, Opinions, Times* (1711) by Anthony Ashley-Cooper, Third Earl of Shaftesbury (1671–1713) were instrumental in conveying this ideal from a distinctively patrician point of view. His own views were derived, in turn, from classical Greek (and particularly ancient Athenian) notions of the civic humanism of a disinterested, rational and educated elite, as well as from a wealth of conduct books and moral commentaries, one of the most influential being *The Book of the Courtier* (1528) by Baldassare Castiglione (1478–1529). Shaftesbury's moral exhortations were based on his view, as a member of the landed gentry, that he might act as a conduit for pronouncements on divine beauty and goodness. His vision of benign aristocratic paternalism in matters of taste and morality was founded on strong notions of class solidarity, and his writings proclaim a confidence that this will generate a pleasurable consensus rather than create dissent.

Earlier thinkers such as Thomas Hobbes (1588–1679) and Bernard Mandeville (1670–1733) had challenged the plausibility of a convivial public-spiritedness (see Chapter 5). Their followers saw Shaftesbury's aristocratic expressions of taste as essentially dishonest and oppressive, humankind being destined for a life of discord, strife and selfishness (Solkin, 1993, 3–25). These divisive qualities were connected increasingly with the threat posed by "sordid" market forces, and indeed Shaftesbury himself would not admit men of commerce to his company. Ironically, it was precisely the burgeoning mercantile classes that appropriated Shaftesbury's validating ideologies. Those belonging or sympathetic to the Whig party were keen to reconcile traditional notions of good breeding with the expanding commercial interests. Commercially developed nations such as Holland had already experienced a similar shift toward a gentrified sociability.

The fashion for "politeness" formed in Britain a means by which all ranks of society (from the "middling sort" upwards) might distinguish themselves from an unrefined populace, while achieving a degree of social harmony. The ranks of the "polite" extended from the most elite parts of society to artisans, shopkeepers, farmers, lawyers, doctors and minor clergy (Solkin, 1993, x). These "middling sorts" were often defined by their property ownership and, by the 1780s, made up nearly 25% of the population in Britain (Brewer, 1997, xvi). "Politeness" combined refined manners (dress, postures, gestures, ways of speaking and even the art of moving gracefully) with a shared sense of benevolence and civic duty previously attributed in many societies to more patrician, aristocratic sensibilities (Craske, 2000, 14–15). Its conventions informed visual culture; for example, through the popular genre of the conversation piece.

A treatise on dancing by Kellom Tomlinson (*c.*1690–1753) conceived of the relevant primary characteristics:

> Let us imagine ourselves, as so many living Pictures drawn by the most excellent Masters, exquisitely designed to afford the utmost Pleasure to the Beholders: And, indeed, we ought to set our Bodies in such a Disposition, when we stand in Conversation, that, were our Actions or Postures delineated, they might bear the strictest Examination of the most critical Judges. (*The Art of Dancing Explained by Reading and Figures*, 1735, cited in Solkin, 1993, 31)

French conduct books were plagiarized by British equivalents, which sought nevertheless to avert the charge of foreign "foppishness" (Solkin, 1993, 77). Membership of "polite" British circles increasingly required sound taste in artistic matters. *The Tatler* (1709–1711), which became in 1711 *The Spectator*, promoted suitable clubs and coffee houses where this might be acquired. These included in London Old Slaughter's Coffee House, patronized by Hogarth and other artists, Garraway's Exchange Alley, a coffee house where exhibitions of paintings and prints were held, and Samuel Johnson's Literary Club, patronized by Reynolds and Burke. Art dealers' premises, newspapers and journals came to be shared by large sections of society, even if the rights to hold political office were still dominated by the nobility (Solkin, 1993, 34–36, 40). Key journals such as *The Gentleman's Magazine* (1731–1922) acted as a mouthpiece for the values of an enlightened, tolerant civility by engaging their readers in an informal style of printed "conversation" on subjects relating to the arts, morals and contemporary manners. Lessons in singing, dancing and drawing and in the writing of diaries, biographies and autobiographies assisted the cultivation of a self-conscious refinement, self-control and correct social conduct (Solkin, 1993, 107–112). Not everyone was complicit in these developments. Hogarth was among those who highlighted the dangers of the contemporary cultivation of social graces, which encouraged artifice of all kinds.

Business contacts were made and business interests served by a protective veneer of sociability. Contemporary debates or moral doubts about new luxuries (tea or chocolate-drinking, interior décor) shared by a wider prosperous constituency were inflected by discussions of the hard work required to achieve them. Material wealth was often validated through the settings, costumes and accessories used in portraiture. As is often the way with social trends, however, once "politeness" became (in the second quarter of the century) the norm of the elegant and the genteel, some sought to set themselves apart by flirting with transgressive modes of behavior and culture. A taste for art or theatre representing rough rural manners, the lower orders or street culture (Solkin, 1993, 97–104) was often defused, however, by the refined settings (such as Vauxhall Gardens or exclusive galleries) in which they were experienced.

The discourses of "politeness" served to unify hitherto disparate elements of the public. The merging of ranks characteristic of the new sociability was not always regarded positively, though many saw it as a good alternative to the political and religious tensions that had prevailed throughout much of the preceding century or, in the case of France, the ancien (pre-Revolutionary) regime as a whole. A review of the 1725 Salon in the *Mercure de France* commented on the mix of sexes and social ranks of viewers (Berger, 1999, 159). When, toward the end of the century, the Louvre opened as a public museum, it was popular with all classes (Berger, 1999, 252), due in part to the growth of literacy, both verbal and visual. As indicated in Chapter 2, a significant blurring of the hierarchy of genres occurred throughout the century, a development analogous to less exclusive social identities. Portraits of the genteel increasingly mitigated grand baroque or court-based conventions by the adoption of a more naturalistic, northern style, although more particular patrons sometimes rejected the latter. The kit-kat portraits popularized by Kneller (and made for members of the Kit-Kat club, who discussed and commissioned art) gave visual expression to "politeness," their sitters in relatively informal poses, their expressions seeming to engage with the viewer in a sociable manner (Solkin, 1993, 35–36). Fragonard's masquerade or 'fantasy' portraits disguised precise social ranks and identities in a way that reflected the covert mixing of classes at masked balls (Percival, 2012, 174–189).

`The private lives of the "middling orders" or *bourgeoisie* became more popular subjects in art. In 1741, an anonymous critical review referred to the way in which the "third estate" or "bourgeois" art of Chardin's *The Morning Toilette* (*La Toilette du matin*, 1741) on display at the Salon had provoked positive responses to his art and the more modest lifestyles it represented:

> It is always the *Bourgeoisie* that he [Chardin] puts into play.... Does a woman of the Third Estate ever pass by without believing that here is an idea of her character, who does not see her domestic surroundings, her countenance, her frank manners, her daily occupations, her morality, the emotions of her children, her furniture, her wardrobe...? (cited in and translated by Crow, 1985, 100)

An emboldened public challenged previous hierarchies of public and private, grand and natural, "higher" and "lower." However, educated taste remained important. David's art remained attached to classical learning and resisted facile populism, even at the height of his popularity.

A merging of private (often family-based) and public subjects became popular in Britain toward the end of the century, inflecting an older insistence on the role of history painting to provide idealized grand narratives with a broader public discourse of heroism. Shaftesbury had focused earlier in the century on grand classical scenes and styles based largely on public life, roles and identities. By the end of the century, private life acquired a more positive connotation. Even before that, with the paintings of Joseph Wright of Derby and the history paintings of Francis Hayman in the 1760s, the cult of sensibility made popular throughout Europe encouraged preferences for art representing more intimate communities and the private lives of "feeling" individuals, which might appeal in turn to the emotional sympathies of viewers (see Chapter 5 and Solkin, 1993, 183–244). Wright's genre subjects were often taken from the lives of the "middling sort"; his style was markedly naturalistic while stimulating the imagination through the use of "sublime" effects of light, thus forming part of a long tradition of chiaroscuro and "candlelight pictures." Unlike Shaftesbury, who had promoted an idealized history genre aimed at an elite group of refined, paternalistic and philosophical viewers, Wright of Derby reached out to a broader public. Hogarth's art conveyed ethical messages infused by the values of a rising middle class. The interests of this class were further reinforced in 1776 by the economic theories in Adam Smith's *The Wealth of Nations*, which made respectable the positive mutual influence of private (commercial) and public benefits.

Public consensus on matters of taste remained a fragile, and perhaps unattainable, ideal. This was particularly the case in France, where the social order fractured so dramatically prior to and during the events of the Revolution. Richard Wrigley (1998, 130–153) has illustrated this difficulty through analysing the changing uses in France of the term *bourgeois*. Used principally to distinguish the members of this class from those of the aristocracy, this term implied prior to the Revolution either a rank of society bound by a restrictive desire to be "normal," or a threat to the existing, aristocratic or "old" social order. As wealthier members of the *bourgeoisie* absorbed some of the cultural tastes and material wealth of the aristocracy, the boundaries between these ranks blurred, although modes of dress in public venues often continued to distinguish between the two. There was some resentment from those whose social superiority was threatened by an ascendant section of society whose preferences were often derided as ignorant and lacking in any true nobility; their tastes in art felt to be over-influenced by dazzling use of color, the sensual and the decorative, and insufficiently by a classical canon. The events of the Revolution temporarily eclipsed the issue, as the term *bourgeois* itself was less commonly used and gave way to patriotic terms such as "citizen" (*citoyen*). Those still labeled explicitly as members of the *bourgeoisie* were often persons of suspicion and there were calls for its members to join with the "people" as part of a united third estate. Meanwhile, those who had thought of themselves before the Revolution as *bourgeois* became resentful of their lack of power, especially as their "vulgar" tastes and methods of acquiring wealth continued to come under fire in the late 1790s, when they were suspected of supporting the demise of grand history painting at the Salons. With such antagonisms rife, and a wealthy middle class pulled between the competing claims of people and nobles, any notion of a unified, national "public" for art remained an ideal rather than a reality (Crow, 1985, 17–20, 178–258).

In Britain at this time social and political divisions – for example, between Whigs and Tories, Catholics and Protestants, Church of England and dissenters – also created differences in taste (Brewer, 1997, xxviii). The Revolution in France provoked there distinctions in the tastes of royalists and anti-royalists, not only in the choice of satirical targets in print culture but also in the extent to which the theme of "liberty" was foregrounded in history paintings. While exhibition crowds included a broadening social range, an increasing emphasis on individualism and private life also served to undermine any possible consensus in taste.

Divergences in taste were inevitable in an age when social hierarchies were modified or softened rather than abolished. In Britain, the 1688 "Glorious Revolution" had proclaimed the potential for all freeborn subjects to lead improving lives. However, both the government and public services remained dominated, throughout the eighteenth century, by the hereditary nobility (Craske, 2000, 14–15). In the art world, the patronage of wealthy aristocrats remained important, alongside the growing power of market forces and the "leveling" principles of conduct drawn from a respect for civic humanism and public spirit. Reynolds expressed the need for Academy artists to prioritize the tastes of an elite public over those of an undiscriminating, less educated crowd (Solkin, 1993, 178, 273; Fenton, 2006, 92–93; Brewer, 1997, 96). Justifying the introduction of a one-shilling entrance charge for exhibitions of the Society of Artists, Samuel Johnson stated:

> ...everyone knows that all cannot be judges or purchasers of works of art. (Society of Artists of Great Britain, *A Catalogue of the Pictures, Sculptures, Models, Drawings and Prints, etc.*, London, 1762, iv–v, cited in Matheson, 2001, 40)

The *dilettanti* (*connoisseurs* and those who "dabbled" in art) and members of the upper echelons of fashionable society attended Reynolds' lectures. Visual representations of the 1781 RA exhibition show a considerable number from such backgrounds in the crowds. Goya was wary of the ignorant multitude, taking against those with insufficient aesthetic awareness to appreciate his early Cathedral paintings. Women at Royal Academy exhibitions were often marginalized as viewers of art, even though they were becoming more frequent buyers: they were regarded as a civilizing influence while also being suspected of trivializing the exhibition experience with gossip and flirtation (Solkin, 2001, 6). The increasing number of learned books and articles on matters of taste also served to exclude the poor from full participation in "high" culture.

The distinction between the uneducated masses and a "proper" audience for art was also important in France. Du Bos, who placed great emphasis on public responses to art as a means of appreciating and validating it *as* art, nevertheless expressed a desire for the art public to be well educated (Wrigley, 1998, 109–111):

> I do not include the low people among the public who are capable of pronouncing on paintings and poems, or to decide what degree of excellence they possess. The word "public" includes here only those who have acquired a certain illumination, either by reading or commerce with the world. (From *Réflexions Critiques*, 1719; cited in Craske, 1997, 13)

Later in the century, the social and cultural commentator Louis-Sébastien Mercier (1740–1814) emphasized the active role of Salon audiences in the 1780s in judging and shaping the kind of art exhibited, and mounted an attack on "snobbish fatuousness" (Crow, 1985, 101). In his *Picture of Paris* (*Tableau de Paris*, 1782–1788), he asked nevertheless "...Does the public exist? What is the public? Where is it?" (cited in Wrigley, 1993, 105; my translation), thus undermining any suggestion of social unity. He generally believed that eventually the public, despite its diverse factions, would arrive at a true judgment of art. The role of the lower orders in this process was, however, restricted: while they might be able to comment on the general effect of a work and its naturalism, and even counter the pernicious effects of over-flattering reviews or of art made for dazzling, opulent interiors, this was not the same as offering a more discriminating judgment (Wrigley, 1993, 106–107; Berger, 1999, 145–148). Even during the Revolution, with the occurrence of the "open Salon" and the shift toward more popular genres, there were fears that mass hedonism would destroy the elevated status of art (Wrigley, 1993, 113). Cochin and Coypel distrusted the judgments of the mob, which they saw as an unstable, dangerous force (Crow, 1985, 10–14). This was a matter of sensibility (feeling and intuition) as well as education or intellect. "New money" was not always welcome in the "community" of taste. Another critic commented:

> Many people have lamented that the most beautiful monuments of antiquity were the prey of barbarians. Without going back to such times past, are we not seeing similar things in our day, when these superb edifices, which should be the residences of princes, become those of financiers? It seems to be a misfortune bound to the richest productions of art, to fall into the hands of people who appreciate less their value than that of the gold used to acquire them. (Louis-Guillaume Baillet de Saint-Julien (1726–1795), *Letter on Painting, Sculpture and Architecture to M**** (*Lettre sur la peinture, la sculpture et l'architecture à M****, 1748) cited in and translated by Ebeling, 2007, 77)

Such attitudes reinforce the view that the "public" was above all a set of representations, constructed from particular ideological or institutional standpoints. The Académie royale had a vested interest in conceiving of a cultivated, elite public to validate its highest aspirations even though it realized the actual public was fractured and at times dissonant.

Painting for an Imperial Public

Eighteenth-century European culture combined an impulse toward a cosmopolitan, universalizing taste, evident for example in its recourse to classical models, with an increasing awareness of national differences and anthropological distinctiveness. Art "publics" were increasingly aware of the colonial territories their nations had established (see Introduction). Western artists in search of new markets traveled to these territories and played an important role in satisfying domestic curiosity concerning unfamiliar lands, peoples and customs. There were few artists permanently resident in colonial territories, Jamaica and North America being exceptional in their ability to offer more secure incomes to resident artists.

Those artists who wished to paint colonial scenes from direct observation often led temporarily itinerant lives. Many works were commissioned for British country houses, some of which have now disappeared from sight: such paintings sometimes included visual references that might be read as justifying the families' means of wealth acquisition (Brown, 2013, 89–97; Longmore, 2013, 43–53). Integral to these developments was a growing awareness of race, described at the time as "human varieties." Eighteenth-century art and literature inspired by colonial enterprise brought their public new opportunities to reflect on its own place and status in a global context and on issues of national identity.

Concepts of race evolved in a context of specific ideas on religion, science and aesthetics. The various editions of the *Systema Naturae* (1735) by Carl Linnaeus (1707–1778) conceived of four races differentiated by continent and skin color (white European, black African, brown Asian and red American), with exploration of the (Pacific) South Seas raising the possibility of a fifth. The work reinforces nevertheless established Christian notions of the inter-relatedness of all peoples, dispersed after the Biblical Fall, and their common origins ("monogenesis") in the Garden of Eden. The naturalist Georges-Louis Leclerc, Comte de Buffon (1707–1788), in his *Natural History* (*Histoire naturelle*, 1749–1804) saw different peoples as located on a spectrum, their precise place on this determined by climate or environment rather than by pre-determined or essentialist "racial" characteristics (Bindman, 2002, 17–21). In the realm of aesthetics, Winckelmann's neoclassical, Greek-inspired concept of ideal beauty (see Chapter 1) depended on an "editing out" from the bodies of gods and men represented in art of ethnically distinctive features. He saw distinctively Chinese or black facial features and skin colors as offending classical notions of "symmetry." He claimed the superiority of white skin lay in its capacity to reflect light. While such statements were made in the name of aesthetic preference, they were succeeded in the nineteenth century by attitudes to race characterized by wider prejudices (Potts, 1994, 160–162; Bindman, 2002, 11, 13, 16, 15–16, 79–81).

A team of scholars, including David Bindman, Henry Louis Gates Jr, Helen Weston, Bruce Boucher and Charles Ford, have recently explored these issues in depth. There were many positive or celebratory visual representations of black subjects, yet eighteenth-century representations of blacks and other native peoples were deeply inflected by western cultural and national values. Implicit hierarchies of power, social standing, political freedom, beauty, skin color and ethical characteristics were common in visual images that included black figures, the term "black" being used here to refer to persons who appear to be of African descent. In the eighteenth century the terms "negro," "Moor" and "Ethiopian" (Greek for "burned face") were common (Bindman and Gates 2011, lx–x, xvi).

The stereotypical view was that the racial characteristics of this group were "thick lips, flat nose, and woolly hair". Very few Europeans distinguished between North African and sub-Saharan peoples or other more localized ethnic groups. It was also common for artists to confuse black Africans with those from the Caribbean – or even American Indians (Bindman, Kaplan and Weston, 2011, 196). Generalized Africans or "blackamores" featured in European paintings, sculptures, porcelain, furniture (e.g.chair legs, gueridons and vase supports), trade cards, maps and shop signs, where they evoked exotic luxury. They often appeared as "jolly" servants, sailors, soldiers, musicians, beggars and street-sellers, or as plantation workers, their subjection to contemporary colonial commerce often represented as benign (Dabydeen, 1985, 17–20, 114; Bindman, Boucher and Weston, 2011a, 34–40; Bindman, Kaplan and Weston, 2011, 172).

Reynolds was among those prepared to concede that the association of white skin with beauty was merely customary, and that the link between skin color and beauty was relative rather than absolute:

> ...it is custom alone determines our preference of the colour of the *Europeans* to the *Aethiopians*; and they, for the same reason, prefer their own colour to ours. I suppose no body will doubt, if one of their painters were to paint the goddess of beauty, but that he would represent her black, with thick lips, flat nose, and woolly hair; and, it seems to me, he would act very unnaturally if he did not; for by what criterion will any one dispute the propriety of his idea? (From *The Idler*, 1759, cited in Bindman, with contributions from Boucher and Weston, 2011, 6)

He nevertheless perpetuated in his art the "custom" of white preference. The aesthetic of the sublime associated blackness and darkness with terror; Buffon conceived of black skin as white skin ruined by the sun; and there were frequent metaphorical associations between blackness, bile (melancholy) and biblical curses. Black skin signified within a structure of thought that assumed white skin as the norm. The naturalist Pieter Camper (1722–1789) used skull measurements to compare racial types and to suggest degrees of degradation from the "ideal" profile offered by the *Apollo Belvedere*, although there was generally much less pseudo-science of this kind than in the following century. Diderot came down categorically on the side of white skin: "I believe that negroes are less beautiful to themselves than white to negroes and to other whites" (*Salon de 1767*, cited in Bindman, with contributions from Boucher and Weston, 2011, 7–9; and see Bindman, Boucher and Weston, 2011b, 115–117). Theories of beauty were, for much of the eighteenth century, connected with those of morality (see Chapter 5). Global anxieties about race were evident in and exacerbated by colonial relations; for example, in the *casta* paintings of New Spain (present day Mexico), a new eighteenth-century genre that recorded through individual and group figure studies the different racial types and lineages evident in Mexico at the time, arising from inter-marriage between colonial Spanish, South American Indian and other races. These paintings documented the perceived degrees of divergence of such types from "pure" Spanishness (Ford, Cummins, McCrea and Weston, 2011, 246–59).

Western visual representations of blacks were characterized, in the eighteenth century, by stereotype and fiction. Blacks were seen variously as "noble" (due to their association with more "primitive" and therefore more "innocent" lifestyles), evil or savage. Negative associations were made with the diabolical, the primeval, witchcraft, paganism, animal lust, unnatural sexual desire (Othello was seen to embody this particular characteristic), idolatry, religious enthusiasm, nakedness, dishonesty, heavy drinking and a lack of modesty. These characteristics marked out blacks as "other" to the European Enlightenment ideal in a way that would fail to satisfy more recent notions of racial and cultural relativity (Bindman and Gates, 2011, xiv). It has been argued that Hogarth played on these negative stereotypical representations and risked misinterpretation by his contemporaries, some of whom did not understand that black figures were often used in his art as a means of exposing the vices, prejudices and social climbing of their white masters (Dabydeen, 1985, 130–131).

By contrast, black figures were often imagined as representing the ideal, uncorrupted human being. The association of blacks with goodness, innocence, antique wisdom and heroism is now referred to as the "noble savage" tradition, and derived from earlier writers, many inspired by overseas exploration, such as Michel de Montaigne (1533–1592) and John Dryden (1631–1700); and from Rousseau's concept of the "good savage," as expounded in his *Discourse on Inequality*. Rousseau didn't use the term "noble savage" itself. The "noble savage" was associated with the simple hunter-gatherer stage of humankind's development, before corrupt motives and behavior became widespread. The type had been made familiar in the novel *Oroonoko; or, The Royal Slave: A True History* (1688) by Aphra Behn (1640?–1689), in which the virtuous black heroine, Yarico, falls victim to the machinations of the wicked Englishman, Inkle. In Samuel Johnson's fictional work *The History of Rasselas, Prince of Abissinia* (1759) Abyssinia is represented as a paradise governed by noble savages. The other positive stereotype was that of the "gallant Moor" – the good, genteel black familiar from the mid-seventeenth century onwards in ballets, carnivals, *fêtes galantes* and the *commedia dell'arte* (Bindman, Boucher and Weston, 2011b, 104; Bindman and Weston, 2011, 156–158).

Fantasy, fiction and the discourses of empire often combined with confused and inconsistent iconography in representations of the home nations and continents of black subjects. For much of the eighteenth century the parts of Africa best known to Europeans were its western and southern coastal regions, although knowledge of the continent increased throughout the century. Benjamin West's late-eighteenth-century paintings distinguished between the physical characteristics of North Africans, deemed to share the ancient wisdom and spirituality of Egyptians, and sub-Saharan African peoples. Distinctions were made increasingly between different tribes. However, stereotypical allegorical representations of Africa, as well as of the other "three" continents (identified from the sixteenth century as Europe, Asia and America) persisted, especially in public art where notions inherited from antiquity and outdated travel literature still prevailed. The attributes of Africa included the classical motif of the cornucopia, a reference to its wealth and natural resources such as ivory and gold, a black magus, and wild animals – for example, elephants' tusks and heads, or crocodiles.

Allegorical representations of Africa were frequently confused with those of Asia and America (Bindman, Boucher and Weston, 2011a, 18–20, 117, 209–215). America was often represented allegorically as a semi-naked Indian, with headdress, bow and arrow; Asia as a source of sensory pleasure such as floral perfumes. Decorative tapestries, for example, Desportes' "New Indies" series, contained a profusion of exotic costumes, flora and fauna. These generally revealed little respect for geographical or ethnographic accuracy, their main aim being to express pride in French exploration and in the hold of the Bourbon monarchy over its colonial territories and trading bases. Their representations of flora and fauna revealed some new knowledge of the natural world, but also some glaring errors, such as a confusion of the "New" Indies with the "Old." Essentially works of fiction and state propaganda, they were based on earlier seventeenth-century designs by the Dutch artist Albert Eckhout (*c.*1610–1665), which had actually represented Brazilian scenes (Ford, Cummins, McCrea and Weston, 2011, 259–288).

The 1593 allegorical representation of Europe in the *Iconologia*, the manual of emblems by Cesare Ripa (*c.*1560–*c.*1622), was among many others that stressed the cultural superiority of the continent. Europe was often represented as bestowing on the "lower" continents the gifts of prosperity, knowledge, the arts and religion, as is seen in Giambattista Tiepolo's ceiling painting at the Würzburg Residenz, in which Apollo (representing ancient European culture) brings enlightenment and the arts to the world (Bindman, Boucher and Weston, 2011a, 26–31). It was common in prints, map illustrations, decorative wall and ceiling paintings for the other continents to be represented paying homage to Europe.

In some contexts representations of black subjects demonstrated a greater concern for closer, more accurate observation. As black peoples became more visible in urban life; for example, as assistants or servants in artists' studios, artists responded by attempting more detailed and diverse facial likenesses, including subtler gradations of skin color. Watteau, Hogarth, the painter, dramatist and set designer Louis Carrogis Carmontelle (1717–1806), the pastellist Quentin de la Tour and the sculptor Pigalle, experimented with observational accuracy as scientific interest increased in the causes of differences in skin color and hair texture. Watteau used his "three color" pastel technique to catch the nuances of light falling on black skin and made black subjects as individualized as white figures (Bindman, Boucher and Gates, 2011b, 96–97). The "Head of a Black man" (1777–1783) by Singleton-Copley (Figure 3.7) demonstrates an unusual naturalism. The sculpture "Bust of a Man" (1758) by

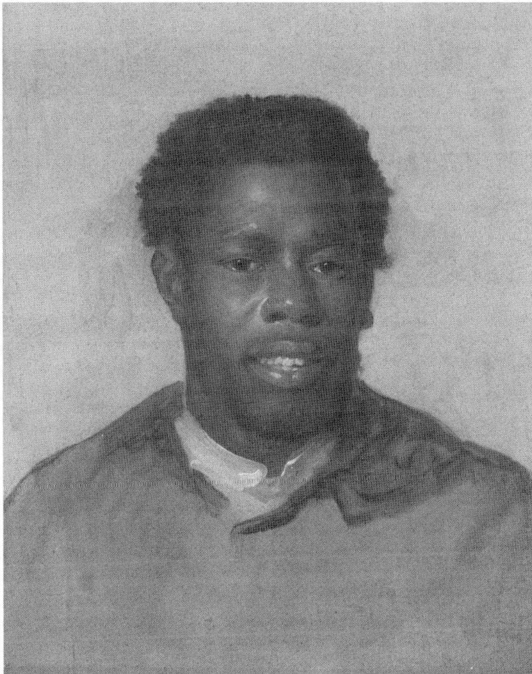

Figure 3.7 John Singleton Copley: *Head of a Negro*, oil on canvas, 53.3 × 41.3 cm, *c.*1777–1778. Detroit Institute of Arts. Source: Detroit Institute of Arts, USA/ Bridgeman Images.

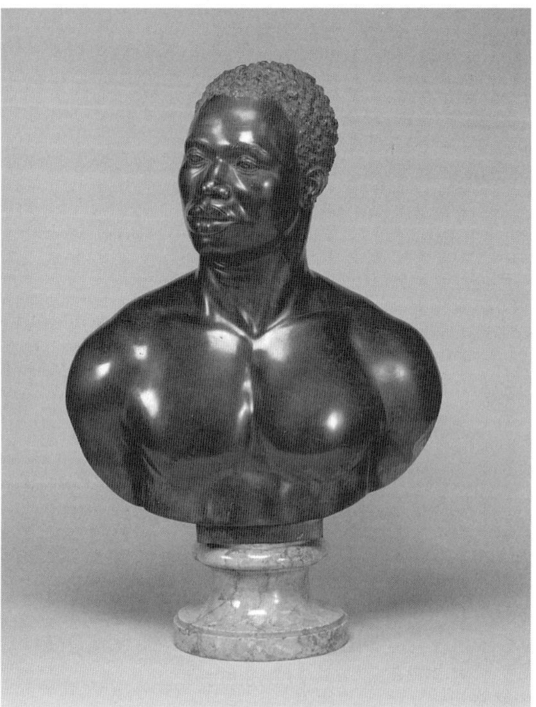

Figure 3.8 Studio of Francis Harwood: *Bust of a Man*, black limestone on a yellow marble socle, overall: 71.1 x 50.8 x 26.7 cm; base or socle: 21.6 cm, *c*.1758. Yale Center for British Art, Paul Mellon Collection. Source: Yale Center for British Art, Paul Mellon Collection, USA / Bridgeman Images.

Francis Harwood (active 1748–1783) (Figure 3.8) combines a traditional, classical mode of representation, possibly that of the noble warrior, with some individualized features (Bindman and Gates, 2011, vii–viii; Bindman, Boucher and Weston, 2011b, 121; Bindman and Weston, 2011, 125–128; Bindman, Kaplan and Weston, 2011, 172–175; Trusted, 2008, 27).

Western paintings featuring black servants were, as in the preceding century, very common. It was fashionable for those living in affluent households to participate in the fashion for the possession and display of black servants that waned only from the 1770s, when anti-slavery debates became more prominent and overt displays of wealth became regarded as vulgar ostentation (Bindman and Weston, 2011, 146–148). Most blacks outside Africa were either slaves or descended from slaves. Black servants and pages featured extensively in grand manner portraits, conversation pieces and genre scenes, and were often used to suggest colonial landownership (Retford, Perry and Vibert, 2013, 24). An iron or silver slave collar (sometimes inscribed with their owner's name or coat of arms) or earring often signified their servitude. They were represented in many forms of domestic service, taking part in court pageants or in musical performances. Highly fashionable at the French court, black servants were sought increasingly by other courts such as those in Prussia and Saxony. English court portraits often included a black servant as a means of signifying an adherence to continental fashions. The social prestige gained through ownership of a black servant was further enhanced by the European fashion of giving them, like white servants, names drawn from European literature, history or mythology, a striking demonstration of their appropriation by white culture. Black servants were rarely named in portrait titles.

The fashion for keeping and representing black servants reached its peak in France during the Regency of 1715–1723. A French edict of 1716 allowed aristocrats and wealthy financiers to bring slaves back from the colonies. The intention was that they should eventually be returned but many stayed on as servants (Bindman, Boucher and Weston, 2011b, 90–91). The practice of keeping black servants spread down the social scale, from court to private mansions. As the century progressed black servants were generally represented in art in less ceremonial, more integrated household roles or informal social gatherings, those serving male masters often carrying out the role of groom or gentleman's page. Such roles offered some hope of a reasonable education or, in rare cases, social advancement, especially when servants had converted to Christianity (Bindman, Kaplan and Weston, 2011, 202–203). In England, however, the resurgence in aristocratic pride and values represented by the vogue for Reynolds' grand portraits led to the representation of more subservient roles. Blacks serving women members of a family were often represented, alongside dogs, parrots and monkeys, as accessories, playthings or pets (Dabydeen, 1985, 28–30). They could signify their owners' wealth or serve as foils to their owners' white-skinned beauty. In diplomatic portraiture, as in a 1780 portrait of George Washington by John Trumbull (1756–1843), a black servant might signify his owner's ancient rank and chivalry at a time when America was seeking allies in established European nations (Bindman and Weston, 2011, 125–144).

The roles played by black servants in aristocratic visual compositions and narratives were generally marginal, at times solitary, and always subordinate to those of white figures. In Watteau's *fêtes galantes* black servants at times interact with and at other times stand apart from their white companions, serving as proxy viewers of their moods and activities. Some, overlooked by their white companions, appear to serve as witnesses to scenes of sexual intrigue or flirtation (Bindman, Boucher and Weston, 2011b, 91–99). Their other roles included those of messengers, for example. in courtship scenes; luxury possessions; fashion statements; or children of nature looking in adoration at their "superiors," who were intended to represent, by these means, social and cultural authority. Black servants were usually placed on the left-hand side of a painting, traditionally the "dark" or "sinister" (from the Latin for "left") side. Some, especially when wearing turbans or (incongruously) Turkish dress, evoked sexual license (Bindman and Weston, 2011, 152–163). Black subjects were consigned, like many female figures, to decorative or erotic roles designed to meet the gaze of the "curious."

Slave trading was, for much of the eighteenth century, regarded as a gentlemanly pursuit, plantation owners in the Caribbean and other places often commissioning portraits of themselves with their black servants as a means of complying with conventions of gentility (Ford, Cummins, McCrea and Weston, 2011, 259). Landscape views of plantations, frequently made by artists such as Thomas Hearne for their absentee colonial owners, captured locations such as the thriving sugar plantations of Jamaica and the Leeward Islands. Sugar plantations were at their peak from the 1730s to the early nineteenth century and were often overseen on behalf of absentee English owners by Irish or Scottish estate managers. While these images exploited the exoticism and actual appearances of the locales represented, they also used a European picturesque aesthetic to defuse the horrors and tensions of actual slavery and make it appear "natural." Geoff Quilley has deconstructed the representations of Jamaican landscapes commissioned by William Thomas Beckford (1760–1844), a British art collector from a family with colonial interests in the country, as uneasy hybrids of the exotic and the classically beautiful: they served as evasions, "displacements" or "surrogations" of the actual spaces of empire and the harsh conditions of slavery, thereby expressing indirectly the complex, colonial identity of Beckford himself (Quilley, 2003, 106–124). Plantation views also show the replication abroad of British Georgian mansions as second homes for their owners (Barringer, Quilley and Fordham, 2007, 12–13; Crowley, 2011, 111–128; Leech, 2013, 54–58). Many such images were exhibited at the Incorporated Society of Artists and at the Royal Academy.

Images representing the lives of slaves mostly glossed over the traumas and horrors they faced, which tended to feature more largely in literature and politics. Most Enlightenment thinkers, informed by reformist ideas on politics, economics and religion, abhorred the practice of slavery. *The Spirit of the Laws* (1748) by Charles-Louis de Secondat, Baron de la Brède et de Montesquieu (1689–1755), and the *History of the Two Indies* (1770) by Guillaume-Thomas-François Raynal (1713–1796), Diderot and others, were among those texts that spoke for universal freedom and equality. Adam Smith argued on economic grounds against the institution, as he felt that free men were able to work more productively: he was also a defender of "liberty" in the broader sense. But pro-slavery arguments remained influential for much of the century. Edward Long (1734–1813), champion of the West Indian slave owners, justified slavery on grounds of racial difference, regarding the "White" and the "Negroe" as two different species (Bindman and Gates, 2011, xx). France tried to limit, from the 1770s, the number of blacks coming to the country, as fears grew of inter-racial breeding and the depletion of plantation staff. This was perhaps a response, also, to the growing numbers of blacks employed in Paris, Marseilles, Nantes and Bordeaux. In 1802 Napoleon reversed the country's 1791 decree to grant liberty to all persons of color and its 1794 decision to abolish slavery.

There were very few images explicitly condemning the slave trade and most of these focused on the terrible conditions of the "middle passage" or sea crossing between Africa and the Caribbean. A print entitled "Description of a Slave Ship" issued in 1789 by the Society for the Abolition of the Slave Trade, proved to be instrumental in constructing modern abolitionist sympathies. This print represented in graphic, diagrammatic fashion the cramped, inhuman conditions in which slaves were kept (Wood, 2000, 19). George Morland was relatively rare in his pictorial exposure of some of the cruelties of slavery, contrasting African hospitality to western visitors with slave traders' breaking up of the families of kidnapped slaves in his *Execrable Human Traffic* (1788) (Figure 3.9) (Bindman and Weston, 2011, 166–170). Hogarth's prints were also exceptional in representing black servant-slaves as the victims, along with poorer white subjects, of a callously commercial society in which they threw into relief the corruption, artificiality and pretentiousness of a contemporary white elite (Dabydeen, 1985, 11, 36–37, 101–132).

Images of blacks as active subjects became more common later in the century. Britain abolished the slave trade in 1807 and (in principle if not in practice) slavery itself in 1830. In general more positive images of black subjects emerged as anti-slavery writers and campaigners such as Phyllis Wheatley (1753–1784), Ottabah Cugoano (*c.*1757–after 1791) and Olaudah Equiano (*c.*1745–1797) visited Europe; as did the musician Ignatius Sancho (*c.*1729–1780) painted by Gainsborough: he had been born into a slaving family before coming to Britain. Plantation households themselves sometimes developed class divisions between slaves, some rising to more responsible household positions.

These small changes to the status of blacks meant that some were represented as European gentlemen (occasionally undertaking the Grand Tour)

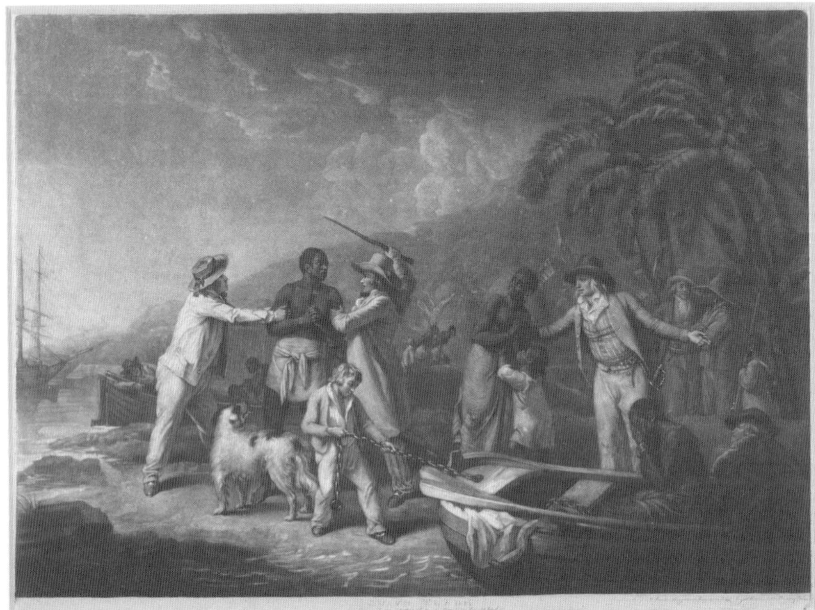

Figure 3.9 John Raphael Smith, after George Morland: *Execrable Human Traffic or The Affectionate Slaves*, mezzotint, etching on paper, 46.3 × 64.8 cm, 1791. British Museum, London. Source: © The Trustees of the British Museum.

or antique heroes (Ford, Cummins, McCrea and Weston, 2011, 262, 271–281). History painting also offered some limited but significant improvements in the roles allocated to black figures, since the singularity of the event represented could normally allow this to happen in a relatively non-threatening way. Black figures featured prominently in some French, Italian and British works on Christian and antique themes, even if they remained subordinate to the narrative and compositional roles of white figures (Bindman, Boucher and Weston, 2011b, 105–114, 118–123; Ford, Cummins, McCrea and Weston, 2011, 288–297). In this respect, however, there was little or no advance on the situation in the Renaissance and seventeenth century, when artists such as Veronese, Rubens and Titian used black figures principally to create dramatic, exotic effects. Empire and slavery generally failed to provide the frameworks of equality necessary to establish models of autonomous, black agency of the kind we currently assume to be part of "modernity."

Eighteenth-century European representations of American Indians were, like those of other peoples, deeply inflected by "allegorical symbolism, voyages of discovery, imperial or colonial expansion and trade" and by discourses of imperialism (significant in the Americas from the sixteenth century) involving "power, fear and fantasy" (Pratt, 1998, 135). The stereotype of the "noble savage" was applied with most enthusiasm and frequency to American Indians, conceived by Locke as surviving testimony of the human race's earliest (and therefore least corrupt) stage of development (Wood, 2012, 279). The *Essay on Man* (1734) by Alexander Pope (1688–1744) reinforced this view:

> "Lo, the poor Indian! whose untutor'd mind /
>
> Sees God in clouds, or hears him in the wind; / His soul proud Science never taught to stray / Far as the solar walk or milky way; / Yet simple Nature to his hope has giv'n, / Behind the cloud-topp'd hill, a humbler heav'n; / Some safer world in depth of woods embrac'd, / Some happier island in the wat'ry waste, / Where slaves once more their native land behold, / No fiends torment, no Christians thirst for gold! / To be, contents his natural desire; / He asks no angel's wing, no seraph's fire: / But thinks, admitted to that equal sky, /
>
> His faithful dog shall bear him company. (Epistle I ll. 91–112, in Pope, 1950 [1734], 27–28)

The native peoples of present-day Canada, North and South America were conceived ideologically within liberal culture as "innocent" and "natural" foils to the excesses and pretentiousness of contemporary European civilization (Bindman, 2002, 11–16, 29–78). They also served as exotic motifs in tapestry designs (Scott, 1995, 34–36). To many colonial publics, however, they were associated with superstition and savagery and the "need" for western supervision. Joseph Wilton's *Monument to General James Wolfe* (erected in Westminster Abbey in 1772), the British hero of the Québec campaign, contrasts the general's bare-breasted vulnerability and nobly classical nude body with the hatchets and scalping implements representing the brutality of American Indians (Fordham, 2007, 102–119). This was one of several monuments that established Britain's colonial adventures and identity, in a conventional visual language used to highlight political rupture. In Hogarth's *The Gaols Committee of the House of Commons* (*c.*1729), a painting representing an investigation into the Fleet Prison, a kneeling prisoner appears as a submissive American Indian dependent on the clemency of western authority.

The American artist Benjamin West created fashionable history paintings for an imperial British public that included American Indians. West was actually descended from farmers, soldiers and craftsmen, his own father being a tavern owner, yet he cultivated in Britain, in response to the "noble savage" myth, the persona of a simple backwoodsman, skillfully combining this with the sophistication required of a member (and eventually leader) of the Royal Academy (Abrams, 1985, 35–39; Fenton, 2006, 151–163). Paintings such as West's *Penn's Treaty with the Indians* (1771–1772) omitted overt references to violence in order to represent western interactions with American Indians as benign affairs. West's "Indians" often played on the conventional association of the noble savage, with the classical hero, ancient Greek and Roman statuary warrior poses supplying a suitable pictorial idiom.

Reynolds was among those artists who sought to reconcile images of American Indians with more relativist conceptions of "nobility," "civilization" and "barbarity" in a sideways attack on the European fashion for wigs that would appeal to a metropolitan public sensitized to colonial issues and ambiguities:

> If an European, when he has cut off his beard, and put false hair on his head, or bound up his own natural hair in regular hard knots, as unlike nature as he can possibly make it; and after having rendered them immoveable by the help of the fat of hogs, has covered the whole with flour, laid on by a machine with the utmost regularity; if, when thus attired he issues forth, and meets a Cherokee Indian, who has bestowed as much time at his toilet, and laid on with equal care and attention his yellow and red oker on particular parts of his forehead or cheeks, as he judges most becoming; whoever of these two despises the other for attention to the fashion of his country, which ever feels himself provoked to laugh, is the barbarian. (Reynolds, 1975 [1797], 137)

In fact, the "other" (American Indian) peoples in question here displayed in the early and middle decades of the eighteenth century an unexpected agency and activism in colonial negotiations, since they were anxious to establish benefits, including protection, in response to European (specifically British and French) competition to "claim" their valuable resources of farmland and trading routes. American Indian delegations in 1710, 1734 and 1762 to the British royal court presented the occasion for formal commemorative portraits. The 1710 portrait series "Four Indian Kings" by Jan Verelst (b. 1648; still active 1719) shows representatives of the Iroquois and Algonquian nations. These portraits combine the conventional poses, gentlemanly bearing and classical dress of European grand portraiture with stereotypical allusions to the noble savage, backgrounds of exotic vegetation, fierce fighting skills (signified by weaponry), and features read as "native," such as tinted skin colors, ornaments and hairstyles (Pratt, 2003, 66–67; Truettner, 2010, 34–39; note the toga-like garment in Figure 3.10, see color plate section). It has been suggested that such hybrid exotic–western representations defused the threat that more truthful representations might have posed to western viewers by presenting visual continuities with the classical tradition (Pratt, 2003, 60–67; Fordham, 2007, 104–110). Poor European knowledge of American Indian languages and culture led to serious misunderstandings and inaccuracies with regard to the traditions and dress of specific tribes, as did widespread western tendency to confuse American Indians with inhabitants of the East and West Indies, and even Africa (Berlo and Phillips, 1998; Pratt, 2003, 72; Wheeler, 2003, 38, 54). The visiting "Kings" were turned into fairground attractions as they could earn money by exhibiting themselves in public, a practice satirized by Hogarth in his *The Times I* (Dabydeen, 1985, 124–125). American Indians tired of European diplomacy later in the century, as it began to jeopardize their local tribal negotiations and loyalties, and as they experienced armed conflict and disease brought by occupying imperial forces (Pratt, 1998, 135–149).

Landscape representations of the United States and Canada were often dominated by fantasy or fiction. Scholars now read the visual foci and compositional formats of colonial landscapes as indicators of the state of imperial politics. Prior to the Seven Years War, many colonial landscapes were a product of artists' imaginations. Once "ownership" of territories had been agreed, a proliferation of new maps, topographical paintings and prints encouraged the peoples of "conquering" nations to feel reassured about and take pride in the imperial project (Crowley, 2011, 47–73). Coastal views were produced as navigational aids to those likely to follow in the tracks of early explorers and sometimes adopted the format of the sea chart, which used both plan and elevation views to place emphasis on the mercantile culture, trade and commerce that dominated many of Britain's eighteenth-century colonial relations (Crowley, 2011, 47–73; Muller, 2012, 48–55). Some eighteenth-century topographical prints of the United States and Canada have been discussed with regard to their application of picturesque composition, a sign of European gentility, to fashionable, local, "exotic" flora and fauna. It was some time before American-born artists developed, post-independence, languages of visual representation expressing the tastes of their own critically active "publics" (Crowley, 2011, 142–165).

Britain did not make any territorial claims in the South Sea (Pacific) islands for some time, as Spain had a monopoly there, but it did claim and settle what we now know as Australia and New Zealand. Tahiti was colonized by the end of the eighteenth century, by British missionaries. New dimensions to European fantasies of the "exotic" appeared as a result of voyages of discovery by Samuel Wallis (1728–1795) and other explorers, including James Cook (1728–1779), whose voyages in the years between 1768 and 1780 to Tahiti, Australia and New Zealand were recorded pictorially by the artists Sydney Parkinson (*c.*1745–1771), William Hodges and John Webber (1751–1793) (Smith, 1985, 8–132; Wood, 2012, 264–269). Cook's *Voyages of the South Seas* (1768–1771) sold well and included a separate volume of 61 illustrations. Joseph Banks, whose interests covered both art and science, joined Cook's first voyage and played a major role in coordinating the visual records made. A member of the Royal Society, the Society of Arts and the Society of Antiquaries, he saw the need to satisfy the need both for scientifically accurate, closely observed landscapes, naturalist studies and coastal profiles, and for providing "pleasing" pictures for audiences at home (Smith, 1985, 13–14). Bernard Smith has described the new colonial genre of the "typical" landscape, "a form of landscape the components of which were carefully selected in order to express the essential qualities of a particular kind of geographical environment" (Smith, 1985, 4). Such landscapes aimed to create a new type of visual unity derived from scientific observation by explorers of different environmental and climactic locations.

As with European images of encounters with American Indian settlements, however, extensive use of classical motifs, for example, antique statuary poses, or indirect references to a Golden Age in ancient Greece, mediated many "documentary" records of newly discovered South Seas peoples (Smith, 1985, 40–43). Smith has discussed in detail the efforts made by artists such as Hodges, on voyages of exploration to the Pacific, to balance the requirements of documentary or topographical accuracy with established European landscape traditions including the neoclassical, the arcadian, the picturesque and the sublime. Hodges went beyond an "eyewitness" approach necessary to lend authenticity to his compositions to develop his own style, in line with ideas on the "genius" or "free spirit" that were gaining currency in British art (see Chapter 1; also Smith, 1985, 1–7, 54–80; Quilley and Bonehill, 2004; McLean, 2007, 26; Quilley, 2011, 16–78; Wood, 2012, 270–284). After his voyages to the Pacific and other parts of the globe, Hodges produced large canvas works likely to appeal to Royal Academy audiences (Quilley, 2011, 42–44). European artists informed their domestic audiences of new additions to Britain's geographical discoveries, trading posts and empire, by providing topographical, "on-the-spot" studies inspired by antiquarian and ethnographic interests that suggested respect for the attributes and actual appearances of newly discovered lands while catering for the aesthetic standards of the European collector or "man of taste."

Hybrid representations of this kind made the unfamiliar more familiar, and newly discovered lands became more readily visualized and emotionally engaging as part of a global national identity developing in the British public (Smith, 1985, ix; Crowley, 2011, 1–11; Quilley, 2011, 32). By such means, colonial landscape art may help to legitimize imperial power. According to one commentator it "naturalizes a cultural and social construction, representing an artificial world as if it were simply given and inevitable" (W.J.T. Mitchell, *Landscape and Power*, 1994, cited in Crowley, 2011, 1). The picturesque, rooted in the arcadian classicism of Claude Lorrain, and so familiar from its presence in English landscape design, also functioned as a visual language of loss for the British gentry. It evoked the loss of their aesthetic elitism due to the rise of the middle classes in the new "public" for art and, if they actually traveled abroad, the loss or absence of their home (McLean, 2007, 26).

Tahiti lent itself to a western landscape aesthetic in a way that other colonial territories failed to do. Australia was first settled by the British in 1788 as a penal colony. For some years, colonial artists there, mainly army and navy officers and convicts, focused on the relatively "safe" motifs of settlement buildings and "exotic" (aboriginal) cultural, animal or botanical details rather than on the slightly intimidating local landscape views, less easily circumscribed within a picturesque format (Radford, 2013, 92). Vast wildernesses were more problematic, their "sublime" dimensions often perceived as threatening (Crowley, 2011, 216). Even at Sydney Cove, however, artists used a picturesque idiom in order to establish a colonial identity (McLean, 2007, 23, 37).

Art produced by native Pacific peoples – cloaks, baskets, canoe paddles, carved wooden bands, non-representational figures, tattoos and totems – were given to visiting European explorers as part of a process of bargaining and exchange but, like many Chinese artifacts or "curiosities," these were poorly understood at the time by western publics and were often regarded as ethnographic evidence rather than as a source of aesthetic experience. However, as the Romantic movement developed, such artifacts came to be appreciated for the appeals to feeling and imagination of their "primitivism," a quality increasingly acknowledged to have existed even in pre-classical Greek art, the fount of European civilization (Smith, 1985, 123–130; Wood, 2012, 285–295).

The tendency to judge degrees of "progress" or "civilization" by European standards was well established (Quilley, 2011, 53–78). Harriet Guest has deconstructed Hodges' images of South Seas peoples as part of an attempt by Europeans to theorize cultural differences in a way that brought as much attention to their own values as to those of the peoples they observed (Guest, 2007, 5–6, 11–17, 22–24, 169–198). Reynolds' 1775–1776 portrait of Omai (*c.*1751–1780) or Mai, as he should have been known (Figure 3.11, see color plate section), represents an inhabitant of an island near Tahiti, employed as an interpreter, who was brought back to Britain by Cook. The portrait serves as an example of the "civilizing" tendency in European representations of native peoples. Like Verlest's work it demonstrates a fusion of "exotic" difference with an impulse to defuse or domesticate it. Omai is represented as a noble savage in loose, dignified, Orientalized dress and with a pose reminiscent of that of a classical god. He conforms to contemporary western conventions of masculine aristocratic gentility. However, both the stereotypical exotic setting and the presence on his hand of a tattoo undermine any suggestion of western patrician status. Reynolds, who was quite broad-minded with regard to cultural and aesthetic relativity, saw tattooing as a step too far as it literally cut into the skin in barbarous fashion, as well as evoking suspect feminine (as well as un-British) associations with "ornament" (Guest, 1992, 101–134; 2007, 21–22, 68–69). Hodges painted a more realistic portrait of Omai (Smith, 1985, 80–82). These portraits indicate the competing values of tolerance, acceptance and fear in British responses to colonial identities.

Representations of South Seas life combined an Enlightenment desire for new knowledge with transgressive aspects of a European fascination with "non-western" cultures. Diderot's *Supplement to Bougainville's "Voyage"* (*Supplément au "Voyage" de Bougainville*) was first published in 1772, in Friedrich Melchior Baron von Grimm's (1723–1807) *Correspondance Littéraire* (*Literary Correspondence, 1753–1790*), in response to the 1771 *Voyage autour du monde* (*Journey around the world*) by the explorer Louis-Antoine de Bougainville (1729–1811), who had "claimed" Tahiti and other Pacific islands for France. As with the visual sources discussed above, Diderot's text demonstrates conflicting aspects of western perceptions of "other" cultures. The author marvels at the new knowledge gained of local customs while delighting in positive references to the sexual permissiveness of native peoples, including the offering of local girls to Bougainville's crew, which challenged a conventional Catholic and Parisian bourgeois morality. Less commonly, Diderot also offers, through the fictional farewell speech of a wise native old man, a critique directed at Bougainville of the corrupting influence, both morally and in terms of physical disease, of European powers. Such reservations were relatively rare at the time.

The exoticization or idealization of landscapes and peoples was "anti-modern" in the sense that, like the picturesque, it froze visual representations within a past golden age inspired by the bucolic tradition of antiquity.

Deployed in hierarchic cultural relationships and for the benefit of an imperial public, it hindered the kind of liberal values and cultural equality essential to present-day notions of modernity. To the eighteenth-century public it served as a vehicle for familiarization with dramatically new lands, peoples and customs, but this manifestation of a forward-looking quest for new knowledge was heavily mediated by the discourses of empire and fashion.

Questions of Modernity

The term "modernity" is often applied to eighteenth-century art because this is the period that witnessed the introduction of a thriving market for art, both within and across nations, that was for the first time able to challenge the previously over-riding authority of governments and institutions in forming taste and artistic practice. In previous eras political and social rituals and celebrations and the patronage of dominant elites had provided the greatest opportunities to view art. Now changes in the social order, created by a new emphasis on commerce and consumerism, as well as a new discursive formation, a "public" for art, brought a much wider section of society into a closer acquaintance with the work of artists and blurred some of the older hierarchies of rank and taste, especially between the highest and middling orders of society.

This public began to refine their aesthetic judgments and self-consciously cultivated the attribute of good taste. There were more opportunities than ever before to view art, both in formal academy settings and in more popular venues. While many private collections remained dominated by an established discourse of "the old masterpiece" (Link, 2013, 115), "modern" (in the sense of contemporary) art became more widely valued and the latest French tastes in particular created excitement throughout continental Europe. An educated public, empowered by the critical spirit at the heart of the Enlightenment, was able to challenge some of the dominant structures of traditional thought, particularly the hierarchy of genres, which began to dissolve under the pressure of commercial demand and the views of artists and critics.

Global exploration and the dissemination through art of scenes representing the world beyond Europe were in many respects illustrations of the Enlightenment's search for knowledge. Documentary studies of hitherto unfamiliar peoples and lands contributed to the contemporary thrust toward progress. However, the exoticization, or idealization of these landscapes and peoples. It imposed western visual schemata on "other," different lands. Dominant visual tropes of blackness also often demonized or diminished "other" peoples. The discourses of empire stalled the debates on rights and equalities stimulated by the Enlightenment. Eighteenth-century colonial art in Europe often embodied the excitement, nervousness and moral myopia of a public confronted with increasingly frequent encounters with the unknown.

Further Reading

Bindman, David and Henry Louis Gates Jr (eds). 2011. *The Image of the Black in Western Art* vol. III Part 3 "From the 'Age of Discovery' to the Age of Abolition: The Eighteenth century." Cambridge, MA, and London: The Belknap Press. A groundbreaking introduction to the representation in eighteenth-century western art of black peoples.

Brewer, John. 1997. *The Pleasures of the Imagination: English Culture in the Eighteenth Century.* London: Harper Collins. An excellent introduction to eighteenth-century English art and its publics.

Craske, Matthew. 1997. *Art in Europe 1700–1830.* Oxford and New York: Oxford University Press. An excellent survey of the complex relationships between eighteenth-century and early nineteenth-century European art and wider developments in politics, urbanization and economics.

Crow, Thomas E. 1985. *Painters and Public Life in Eighteenth-Century France.* New Haven, CT, and London: Yale University Press. An excellent study of the relationship between eighteenth-century French art and increasingly politicized notions of the "public." The final chapter focuses on David.

Guest, Harriet. 2007.*Empire, Barbarism, and Civilisation: James Cook, Wlliam Hodges, and the Return to the Pacific.* Cambridge: Cambridge University Press.

Quilley, Geoff and Kay Dian Kriz (eds). 2003. *An Economy of Colour: Visual Culture and the Atlantic World, 1660–1830.* Manchester: Manchester University Press. Includes useful studies on colonial identities.

Solkin, David. 1992. *Painting for Money: The Visual Arts and the Public Sphere in Eighteenth-Century England.* A useful study of new notions of the "public" in relation to developments in British art.

Smith, Bernard. 1985. *European Vision and the South Pacific.* New Haven, CT, and London: Yale University Press.

4

Taste, Criticism and Journalism

Identifying Beauty and Good Taste

The concept of taste acquired great significance in the eighteenth century and was the subject of much debate. As the idea of a public for art took hold, so did a concern that this public, more inclined to offer opinions on art, should do so in an informed and appropriate manner. This public expected sound, reliable criteria in the judgments of critics and amateurs. To be a "man of taste" (the distinction was rarely applied to women) became a sign of social cachet as well as the height of fashion:

> ...for some years a reputation as a man of taste has been as sought after among those who would distinguish themselves as was, in Molière's time, that of a man of wit ... there are teachers of this skill as well as proselytes; the accomplished wit has been replaced by the *virtuoso*, each house wishing to have its own. (*Mercure de France*, 1754, cited in Wrigley, 1993, 192; my translation)

Particular themes run through eighteenth-century debates on taste and criticism. First, there were varying opinions on whether it was possible to identify an objective standard of beauty and taste, or whether this was difficult due to the fact that individual assessments of artworks were bound to be subjective or relative. Second, there was the issue of whether beauty became evident to the man of taste through a process of abstract reasoning, or whether the identification of beauty central to the operations of taste was essentially empirical – a matter of practical experience – of comparing, contrasting and forming an opinion on works of art in order to

A Guide to Eighteenth-Century Art, First Edition. Linda Walsh.

Companion website: www.wiley.com/go/walsh/guidetoeighteenthcenturyart

cultivate sound judgments on their merits. Finally, there was the matter of whether judgments of the beauty or aesthetic value of works of art could be separated from an evaluation of their moral qualities – a subject to which we shall turn in Chapter 5. A wide variety of issues has been raised in more recent academic debates on the methods used by eighteenth-century critics and commentators on taste. These include questions of the degree to which art criticism should share the concerns of literary criticism (e.g. by focusing on narrative details, character and expression), the matter of an appropriate register for the writing of criticism (from the formal and academic to the literary and irreverent) and the degree of erudition (in the case of history painting) or technical knowledge (in respect of all art) that a good critic should be expected to possess. There is also the matter of the extent to which eighteenth-century critics and commentators perpetuated the previous century's emphasis on the "perfect forms" and inspiring narratives of history painting.

The first person identified as using the term "aesthetics" in the modern sense (i.e. the philosophy of the beautiful or the principles underlying good taste) was Alexander Gottlieb Baumgarten (1714–1762), Professor of Poetry at the University of Frankfurt an der Oder. In his *Aesthetica*, of which the first two volumes were published in 1750 and 1758, respectively, he defined aesthetics as the "science of sensible knowledge," the term "sensible" meaning, at this time, "pertaining to the senses." According to his empirical view of taste, good judgment was the result of wide sensory experience. Because artistic works affect their audiences through their impact on the senses; for example, sight and hearing, which move the imagination in vivid ways, taste may not be reduced to the clarity of logic (Gaiger, 2002, 7–8). He and others in the eighteenth century stressed that a kind of accumulated "knowledge," derived from the senses but ultimately more sophisticated in form, was involved, and that taste could not be a simple matter of isolated, spontaneous responses to art but must evolve as an intellectual attribute, the senses nourishing the mind. This tendency to emphasize the role of the mind's internal operations in the formulation of judgments of taste reached a climax later in the century in the writings of Immanuel Kant (1724–1804). One of Baumgarten's achievements, also developed by Kant, was to separate the realm of the "aesthetic" (artistic form) clearly from the moral content of a work of art (Kaufman, 1995, 455).

In his essay *Of the Standard of Taste* (first published in 1757), David Hume was also keen to explain the workings of taste as the formulation of empirical knowledge: data received by the senses and through experience formed its basis. Empiricism was a core Enlightenment value, drawn from the realm of scientific enquiry and, in particular, from the methodological principles of the seventeenth-century philosopher John Locke, who had regarded knowledge as the result of experiential learning rather than of purely abstract reasoning (Locke, 1694). Hume argued that in the workings of taste sense data were filtered through the mind's capacity to store and compare previous experiences of art and of human nature: in order for a specific judgment to be right, our immediate pleasure or displeasure in front of a work of art must be mediated by "A perfect serenity of mind, a recollection of thought, a due attention to the object" (cited in Harrison, Wood and Gaiger, 2000, 509). For Hume, taste was a matter of "sentiment" in the eighteenth-century sense of finely tuned intuitions (or "delicacy") of the mind. It was nourished by reason and education, as well as by the imagination. True men of taste were therefore rare (Harrison, Wood and Gaiger, 2000, 515).

Most eighteenth-century theorists of taste wished to avoid the conclusion that it was to any significant degree arbitrary or subjective. While some deployed the arguments above (that taste was derived from, but not reducible to individual sense impressions or the pleasure to which these gave rise), others argued that a universal view of beauty could be derived from identifying the qualities determining an object's "perfection." The latter notion was derived from Plato's notion of "perfect" or "ideal" forms. Plato had conceived, in his work *De Republica* (*The Republic*, written *c.*380 BCE) of "Eternal forms," "Ideas" or prototypes from which all (less perfect) earthly forms were derived. A central part of the classical aesthetic was the belief that it was the role of the artist to create forms resembling as closely as possible these ideal forms, through the application of beautiful proportion and harmonious composition. In the eighteenth century many still believed this had been achieved by the artists and sculptors of classical Greece and Rome, who had studied natural forms in order to derive from them and refine models of perfect beauty. Winckelmann played a key role in promoting such views, his admiration for purer antique forms serving also to undermine the fashion for the rococo (see Chapter 1; see also Kaufman, 1995, 446–449; Walsh, 2012, 231–232).

Several of Winckelmann's German compatriots, such as Gotthold Ephraim Lessing (1729–1781) and Johann Georg Hamann (1730–1788) wished to challenge or modify his rationalizing neoclassicism (Kaufman, 1995, 446–457). For Francis Hutcheson (1694–1746), Hume and others, any standard of taste developed in this way would risk the kind of arid and formulaic classicism promoted often dogmatically by the academies. They preferred a practical view of taste that relied less on prescribed visual formulae and allowed for its relativity, while distancing it from the purely arbitrary or "vulgar" (Macmillan, 1986, 23–26). Hutcheson paid great attention to the "essential" neo-platonic qualities of beauty, while stopping short of reducing beauty and taste to formulaic definitions. In 1725 he had argued, in his *An Inquiry into the Original of our ideas of Beauty and Taste*, that taste was exercised by an "inner sense" or intuitive appreciation of beauty. This "sense" was informed by a recognition of the principles of neo-platonic beauty, which had guided many seventeenth-century artists but was reducible neither to such rational certainties nor to the physical senses. This left some room for individual, subjective responses to works of art, as well as culturally relative tastes:

> These *Determinations* to be pleas'd with any Forms, or Ideas which occur to our Observation, the *Author* chooses to call *Senses*; distinguishing them from the Powers which commonly go by that Name, by calling our Power of perceiving the *Beauty* of *Regularity, Order, Harmony*, an *Internal Sense*;.... (Cited in Harrison, Wood and Gaiger, 2000, 403, original emphasis)

Hutcheson's "inner sense" theory influenced Hume, Alexander Gerard (1728–1795) and other thinkers, and became a marker of the "polite" and informed amateur. Hume's view of taste also allowed for some subjective variation through his theory of associationism, inherited from classical philosophy, according to which we find beauty in things when they arouse certain associations or memories in our minds. In 1790, Archibald Alison (1757–1839) developed a similar view, in his *Essays on the Nature and principles of Taste*. For Alison, any formulaic classical idealism would offer too restrictive and "aristocratic" an approach, given the complexities of human nature and taste:

> If ... in the human countenance and form, there were only *certain* colours, or forms, or proportions, that were essentially beautiful, how imperious a check would have been given, not only to human happiness, but to the most important affections and sensibilities of our nature! ... an Aristocracy would be established even by Nature itself, more irresistible, and more independent either of talents or virtue, than any that the influence of property or of ancestry has ever yet created among mankind. (Cited in Macmillan, 1986, 129)

Unlike the skeptic Hume, however, Alison reinterpreted the workings of taste in a way that devoted a large role to Christian spirituality (Macmillan, 1986, 149). Such approaches allowed for some variations in taste, while retaining its exclusivity within the domain of the educated and refined. Artists themselves were often barred from the category of "man of taste" because of their close proximity to the messy, material world of paint (Brewer, 1997, 88–92).

Neo-platonic conceptions of beauty were "formalist" in the sense that they placed emphasis on aspects of an object's form: in the eighteenth century these normally included regularity, order and harmony in, for example, the composition of a work or in the drawing of a figure. Such conceptions of beauty also had the advantage of offering a universal explanation of its cause and of its effects on viewers. Enlightenment thinkers generally sought the rational, universal principles underlying phenomena. For this reason neo-platonic explanations of beauty continued to be influential throughout the eighteenth century, increasingly modified, however (as in Hume's case), by a greater acknowledgement of empirical or "scientific" method. Hybrid neo-platonic-empiricist approaches were common. In his *A Notion of the Historical Draught of the Tablature of the Judgement of Hercules* (published in English in 1713), Shaftesbury saw taste as a particularly refined form of empiricism based on a patrician experience of art and informed by a universalizing neo-platonic view of beauty based on the idea of visual harmony. He was also strongly influenced by a traditional emphasis on the narrative, quasi-literary effectiveness of history paintings (Harrison, Wood and Gaiger, 2000, 373).

Other theorists who applied neo-platonic principles included Hogarth in his *The Analysis of Beauty* (1753), who identified a formal cause for beauty and grace: the use of waving and serpentine lines, the latter consisting of a three-dimensional, spiraling version of the former, in, for example, the twisting forms of a dancer's body. Hogarth placed the waving line, derived from beautiful natural forms, at the heart of his rococo aesthetic. His very particular formalist approach to taste has been seen as an attempt to distance himself from the prevailing taste for works by foreign, often Catholic, old masters, too influenced by less natural antique forms (Craske, 2000, 19). Additionally, like other critics, including Du Bos and the philosopher Louis-Jean Lévesque de Pouilly (1691–1750) in his 1736 *Theory of Agreeable Sentiments* (*Théorie des sentiments agréables*), Hogarth placed great emphasis on good sense and hedonism, or the pleasures of the physical senses, particularly the eye, which was to be entertained by "chasing" or following waving lines on a canvas in a way we have already encountered in the picturesque landscape aesthetic and in the rococo (see Chapter 2).

In his *Essay on Taste* (*Essai sur le gout*) for the French *Encyclopédie*, Montesquieu saw beauty as the product of "order," in, for example, figure groupings and composition, and a judicious amount of visual "variety." Variety could be taken to excess, however, in styles such as the Gothic. The latter was anathema to those who, like Montesquieu, derived their ideal forms from the more restrained and harmonious models of Greek art and architecture, which they felt were sure to please the mind of the observer (Harrison, Wood and Gaiger, 2000, 526–528). He had little faith in any universal or absolute standard of taste, emphasizing that the criteria applied by specific institutions, customs and habits might militate, in practice, against any essentialist view of beauty. Other Enlightenment thinkers, such as Voltaire, were bolder in their statements about the universalizing operations of taste, which they linked quite overtly with current Eurocentric (and aristocratic) values (Harrison, Wood and Gaiger, 2000, 531). Kant reconciled the notion of variations in individual taste with a quest for universally valid judgments by aligning the judgments of the true man of taste with those of a *sensus communis* or "communal sense" through which individuals placed their own subjective judgments in the context of "the collective Reasoning of humanity" (Harrison, Wood and Gaiger, 2000, 779–782).

Less easily reconciled with universalizing or neo-platonic views of taste were approaches that, particularly from the mid-century, drew on the cult of sensibility that emphasized the importance to taste of the viewer's emotional reactions to art. Edmund Burke's views on aesthetics stressed the importance of our emotions in identifying the beautiful (see Chapter 2), and by these means might have been thought to licence subjectivity in matters of taste. He countered such misconceptions by suggesting that the same emotions ("love, or some passion similar to it"; Burke, 1998, 28) were caused uniformly by any beautiful object with essential qualities such as smallness, smoothness, softness and delicacy. At the same time, he objected to more conventional neo-platonic criteria for beauty such as the beautiful proportions observed in antique sculpture, or any notion of "perfect" form. His approach to the sublime was characterized by a discussion of "wild" feelings responding to stimuli in a uniform way.

The critic Denis Diderot made constant reference, in his *Salons* (1759–1781), to the need for *pathétique* (pathos-arousing) effects in art, as he became a vehement advocate of the moral, social and cultural advantages of possessing a keen emotional sensibility. From the 1760s, such beliefs also infused responses to literature, the fashionable, tear-inducing novels of Samuel Richardson (1689–1761) providing a vivid example. Diderot was among other critics such as Du Bos and the Abbé Marc-Antoine Laugier (1713–1769), who expected similarly literary, emotive effects in art (Berger, 1999, 141–148). This led him to a warm appreciation of the genre paintings of Greuze until the artist tried to outreach his talent by tackling very unsuccessfully the genre of history. In response to Greuze's *The Paralytic* (*La Piété Filiale*), a moving representation of a family tending to a suffering elderly man, exhibited at the Salon of 1763, Diderot stated:

> When I saw this eloquent old man, full of pathos, I felt ... my soul become tender and tears ready to fall from my eyes. (Diderot, 1984, 353; my translation)

Diderot also expected plausible characters, actors, compositions and expressions in history paintings, so that these would rouse the imagination and emotions of the beholder. Most kinds of emotional stimulation were welcomed: horror, melancholy, love and fear among them. Diderot's critical approach was not, however, a simple submission to subjectivism in matters of taste. Many of his emotional reactions to paintings became exercises in his own creativity, as he invented stories, dialogues and witty anecdotes prompted by paintings. Also, he showed an increasing awareness of the need for critics to develop an understanding of the specialist, technical issues of the visual arts. He reinforced his traditional, literary criteria of judgment (ideas on narrative, character, expression and a generally plausible representation of an event) with those related to ocular discrimination: the use of light, color, figure groupings, drapery, drawing and the application of paint. While Diderot placed great emphasis on his powers of empathy when viewing art, he wished to emphasize that his taste carried the force of rational principle:

> If taste is capricious, if there are no rules determining beauty, then what is it that prompts these delicious feelings that arise so suddenly, so involuntarily, so tumultuously in the depths of our souls, dilating or constricting them, forcing our eyes to shed tears of joy, pain, and admiration, whether in response to some grand physical phenomenon or to an account of some great moral action?.... You'll never convince my heart that it's mistaken in skipping a beat, nor my entrails that they're wrong to contract from profound emotion. (From "Notes on Painting" in Diderot, 1995a, 237–238)

The critic felt his "heart" was right in these matters because he could, if necessary, justify its responses with reference to identifiable standards of beauty. He included in these an essentially classical, harmonious relationship or unity of the different parts of a painting to its whole. His acquisition of the technical vocabulary of art was exceptional for a non-artist. Like many eighteenth-century theorists and critics, Diderot sought to protect an objective, professional form of aesthetic judgment within a framework of individualized, personal responses to art (Furbank, 1992, 276–277). In stressing the broader relevance of personal feeling in matters of taste, he joined other eighteenth-century commentators who conceived of shared "public" judgments originating from the realm of private experience. The fact that Diderot demonstrated this in the context of Greuze's *The Paralytic*, a painting concerned explicitly with the family, further emphasizes the growing interdependence of private and public realms in social and aesthetic matters.

Theorists in other countries sought different validations of subjective experience. In Scotland the emphasis of the philosopher Thomas Reid (1710–1796) on pure perception challenged aesthetic theories based mainly on intellect or analysis. For Reid, no "idea" intervened between an object and our perception of it, and it was the job of an artist to translate into paint the raw material of perception, rather than attempting to represent any clear idea of the thing represented. His view influenced Henry Raeburn in the 1790s in the sense that an emphasis on color, light and brushwork helped the artist to suggest rather than clearly define the forms he represented, the analytical work of draftsmanship being much less important. In this "looser" style of painting, the viewer would "complete" the abstract forms in question in a common-sense way, rather than receiving or attempting to describe a clear visual description (Macmillan, 1986, 79–80).

Unsurprisingly, given the Enlightenment's emphasis on the acquisition of knowledge, connoisseurship remained important through the eighteenth century. Kristel Smentek has recently illuminated the ways in which connoisseurs such as the print collector and dealer Pierre-Jean Mariette (1694–1774) developed professional expertise (e.g. in matters of style) through carefully cultivated commercial and social networking (Smentek, 2014). Important models included seventeenth-century scholars and critics, such as André Félibien and Roger de Piles, who had placed great emphasis on matters of attribution, the scholarly study of art, the perception of quality, comparative discussions of artists' techniques and the ability to distinguish copies from originals (McClellan, 2008, 118, 157; Percival, 2012, 99). This skill set often remained exclusive to the *connoisseur*, but sometimes overlapped with more gentlemanly, classical humanist interests in art, such as those expressed by Shaftesbury, the architect and garden designer William Kent and others who sought familiarity with art without aspiring to the exclusive, specialist domain of the connoisseur. Jonathan Richardson, who was influenced by de Piles, sought some connoisseurial engagement with art (Brewer, 1997, 215–217). Richardson subsequently played an important role in popularizing through his writings de Piles' critical criteria, which included the technical issues of how the parts of a painting relate to the whole, correct drawing, appropriate use of color, the use of appropriate facial expressions and the importance of producing a plausible representation of a subject (Brewer, 1997, 276). In France

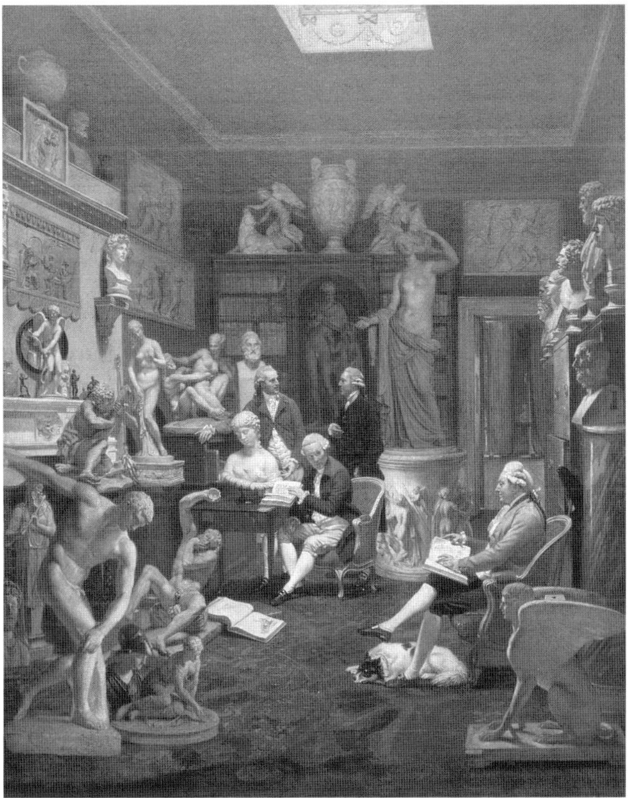

Figure 4.1 Johan Zoffany: *Charles Townley and Friends in His Library at Park Street, Westminster*, oil on canvas, 127 × 99.1 cm, 1781–1790 and 1798. Towneley Hall Art Gallery and Museum, Burnley. Source: DeAgostini/Getty Images.

Cochin, who saw himself as the guardian of the values of classicism and state culture, while often being more flexible in practice, was also keen to comment on technical matters (Wrigley, 1993, 279).

British artists were often wary of connoisseurs' approaches to assessing their work, seeing them as too concerned with correctness in matters of attribution and the identification of the "hand" of a specific artist, and too much immersed in the fine detail and finish of Dutch works in particular (Mount, 2006, 176–177). Connoisseurs were seen as preserving through such erudition the elitism and professional "mystique" of their work (Mount, 2006, 180) (Figure 4.1). In visual representations of connoisseurs at work scrutinizing paintings, use of a magnifying glass signifies their close attention to detail. There remained, however, a distinction between the expert and the educated public (Wrigley, 1998, 232–233). The precise blend of critical methods deployed varied according to whether an author was addressing the public at large, more educated or specialist readers, or adopting a kind of literary ("man of letters" - *littérateur* - or *amateur*) focus on the story, history, costumes and emotional experiences represented in the paintings seen. Practitioners of this latter genre of art writing included, in Britain, Shaftesbury and Richardson (who, as we have seen, combined it with more technical and specialist approaches) and, in France, Laugier, Jean-Baptiste de La Curne de Sainte Palaye (1697–1781), Caylus and Louis Petit de Bachaumont (1690–1771).

Journalism

After the resumption in 1737 of more regular Salons in Paris, there emerged a proliferation of *brochures* (pamphlets) and periodicals bearing critical accounts of the exhibitions (McWilliam *et al.*, 1991). These were sold at bookshops, by street hawkers or at the foot of the stairs leading to the Salon exhibitions themselves. The popular press in France had grown since the preceding century. Most people from the artisan class upwards could afford its publications, many of which appeared in the regions as well as in the capital. The most resilient new journals were the *Literary Year* (the *Année littéraire*, 1754–1791), *The Encyclopaedic Journal* (*Le Journal encyclopédique*, 1756–1794), *The Herald* (*L'Avant-Coureur*, 1760–1773) the *Paris Journal* (*Le Journal de Paris*, 1777–1840), the *Journal of Literature, Sciences and the Arts* (*Journal de litérature, des sciences et des arts*, 1779–1782) and *Notices, Announcements and Opinions on Various Matters* (*Affiches, annonces et avis divers*, 1783–1814) (Wrigley, 1993, 158; Berger, 1999, 91–124). Publications such as the *French Gazette* (*Gazette de France*) and the *Scholars' Journal* (*Journal des savants*), both founded in the seventeenth century, survived until 1792, the *Journal des Savants* being relaunched in 1816. The *Gallant Mercury* (*Mercure Galant*), also established in the seventeenth century, lasted until 1791. By this time the court and aristocratic bias of these publications failed to serve a newly politicized public (Berger, 1999, 91–100). The academic Jesuit publication, the *Journal de Trévoux* (also known as *Memoires of Trévoux*, 1701–1777), predecessor of the *Journal de litérature, des sciences et des arts*, did much to educate the public, but struggled to survive from 1762 when members of this Catholic sect were expelled from France.

Many French journal and newspaper critiques of art were written in a way that offered little challenge to authority, political or cultural, in order to avoid censorship. They often had smaller print runs than the *brochures*, which took greater risks and were less deferential. Journals were often collaborative affairs and sometimes covered the arts in general. Very few writers could earn a living from criticism itself, so had to write for a range of publications. It was common to plagiarize other writers' work, hence the close similarities of many Salon reviews. Those *brochures* that had to be printed illicitly, such as the *libelles* (lampoons) often written by authors unsupported by patrons, were very popular with readers of all backgrounds who were tired of anodyne or elitist commentaries on art. *Libelles* thrived on parody, the burlesque and the carnivalesque (Crow, 1985, 93–94). Diderot's critical accounts of the Salons held between the years 1759 and 1781 were circulated in the journal the *Literary Correspondence* run by his friend Grimm. This was circulated in manuscript form to a few (mainly foreign) clients, including monarchs and wealthy dignitaries. Freed from censorship, Diderot was able to express his personal views with some frankness. Like the *Secret Memoires* (*Mémoires Secrets*, 1762–1787), unpublished until 1783–1789 in London and the nineteenth century in France, another clandestine journal, Diderot's *Salons* were published much later than written.

The heavy intervention of the state in France's cultural life delayed the foundation of an independent, specialist art press there until after the Revolution: the first specialist art journal was established in 1799. Such developments occurred much earlier in other nations, such as Germany and Italy (Wrigley, 1993, 201–206, 230), where specialist art periodicals appeared from the 1770s, including the *Artistic Miscellany* (*Miscellaneen artistischen Inhalts*, 1779–1787) and its various successor journals, which ran into the nineteenth century; Goethe's *Proplylaea* (*Die Propyläen*, of which the title refers to the gateway to the Acropolis; 1798–1801); and the *Memoirs on the Fine Arts* (*Memorie per le Belle Arte*; 1785–1788) (Burton, 1976, 3–4). Criticism had its place as a sub-genre of journalism for much of the century, except at times of political turmoil. It was frowned upon for much of the eighteenth century in France for artists to turn their hand to reviewing the work of their peers or tread on the territory of the Académie royale. However, some wrote critical accounts in defense of the work of friends and relatives whose reputations had been compromised by critics.

More controversial pamphlets and reviews were often published anonymously, resulting in the need for some authors to issue denials that they were responsible for them. Competition for sales and publicity meant that authors often used accessible or witty titles to lure readers, or made great efforts to display their erudition and credentials as critics. Charles-Joseph Mathon de la Cour (1738–1793) and Raphael David Daudet de Jossan (dates unknown) were among those who used their critical writings as a means of career and social advancement (Wrigley, 1993, 193–195), although the former became more radical in his approach once established. In order to be taken seriously by the educated world, critics had to adopt a suitably austere tone that set them apart from the banter offered by "lesser" writers. From the 1750s, they often quoted the principles or rules underlying the arts as set out by the seventeenth-century poet and scholar Nicolas Boileau (1636–1711). Some critics saw their role as instructive, helping the public to understand art in the manner previously established by Félibien and de Piles. Dictionaries of art became more popular from the mid-century in order to assist more educated viewers (Wrigley, 1993, 258), and to help bridge the gap between *connoisseurs* and the general public. Even pamphlet literature was increasingly infused by the technical terminology of art. The wider public also assimilated such terminology through conversation with dealers.

In less formal criticism wit, humour, slang and literary tableaux (imaginary "stagings" of painted scenes) were increasingly incorporated into reviews in a spirit of *ekphrasis*, the ancient Greek device of a vivid verbal description of a work of visual art for rhetorical purposes. This was particularly appropriate where paintings themselves resembled theatrical tableaux, as was the case with many of Greuze's genre paintings, which gave the impression of "freezing" figures into fixed positions. Such devices could also distance the authors of reviews from any charge of assaulting artists' reputations or prevent them from incurring the wrath of the public censors. It was important to know the rules governing the use of such writing techniques, however, since reference to boulevard or street theatre would be seen as an insult to any paintings to which they were applied: "bad" forms of theatricality in art included the use of blatantly unnatural, "stagey" gestures, poses and expressions. The reputations of critics often hung on their finesse in making such distinctions and on their tone, knowledge and conformity with the principles guiding the academies.

Most art criticism in France was related to the Salon exhibitions and these provided the main opportunities to educate the public, prior to the introduction of public museums. Reviews of the Salons also reflected changes in public taste and broader social tensions, serving as an intermediary between the official concerns and policies of the state and the views of a broader public (Wrigley, 1993, 161). There was a standard agenda (inherited from the seventeenth century) of items to be discussed in relation to each work discussed: expression, composition, costume, drawing, color, chiaroscuro, *airs de tête* (the expressions of heads and faces) and drapery in the case of paintings; with notions of grandeur, nobility, dignity and respect for classical prototypes featuring heavily in discussions of history painting. There was a general avoidance of the esoteric, dwelling rather on how plausible a painting's system of representation was to the general viewer. Salon criticism and "men of taste" more broadly could in theory pose a significant threat to the Académie royale and its authority. After the demise in the early century of the Académie's lectures and debates on art, "theory" became the concern of circles of authority outside the institution, such as that led by Pierre Crozat, who served as artistic adviser to the Duc d'Orléans and enjoyed strong relations with the Regency Court and the Palais Royal. He gathered at his home other collectors, theorists and critics such as Pierre-Jean Mariette, Jean de Jullienne, Du Bos, Caylus and Bachaumont (see Chapter 2; Crow, 1985, 22–41).

The relationship between art criticism and centers of power was among the reasons for the growing politicization of this genre of writing. Wrigley (1998, 136–137) argues that, in France, political debate and dissent were often displaced into art criticism because they were forbidden in public. In turn, art criticism affected the "material and discursive matrix" (the social conditions and representations of power) in contemporary art (Wrigley, 1993, 4). When La Font de Saint Yenne launched, in his 1747 *Reflexions*, an attack on decadent (rococo) art, he allied aesthetic with political causes, from notions of civic duty to support for the *Parlements* and their challenge to royal authority (Wrigley, 1993, 185–186). As pamphlet literature proliferated in the two decades preceding the Revolution, much of it had an anti-court flavor, as well as challenging the authority of the Académie in the name of the public (Crow, 1985, 180–186). After the Revolution there were some largely unsuccessful attempts by art critics to bring order to society (Wrigley, 1993, 166–167). Even in nations where political tensions were less acute, art criticism often served as commentary on the health of nations and societies. Myth-making grand narratives and historicist accounts of art served the interests of reform movements by identifying cycles of health, decadence, death and regeneration in a range of civilizations, from Italy (felt to be a "dying" civilization in the eighteenth century, its visitors dazzled mainly by its distant past) to the prospering societies and cultures of France, Britain and Germany. The growing fashions for neoclassicism and primitivism in art were associated with a quasi-biological regeneration of late eighteenth-century civilizations (Craske, 1997, 219–250). Such ideological reconstructions of history suited the new taste for national schools and histories of art. In 1745 Antoine-Joseph Dezallier d'Argenville (1680–1765) published the first part of the first history of French painting, his *Summary of the Lives of the Most Famous Painters* (*Abrégé de la vie des plus fameux peintres*), based on celebrity biographies in the manner of Vasari's 1550 *Lives of the Most Excellent Painters, Sculptors and Architects* (*Le Vite de'piu eccellenti pittori, scultori, e architettori*) (Berger, 1999, 233).

It was rare for journals to have an explicit polemical allegiance. However, the *Année Littéraire* founded by Élie-Catherine Fréron (1718–1776), professor and professional critic, was openly hostile to key Enlightenment thinkers, such as Voltaire. Censorship laws did little to curb the efforts of critics who went on the offensive, as these laws tended to be enforced strictly only during political crises, such as those provoked by the Maupeou affair and the end of Louis XVI's reign: René Nicolas-Charles-Augustin de Maupeou (1714–1792) was the chancellor who challenged the power of the Paris *Parlements.* The establishment could rally its support if under attack. La Font's rare, virulent assault on contemporary art at the Salons invoked a plethora of counter-attacks. Cochin was among those who, as Secretary to the Académie royale, tried to moderate the virulent attacks of critics. In 1763, he published his *Les Misotechniques aux enfers*, an indictment of the views of La Font de Saint Yenne and his followers, including Jean de Jullienne (Berger, 1999, 182–186) and of all ill-informed critics. The art critic Le Blanc also circulated views in defense of rococo artists (Crow, 1985, 7), as did Coypel, through his *Dialogue by Monsieur Coypel, First Painter to the King, on the Exhibition of Paintings at the Salon of the Louvre, in 1747* (*Dialogue de M.Coypel, premier peintre du Roi, sur l'exposition des tableaux dans le Salon du Louvre, en 1747*) (Berger, 1999, 186–191). Cochin insisted in 1767 that critics should put their names to their publications so that they could no longer hide behind anonymity and, in 1787, he lobbied d'Angiviller, then-Director of Public Buildings, in a further attempt to curb destructive criticism (Wrigley, 1993, 100–155). His efforts did suppress some negative Salon criticism, but were hampered by the fact that many members of the court and the wealthy elite of Paris enjoyed and encouraged pamphlet wars and lively assaults on artists.

Meanwhile, many critics had gained a reputation for self-seeking publicity stunts. Laugier's request to establish a new monthly review of the arts provoked the following cool reception from Cochin:

> This sort of publication can degenerate in no time to criticisms, mockery, and baseless judgements. Any writer will soon persuade himself that negativity amuses the public and can sell his work. Self-interest runs the show, and it will become no more than a periodical series of insults which would aggrieve our artists, close the studios, and ruin public exhibitions, which are more useful to the arts than are the arguments of literary men who know next to nothing. (Cited in Crow 1985, 9)

A turbulent critical culture returned in the 1770s and 1780s, when Terray (Director of Public Buildings in 1773–1774) relaxed Cochin's reforms. France was exceptional in the virulence and conflicts of its art critics. In Britain it was much more common to know and write about literature than painting, although Reynolds' lectures at the Royal Academy brought some advancement in this respect. Critics such as Shaftesbury and Jonathan Richardson, and newspaper and journal reviews such as those in *The Tatler*, *The Spectator* and *The Gentleman's Magazine* did much to educate (and shape) the art public, as did the founding of a specialist journal, *The Artist's Repository and the Drawing Magazine* (1785–1795). Britain's first art periodical, Charles Taylor's *Artist's Repository*, was launched in 1785. As in France, there was a range of registers used in the writing of criticism, from serious philosophical discourse to gossip, satire and the burlesque (Kriz, 2001, 62). Much negative criticism was, however, defused through satire and, at least outside the professional disputes of academicians, there was a greater emphasis on a public consensus of taste than in France. Reynolds, Richardson and Shaftesbury wrote for and helped to mold this relatively consensual, genteel art public (Solkin, 1993, 248–259). Differences in emphasis in critical writings tended to be more subtly graduated but could be polarized in response to developments on the continent, such as the French Revolution or American War of Independence, which led many (mainly of Tory sympathies) to declare their allegiances to a more conservative, aristocratic (and implicitly royalist) taste (Hoock, 2003, 130–135). Edmund Burke was among those who wrote against French attacks on the monarchy. Both Hogarth and William Blake declared their sympathy for disadvantaged sections of society. They also expressed resentment, the former in his 1753 *The Analysis of Beauty*, and Blake in his annotations on Reynolds' *Discourses*, of the power of the Royal Academy. However, Hogarth's "waving line" aesthetic was essentially an aspect of rococo aristocratic taste and he painted some aristocratic subjects; Blake was not anti-classical in his tastes: neat alignments of culture and politics were, as on the continent, quite rare.

Questions of Modernity

The unprecedented growth in the eighteenth century of art criticism and aesthetics further empowered an art public already made assertive through an expanding art market. Writers used a range of tones, from the gravely philosophical to the comic, to encourage the development of enlightened, critical and reflective taste. They disseminated an acquaintance with technical issues and with canonical religious and mythological narratives. Eighteenth-century critics often followed templates for the analysis and evaluation of art established in the preceding century, but the emphases on "nature" and feeling were new. If we think of change in terms of momentum, the period stands out for the increasing power of an art public encouraged to be reflective, critical and even irreverent about art.

Further Reading

Harrison, Charles, Paul Wood and Jason Gaiger, eds. 2000. *Art in Theory 1648–1815: An Anthology of Changing Ideas.* Oxford: Blackwell.

Wrigley, Richard. 1993. *The Origins of French Art Criticism: From the Ancien Régime to the Restoration.* Oxford: Clarendon Press.

5

Seeking a Moral Order

The Choice between Virtue and Pleasure

Art as a School of Morals

The process of viewing art, which incorporates both looking and seeing, was in the eighteenth century a deeply moral issue. Forms of looking varied from the voyeuristic to the enlightened, motivations from a search for moral inspiration or knowledge to a quest to please the senses, or the temptation to indulge in visual illusion. As these forms of looking involved not just the sense of sight, but also differing degrees of mental discrimination or judgment, they were associated with a particular viewer's moral constitution or public status. There was, around the middle of the century, a strong desire to enhance art's ability to convey messages relating to both private and public morality. The cult of sensibility emphasized the role of subjective responses (such as weeping) to works of art, as part of a wider engagement with issues of domestic and public morality. Lewd references in works of art often attracted mildly satirical responses, but as the century progressed the increasing desire to exploit the didactic or reformist potential of art made such references seem to many an unwelcome distraction. There were some exceptions, such as the socially segregated circles of some established *connoisseurs*, who continued to seek out the more vicarious attractions of art. Orientalist painting also offered sensual pleasure. By the end of the century there was widespread institutional approval of art related to themes of public utility and virtue, while a considerable underbelly of less moral, scurrilous works persisted.

The desire to attribute a moral purpose to art was inherited from antiquity and had been reinforced by the dominance of the Christian tradition.

A Guide to Eighteenth-Century Art, First Edition. Linda Walsh.

Companion website: www.wiley.com/go/walsh/guidetoeighteenthcenturyart

In his *Nichomachean Ethics* (350 BCE) Aristotle outlines an ideal manner of living:

> Every art and every enquiry, and similarly every action and pursuit, is thought to aim at some good; and for this reason the good has rightly been declared to be that at which all things aim. (Aristotle, 1954 [350 BCE], chapter 1, 1093)

In the early eighteenth century a similar philosophy underlay the views of Shaftesbury. He distinguished between public virtue (as demonstrated through one's role and responsibilities in the social order) and a looser kind of "social" or "natural" affection, but saw the latter as a prerequisite for the former. A "sense of fellowship" was in his view essential to the cohesion of society. He identified decency toward others with beauty in the arts, fusing ethical and aesthetic concerns in the interests of a general harmony or order (Solkin, 1993, 10–12). Such ideals depended heavily on the idea of a universal "high" taste that would lead the (educated) public toward the simultaneous appreciation of beauty and morality located in grand classical and history painting. Shaftesbury's ethics were based on the ideal standards of the ancient Roman Republic, and were exemplified in his discussion of the human dilemma of being torn between the paths of pleasure and virtue (Solkin, 1993, 63–64, 203–204). When envisaging this dilemma, he referred to the mythical tale of Hercules as he faced such a choice. He saw the theme as one of the most elevated that might be tackled by a history painter, and offered detailed advice on how it might be represented visually. The artist Paolo de' Matteis (1662–1728) subsequently followed Shaftesbury's advice in his rendering of the subject. In approaching this mythical moment of crisis, Shaftesbury outlined an area of tension that was to characterize much eighteenth-century artistic debate and practice: the choice between the "superficial" pleasures of the senses and the deeper joys of moral consciousness. Further to this was the type and degree of pleasure to be sought, from that of polite refinement to the excesses of luxury and ostentation; from uncontrolled appetite to its regulation. Shaftesbury's conflation of art with ethics was a common idea by the second half of the eighteenth century. For the judge, philosopher and writer Henry Home, Lord Kames (1696–1782):

> A just taste in the fine arts, by sweetening and harmonizing the temper, is a strong antidote to the turbulence of passion and violence of pursuit. Elegance of taste procures to a man so much enjoyment at home, or easily within reach, that in order to be occupied, he is, in youth, under no

temptation to precipitate into hunting, gaming, drinking; nor, in middle age, to deliver himself over to ambition; nor, in old age, to avarice. (Home, *Elements of Criticism*, 1762, cited in Solkin, 1993, 169)

The "Instrument of Foundation" document of the Royal Academy in London commented that its members would be "men of fair moral characters" (cited in Saumarez Smith, 2012, 69). To Reynolds, knowledge of beauty and refined taste could reach so far "... till that contemplation of universal rectitude and harmony which began by Taste, may, as it is exalted and refined, conclude in Virtue" (cited in Brewer, 1997, 293; and see Kriz, 2001, 55). And yet there was by the end of the century a growing recognition of the separate rather than shared spheres of art and morality.

Moral values depended on the interests of dominant social, political and cultural constituencies. In Britain the moral satires or "modern moral subjects" invented by Hogarth as a distinctively British form of art were grounded in the values of free will and Protestant reform used to challenge the traditional messages of continental Catholic art (Simon, 1987, 13). While such art had propagated the belief that the rewards of virtue might be found in heaven, in Hogarth's modern narrative series these rewards are to be found in the contemporary, human world, as a consequence of the just exercise of our free will and impulse toward self-improvement, with some additional help from a quasi-puritan "providence" arranging the salvation of souls and the wages of sin in a way made acceptable and understandable to a predominantly Anglican Britain (Webster, 1979, 34, 48; Craske, 2000, 16, 22–6, 56–63; Haynes, 2006, 9–10). This didactic strain was linked in Hogarth's work with imaginative story-telling that combined the virtues of "entertainment" with the "higher" realm of the ethical, a combination that would have been problematic to those sharing Shaftesbury's more patrician style of moralizing. Nor was the relationship between art and religion unproblematic. Much of the Italian art valued for its canonical aesthetic value was at the same time a dubious source of "idolatry" or superstition for those committed to more austere Anglican views. Clare Haynes has analyzed these tensions in depth (Haynes, 2006, 1–13). In Britain, national identity was defined, from the Reformation, in opposition to the Catholic Church; church ornamentation was, for example, carefully adapted to specific liturgical traditions (Haynes, 2006, 102–135).

References to human vice and depravity were often secularized in the satirical works of artists such as Hogarth and Goya, through, for example, scatological, pathological, "foppish" and caricatural representations of the human body (Craske, 1997, 235–255). This corresponded with an increasingly critical Enlightenment attitude to religions in general. Poverty, crime and corruption were often associated in satirical art with the Catholic Church in countries such as France, Italy and Spain. Goya's monks are among his most depraved subjects. In mainstream history painting, meanwhile, continental art continued to rise to governmental challenges to proclaim a more positive Catholic morality (see Chapter 2). Nationalistic agendas, such as Hogarth's xenophobia or the French government's desire to consolidate the united powers of church and state, played their part in the determination of the moral values to be promoted (Craske, 2000, 31–33). In secular contexts, a universalizing moral agenda based on the values of ancient Greece and Rome was championed by many Enlightenment thinkers, but often challenged by an increasingly divergent art market. As nations developed their empires, neoclassical values of beauty and morality often came to the fore again, sometimes in order to justify the dominance of western cultures.

The patrician and Christian values upheld in the early part of the century by Shaftesbury and his followers, such as Joseph Addison (1672–1719) and Sir Richard Steele (1672–1729), continued to serve for many throughout the century as a moral exemplar, even when evidently under attack from sources of corruption and dissent. These values encompassed a condemnation of ostentation, duplicity, deceit, fanaticism, avarice, depravity, pretension and cowardice as well as a love of "virtue" and "wisdom." To Shaftesbury such values were gendered as male (Donald, 1996, 32, 81). It was often felt that women must mitigate their "natural" irrationality by cultivating modesty and restraint, if they were to avoid sinking into the vice, depravity and degeneracy captured in images such as Hogarth's *Gin Lane* or his *Marriage à-la-mode* (Donald, 1996, 11; Craske, 1997, 227). However, Hogarth's male figures also exhibited many vices. The most important moral value of the eighteenth century was perhaps moderation. Hogarth's art acknowledged the importance of pleasure; for example, the relatively healthy and modest pleasures of drinking beer, while being opposed to excess of any kind in personal conduct, as in the contemporary love of gin-drinking so prevalent in London from the 1720s to 1750 (Riding, 2006e, 181). Scenes located in familiar urban locations, showing rakes, procuresses, prostitutes, usurers, gamblers and the corrupt, idle and vain, expressed biting visual satire of all social ranks (Webster, 1978, 31, 47, 60; Craske, 1997, 11, 43, 47, 64–68; Krysmanski, 1998, 399–403 Hallett, 2006a, 15; Riding, 2006b, 73–75; 2006c; 2006d, 141). Moderation was regarded as a sign of good breeding and prevented the social disorder so feared in Britain, especially as the Revolution struck in France. Hogarth's morality appealed to the kinds of portrait sitters with whom he mixed: these were from mercantile, professional, ecclesiastical and scientific backgrounds, and in them he often exemplified the "solid" virtues of directness, benevolence, energy and lack of pretension valued in male subjects, or the modesty, politeness, "sincerity" and social ease in their female equivalents (Hallett, 2006d, 160). In his xenophobic view of the continent, such values stood against "foreign" refinement of an overblown or insincere kind.

In France itself, however, "politeness" and a concern with virtue also bound together the moral aspirations of those in the middling ranks and above. The art of Greuze provided, in the middle decades of the century, fashionable scenes of virtuous domesticity. Moral values acquired a different inflection in distinctive political contexts. The autocracy of the French government and the power of the Catholic Church prompted Enlightenment thinkers such as Diderot, Voltaire and Rousseau to prioritize the virtues of tolerance, rationality and the acquisition of knowledge: they stood against ignorance, irrationality, religious superstition and court corruption. This situation contrasted with the generally *bourgeois* court of George III, which attracted less scandal (Brewer, 1997, 16, 19, 21). In both countries, however, the general intellectual climate was against asceticism – "pleasurable living" and sociability being desirable ideals. The pursuit of happiness was a central part of Enlightenment ideology (Porter, 2000, 262–275). There was amongst the French intelligentsia a backlash against official Catholic moral codes, which were distrustful of the senses. Many of Diderot's critical judgments on Greuze's swooning maidens are problematic precisely because they attempt to reconcile sympathy for injured innocence with a "pleasurable" masculine desire (Walsh, 1994, 162–181).

The idea of "Nature" as an ideal moral standard was important in ethical debates across Europe, especially once the ideas of Rousseau, popularized in his international best-selling 1761 novel, *Julie, ou la Nouvelle Héloïse* (*Julie, or the New Heloise*), had taken hold. In Britain the theologian George Turnbull (1698–1748) stated in his 1740 *A Treatise on Ancient Painting, Containing Observations on the Rise, Progress, and Decline of that Art Amongst the Greeks and Romans*, the importance of following the "Order in nature" in both life and the imitations of art:

> A sound and thorough Sense of Beauty, Greatness, and Order in Nature, in Life, or in the fine Arts, will … be best form'd, by such a Course of Instruction and Education, as exercise the Mind in passing from Nature to Imitations, and reciprocally from Imitations to Nature; and in observing that the Beauty and Perfection of Arts, of Life, and of Nature, is the same. (cited in Solkin, 1993, 220)

A concern with "Nature" underlay widespread aversion to affectation of all kinds (Porter, 2000, 295). The advances of civilization should not develop at the expense of the natural world or of reasoned, moderate behavior. Art should improve on, rather than deny or destroy, natural forms (Michel, 2007, 283–284). Truthfulness of the affections should predominate over more superficial forms of gallantry, artifice or affectation, as demonstrated by a developing preference for the conventions of comic or "bourgeois" forms of theater over high-blown serious opera or stage tragedies (Wrigley, 1993, 255; Pointon, 2001, 123).

The question of nudity in art was a testing ground for such values – a respect for the aesthetic attributes of antique nudes or for the "natural" body on which these were based often being weighed against the need for the decency provided by clothing; for example, in the "high style" of art where classical drapery was often used. David's history paintings and Canova's nude sculptures provoked such debates in the late eighteenth and early nineteenth centuries. Contemporary fashions in dress also fueled anxieties. Clothing in the form of extreme or unnatural fashions might distort the body and undermine any suggestion of moral innocence. Those who saw art as a source of moral probity generally disapproved of the overtly erotic (Ledbury, 2007, 201). It has been pointed out, however, that in the eighteenth century the term "erotic" itself signified an association with the affairs of love and the heart; the terms *grivois* ("saucy") and "obscene" being associated more closely with indecency (Michel, 2007, 278). The traditional mythology of antique art could blur the distinction between acceptable and unacceptable nudity through its representations of divine beauty, but the issue was of concern to many critics aware of the potential invasion of moral subjects by distracting sensual detail. Many artists based in Rome painted bacchanalian subjects or motifs: these were popular with Grand Tourists as representations of a culturally endorsed sexuality. Some connoisseurs, especially those associated with the Society of Dilettanti (see Chapter 1), including the connoisseurs Richard Payne Knight (1750–1824), William Hamilton, Charles Townley and Pierre-François Hugues d'Hancarville (1719–1805), reveled in the more licentious aspects of antique art representing fertility rites and primitive religions such as the cult of Priapus (Brewer, 1997, 270–276; Craske, 1997, 241–242; Porter, 2000, 273–274).

While such developments resonated with the more libertarian ideals fostered by Enlightenment thinkers, there was in the 1780s and 1790s a more conservative reaction in social and artistic institutions to such "licence" (Crow, 1985, 105–109). There was concern in the 1780s in France about the fashion for licentious prints (Smentek, 2007, 229). We have already seen in Chapters 2 and 3 how the French state sought to commission history paintings of a more edifying nature. Commentators in Britain and members of the Royal Academy also objected to the "perverted" values of licentious taste. In 1781, the Academy was forced to place plaster fig leaves on exhibited casts and copies of nude sculptures (Brewer, 1997, 242, 275–276), and in the 1790s the decision to place on public display in the Tuileries similar examples of antique statuary led to moral objections (Berger, 1999, 274–279). There were also concerns in Britain about the exposure of female viewers to antique nude exhibition pieces (Kriz, 2001, 58), and artists who refused to seek their female models in brothels were singled out for praise – Reynolds and Gainsborough being among reputable examples.

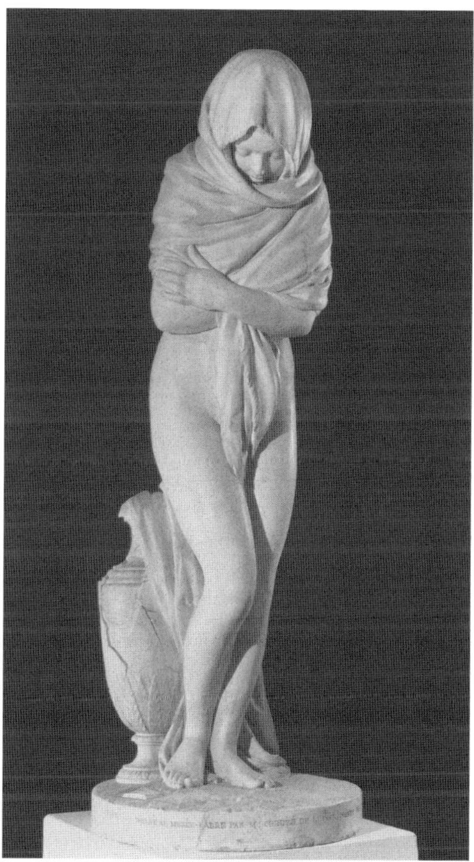

Figure 5.1 Jean-Antoine Houdon: *Winter, or The Chilly Woman*, marble, height 145 cm, 1783. Musée Fabre, Montpellier. Source: Musée Fabre, Montpellier, France/Bridgeman Images.

A classic example of this renewed moralism was the reception of Houdon's sculpture *Winter* (paired with another work, *Summer*) (Figure 5.1) intended for display at the 1785 Salon in Paris. The sculpture represented a part-draped female figure whose "dress" was considered indecent as it achieved little more than drawing attention to the nudity and sexual vulnerability of much of her body. Pierre, then-Director of the Academy, wrote to d'Angiviller to express his concerns about the suitability of this piece for public exhibition and it was subsequently banished from the Salon:

> Two small, half-size figures by M.Houdon were brought in: one, which is draped [*Summer*], is not wonderful, the other might not pass because of the kind of nudity it displays. A completely nude figure is less indecent than those draped with false modesty … let me observe, however, that this figure is the better of the two and that it will be hidden away in a corner. (cited in Poulet, 2003, 225–229)

The work was disturbing in all kinds of ways that unsettled conservative moral and aesthetic hierarchies. It represented an adolescent girl with a water urn in a morally spurious tradition of antique sculpture, specifically the *Callypgian Venus* (*Venus of the Beautiful Buttocks*), a Roman statue from the first or second century BCE believed to be a copy of a Greek original; one version of this sculpture was on display at Versailles. In the 1760s, Greuze's portraits of *ingénues* or part-undressed "innocents" had achieved popularity through their combination of vulnerability (stimulating the moral "sensibility" of the viewer) with a frisson of sexual appeal. By the 1780s, however, not only was social unrest a real concern in France, but Louis XVI had also launched a crusade against licentious art of the kind found in the novels of the Marquis de Sade (1740–1814) in which predatory sexual behavior featured heavily. Increasingly, art critics distinguished between the "legitimate" nudity of elevated history subjects; for example, gods and goddesses representing human and divine attributes, or biblical subjects such as Adam and Eve, and more suspect representations, including the partially clothed or suggestively disrobing female figure (Wrigley, 1993, 309–313).

Houdon's sculpture raised issues connected with the distinction made in our own times by Kenneth Clark (1903–1983) in his *The Nude: A Study of Ideal Art* (1956, 1–25) between the aesthetic qualities of the "nude" and a less morally acceptable form of "nakedness." It was common in the 1780s for neoclassical nudes to invoke ideas of androgyny or sexlessness as a means of editing out of the human body any individual characteristics and emphasizing an antique-inspired process of idealization. But Houdon's figure is given a smile that seems to be complicit with the male gaze and undermines any pretensions to "higher" ideals. She also offends contemporary concerns with female modesty and the physiological vulnerability of adolescents as described in Pierre Virard's 1776 medical text *Essay on Adolescent Girls* (*Essai sur la santé des filles nubiles*). According to Virard, such girls "… should never forget that they carry a treasure [i.e. their virginity] in fragile vases" (Virard, 1776, 38, my translation). The vase was a common emblem of the womb and in Houdon's sculpture it has been shattered by freezing water. The moral reference did little, however, to absolve the work from a charge of licentiousness, in the morally conservative, official artistic culture of the 1780s. Rather, the sculpture played on persistent libertarian tendencies to take pleasure in art from the immoral (Ganofsky, 2015, 24–25).

Ways of Looking, Ways of Seeing

Ways of looking at art had moral implications. Eighteenth-century art often drew attention to its own artifice, its ability to conjure up illusions that could deceive the eye. Such works exploited contemporary obsessions with popular entertainment such as fair pavilions, street theater, masquerade, fancy dress and magic lanterns The Eidophusikon, an entertainment developed in London by Philip-Jacques de Loutherbourg, consisted of images made to appear as if in motion, through the use of mirrors and pulleys, and combined modern technology with "high art" themes. The "panorama" (a term invented in 1788 by Robert Barker, 1739–1806) became a popular tourist attraction consisting of a 360-degree painted representation of a view – in Barker's case *A View from the Top of Carlton Hill, Edinburgh* (Macmillan, 1986, 144; Porter, 2000, 267–268). The crowds also loved puppeteers, magicians and alchemists. A preference for experiencing popular diversions was often associated most closely with the "common" people and with the "lower" genres, such as topographical landscape and still lifes, which gave priority to conjuring up illusions of real objects and places. Contemporary audiences were also interested in more self-centered forms of artifice, altering their physical appearance, for example, through fashion, hairdressing and cosmetics.

Meanwhile, artists often reacted to views of their trade that reduced it to artifice and illusionism. In Goya's print series *Los Caprichos* he satirized the self-delusion and vanity of an obsession with superficial appearances and forms of disguise. In the print *Until Death* (Plate 55, *Hasta la muerte*) an old woman pays embarrassing attention to her reflection in a mirror,

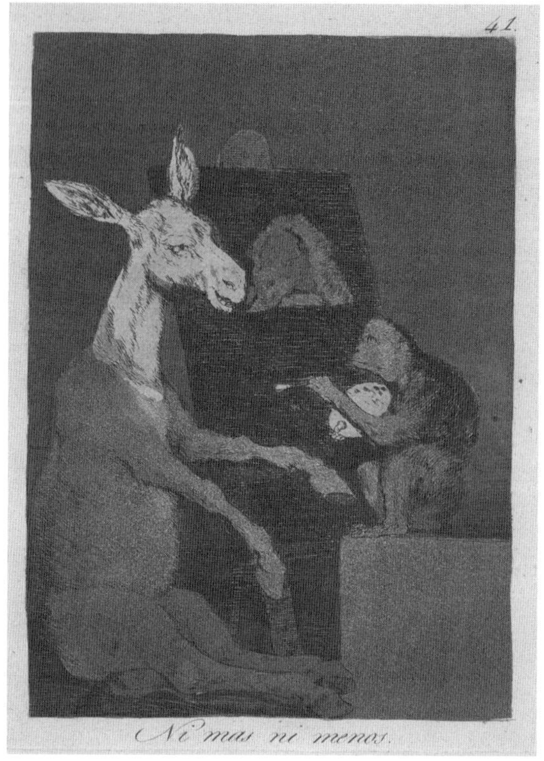

Figure 5.2 Goya (Francisco de Goya y Lucientes): Plate 41 from "*Los Caprichos*": *Neither more nor less (Ni mas ni menos)*, etching, burnished aquatint, drypoint and burin, plate: 19.7 × 14.8 cm; sheet: 29.5 × 20.9 cm, 1799. The Metropolitan Museum of Art, Gift of M. Knoedler & Co., 1918, Acc. No: 18.64(41). Source: The Metropolitan Museum of Art, www.metmuseum.org

and in *Neither More nor Less* (Plate 41, *Ni mas ni menos*) (Figure 5.2) an artist represented as a monkey attempts to create a physical likeness of an aristocrat depicted as a wig-wearing donkey. These 1799 prints show how, at the turn of the century, artists were preoccupied with the morally questionable practice of conjuring or being seduced by appearances. Perspicuity or clear-sightedness found a stylistic analogue in the morally elevated, "virile," linear clarity and spatial logic of David's neoclassical style. They were seen increasingly as an essential requisite of moral viewing (Crow, 1985, 221; Craske, 1997, 230).

Earlier in the century, Hogarth had been interested in a similar theme. His narrative series on a "modern moral subject," *A Rake's Progress*

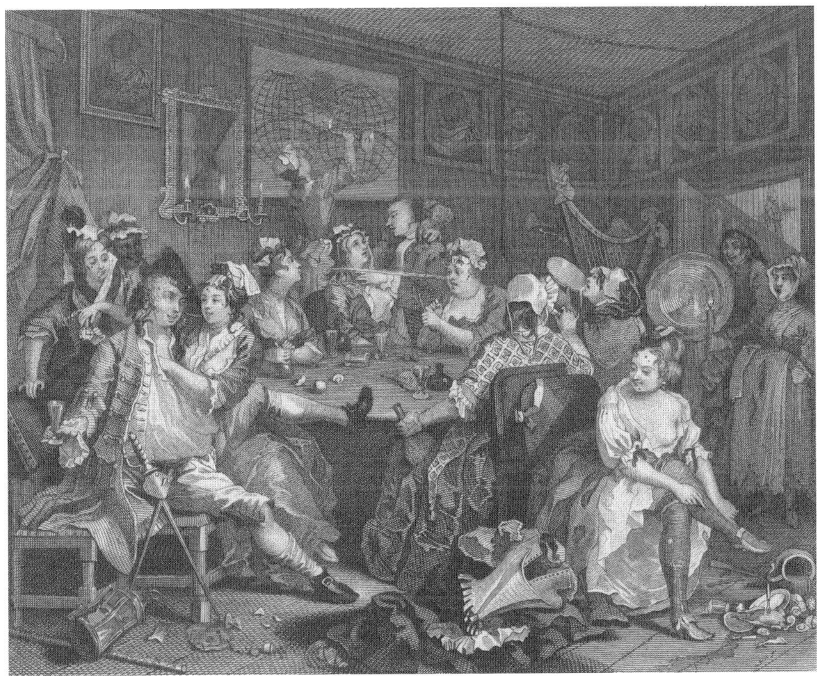

Figure 5.3 William Hogarth: *A Rake's Progress* (Plate 3), etching and engraving on paper, 31.8 × 38.7 cm, 1735. Tate Gallery, London. Source: Hulton Archive/Getty Images.

(painted 1733–1734 and subsequently issued in print form) (Figure 5.3), satirizes the protagonist Tom Rakewell's obsession with appearances as a means of increasing his social standing. *A Harlot's Progress* (which was painted and attracted print subscriptions in 1731) links the deceptions of the masquerade with those of prostitutes, represented as a threat to the moral order (Carter, 1999, 57–79). Such examples relate to concerns about "superficial" forms of representation and looking and are understandable in the context of the Enlightenment, which valued the importance of information gained from the physical senses (including sight) as sources of knowledge and reasoning, rather than as a means of disguise and deception. In such a context the inclusion in Hogarth's titles of the term "progress" appears as a deeply ironic comment on the betrayal of a key Enlightenment value. The theme recurs in those paintings and prints that refer to tricksters and charlatans of all kinds, and was often emblematized (as in Goya's work) through motifs such as the blindfold, the mirror (a symbol of vanity) or card tricks that aimed to deceive the eye. "Seeing" of a moral kind must penetrate the surface of things (Craske, 1997, 44, 145–216). Goya's prints often feature those who cannot see "properly," either because literally blindfolded or myopic in a more general sense, in order to comment satirically on those who misuse sight or surrender to superstition and ignorance rather than the evidence-based knowledge sought by Enlightenment thinkers (Schulz, 2000, 153–181). The sexualized "leer" was also identified as a moral hazard; for example, in Traversi's *The Sitting* (*La Seduta*, 1754) (Figure 5.4), which shows an old woman raising an artist's head so that he focuses on the face, and not the breasts, of his female sitter. On the other hand, the more "open" meanings, loose style of painting and primacy of imaginative effect of Fragonard's art relied on a view of creativity that minimized clear, rational vision (Milam, 1998, 17–23).

The theme of dressing up resonated throughout the century. Paintings on this subject sometimes appealed to the sophisticated insights of the cognoscenti rather than condemning unambiguously their love of playful disguise. Watteau's *fêtes galantes* celebrated the wearing of theatrical costumes, particularly those of his *commedia dell'arte* figures, while evoking a melancholic mood that suggested the fragility of such pleasures.

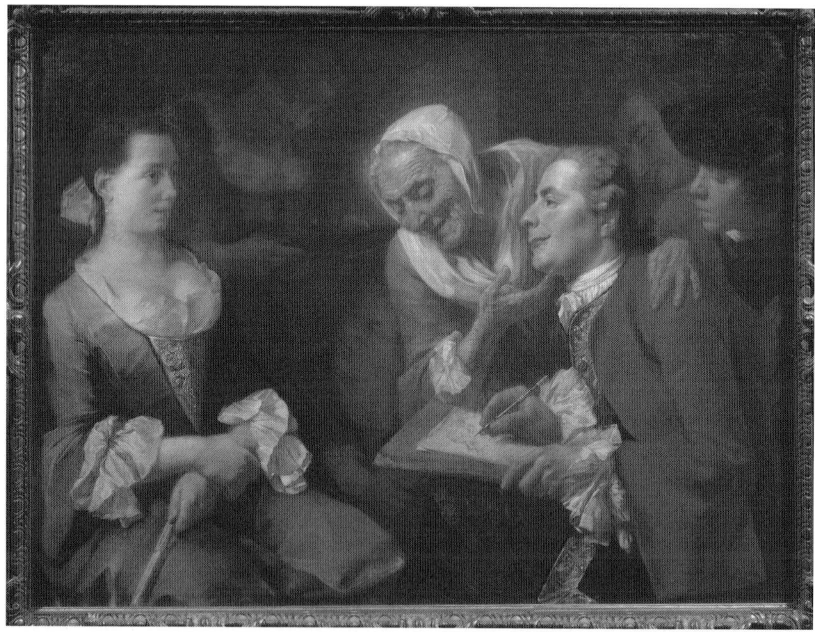

Figure 5.4 Gaspare Traversi: *Posing for a Portrait*, oil on canvas, 100 × 131 cm. 1754. Paris, Musée du Louvre. Source: © 2015. © Photo Josse/Scala, Florence.

The engravings of Jean-Michel Moreau the Younger (1741–1814) also reflected a concern with the deceptive appearances of the theater, represented initially as unproblematic but later (during the Revolution) more negatively (Craske, 1997, 167–168). Fragonard's fantasy figures are often represented in fancy dress (e.g. in a fashionable "Spanish costume") in order to proclaim a form of self-confident social display and appeal to those viewers familiar with deliberately confusing and fantastical social masquerade balls. In Italy, Longhi's images appealed to the Venetian elite by playing on references to the theatrical and deceptive nature of the masquerade and its costumes, while assuming also in the viewer a capacity for clear-sightedness. Longhi exposed the superficial thrill of "looking" in his *Clara the Rhinoceros* (*Clara la rinoceronte*, 1751) representing a crowd of visitors in masquerade costume, including face masks, gawping at a "curious" unfamiliar animal while engaged in carnivalesque concealment of their own bodies: the whole represents to the discerning viewer a travesty of the Enlightenment's search for scientific knowledge. The Macaronies in Britain were a group of aristocrats who, in the 1770s, deliberately sought out and wore outrageous costumes and hairstyles influenced by continental court fashions, such as those associated with Marie Antoinette (Tullett, 2015). Masked balls remained popular in France until the end of the century. There was, however, gathering criticism outside France of such trends (Craske, 1997, 157–160), and even within France the daring fashions of Marie Antoinette identified her eventually as an enemy of the people.

As discussed in Chapter 4, empiricist aspects of Enlightenment ideology placed great emphasis on the impressions or "data" gained by the five senses in the formulation of knowledge and taste, but "sensations" or the crude reflex responses of sense experience were not deemed in themselves to be sufficient to form true knowledge or insight. John Locke had highlighted the role of "sensations" in forming simple ideas in the mind such as brightness, hardness and so on. In the thinking person, however, these data had to be combined and reflected upon in order to allow the formulation of "complex" ideas such as beauty or truth (Locke, 1694, 41, 48, 75, 79). For "sensationist" philosophers throughout the eighteenth century, such as Diderot, Julien Offray de La Mettrie (1709–1751), Claude-Adrien Helvétius (1715–1771) and Étienne Bonnot de Condillac (1714–1780), raw data provided by the sense of sight must be refined in order to form rational ideas about morality or taste.

There were strong views from Enlightenment thinkers on such issues, since an interest in the supernatural, the superstitious, occult and mystical often challenged the rationalism that eighteenth-century thinkers tried so hard to instil in their readers. Giovanni Battista Tiepolo, who held strong Catholic beliefs, continued to be influenced by the supernatural, and his engraved *capriccios* series (*c.*1740–1743) defies rational analysis. Such trends in Venetian art became fashionable in Paris but also lie behind the dark fears represented in Goya's *Los Caprichos, The Sleep of Reason Produces Monsters* (*El sueño de la razon produce monstruos*, Plate 43). Occultist freemasonry was popular in late eighteenth-century Sweden and appealed to the superstitious beliefs of the court of Gustav III (reigned 1771–1792). Spiritualism and the study of dream states had become fashionable there through the influence of the scientist and thinker, Emanuel Swedenborg (1688–1772). Many eighteenth-century artists, including the sculptor Houdon, were also freemasons, a movement imbued with magic and mysticism, although some tried to reconcile such interests with a more rational approach.

Given the complex ways in which vision might influence beliefs or ideas, it is interesting to discover in eighteenth-century art many visual representations of an interest in the processes of looking and seeing. Watteau's *Shop Sign of the Art Dealer Gersaint* (*L'Enseigne de Gersaint*, 1720–1721) (Figure 3.2) provides one such representation of looking at art, within a shop setting. Here some prospective buyers examine, in the background, a circular painting of nymphs in the rococo style. A man indulges in the kind of "close up" looking that expresses both ignorance (the work might be better viewed from afar) and lewdness. Many satirical images used the eyeglass as a signifier of voyeuristic viewing. It might also be used by the *curieux* collector and was seen as a sign of pedantry, lust or moral and intellectual myopia (Wrigley, 1993, 273; Brewer, 1997, 279–81; Craske, 1997, 148–151). This form of looking was often associated with gentleman's club humor or with societies such as the Society of Dilettanti. Zoffany's *The Tribuna of the Uffizi* (1772–7) represents a crowd of male connoisseurs taking advantage of an opportunity to view from close up the anatomical detail of Renaissance and antique nude female figures.

Prints representing exhibition crowds highlighted different ways of seeing and looking: the connoisseurs they featured often representing a patriarchal influence on these processes, mediating the viewing practices of women (Matheson, 2001, 48–53). By the 1780s, the "decorous" influence of women at such exhibitions had also become much more noticeable (Perry, 2007, 64). Prints representing exhibitions emphasized the importance of social interaction in the eighteenth-century viewing of art, as well as the direction and height of the viewer's eye and gaze, not always helpfully aligned, given the crowded wall spaces and throngs of viewers, with the perspective lines in works of art (Solkin, 2001, 1–6). In such a context, the act of looking could be quite chaotic. Viewers might provide as much eye fodder as the works on display, with male viewers just as likely to leer at their female companions as at the women represented in the works displayed, while the women themselves appeared anxious to "study" the appearances of their social equals or betters. Rowlandson's satirical prints represent such complex "looking" as a joke for those who have experienced such events, in which notions of the "civic" and the "polite" may appear precarious (Kriz, 2001, 57–62). Particular types of work, such as actress portraits, seemed to provoke a kind of "flirtatious" male viewing (Perry, 2007, 7–21).

The advances made in the Enlightenment's quests for knowledge and a "true" standard of taste were represented more closely in more serious treatments of the act of looking. Wright of Derby's *Three Persons Viewing the Gladiator by Candlelight* (1765) focuses both on the antique sculpture that gives the painting its title and on the expressions and experiences of those viewing it, as a means of developing their knowledge of antique art. In such paintings the figures become surrogates of the actual viewer. Philippe Mercier's (1689–1760) *The Sense of Sight* (*c*.1744–1747) (Figure 5.5) includes emblematic references to the sense of sight, within a

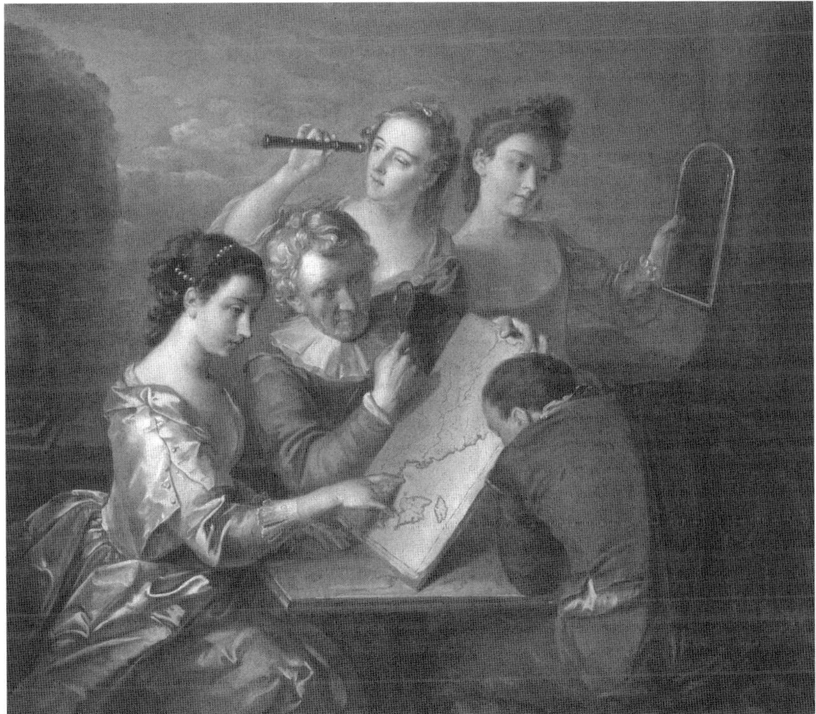

Figure 5.5 Philippe Mercier: *The Sense of Sight*, oil on canvas, 132.1 × 153.7 cm, 1744–1747. Yale Center for British Art, Paul Mellon Collection. Source: Yale Center for British Art, Paul Mellon Collection.

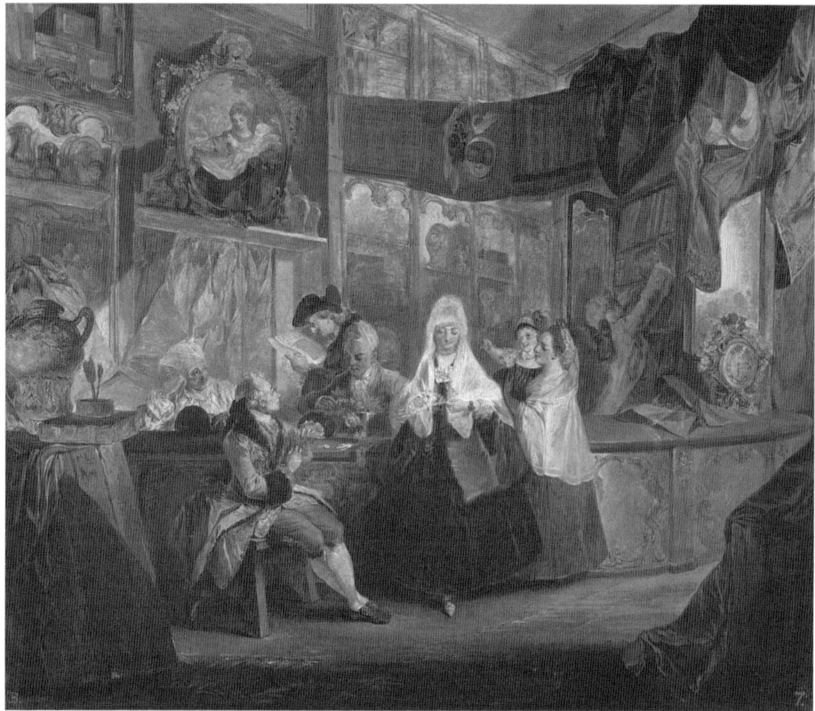

Figure 5.6 Luis Paret y Alcazar: *The Art and Antique Shop*, oil on board, 50 × 58 cm, 1772. Lazaro Galdiano Museum, Madrid. Source: akg-images/Album/Oronoz.

more private yet sociable, "polite" grouping of figures carrying a mirror, eyepiece and magnifying glass as viewing aids.

Viewing, Consumerism and Luxury

Representations of the acts of viewing and seeing, whether in the context of the public exhibition, shop, private collection or domestic life, could provoke ideas about art works as objects of consumerism. Luxury and the acquisition of material goods were among those preoccupations that "polite" society enjoyed yet viewed as a potential threat to more disinterested moral standards. *The Art and Antique Shop* (*La Tienda del anticuario*, 1772) (Figure 5.6) by the Spanish court artist Luis Paret y Alacazar (1746–1799) represents in quite a sympathetic manner a shop setting in which customers are presented with a dazzling array of paintings, rugs, drapes and ornaments that recalls the free play of artistic and decorative objects in rococo interiors. Later, Goya was to adopt a less positive attitude to Spanish attitudes to finery and artifice (Craske, 1997, 170–171). There was no straightforward response, among Enlightenment thinkers, to luxury and its influence on the arts. In France, debates about luxury were often bound up with those concerning the desirability or otherwise of commerce. These were influenced in turn by developments in international trade, colonialism, economics and politics.

It has been suggested that economics as a discipline developed in mid-century France, around the court of Louis XV (Terjanian, 2013, 2–3). The economic devastation provoked by the Seven Years War acted as a catalyst for this, as did Enlightenment figures such as François Quesnay (1694–1774), leader of the Physiocrats, who centered their economic philosophy on the idea that true wealth was to be derived from productive land, or agriculture, and from the free circulation of goods, as was perceived to be the case in England (Terjanian, 2013, 4–5). The Physiocrats believed that trade should be freed so that agricultural prices might rise and the profits be reinvested in this "healthy" and "natural" form of wealth (Terjanian, 2013, 33). Such theories were perceived as a threat to traditional mercantilism, favored by the French government and based on the idea that the world contained finite resources or wealth that should be seized and controlled by the state through, for example, state-run monopolies, aggressive military conflict and colonial enterprise. Voltaire, offended by Christian asceticism, saw commerce as a valuable means of increasing social prosperity. The poem *Commerce* by Firmin Douin, published on the eve of the Seven Years War, was awarded a certificate of merit by the French Academy. It asserted obsequiously that commerce would render "the Empire of Lilies [the Bourbons] even more flourishing,/The French happier and Louis more powerful" (cited and translated in Terjanian, 2013, 1). Other Enlightenment thinkers made careful distinctions between good and bad types of commerce. Montesquieu felt that commerce could both civilize and corrupt. The *Histoire des deux Indes* (*History of the Two Indies*), edited and part-written by Raynal, Diderot and others and published in 1770, had a massive impact on contemporary readers, with 48 editions published between 1770 and 1795, and translations in English, German, Russian, Italian, Spanish, Dutch, Danish, Swedish and Hungarian. It was banned in 1772 by the French government in response to its critical attitude to empire, which it saw as a source not only of national glory, but also of piracy, trade monopolies and slavery.

A similar ambivalence characterized views on luxury, sometimes confused with commerce and at other times distinguished from it, embodied in the eighteenth century through the visible increase in global trade in coffee, chocolate, silk, fine porcelain and the decorative arts. Attitudes varied according to whether luxury was conceived as "abundance" or "superfluity" (Terjanian, 2013, 46–51). There was a sense that the lifestyle associated with such luxuries was new, even though ancient civilizations had previously enjoyed similar peaks in material wealth (Terjanian, 2013, 30). The "modern" tastes of polite society embraced the association of luxury with economic benefit and refinement, while the more conservative saw it as potentially corrupting and unhealthily ostentatious. Colonial commerce in luxury items attracted criticism, but was often excused in the name of a burgeoning national pride (Quilley, 2011, 145–164). Diderot, who enjoyed, like many Enlightenment thinkers, the life of a *bon viveur*, distinguished between the "good" kind of luxury derived from a soundly founded national wealth and "bad" luxury, a kind of excess or greed that thrived in a political climate of corruption and had a pernicious effect on the arts:

> ... it's this [kind of luxury] that degrades and destroys the fine arts, for their continued health and progress require genuine opulence, whereas this brand of luxury does nothing but fatally mask a misery that's almost general, which it aggravates and encourages. It's under the tyranny of this luxury that talents are wasted or sidetracked. It's in such circumstances that the fine arts must make do with the dregs left to those of inferior status; it's in such extraordinary, perverse circumstances that they're either subordinated to the fantasy and caprice of a handful of rich, bored, fastidious men, their taste as corrupt as their morals, or they're abandoned to the mercy of the indigent multitude, which strives, with poor work in all genres, to take on some of the credit and the lustre associated with wealth. In the present century and under the present reign the impoverished nation has framed not a single grand enterprise, no great works, nothing that might nourish the spirit and exalt the soul. At present great artists don't develop at all or are compelled to endure humiliation to avoid dying of hunger. At present there are a hundred easel paintings for every large composition, a thousand portraits for every history painting; mediocre artists proliferate and the nation is flooded with them. (Diderot, 1995b, 77)

Rousseau, who adopted a bleak view of the ways in which civilization had corrupted nature and morality, was also eloquent in his condemnation of this kind of luxury, which he saw as a threat to our humanity and a source of unhealthy inequalities (Terjanian, 2013, 34–39).

In Britain and Holland, a number of moral thinkers participated in a lively debate on luxury. The Dutch philosopher and economist Bernard

Mandeville strove, in his 1705 poem *The Fable of the Bees or, Private Vices, Public Benefits*, to undermine Shaftesbury's view that social affections and a sense of rational restraint could help to mitigate the selfishness underlying an enjoyment of material wealth. To Mandeville, what appears as virtue is often actually vice (pride, vanity, egoism) in disguise. He considered, however, that vices such as self-indulgence in luxury had a positive role to play in stimulating the wealth and well-being of a nation: where, for example, would the fashion industry be, without the "vice" of pride? In this way, private vices might produce public virtue, rather than having to be mitigated by personal virtues. Other theorists praised the potential of luxury while failing to identify it, as Mandeville had done, as a by-product of vice. Jean-François Melon (1675–1738) in his *Essay on Commerce* (*Essai sur le commerce*, 1734), Voltaire in *The Worldly One* (*Le Mondain*, 1736), Jean-François de Saint Lambert (1716–1803) in his article "Luxury" (*Luxe*) in the *Encyclopédie* and Georges-Marie Butel-Dumont (1725–1788) in his *Theory or Treatise on Luxury* (*Théorie ou Traité du luxe*, 1771) helped to popularize similar messages about the benefits of luxury, variously perceived as the marker of a civilized nation, a stimulus to employment and generator of wealth. Francis Hutcheson challenged Mandeville's elevation of "vice," questioning the social usefulness of spending on luxuries and reasserting the importance of a "moral sense" in human beings that was compatible with the pleasures gained from wealth, especially when gained from industriousness. This positive ideology informed many portraits of elite families, such as Hogarth's *Wollaston Family* (1730).

David Hume also took a more positive view of the possibility of combining strong moral impulses with the pursuit of material wealth essential to a commercial society (Susato, 2006, 167–168). In his essay "Of Refinement in the Arts" (1752), he saw wealth derived from knowledge and industriousness as an asset, rather than as a deterrent, to refined manners and humanity. Of the wealthy, he said:

> They flock into cities; love to receive and communicate knowledge; to show their wit or their breeding; their taste in conversation or living, in clothes or furniture.... Both sexes meet in an easy and sociable manner; and the tempers of men, as well as their behaviour, refine apace. So that, besides the improvements which they receive from knowledge and the liberal arts, it is impossible but they must feel an encrease [sic] in humanity... (Cited in Solkin, 1993, 157)

A blending of wealth with humanity was visible in the eighteenth-century propensity of the rich to support and visit charitable institutions such as the Foundling Hospital, where they were received in splendidly decorated public rooms (Solkin, 1993, 159–162). Adam Smith, a student of Hutcheson's, situated the debate about material wealth in a historical context, in his *The Wealth of Nations*, by explaining how societies had evolved over the centuries away from a concern with the basic necessities of life to a concern with "amusements" or "luxury," as opulence spread more widely across populations. While seeing commerce as a positive force in society, he did not approve of greedy or irresponsible companies, thus highlighting more than Mandeville the human virtues of restraint and social responsibility (Smith, 1970, 480). To Louis-Sébastien Mercier, however, in his utopian work of 1770, *The Year 2440: A Dream if Ever There Was One* (*L'An 2440: rêve s'il en fut jamais*), the taste for luxury generated colonial bloodshed, mental dysfunction and moral bankruptcy (Terjanian, 2013, 51–53); and Voltaire became less positive about the effects of luxury in the wake of the race for colonial riches that constituted the Seven Years War (Terjanian, 2013, 54). As European countries established their colonies in North America, the quest for riches became associated with absentee landlords of slave plantations, neglect of their homeland estates, the excesses of royal estates, servitude, addiction and personal debt (Terjanian, 2013, 57–67).

Genre and audience played important roles in the approaches to luxury in visual culture. Artists such as Paret y Alcazar, Hogarth and Joseph van Aken (*c*.1699–1749) completed conversation pieces or serious genre paintings, such as the latter's *An English Family at Tea* (*c*.1720; see Solkin, 1993, 67), which took seriously both the wealth and the virtue of those who had commissioned their works. Hogarth's satirical series presented an opportunity for more independent comment. His unusually independent status within the art market meant that he was able to satirize the pretensions of wealth, particularly the aping of foreign fashions, in narrative series such as *Marriage à-la-Mode*. Ironically, he marketed such series in both popular and luxury (framed) editions (Donald, 1996, 78–85; Riding, 2006d, 141–142). Women were often blamed for an unhealthy consumption of luxury goods (Donald, 1996, 78–80; Brewer, 1997, 81; Perry, 2007, 189).They were held responsible, for example, for encouraging others to peer into – and perhaps purchase from – print shop windows exhibiting "impure" images, thereby posing a threat to the realms of "higher," genteel taste (Brewer, 1997, 76). Their obsession with fashion was also blamed for making men effeminate and undermining more "natural" values (Donald, 1996, 86–89; Kriz, 2001, 60).

Attitudes to wealth and luxury varied in accordance with national economics and politics. Hogarth's 1721 print *The South Sea Scheme* offers critical comment on a recent public–private initiative in Britain, the foundation in 1711 of the South Sea Company, which traded in stock that was intended to help reduce the national debt. After rising in value, the stock rapidly declined, however, thus creating a "bubble" effect that was to prompt suspicion on a massive scale of financial speculation, corruption or gambling of all kinds (Craske, 2000, 44–45; Walcot, 2012, 413–432). Like many other eighteenth-century artists and thinkers, Hogarth preferred more moderate wealth built on solid foundations. In France, prior to and during the Revolution, debates about luxury coincided with those on the need to regenerate society (Wrigley, 1993, 204–206). Meanwhile in Britain, French fashions were both a source of desire and symbols of the political bondage or corrupt court behavior of their nation of origin (Donald, 1996, 81). Resistance to such trends was particularly marked in rural areas, which popular prints often represented as at risk of pollution by "city ways" (Donald, 1996, 82–83).

Important shifts in attitude occurred. Across Europe, toward the end of the century, it became more acceptable to separate the realms of art and taste from those of politics and public morality, as conceptions of an autonomous subjectivity in matters of taste became more common due to the development of a diversified, market-led culture. As a wider public engaged with art, so the language of self-denial became less important and it became more acceptable for private individuals to enjoy some of the more sensuous and delicate effects of art: this development allowed Benjamin West, for example, to draw freely on the coloristic and sensuous brushwork effects of artists such as Titian and Correggio (Solkin, 1993, 181–97). In the aftermath of the French Revolution, leisure and entertainment industries revived, so that aesthetic, rather than political, critiques of art and fashion became more common (Donald, 1996, 89–108). This separation of the realms of the aesthetic and the ethical was among the issues examined by Kant. He developed the views of Baumgarten (Kaufman, 1995, 449–458; and see Chapter 4), who saw a sense of the beautiful in art (as opposed to nature) as separate from the concerns of morality:

> Now I am quite willing to concede that an interest in the *beautiful in art* (in which I include the artistic use of natural beauties for our adornment, and hence for vanity's sake) provides no proof whatever that [someone's] way of thinking is attached to the morally good, or even inclined toward it. (*Critique of Judgment*, 1790, in Kant, 1987 [1790], 165)

This separation of the ethical and the aesthetic had been at most a sporadic or implicit undercurrent earlier in the century, particularly at the height of the fashion for the rococo. For example, the sensuous and successful appeal of the works of artists such as Watteau, Fragonard and Boucher had claimed few moral or didactic aims (Crow, 1985, 70; Wrigley, 1993, 280; Plax, 2000, 81; Barker, 2005, 119; Michel, 2007, 286). Even art that represented more humble or restrained moments of contemporary life, such as Chardin's genre paintings, could be valued for its formal values (use of color, light and composition) and appeal to the senses rather than for its moral content. However, there was a compulsion among the wider public to "textualize" such images through the addition, often in engraved copies, of explanatory captions that turned them into moral emblems or narratives (Crow, 1985, 137; Wrigley, 1993, 297–298). Prints became, from the middle of the century, a popular vehicle for the ideals of domestic, sentimentalized moral values (Retford, 2006, 17). Private scenes from the life of the "polite" became a more promising ground for moral edification at times when faith in the ability of the history genre to embody such noble aims was relatively low. Through the middle decades of the eighteenth century, genre paintings in France began to place significant emphasis on moral themes. Theorists began to see the "naïve" or everyday as an alternative means of moral instruction to the grand style of history, their "truth" replacing an emphasis on the sublime or heroic (B. Gaehtgens, 2003, 52–56).In Britain too, private life became the most fertile context for the dissemination of moral messages or themes in art, as the values of civic humanism, formerly the preserve of the elite, were transformed into a wider public discourse of virtue and sentiment (Solkin, 1993, 169).

Toward the end of the century, however, art free of any overt moralizing function became more common. Artists such as Rowlandson, Barry and Fuseli openly prioritized (in the case of Rowlandson) humor and social satire, or (in the case of the others) drama or the terrors of the essentially amoral sublime (Craske, 1997, 27, 183–188). Rowlandson built on the tradition of Hogarth and other earlier satirists in using humor to provide a kind of social and moral self-regulation that was the antithesis of the ambition of grand history painting to make moral pronouncements from on high (Craske, 2000, 11–13, 35–36). The use of satirical or subversive prints was effective in a climate of taste sufficiently consensual to make evident the targets of their humor, and in a climate that was the product of an open-minded context of "civic accord" (Craske, 2000, 11). The novelist Henry Fielding (1707–1754) had helped the public to distinguish between serious-minded satire and mere entertainment or caricature, distancing Hogarth's works from the latter. Even grotesque or caricatural distortions became more acceptable later in the century, however, as the public saw humor and social comment as mutually reinforcing.

The grotesque bodies of Rowlandson's figures provided a counterpoint to idealized classical figures or to the "polite" modes of representation typical of genteel conversation pieces (Kriz, 2001, 62).

The victims or targets of satirical prints in Britain rarely prosecuted caricaturists or print-sellers for libel, choosing instead to buy up all offending copies of a print run: this happened in the case of prints mocking the Prince of Wales. In post-Revolutionary France similar prints on the nation's leading citizens brought at most warnings issued by the judiciary (Donald, 1996, 15–16). Satire became increasingly valued as the sign of a politically free nation in which free speech might thrive and, as the century wore on, as a vehicle for good humor rather than venomous lampoons. This development was marked in France after the end of the Revolution, during which satirical prints (especially those aimed at the royal family) had reached new depths of savagery (Donald, 1996, 31–34). The self-ordering society, able to regulate its moral standards through standing back and scrutinizing its own follies and foibles, and able to share on a wider basis the cultural references to allow this, contrasted with earlier ideals of court or patrician leadership that had seemed to demand a more explicit form of didacticism. Social and moral satire became gentrified as, in the hands of Rowlandson and others, it changed its emphasis from morally incisive comment to gentlemanly ribbing (Donald, 1996, 34–35, 75–108).

Exploring Moral Boundaries: Orientalism, the Senses and the Imagination

The eighteenth-century taste for Oriental themes in art expressed a further indirect means of exploring moral issues. In inspiring fantasies of "other" cultures and lifestyles, it was attuned to the mode for sensuous luxury. It resonated with the Enlightenment impulse to examine all conventions, including those of morality, in an open fashion and celebrated the growing status in thinking on art of the creative imagination (Chapter 1). For those keen on masquerade, adventure and disguise, Orientalist art provided an opportunity to explore through the imagination new identities.

Edward Said's "Orientalism" (1978) established a scholarly tradition of examining critically western representations of the "East," especially the Middle East, Islamic peoples and Arab cultures. By imagining and (mis-) representing such peoples and cultures as "other" to themselves, western writers and artists could turn them into objects of curiosity, fantasy and exoticism, which justified their own imperial sense of moral superiority while at the same time creating desirable visions of the transgressive. Although Said subsequently modified his views on "otherness" (Barringer, Quilley and Fordham, 2007, 5), he considered that the "Orient" may be seen as a "semi-mythical construct" or ideological generalization (Said, 2003 [1978], xiii) acting through history as a convenient foil to over-simplified western values such as democracy, enlightenment and modernity. Said identifies the eighteenth century as a period that prepared the ideological ground for Orientalism as a discrete area of study (cultural, political and ideological) in the nineteenth century.

The eighteenth-century Enlightenment broadened, through its travel literature, fictional utopias and voyages of exploration, earlier identifications of the "Orient" with Islamic lands of the eastern seaboard of the Mediterranean (unfamiliar and therefore intriguing to many Europeans until the nineteenth century), and opened them up to include China, Japan, India, Africa (represented in exotic splendor in the "Africa" ceiling at the Würzburg Residenz by Giovanni Battista Tiepolo), America and even those unfamiliar aspects of Spain, Russia and Greece mythologized as "primitive" (Michel, 2003, 106; Lemaire, 2013, 7). The Enlightenment began a trend, for example, in the writings of the historian Edward Gibbon, for comparing contemporary European experience and values with those of other, older civilizations and, beyond that, engaged sympathetically with such civilizations. Its writers often applied a scholarly approach we would now characterize as historicist (seeing a culture from the perspective of its own time) and humanist (reflective scholarship approached in a spirit of community with, rather than hostility toward, the cultures studied). Attitudes to the "east" became increasingly secularized. Christian attitudes toward it were challenged by geographical and historical reference points extending beyond those of the Bible and were reconstructed as and naturalized within the emergent discipline of anthropology (Said, 2003, 116–121). However, the "Orient" was also viewed at times in a sensationalized way, as a popular vogue in the late eighteenth century. New developments in knowledge could also produce reductive perspectives on the east.

Orientalist images could be historically specific and documentary in nature. Many artists strove to document with some accuracy the costumes, settings and daily life encountered in these regions (Tarabra, 2006, 296; Bindman, Boucher and Weston, 2011b, 79; Lemaire, 2013, 66–76, 118; Ribeiro, 2015, 38–39). Orientalist painting may be interpreted as one of the outcomes of the Enlightenment's quest for critical scholarship (Craske, 1997, 117, 129). Arabic and Persian literature became available in translation; scientists, explorers and the visits of ambassadorial staff facilitated east–west exchanges. The letters of Lady Mary Wortley Montagu (1689–1762), wife of the British Ambassador to Constantinople (present-day Istanbul), were published posthumously in 1763. In France, Enlightenment intellectuals such as Montesquieu, in his *Persian Letters* (written in 1721), Voltaire, in *Zadig* (1747), and Diderot, in his *The Indiscreet Jewels* (published anonymously in 1748), wrote works of philosophically inclined fiction in which the west was "seen" or represented obliquely and often satirically through Orientalist narratives. Although these narratives were fantasy tales, they took seriously the moral and political lessons to be learned from contact with the wider world. There were also an increasing number of European Orientalist scholars interested in anthropological enquiry, including comparative religion, Richard Payne Knight being among their number.

It was common, however, for Orientalist paintings to be infused by the "exotic" (a term not used in the eighteenth century itself), a voyeuristic fantasy of the east that often removed "Oriental" subjects from specific historical, cultural or geographical contexts, inscribing them instead with an "acultural illegibility" that enabled vicarious forms of pleasure (Guest, 1992, 102–104). Western artists specialized in ethnographic, documentary or fantasy images of the east depending on their accustomed styles of painting. Most of their representations remained figurative, even though much art from the east itself, particularly from Islamic cultures, was non-figurative: the style or manner of painting of western artists was not affected to any significant degree by the sights they had witnessed or imagined. The Ottoman Empire had inspired from the seventeenth century both fear and wonder and was mediated in the eighteenth century through western interests not just in the ethnographic but also in the decorative and the beautiful. As has already been seen with *chinoisierie*, some western styles such as the rococo were thought to provide a suitable stylistic language for Orientalist subjects.

Documentary interests could easily spill over into a celebration of the "exotic." In 1748 Vien organized at the French Academy in Rome an "exotic" carnival of Muslim culture and costumes based on a documentary series of costume studies, and held in honor of the visit to the Academy by Dominique, Cardinal de la Rochefoucauld (1712–1800) (Bindman, Boucher and Weston, 2011b, 86–89). Orientalist subjects were easily subsumed within the western imaginary. The vogue for Orientalism peaked in the first half of the eighteenth century and re-emerged in the 1780s. Europeans commissioned portraits of themselves in Turkish dress in order to explore new, fantasy identities (Lemaire, 2013, 58, 109–111)

(Figure 5.7, see color plate section). Venetian artists, including Francesco Lazzaro Guardi (1712–1793), popularized the "Turkish look" (Lemaire, 2013, 54–66). At the French court, Mme de Pompadour, Mlle de Clermont (full name Louise-Marie-Anne de Bourbon-Condé, 1673–1743) and Marie Antoinette were among those represented in portraits as a Turkish Sultana, sometimes to mark lavish court receptions in honor of visiting Persian and Turkish dignitaries.

These images formed part of the discourse of luxury and celebrated indirectly European commercial pre-eminence (Bindman, 2008, 16; Bindman, Boucher and Weston, 2011b, 79–83). Zoffany's British portrait of Queen Charlotte with her two sons follows implicitly in this tradition (Pointon, 1993, 163). It overflows with Chinese motifs, Turkish carpets and costumes, as well as luxury goods from Germany and Flanders, that underline the Queen's possession of the highest quality goods from all over the world. Such positive, emotive representations of overseas trade and exotic wealth, expressed even in the children's costumes, could serve simultaneously to express and justify an imperialist mentality, "ownership" of foreign cultures and the following of fashion (Solkin, 1993, 195). Augustus the Strong of Saxony commissioned Turkish subjects from Johann Samuel Mock (1687–1737).

In paintings such as Boucher's *Odalisque*, the east became the loosest possible excuse for the representation of erotic subjects on the general theme of the courtesan or the harem – the latter made more familiar to westerners through works such as *A Full and Just Account of the Present State of the Ottoman Empire* (1709) by Aaron Hill (1685–1750). Turkish dress often allowed western sitters to expose more of their bodies in a way that was prevented by conventional fashions. Liotard, who had also painted more documentary eastern scenes, participated actively as an artist in the construction of such fictions, dressing himself in a caftan as he worked. The artistic vogue for *turqueries* coincided with and was reinforced by social practices such as the masquerade.

Vicarious pleasure in "Oriental" adventure was often based on racial stereotyping and muddled western thinking. Anthropological understanding of racial difference is thought to have originated in the later Enlightenment. Earlier in the eighteenth century, western representations of "other" races were often based on stereotypes or composites: Chinese–Japanese–Indian "hybrids" being symptomatic of the latter. The stereotypical view of Turks veered in the eighteenth century between that of the brutal warrior and its counterpart: the languid, sensual man or woman at ease. The court of the Ottoman Empire at Constantinople was associated in the early part of the century with power, affluence, military valor, cruelty (e.g.in succession killings), mythic female beauty and a liberal sexuality that nourished western fantasies. By the end of the century, there was a greater awareness of larger racial groupings; for example, the inclusion of Turks in the "family" of Indo-European ethnicity. For much of the century, however, loosely defined "Orientals" remained a common fantasy of western art.

Moral Feeling, Moral Looking

If Orientalist art celebrated the "senses," the development of a cult of "sensibility" created a moralizing strain of artistic production. In the same way as crude "sensations" or sense impressions were felt to be inadequate in themselves for the development of cognitive processes, more sophisticated modes of feeling were theorized, in the eighteenth century, as the basis of our moral impulses. The middle decades of the century have been characterized as the high point of the cult of "sensibility" (*sensibilité*) in the sense of refined moral feelings (Pagden, 2013, 53–78). Manifestations of this movement in art and culture are often referred to as sentimentalism. Although eighteenth-century culture, particularly in science and philosophy, promoted the use of reason, this was not felt to be incompatible with the private cultivation and public display of emotion; for example, in response to scenes of virtue in distress. In the early decades of the century "sensations" (of sight, hearing, touch and so on) were regarded as useful empirical sources not only for the formulation of our more complex ideas and knowledge generally, but also for the formulation of subtler feelings or intuitions about what was morally acceptable. "Sensations" had an affective dimension as they were deemed, even in their crudest form, to be "agreeable" or "painful." This was acknowledged in the 1736 work, *Theory of Agreeable Sentiments* (*Théorie des sentiments agréables*) by Lévesque de Pouilly. Sometimes the term "sensation" was used interchangeably with other terms indicating the emotions in general. The term *sentiment* was normally reserved, however, for feelings (or mental intuitions) of a more refined nature, qualified or sanctioned by our powers of reason. It was this kind of feeling that lay behind many of the mid-century pronouncements of critics and the general public about their moral responses to art.

When the fashion for sensibility was at its height, the viewer's capacity for "sympathetic imagination" or for empathy with the figures in paintings and sculptures was very important. The emotions indicated by a figure's facial expression, pose or general context could all play a part in activating these channels of sympathy:

> It is the hidden relationship of these different expressions with our own individual states of mind, that brings sympathy into play. (Lévesque de Pouilly, 1971 [1747], 74; my translation)

Moral "sentiments" were distinguishable from the anarchy and violence of "passion." Facilitating a viewer's sympathetic engagement with the concerns of figures represented in art, "sentiments" could turn art into a school of morals:

> Every piece of sculpture or painting must express a great maxim, a lesson for the spectator; otherwise it is mute. (from *Diverse Thoughts on Painting* or *Pensées détachées sur la peinture*, 1772 in Diderot, 1968, 765; my translation)

Artists devised a range of strategies in order to engage the viewer imaginatively in morally significant scenes. These ranged from a deployment of the explicitly coded expressive stereotypes of Le Brun, to representing more "absorptive" or meditative expressions that of emotion engaged the viewer while seeming implicitly to indicate less awareness of the viewer's presence (Walsh, 1996, 523–524).

Moral looking was inflected by the viewer's position in the social order in relation to those of the figures and situations represented in a work of art. This was particularly the case with genre paintings relating to contemporary life. Greuze's genre paintings were popular from the mid-1750s to the early 1780s. Emma Barker has argued that the artist's carefully composed, emotive scenes treated themes of genuine relevance to his contemporaries and in a way that they found aesthetically desirable (Barker, 2005, 3–9). His genre paintings often drew on fashionable contemporary literary themes such as those explored in the novels of Samuel Richardson, including his *Clarissa: or the History of a Young Lady* (1748), in which virtuous (and less socially secure) heroines fell victim to deceiving rakes of 'superior' social status enabled by a seemingly complicit society. Other influences included tearful comedies written by Pierre-Claude Nivelle de la Chaussée (1692–1754); and Rousseau's *Julie, or the New Héloïse* (*Julie, ou la nouvelle Héloïse*, 1761), in which the highly sensitive (*sensible*) heroine Julie both sheds and provokes tears as she wrestles with a conflict between personal inclination and social duty, in matters of the heart.

The tears shed over such subjects, whether provoked by Richardson's novels or Greuze's paintings, helped to create a community of feeling that spread from private and subjective to publicly shared responses (Barker, 2005, 52–54). Sarah Maza has argued that the high valuation of family sentiment crossed class boundaries (Maza, 1997). The social values (e.g. meritocracy) that developed as a consequence of such shared concerns began to challenge those of an older aristocratic order. The realms of the family and of civil society represented in genre paintings, relatively private by comparison with those of the church and state, educated the bourgeoisie in the values they might now embrace as a new, economically active public (Barker, 2005, 15). Greuze's *The Village Bride* (*L'Accordée de village*, 1761) (Figure 5.8, see color plate section), in which a young girl's dowry is presented by her father, and in the presence of her family, to her prospective bridegroom, could be read as a representation of a rural family generating the "good wealth" arising from productive cultivation of the land that was so valued by the Physiocrats (Barker, 2005, 46–64). Additionally, the (male) viewer might "enter" the painting by proxy, perhaps identifying with the girl's fiancé and being "seduced" into protecting her virtue through the arousal of his own desire (Barker, 2005, 52–54).

In order for such subjects to convey moral messages, a particular kind of ideal viewer was often assumed: male (often susceptible to the sight of attractive, vulnerable women), patriarchal, sympathetic and receptive to reformist ideas. A viewer of this kind might even be imagined as inscribed into the fabric of such works, which dealt with socially relevant themes such as the legal and social aspects of marriage, models of good fatherhood or the way in which families treat older people (Crow, 1985, 163). Greuze's works suggested little by way of a different life for women, except insofar as they might benefit from the better morals of those men who surrounded them (Barker, 2005, 75, 238–240). Later in his career the content of Greuze's work was less idealistic, yet continued to inspire many imitators, including Étienne Aubry (1745–1781) and Lépicié (Brookner, 1972, 138–155; Conisbee, 1981, 168). His failure to acquire the status of history painter (see Chapter 2) and growing criticism of his technique; for example, in his figure drawing, which was increasingly, from the 1780s, compared negatively with David's, played their part in the collapse of his career. In addition, Greuze realized perhaps that the kind of reforms at which his works hinted were not yet welcomed by more self-seeking constituents of the public – as we have seen, immorality remained a common concern in France in the 1780s. Fragonard's art continued at that time to appeal to those who sought a freer style of painting in which looser brushwork and amoral subject matter flattered older, aristocratic tastes (Barker, 2005, 115–119). Greuze's reputation as an accomplished painter of portraits began to outshine his efforts to instil through genre painting the kind of moral gravity consonant with reformist Enlightenment values.

During the French Revolution the moralizing potential of genre paintings, now more prevalent in the Salons, found fresh resonance in the new political climate. A new emphasis on family values, freedom and Nature was commonly expressed. Children began to be represented as freer and more spontaneous and not, as before, as convention-bound miniature adults (Kayser, with Salmon and Hugues, 2003, 14). Notions of the family were deployed in a polemical way, the concept of the "fatherland" being central to the Revolution's ideology. Due in part to the influence of Rousseau, children were often represented in family scenes as embodiments of the kind of natural innocence that had preceded a corrupt society (Schama, 1989, 770).

In Britain, contemporary experiences of empire; for example, through images of sea voyages and shipwrecks, were represented in an emotive way in order to assert the values of sentiment, family, community, heroism and sacrifice increasingly identified as core elements of a national identity (Quilley, 2011, 113–164).

The cult of sensibility has often been viewed retrospectively as inauthentic or shallow; as a conflicting nexus of feelings that evoked "virtuous" responses infused by sexual impulses: a charge increasingly laid against the responses of male viewers to Greuze's seductively wilting heroines. In the eighteenth century itself the responses of Diderot and the art critic Mathon de la Cour initiated a tradition of the "Greuze girl" as a moral enigma representing, like the Houdon figure discussed above, both the kind of lost innocence that might evoke paternal responses and a more provocative voluptuousness evident in an age of "modern" ideas on sexuality (Fort, 2007, 142–143; Lajer-Burcharth, 2007, 201–207; Barker, 2012b, 86–87, 93). The mode for sensibility has also been suspected of arousing the facile sensations associated with those experienced at popular theater performances. Audiences wept copiously while viewing a new style of bourgeois drama focusing on issues from contemporary life (Ledbury, 1997; Barker, 2005, 3–9; Fort, 2007, 130). However, sentimentalism in art enjoyed in the eighteenth century a more positive reception. It was regarded initially as an authentic and welcome reaction against artifice, and as a badge of social and moral virtue (Brewer, 1997, 113–114, 118–121). In Britain, its reputation suffered toward the end of the century, when it was seen increasingly, and in its more extreme forms, as an unpatriotic surrender to the pernicious influence of "foreign" thinkers such as Rousseau and Goethe. The latter's *The Sorrows of Young Werther* (*Die Leiden des jungen Werther*, 1774), an epistolary novel in the mode of Rousseau's *Julie, ou la nouvelle Héloïse*, dwelled on the solipsistic emotions of its hero in a way that undermined more socially unifying forms of feeling. Ironically, the concern with subjective feeling that the cult of sensibility had fostered led, at times, to a taste for intense introspection that could be harnessed to validate the pre-eminence of the personal and individual over the rights of "fellow feeling," in much the same way as the commercialization of society had enabled a preoccupation with private, as well as public, gain (Porter, 2000, 279).

Before such fears emerged on any significant scale, more positive connotations of sensibility prevailed. In Britain, Shaftesbury's view that "natural affections" between family members might lead to a broader, unifying sociability, was succeeded by the views of other British thinkers such as Hume, who explored in his *Enquiry Concerning the Principles of Morals* (1751) the importance of fellow feeling (or "benevolence") in forming social bonds. Many artists produced works that might promote feelings of benevolence in their viewers and exhibited them at Vauxhall Gardens, the Foundling Hospital and other public venues (Solkin, 1993, 11, 155–157, 168–169). Hogarth's history paintings for the Foundling Hospital treated subjects such as the Good Samaritan and others relating to Protestant ethics (Webster, 1978, 72–77). Works such as Wright of Derby's *An Experiment on a Bird in the Air Pump* (1768) (Figure 5.9, see color plate section) shows an itinerant lecturer demonstrating the threat to a bird of air deprivation, as the result of the creation of a vacuum. Those observing the experiment are bound by the ties of sympathy and support assumed in the putative viewer of the painting, who is expected to share the figures' distress at the imminent demise of the bird.

The work of past artists was also viewed through the lens of sensibility. The work of Nicolas Poussin began to be valued more for its expression of emotion than for its dignified classical forms. Emotion of any kind came to signify cathartic processes that would assist viewers to develop moral standards (Brookner, 1972, 9–10; Solkin, 1993, 171). In the later decades of the century, British and French history paintings adopted some of the conventions of sentimental genre scenes, placing more emphasis on the emotions experienced by their protagonists or on moving narrative episodes such as the spectacle of women in distress. This method succeeded due to the adoption of more "natural" or familiar human situations. Paintings by British history painters such as West, Turnbull, Edward Penny (1714–1791) and Hayman used themes from the theater, ancient and contemporary history and religion that incorporated references to the sense of justice, benevolence and loyalty of their protagonists: Penny's *The Marquis of Granby relieving a Sick Soldier* (*1764*) exemplifies such trends (Abrams, 1985, 70; Solkin, 1993, 170–172, 205). This transposition of private feeling to history subjects worked well, however, only when handled by artists possessing the full range of skills normally expected of a history painter. Greuze's use of the artistic conventions of sensibility, in which the poses, expressions and compositional contexts of figures often emphasized their vulnerability, was less successful when he transferred these to grand history painting, as in his reception piece for the Académie royale, his *Septimius Severus and Caracalla* (1769) (Crow, 1985, 164). Much of his failure was due to an inability to match visually, and with sufficient technical expertise, the gravity inherent in the antique narratives he chose to represent.

Wright of Derby's *An Experiment on a Bird in the Air Pump*, a genre painting on a grand scale, demonstrated within genre painting itself the kinds of familial and affective bonds that might appeal to the growing ranks of the commercially successful classes who featured in such scenes. Angelica Kauffman's portraits represented their female subjects in a way that appealed to the bonds of affection that might be formed imaginatively with viewers who moved in the circles of the "polite," their expressions consisting of the kind of melting tenderness that flattered viewers implicitly for their own capacity for intense natural feeling (Rosenthal, 1992, 105). The bonds of feeling openly celebrated in such works contrast with works earlier in the century in which sentimentalism had not enjoyed such sway; for example, Hogarth's satirical works, in which sentiment was offset by humor and ridicule. Hogarth drew freely on history painters' repertoire of facial expressions; and related his narrative series to contemporary themes in literature, the theater and society; but his use of satire and realism in these series had served a more Puritan agenda, in which uninhibited indulgence in feeling was slightly suspect (Webster, 1978, 32; Riding, 2006a, 34).

Questions of Modernity

A common historiographical approach in discussions of the relationship between eighteenth-century art and moral values is to describe it as a progression from the amoral, pleasure seeking art of the early century (e.g. in the taste for the rococo and the decorative) to the moral gravity, elevating patriotism and public virtues of David's antique subjects, a process aided by reformist ideals of the Enlightenment that held sway across Europe. Thomas Crow characterizes this commonly perceived progression as a trajectory from the sensual and the private to the classical and didactic, instigated in part by La Font de Saint-Yenne's anti-rococo and anti-commercialism polemic (Crow, 1985, 6–7). Matthew Craske has indicated the nineteenth-century origins of "degeneration to regeneration" art-historical narratives relating to the eighteenth century, which sometimes cast Boucher and his rococo colleagues in the role of villains (Craske, 1997, 226–229, 247–248). There is certainly a great deal of evidence from eighteenth-century art criticism that concerns about the declining moral vigor of art ran throughout the century. Debates on luxury acted as a focal point for these. Rousseau wrote eloquently on the subject in his 1750 *A Discourse on the Arts and Sciences*, in which he refers to artists who created rococo works:

> It is thus that the dissolution of morals, the necessary consequence of luxury, brings with it in its turn the corruption of taste. Further, if by chance there be found among men of uncommon ability, an individual with enough strength of mind to refuse to comply with the spirit of the age, and to debase himself by puerile productions, his lot will be hard. He will die in indigence and oblivion. This is not so much a prediction as a fact already confirmed by experience! Yes, Carle Vanloo and Pierre [history painters], the time is already come when your brushes, destined to increase the majesty of our temples by sublime and holy images, must fall from your hands, or else be prostituted to adorn the panels of a coach with lascivious paintings. And you inimitable Pigalle [French sculptor], rival of Phidias and Praxiteles [ancient Greek sculptors], whose chisel the ancients would have employed to carve them gods, whose images almost excuse their idolatry in our eyes; even your hand must condescend to fashion the belly of a porcelain monkey, or else remain idle. (*Discourse on the Arts and Sciences* (*Discours sur les sciences et les arts*, 1750) in Rousseau, 1973, 20)

Quite apart from the fact that Rousseau later became less critical of the arts in general, especially as his own writing became so popular, the problem with the regeneration narrative is that it ignores the continuing interest in sensual art evident in the work of Fragonard, Fuseli, Orientalist and other artists. Additionally, La Font de Saint-Yenne's anti-rococo views were quickly subjected to counter-attack by other commentators (Crow, 1985, 6–7). The moral order in eighteenth-century art continued to display a divergence of formal academic priorities and hierarchies from the preferences of the increasingly important art market. Grand history painting at the end of the century contributed to moral regeneration only because it reformed itself in line with the priorities of "sensibility" that had arisen mainly within the lower genres. Furthermore, neoclassicism did not always produce the kind of morally elevating art that the regeneration myth suggests. Houdon's sculpture of *Winter* was banned from the Salon in 1785 and the plaster model of Pajou's later *Psyche Abandoned* was banned from the same Salon on the grounds that it used a mythological subject as the pretext for eroticism (Walsh, 2012, 234–235). An ethics of sensuous and sensual pleasure remained important to the end of the century, if suppressed temporarily during the Revolution: the marble version of Pajou's sculpture was well received in 1791.

In terms of ethics, the modernity of eighteenth-century art lay not so much in the grand statements of neoclassical art or in a rejection of old-regime degeneracy as in the ability of the higher genres to absorb and transform the moral sensitivities brought to art by its exposure to a wider public, a process in which La Font's critical voice played a part. Also "modern" was an incipient awareness that art and morality might each require distinctive processes and standards of judgment, and that the aesthetic might inhabit a "disinterested" or autonomous dimension of human experience.

Further Reading

Barker, Emma. 2005. *Greuze and the Painting of Sentiment.* Cambridge: Cambridge University Press. An excellent scholarly analysis of the cult of sensibility through a historicized reading of Greuze's paintings.

Hallett, Mark and Christine Riding, with an essay by Frédéric Ogée and Olivier Meslay and additional catalogue contributions by Tim Batchelor. 2006. *Hogarth* (exh. cat.). London: Tate. An excellent introduction to the moral and social issues represented in Hogarth's art.

Conclusion

The eighteenth century was poised between centuries of artistic production in which court-dictated and church-dominated priorities and hierarchies had prevailed, and the nineteenth century, which witnessed the height of the fashion for Romanticism, when individual creativity and the breaking of conventions came to the fore. The beginnings and endings of centuries present crude units for analysis. It would be misleading to "read back" into the eighteenth century the seeds of later developments, as cause and effect rarely occur in such neatly linear ways. It was certainly, however, a century in which the production and reception of art underwent many changes. It is sometimes characterized as the period in which modernity first came into focus, as an expanding art market and art public stole some of the momentum previously guarded by an elite and shaped changes to the old order. By the end of the century, academies of fine art remained important in Europe, as did specialization in specific genres and media. Yet the established statuses of art and artists began to change, particularly as the "lower" genres challenged more significantly the primacy of grand history painting.

Subjectivity, the awareness of viewers of their own role in the interpretation and assessment of art, was nourished by a burgeoning literature in art criticism and aesthetics. Many became conscious of the ways in which art reflected back to them their own values, ideals and desires, although such insights had not yet attained the sophistication arising from later developments in psychology and psychoanalysis. Enlightenment writers and artists applied a critical eye to the workings of taste. Ultimately, this led to unprecedented scrutiny of the moral implications of the act of looking itself.

A Guide to Eighteenth-Century Art, First Edition. Linda Walsh.

Companion website: www.wiley.com/go/walsh/guidetoeighteenthcenturyart

References

Abrams, Ann Uhry. 1985. *The Valiant Hero: Benjamin West and Grand-Style History Painting*. Washington DC: Smithsonian Institution Press

Académie française. 1762. *Nouveau dictionnaire de l'Académie*, quatrième édition. 2 vols. Paris: Bernard Brunet

Alexander, David. 1992. "Kauffman and the Print Market in Eighteenth-Century England." In *Angelica Kauffman: A Continental Artist in Georgian England*, edited by Wendy Wassyng Roworth, 141–178. London: Reaktion Books

Alexander, David. 1998. *Richard Newton and the English Caricature in the 1790s*. Manchester: Manchester University Press

Allen, Brian. 1987. *Francis Hayman*. New Haven and London: Yale University Press

Andrews, Malcolm. 1989. *The Search for the Picturesque*. Aldershot: Scholar Press

Andrews, Malcolm. 1999. *Landscape and Western Art*. Oxford: Oxford University Press

Aristotle. 1954 [350 BCE]. *Aristotle: The Nicomachean Ethics*, trans. and introduced by David Ross. London: Oxford University Press

Bailey, Colin B. 2000. "Anglo-Saxon Attitudes: Recent Writings on Chardin." In *Chardin* (exh.cat.), 77–98. London: Royal Academy Publications

Bailey, Colin B. 2003. "Surveying Genre in Eighteenth-Century French Painting." In *The Age of Watteau, Chardin and Fragonard: Masterpieces of French Genre Painting* (exh. cat.), edited by Colin Bailey, 2–39. New Haven and London: Yale University Press

Bailey, Colin B. 2007. "'A long working life, considerable research and much thought': An Introduction to the Art and Career of Jean-Baptiste Oudry (1686–1755)." In *Oudry's Painted Menagerie: Portraits of Exotic Animals in Eighteenth-Century Europe* (exh. cat.), edited by Mary Morton, 1–29. Los Angeles: The J. Paul Getty Museum

Banerji, Christiane and Diana Donald. 1999. *Gillray Observed: The Earliest Account of his Caricatures in 'London und Paris'*. Cambridge: Cambridge University Press

A Guide to Eighteenth-Century Art, First Edition. Linda Walsh.

Companion website: www.wiley.com/go/walsh/guidetoeighteenthcenturyart

Barker, Emma. 2005. *Greuze and the Painting of Sentiment*. Cambridge: Cambridge University Press

Barker, Emma. 2007. "Putting the Viewer in the Frame: Greuze as Sentimentalist." In *French Genre Painting in the Eighteenth Century*, edited by Philip Conisbee, 105–127. New Haven and London: Yale University Press

Barker, Emma. 2009. "Rehabilitating the Rococo." Oxford Art Journal 32(2): 306–313

Barker, Emma. 2012a. "Inventing the Romantic Artist." In *Art and Visual Culture 1600–1850: Academy to Avant-Garde*, edited by Emma Barker, 299–335. London: Tate

Barker, Emma. 2012b. "Reading the Greuze Girl: The Daughter's Seduction." Representations 117: 86–119. DOI: 10.1525/rep.2012.117.1.86

Barnard, Frederick M. 2003. *Herder on Nationality, Humanity and History*. Montreal: McGill-Queen's University Press

Barringer, Tim, Geoff Quilley and Douglas Fordham. 2007. "Introduction." In *Art and the British Empire*, edited by Tim Barringer, Geoff Quilley and Douglas Fordham, 1–19. Manchester: Manchester University Press

Barroero, Liliana and Stefano Susinno. 2000. "Arcadian Rome, Universal Capital of Europe." In *Art in Rome in the Eighteenth Century* (exh. cat.), edited by Edgar Peters Bowron and Joseph J. Rishel, 47–75. Philadelphia: Philadelphia Museum of Art

Berger, Robert W. 1999. *Public Access to Art in Paris: A Documentary History from the Middle Ages to 1800*. Pennsylvania: The Pennsylvania State University Press

Berlo, Janet C and Ruth B. Phillips. 1998. *Native North American Art*. Oxford: Oxford University Press

Bignamini, Ilaria. 1989. "'The Academy of Art' in Britain before the Foundation of the Royal Academy in 1768." In *Academies of Art: Between Renaissance and Romanticism*, edited by Anton W.A. Boschloo *et al.*, 434–450. 's-Gravenhage: SDU Uitgeverij

Bignamini, Ilaria. 1991. "George Vertue, Art Historian, and Art Institutions in London, 1689–1768." Journal of the Walpole Society. LIV: 1–148

Bindman, David. 2002. *Ape to Apollo: Aesthetics and the Idea of Race in the Eighteenth Century*. Ithaca, New York: Cornell University Press

Bindman, David. 2008. "Introduction to The History of British Art 1600–1870." In *The History of British Art 1600–1870*, edited by David Bindman, 16–17. London: Tate Publishing

Bindman, David and Henry Louis Gates Jr. 2011. "'Preface." In *The Image of the Black in Western Art*, vol. III, Part 3 "From the 'Age of Discovery' to the Age of Abolition: The Eighteenth Century," edited by David Bindman and Henry Louis Gates Jr, ix–xxi. Cambridge, Massachusetts and London: The Belknap Press

Bindman, David and Helen Weston. 2011. "Court and City: Fantasies of Domination." In *The Image of the Black in Western Art*, vol. III, Part 3 "From the 'Age of Discovery' to the Age of Abolition: The Eighteenth century," edited by David Bindman and Henry Louis Gates Jr, 125–170. Cambridge, Massachusetts and London: The Belknap Press

Bindman, David, with contributions from Bruce Boucher and Helen Weston. 2011. "Introduction." In *The Image of the Black in Western Art*, vol. III, Part 3 "From the 'Age of Discovery' to the Age of Abolition: The Eighteenth Century," edited by David Bindman and Henry Louis Gates Jr, 1–16. Cambridge, Massachusetts and London: The Belknap Press

Bindman, David, Bruce Boucher and Helen Weston. 2011a. "The Theater of Court and Church: Blacks as Figures of Fantasy." In *The Image of the Black in Western Art*, vol. III, Part 3 "From the 'Age of Discovery' to the Age of Abolition: The Eighteenth Century," edited by David Bindman and Henry Louis Gates Jr, 17–76. Cambridge, Massachusetts and London: The Belknap Press

Bindman, David, Bruce Boucher and Helen Weston. 2011b. "Between Court and City: Fantasies in Transition." In *The Image of the Black in Western Art*, vol. III, Part 3 "From the 'Age of Discovery' to the Age of Abolition: The Eighteenth Century," edited by David Bindman and Henry Louis Gates Jr, 77–124. Cambridge, Massachusetts and London: The Belknap Press

Bindman, David, Charles Ford and Helen Weston. 2011. "Africa and the Slave Trade." In *The Image of the Black in Western Art*, vol. III, Part 3 "From the 'Age of Discovery' to the Age of Abolition: The Eighteenth Century," edited by David Bindman and Henry Louis Gates Jr, 207–240. Cambridge, Massachusetts and London: The Belknap Press

Bindman, David, Paul Kaplan and Helen Weston. 2011. "The City Between Fantasy and Reality." In *The Image of the Black in Western Art*, vol. III, Part 3 "From the 'Age of Discovery' to the Age of Abolition: The Eighteenth Century," edited by David Bindman and Henry Louis Gates Jr, 171–206. Cambridge, Massachusetts and London: The Belknap Press

Blake, Robin. 2004. "Stubbs and Rockingham's Young Whigs in the 1760s." In *Stubbs and the Horse*, by Malcolm Warner and Robin Blake, with an essay by Lance Mayor and Gay Myers, 43–63. New Haven and London: Yale University Press

Bonehill, John. 2005. "Exhibiting War: John Singleton Copley's The Siege of Gibraltar and the Staging of History." In *Conflicting Visions: War and Visual Culture in Britain and France c.1700–1830*, edited by John Bonehill, 139–167. Aldershot: Ashgate.

Bonehill, John. 2011. "Art History: Re-Viewing Recent Studies." *Journal for Eighteenth-Century Studies* 34(4): 461–470

Bonehill, John and Geoff Quilley. 2005. "Introduction." In *Conflicting Visions: War and Visual Culture in Britain and France c.1700–1830*, edited by John Bonehill, 1–14. Aldershot: Ashgate

Bordes, Phillipe. 2007. "Portraiture in the Mode of Genre: A Social Interpretation." In *French Genre Painting in the Eighteenth Century*, edited by Philip Conisbee, 257–273. New Haven and London: Yale University Press

Brewer, John. 1997. *The Pleasures of the Imagination: English Culture in the Eighteenth Century.* London: Harper Collins

Brookner, Anita. 1972. *Greuze: The Rise and Fall of an Eighteenth-Century Phemonenon.* London: Elek

Brown, Laurence. 2013. "Atlantic Slavery and Classical Culture at Marble Hill and Northington Grange." In *Slavery and the British Country House*, edited by Madge Dresser and Andrew Hann, 89–97. Swindon: English Heritage

Brunel, Georges. 1986. *Boucher.* London: Trefoil Books

Bryson, Norman. 1990. *Looking at the Overlooked: Four Essays on Still Life Painting.* London: Reaktion Books

Bukdahl, Else Marie. 1980. *Diderot critique d'art*, vol. 1, "Théorie et pratique dans les *Salons* de Diderot." Copenhagen: Rosenkilde et Bagger

Burke, Edmund. 1998 [second edition (1759)]. *A Philosophical Enquiry into the Sublime and Beautiful and Other Pre-Revolutionary Writings.* London: Penguin Books

Burton, Anthony. 1976. " Nineteenth-century Periodicals." Art Documents 1 ("The Art Press: Two Centuries of Magazines"): 3–10

Campbell, Malcolm. 2000. "Piranesi and Innovation in Eighteenth-Century Roman Printmaking." In *Art in Rome in the Eighteenth Century* (exh. cat.), edited by Edgar Peters Bowron and Joseph J. Rishel, 561–591. Philadelphia: Philadelphia Museum of Art

Campbell Orr, Clarissa. 2011. "Six Courts and Four Empires: Zoffany as Courtier." In *Johan Zoffany RA: Society Observed* (exh. cat.), edited by Martin Postle, 74–99. New Haven and London: Yale Centre for British Art and Royal Academy of Arts

Carter, Sophie. 1999. "'This Female Proteus': Representing Prostitution and Masquerade in Eighteenth-Century English Popular Print Culture." Oxford Art Journal 22(1): 55–79

Casid, Jill H. "Commerce in the Boudoir." In *Women, Art and the Politics of Identity in Eighteenth-Century Europe*, edited by Melissa Hyde and Jennifer Milam, 91–114. Aldershot: Ashgate

Chongzheng, Nie. 2005. "Qing Dynasty Court Painting." In *China: The Three Emperors 1662–1795* (exh. cat.), edited by Evelyn S. Rawski and Jessica Rawson, 76–115. London: Royal Academy of Arts

Clark, Anthony M. 1966–1967. "The Development of the Collections and Museums of Eighteenth-Century Rome." Art Journal 26(2): 136–143

Clark, Kenneth. 1956. *The Nude: A Study of Ideal Art.* London: Penguin

Clayton,Tim. 1997. *The English Print 1688–1802.* New Haven and London: Yale University Press

Clunas, Craig. 1999. "What about Chinese Art?" In *Views of Difference: Different Views of Art*, edited by Catherine King, 121–141. New Haven and London: Yale University Press in association with The Open University

Colley, Linda. 1984. "The English Rococo: Historical Background." In *Rococo: Art and Design in Hogarth's England* (exh. cat.). London: Victoria and Albert Museum

Collins, John, with the assistance of Penny Sullivan. 2003. "Genre Paintings Exhibited at the Salon, 1699–1789." In *The Age of Watteau, Chardin and Fragonard: Masterpieces of French Genre Painting* (exh. cat.), edited by Colin Bailey, 393–404. New Haven and London: Yale University Press

Coltman, Viccy. 2006. *Fabricating the Antique: Neoclassicism in Britain, 1760–1800.* Chicago and London: University of Chicago Press

Coltman, Viccy. 2009. *Classical Sculpture and the Culture of Collecting in Britain Since 1760.* Oxford: Oxford University Press

Conisbee, Philip. 1981. *Painting in Eighteenth-Century France.* Oxford: Phaidon

Conisbee, Philip. 2007. "Introduction." In *French Genre Painting in the Eighteenth Century*, edited by Philip Conisbee, 9–13. New Haven and London: Yale University Press

Craske, Matthew. 1997. *Art in Europe 1700–1830: A History of the Visual Arts in an Era of Unprecedented Urban Economic Growth.* Oxford and New York: Oxford University Press

Craske, Matthew. 2000. *William Hogarth.* London: Tate Publishing

Crow, Thomas. 1985. *Painters and Public Life in Eighteenth-Century Paris.* New Haven and London: Yale University Press

Crow, Thomas. 1995. *Emulation: Making Artists for Revolutionary France.* New Haven and London: Yale University Press

Crow, Thomas. 2005. "Chardin at the Edge of Belief: Overlooked Issues of Religion and Dissent in Eighteenth-Century Painting." In *Land, Nation and Culture, 1740–1840: Thinking the Republic of Taste*, edited by Peter de Bolla, Nigel Leask and David Simpson, 97–113. Hampshire: Palgrave Macmillan

Crowley, John E. 2011. *Imperial Landscapes: Britain's Global Visual Culture 1745–1820.* New Haven and London: Yale University Press

Crown, Patricia. 1984. "Portraits and Fancy Pictures by Gainsborough and Reynolds: Contrasting Images of Childhood." British Journal for Eighteenth-Century Studies 7(2): 159–167

Cumming, Robert. 1985. "Landscape and Still Life." In *Looking into Paintings*, edited by Elizabeth Deighton, 177–266. London and Boston: Faber and Faber with Channel 4

Dabydeen, David. 1985. *Hogarth's Blacks: Images of Blacks in Eighteenth-Century British Art.* Mundelstrup and London: Dangaroo Press

Dandré-Bardon, Michel-François. 1972 [reprint of 1765 edition]. *Traité de Peinture.* Geneva: Minkoff Reprint

Dejean, Joan. E. 2007. "Man of Mode: Watteau and the Gendering of Genre Painting." In *French Genre Painting in the Eighteenth Century*, edited by Philip Conisbee, 39–47. New Haven and London: Yale University Press

Démoris, René. 2000. "Chardin and the Far Side of Illusion." In *Chardin* (exh. cat.), 99–109. London: Royal Academy of Arts

Diderot, Denis. 1968. *Oeuvres esthétiques*, edited by Paul Vernière. Paris: Garnier

Diderot, Denis. 1984. *Essai sur la peinture; Salons de 1759, 1761, 1763.* Paris: Hermann

Diderot, Denis. 1995a. *Diderot on Art I: The Salon of 1765 and Notes on Painting*, edited and translated by John Goodman, with an introduction by Thomas Crow. New Haven and London: Yale University Press

Diderot, Denis. 1995b. *Diderot on Art II: The Salon of 1767*, translated and edited by John Goodman, with an introduction by Thomas Crow. New Haven and London: Yale University Press

Diderot, Denis and Jean le Rond d'Alembert, eds. 2013 [1751–1772] *Encyclopédie, ou dictionnaire raisonné des sciences, des arts et des métiers, etc.*, University of Chicago: ARTFL Encyclopédie Project (Spring 2013 Edition), Robert Morrissey (ed.), http://encyclopedie.uchicago.edu.

Donald, Diana. 1996. *The Age of Caricature: Satirical Prints in the Reign of George* III. New Haven and London: Yale University Press

Duro, Paul. 1997. *The Academy and the Limits of Painting in Seventeenth-Century France*. Cambridge: Cambridge University Press

Eaton, Natasha. 2007. "Critical Cosmopolitanism: Gifting and Collecting Art at Lucknow, 1775–97." In *Art and the British Empire*, edited by Tim Barringer, Geoff Quilley and Douglas Fordham, 189–204. Manchester: Manchester University Press

Ebeling, Jörg. 2007. "Upwardly Mobile: Genre Painting and the Conflict between Landed and Moneyed Interests." In *French Genre Painting in the Eighteenth Century*, edited by Conisbee, Philip, 73–89. New Haven and London: Yale University Press

Egerton, Judy, ed. 1990. *Wright of Derby* (exh. cat.). London: The Tate Gallery

Fahr-Becker, Gabriele, ed. 2006. *The Art of East Asia*. Potsdam: Ullmann

Falaky, Fayçal. 2013. "From Barber to Coiffeur: Art and Economic Liberalisation in Eighteenth-Century France." Journal for Eighteenth-Century Studies 36(1): 35–48

Farr, James. 2000. *Artisans in Europe 1300–1914*. Cambridge and New York: Cambridge University Press

Félibien, André. 1669. Extract from Preface to "Conférences de l'Académie Royale de Peinture et de Sculpture" (1669), trans. L.Walsh. In *Art and its Histories: A Reader*, edited by Steve Edwards, 34–36. New Haven and London: Yale University Press in association with The Open University

Félibien, André. 1967 [Reprint of 1725 edition]. *Entretiens sur les vies et sur les ouvrages des plus excellents peintres anciens et modernes; avec la vie des architectes.* Farnborough: Gregg Press Reprint

Fenton, James. 2006. *School of Genius: A History of the Royal Academy of Arts.* London: Salamander Press

Forbes Adam, Malise and Mary Mauchline. 1992. "Kauffman's Decorative Work." In *Angelica Kauffman: A Continental Artist in Georgian England*, edited by Wendy Wassyng Roworth, 113–140. London: Reaktion Books

Ford, Charles, Thomas Cummins, Rosalie Smith McCrea and Helen Weston. 2011. "The Slave Colonies." In *The Image of the Black in Western Art*, vol. III, Part 3 "From the 'Age of Discovery' to the Age of Abolition: The Eighteenth

Century", edited by David Bindman and Henry Louis Gates Jr, 241–305. Cambridge, Massachusetts and London: The Belknap Press

Fordham, Douglas. 2007. "Scalping: Social Rites in Westminster Abbey." In *Art and the British Empire*, edited by Geoff Quilley and Douglas Fordham, 99–199. Manchester: Manchester University Press

Fort, Bernadette. 2007. "The Greuze Girl: The Invention of a Pictorial Paradigm." In *French Genre Painting in the Eighteenth Century*, edited by Philip Conisbee, 129–151. New Haven and London: Yale University Press

Foucault, Michel. 1969. "What is an Author?" In *The Art of Art History: A Critical Anthology (2009)*, edited by Donald Preziosi, 321–334. Oxford: Oxford University Press

Foucault, Michel. 1972 [1969]. *The Archaeology of Knowledge*, trans. A.M. Sheridan Smith. London and New York: Routledge

Frank, Christoph. 2007. "Pictorial Relations: New Evidence on Jean-Baptiste Oudry and the Court of Mecklenberg-Schwerin. In *Oudry's Painted Menagerie: Portraits of Exotic Animals in Eighteenth-Century Europe* (exh. cat.), edited by Mary Morton, 31–57. Los Angeles: The J. Paul Getty Museum

Furbank, P.N. 1992. *Diderot: A Critical Biography*. London: Secker and Warburg

Gaehtgens, Barbara. 2003. "The Theory of French Genre Painting and its European Context." In *The Age of Watteau, Chardin and Fragonard: Masterpieces of French Genre Painting* (exh. cat.), edited by Colin Bailey, 40–59. New Haven and London: Yale University Press

Gaehtgens, Thomas W. 2003. "Genre Paintings in Eighteenth-Century Collections." In *The Age of Watteau, Chardin and Fragonard: Masterpieces of French Genre Painting*, edited by Colin Bailey, 78–89. New Haven and London: Yale University Press

Gaiger, Jason. 2002. "Introduction." In *Sculpture (Plastik)*, by Johann Gottfried Herder, edited and translated by Jason Gaiger, 1–28. Chicago: The University of Chicago Press

Ganofsky, Marine. 2015. "Illustrating Narrative Seduction: The Example of Choderlos de Laclos's *Liaisons Dangereuses* in the Illustrated Edition of 1796." Journal for Eighteenth-Century Studies 38(1): 1–27

Giviskos, Christine. 2007. "Technique and Tradition in Oudry's Animal Drawings." In *Oudry's Painted Menagerie: Portraits of Exotic Animals in Eighteenth-Century Europe* (exh. cat.), 75–89. Los Angeles: The J. Paul Getty Museum

Goldstein, Carl. 1996. *Teaching Art: Academies and Schools from Vasari to Albers*. Cambridge: Cambridge University Press

Goodden, Angelica. 1997. *The Sweetness of Life: A Biography of Elisabeth Louise Vigée Le Brun*. London: André Deutsch

Green, Georgina. 2015. "Translating Hemp into a Transatlantic 'Bond of Reciprocal Interest': The Society for the Encouragement of Arts, Manufactures and Commerce as a 1760s' Actor Network." Journal for Eighteenth-Century Studies 38(4): 483–495

Goudie, Allison. 2013. "The Wax Portrait Bust as Trompe-l'oeil? A Case Study of Queen Maria Carolina of Naples." Oxford Art Journal 36(1): 55–74

Greig, Charles. 2011. "In Zoffany's Footsteps: Journeys in Upper India, Past and Present." In *Johan Zoffany RA: Society Observed* (exh. cat.), edited by Martine Postle, 140–166. New Haven and London: Yale Centre for British Art and Royal Academy of Arts

Grindle, Nicjolas. 2008. "New Ways of Seeing: Landscape Painting and Visual Culture c.1620–1870." In *The History of British Art 1600–1870*, edited by David Bindman, 121–143. London: Tate Publishing

Guest, Harriet. 1992. "Curiously Marked: Tattooing, Masculinity, and Nationality in Eighteenth-Century British Perceptions of the South Pacific." In *Painting and the Politics of Culture: New Essays on British Art 1700–1850*, edited by John Barrell, 101–134. Oxford: Oxford University Press

Guest, Harriet. 2007. *Empire, Barbarism, and Civilisation: James Cook, Wlliam Hodges, and the Return to the Pacific*. Cambridge: Cambridge University Press

Guiffrey, Jules. 1872. *Livrets des expositions de l'Académie de Saint-Luc à Paris pendant les années 1751, 1752, 1753, 1756, 1762, 1764 et 1774, avec une notice bibliographique et une table*. Paris: Baur et Détaille

Guillomet, J. 1989. "L'École gratuite de dessin de Drouai de 1770 à 1800." In *Academies of Art: Between Renaissance and Romanticism*, by Anton W.A. Boschloo, Elwin J. Hendrikse, Laetitia C. Smit and Gert van der Sman, 255–258. 's-Gravenhage: SDU Uitgeverij

Habermas, Jürgen. 1992 [1962]. *The Structural Transformation of the Public Sphere: An Inquiry into a Category of Bourgeois Society*, translated by Thomas Burger with the assistance of Frederick Lawrence. Cambridge: Polity Press

Hallett, Mark. 2006a. "Hogarth's Variety." In *Hogarth* (exh. cat.), by Mark Hallett and Christine Riding, with an essay by Frédéric Ogée and Olivier Meslay and additional catalogue contributions by Tim Batchelor, 13–21. London: Tate

Hallett, Mark. 2006b. "Pictorial Theatre: The 1720s." In *Hogarth* (exh. cat.), by Mark Hallett and Christine Riding, with an essay by Frédéric Ogée and Olivier Meslay and additional catalogue contributions by Tim Batchelor, 55–71. London: Tate

Hallett, Mark. 2006c. "Pictures of Urbanity: The Conversation Piece." In *Hogarth* (exh. cat.), by Mark Hallett and Christine Riding, with an essay by Frédéric Ogée and Olivier Meslay and additional catalogue contributions by Tim Batchelor, 95–117. London: Tate

Hallett, Mark. 2006d. "The English Face: Hogarth's Portraiture." In *Hogarth* (exh. cat.), by Mark Hallett and Christine Riding, with an essay by Frédéric Ogée and Olivier Meslay and additional catalogue contributions by Tim Batchelor, 159–179. London: Tate

Hallett, Mark. 2006e. "High Art." In *Hogarth* (exh. cat.), by Mark Hallett and Christine Riding, with an essay by Frédéric Ogée and Olivier Meslay and additional catalogue contributions by Tim Batchelor, 197–213. London: Tate

Hallett, Mark. 2006f. "Patriotism, Portraiture and Politics." In *Hogarth* (exh. cat.), by Mark Hallett and Christine Riding, with an essay by Frédéric Ogée and Olivier

Meslay and additional catalogue contributions by Tim Batchelor, 215–241. London: Tate

Hallett, Mark. 2014. *Reynolds: Portraiture in Action*. New Haven and London: Yale University Press

Hargraves, Matthew. 2005. *Candidates for Fame: The Society of Artists of Great Britain 1760–1791*. New Haven and London: Yale University Press

Harrison, Charles, Paul Wood and Jason Gaiger, eds. 2000. *Art in Theory 1648–1815: An Anthology of Changing Ideas*. Oxford: Blackwell

Haynes, Clare. 2006. *Pictures and Popery: Art and Religion in England 1660–1760*. Farnham: Ashgate

Hofer, Philip. 1969. "Introduction." In *Los Caprichos by Francisco Goya y Lucientes*, 1–6. New York: Dover Publications

Hogarth, William. 1968 [wr.1760–1761?]. "Apology for Painters." In "Hogarth's 'Apology for Painters,'" by Mark Kitson. Journal of the Walpole Society XLI: 46–111

Hongxing, Zhang. 2013. "Introduction." In *Masterpieces of Chinese Painting 700–1900* (exh. cat.), 11–39. London: V and A Publishing

Honour, Hugh and John Fleming. 1999. *A World History of Art*, 5th edition. London: Laurence King

Hoock, Holger. 2003. *The King's Artists: The Royal Academy of Arts and the Politics of British Culture 1760–1840*. Oxford: Clarendon Press

Hsieh, Chia-Chuan. 2013. "The Emergence and Impact of the 'Complete Drawing Book' in Mid-Eighteenth-Century England." Journal for Eighteenth-Century Studies 36(3): 395–414

Hughes, Anthony. 1986. "An Academy for Doing: II: Academies, Status and Power in Early Modern Europe." Oxford Art Journal 9(2): 50–62

Hughes, Eleanor. 2007. "Ships of the 'Line': Marine Paintings at the Royal Academy Exhibition of 1784." In *Art and the British Empire*, edited by Tim Barringer, Geoff Quilley and Douglas Fordham, 139–152. Manchester: Manchester University Press

Hunt, Lynn. 1991. "The Many Bodies of Marie Antoinette: Political Pornography and the Problem of the Feminine in the French Revolution." In *Eroticism and the Body Politic*, edited by Lynn Hunt, 108–130. Baltimore: The Johns Hopkins Press

Hutchison, S.C. 1989. "The Royal Academy of Arts in London: Its History and Activities." In *Academies of Art: Between Renaissance and Romanticism*, by Anton W.A. Boschloo, Elwin J. Hendrikse, Laetitia C. Smit and Gert Jan van der Sman, 451–463. 's-Gravenhage: SDU Uitgeverij

Hyde, Melissa and Jennifer Milam. 2003. "Introduction." In *Women, Art and the Politics of Identity in Eighteenth-Century Europe*, edited by Melissa Hyde and Jennifer Milam, 1–19. Aldershot: Ashgate

Jasanoff, Maya. 2011. "A Passage through India: Zoffany in Calcutta and Lucklow." In *Johan Zoffany RA: Society Observed* (exh. cat.), edited by Martine Postle, 124–139. New Haven and London: Yale Centre for British Art and Royal Academy of Arts

Johns, Christopher M.S. 2000. "The Entrepôt of Europe." In *Art in Rome in the Eighteenth Century* (exh. cat.), edited by Edgar Peters Bowron and Joseph J. Rishel, 17–45. Philadelphia: Philadelphia Museum of Art

Johns, Christopher M.S. 2003. "'An Ornament of Italy and the Premier Female Painter of Europe': Rosalba Carriera and the Roman Academy." In *Women, Art and the Politics of Identity in Eighteenth-Century Europe*, edited by Melissa Hyde and Jennifer Milam, 20–45. Aldershot: Ashgate

Johnson, Dorothy. 1993. *Jacques-Louis David: Art in Metamorphosis.* New Jersey: Princeton University Press

Jourdain, Margaret and R. Soame Jenyns. 1950. *Chinese Export Art in the Eighteenth Century.* Middlesex: Spring Books

Kant, Immanuel. 1987 [1790]. *Critique of Judgment*, translated by Werner S. Pluhar. Indianapolis/Cambridge: Hackett Publishing Company

Kaufman, Thomas da Costa. 1995. *Court, Cloister and City: The Art and Culture of Central Europe 1450–1800.* Chicago: University of Chicago Press

Kayser, Christine with the collaboration of Xavier Salmon and Laurent Hugues. 2003. *L'enfant chéri au siècle des lumières: Après l'Émile.* Louveciennes: Musée Promenade de Marly-le-Roi

Kitson, Michael. 1994. "Introduction." In *Painting in Britain 1530–1790* (fifth edition; first published 1953) by Ellis Waterhouse, xi–xxvii. New Haven and London: Yale University Press

Krahl, Regina. 2005. "The Yongzheng Emperor: Art Collector and Patron." In *China: The Three Emperors 1662–1795* (exh. cat.), edited by Evelyn S. Rawski and Jessica Rawson, 240–269. London: Royal Academy of Arts

Krahl, Regina and Jessica Harrison-Hall. 2009. *Chinese Ceramics: Highlights of the Sir Percival David Collection.* London: The British Museum Press

Kriz, K. Dian. 2001. "'Stare Cases': Engendering the Public's Two Bodies at the Royal Academy of Arts." In *Art on the Line: The Royal Academy Exhibitions at Somerset House 1780–1836*, edited by David H. Solkin, 55–63. New Haven and London: Yale University Press

Krysmanski, Bernd. 1998. "Lust in Hogarth's *Sleeping Congregation* – Or, How to Waste Time in Post-Puritan England." Art History 21(3): 393–408

La Font de Saint-Yenne, Étienne. 1747. *Réflexions sur quelques causes de l'état present de la peinture en France.* Paris: Hachette. Accessible online at http://gallica.bnf.fr/ark:12148/bpt6k1132488

Lajer-Burcharth, Ewa. 2007. "Greuze and Sex." In *French Genre Painting in the Eighteenth Century*, edited by Philip Conisbee, 201–219. New Haven and London: Yale University Press

Ledbury, Mark. 1997. "Intimate Dramas: Genre Painting and New Theatre in Eighteenth-Century France." In *Intimate Encounters: Love and Domesticity in Eighteenth-Century France* (exh. cat.), edited by Richard Rand, 49–67. Princeton: Princeton University Press

Ledbury, Mark. 2007. "Greuze in Limbo: Being "Betwixt and Between." In *French Genre Painting in the Eighteenth Century*, edited by Philip Conisbee, 179–199. New Haven and London: Yale University Press

Leech, Roger H. 2013. "Lodges, Garden Houses and Villas: The Urban Periphery in the Early Atlantic World." In *Slavery and the British Country House*, edited by Madge Dresser and Andrew Hann, 54–58. Swindon: English Heritage

Lemaire, Gérard-Georges. 2013. *Orientalism: The Orient in Western Art*, translated by Harriet de Blanco, Peter Field, Françoise Jones and Doris Wolstencroft, in association with Cambridge Publishing Management Editing. Potsdam: Ullmann

Lévesque de Pouilly, Louis-Jean. 1971 [1747]. *Théorie des sentiments agréables.* Geneva: Slatkine Reprint

Levey, Michael. 1959. *Painting in Eighteenth-Century Venice.* London: Phaidon

Levey, Michael. 1993. *Painting and Sculpture in France 1700–1789.* New Haven and London: Yale University Press.

Link, Anne-Marie. 2013. "'The Masterpieces of the World in Small Pages!" In *Patronage, Visual Culture, and Courtly Life in Eighteenth-Century Germany and England*, edited by Catherine Tite, 101–123. New York: Cambria Press

Lock, Leon E. 2010. "Picturing the Use, Collecting and Display of Plaster Casts in Seventeenth- and Eighteenth-Century Artists' Studios in Antwerp and Brussels." In *Plaster Casts: Making, Collecting and Displaying from Classical Antiquity to the Present*, edited by Rune Frederiksen and Eckhart Marchand, 251–268. Berlin and New York: De Gruyter

Locke, John. 1694. *An Essay Concerning Human Understanding*, 2nd edition. London: Dring and Manship

Longmore, Jane. 2013. "Rural Retreats: Liverpool Slave Traders and Their Country Houses." In *Slavery and the British Country House*, edited by Madge Dresser and Andrew Hann, 43–53. Swindon: English Heritage

Losty, J.P. and Malini Roy. 2012. *Mughal India: Art, Culture and Empire: Manuscripts and Paintings in the British Library* (exh. cat.). London: The British Library

Luxenberg, Alisa. 1997. "Figaros and Free Agents: Some Perspectives on French Painters in Eighteenth-Century Spain." In *Painting in Spain in the Age of Enlightenment: Goya and His Contemporaries* (exh. cat.), edited by Ronda Kasl and Suzanne L. Stratton, 39–64. Washington DC: University of Washington Press.

MacDonald, M.F. 1989. "British Artists at the Accademia del Nudo in Rome." In *Academies of Art: Between Renaissance and Romanticism*, by Anton W.A. Boschloo, Elwin J. Hendrikse, Laetitia C. Smit and Gert Jan van der Sman, 77–91. 's-Gravenhage: SDU Uitgeverij

Macmillan, Duncan. 1986. *Painting in Scotland: The Golden Age.* Oxford: Phaidon Press

Macsotay, Tomas. 2010. "Plaster Casts and Memory Technique: Nicolas Vleughel's Display Of Plaster Casts After the Antique in the French Academy in Rome (1725–1793)." In *Plaster Casts: Making, Collecting and Displaying from*

Classical Antiquity to the Present, edited by Rune Frederiksen and Eckhart Marchand, 181–196. Berlin and New York: De Gruyter

Masterpieces of Chinese Painting 700–1900 (exh. cat.). 2013. London: V and A Publishing

Matheson, C. 2001. "'A Shilling Well Laid Out': The Royal Academy's Early Public." In *Art on the Line: The Royal Academy Exhibitions at Somerset House 1780–1836*, edited by David H. Solkin, 39–53. New Haven and London: Yale University Press

Maza, Sarah. 1997. "The "Bourgeois" Family Revisited: Sentimentalism and Social Class in Prerevolutionary French Culture." In *Intimate Encounters: Love and Domesticity in Eighteenth-Century France* (exh. cat.), edited by Richard Rand, 39–47. Princeton: Princeton University Press

McCausland, Shane. 2013. "Categories of Chinese Painting." In *Masterpieces of Chinese Painting 700–1900* (exh. cat.), 41–51. London: V and A Publishing

McClellan, Andrew. 2008. *The Art Museum from Boullée to Bilbao*. Berkeley: University of California Press

McGregor, Neil. 2014. *Germany: Memories of a Nation*. London: Allen Lane

McWilliam, Neil (editor), Vera Schuster and Richard Wrigley, with the assistance of Pascale Méker. 1991. *A Bibliography of Salon Criticism in Paris from the Ancien Régime to the Restoration*. Cambridge: Cambridge University Press

Michel, Christian. 2007. "Nature and Moeurs: Thoughts on the Reception of Genre Painting in France." In *French Genre Painting in the Eighteenth Century*, edited by Philip Conisbee, 275–289. New Haven and London: Yale University Press

Milam, Jennifer. 1998. "Fragonard and the Blindman's Game: Interpreting Representations of Blindman's Buff." Art History 21(1): 1–25

Miles, Ellen G. with contributions by Patricia Burda, Cynthia J. Mills and Leslie Kaye Reinhardt. 1995. *American Paintings of the Eighteenth Century*. New York and Oxford: Oxford University Press

Mitchell, Timothy. 1989. "Orientalism and the Exhibitionary Order." In *The Art of Art History: A Critical Anthology*, edited by Donald Preziosi, 409–423. Oxford: Oxford University Press

Mitter, Partha. 2001. *Indian Art*. Oxford: Oxford University Press

Mount, Harry. 2006. "The Monkey with the Magnifying Glass: Constructions of the Connoisseur in Eighteenth-Century Britain." Oxford Art Journal 29(2): 167–184

Muller, Kevin. 2012. "Navigation, Vision, and Empire: Eighteenth-Century Engraved Views of Boston in a British American Context." In *New Views of New England: Studies in Material and Visual Culture, 1680–1830*, edited by Martha J. McNamara and Georgia B. Barnhill, 47–68. Boston: The Colonial Society of Massachusetts

Murck, Alfreda. 2005. "Silent Satisfactions: Painting and Calligraphy of the Chinese Educated Elite." In *China: The Three Emperors 1662–1795* (exh. cat.), edited by Evelyn S. Rawski and Jessica Rawson, 306–355. London: Royal Academy of Arts

Myrone, Martin. 2008. "The British Artist c.1570–c.1870." In *The History of British Art 1600–1870*, edited by David Bindman, 188–213. London: Tate Publishing

Nivelon, François. 1737. *The Rudiments of Genteel Behaviour*. The British Library: Ecco

Ogée, Frédéric and Olivier Meslay. 2006. "William Hogarth and modernity." In *Hogarth* (exh. cat.), edited by Mark Hallett and Christine Riding, 23–31. London: Tate

Pagden, Anthony. 2013. *The Enlightenment and Why it Still Matters.* Oxford: Oxford University Press

Pasta, Renato. 2005. "The History of the Book and Publishing in Eighteenth-Century Italy." Journal of Modern Italian Studies 10(2): 200–217

Paul, Carole. 2008. *The Borghese Collections and the Display of Art in the Age of the Grand Tour*. Farnham: Ashgate

Paulson, Ronald. 1983. *Representations of Revolution (1789–1820)*. New Haven and London: Yale University Press

Percival, Melissa. 2012. *Fragonard and the Fantasy Figure: Painting the Imagination.* Farnham: Ashgate

Percy, Ann. 2000. "Drawings and Artistic Production in Eighteenth-Century Rome." In *Art in Rome in the Eighteenth Century* (exh. cat.), edited by Edgar Peters Bowron and Joseph J.Rishel, 461–559. Philadelphia: Philadelphia Museum of Art

Pérez-Sanchez, Alfonso E. 1989. "Introduction." In *Goya and the Spirit of Enlightenment*, edited by Alfonso E. Pérez-Sanchez and Eleanor A. Sayre, xviii–xxv. Boston: Bullfinch Press

Perry, Gill. 2007. *"Spectacular Flirtations": Viewing the Actress in British Art and Theatre 1768–1820.* New Haven and London: Yale University Press

Plax, Julie Anne. 2000. *Watteau and the Cultural Politics of Eighteenth-Century France.* Cambridge: Cambridge University Press

Plax, Julie Anne. 2007. "Belonging to the In Crowd: Watteau and the Bonds of Art and Friendship." In *French Genre Painting in the Eighteenth Century*, edited by Philip Conisbee, 49–71. New Haven and London: Yale University Press

Pointon, Marcia. 1993. *Hanging the Head: Portraiture and Social Formation in Eighteenth-Century England.* New Haven and London: Yale University Press

Pointon, Marcia. 2001. "Portrait! Portrait! Portrait!!!" In *Art on the Line: The Royal Academy Exhibitions at Somerset House 1780–1836*, edited by David H. Solkin, 93–109. New Haven and London: Yale University Press

Pope, Alexander. 1950 [1734]. *An Essay on Man*, edited by Maynard Mack. London: Methuen

Porter, David. 2010. *The Chinese Taste in Eighteenth-Century England.* Cambridge: Cambridge University Press.

Porter, Roy. 2000. *Enlightenment Britain and the Creation of the Modern World.* London: Penguin Press

Postle, Martin. 2011. "Johan Zoffany: An Artist Abroad." In *Johan Zoffany RA: Society Observed* (exh. cat.), edited by Martin Postle, 12–49. New Haven and London: Yale Centre for British Art and Royal Academy of Arts

Potts, Alex. 1994. *Flesh and the Ideal: Winckelmann and the Origins of Art History.* New Haven and London: Yale University Press.

Pratt, Stephanie. 1998. "Reynolds' 'King of the Cherokees' and Other Mistaken Identities in the Portraiture of Native American Delegations 1710–1762." Oxford Art Journal 21(2): 133–150

Pratt, Stephanie. 2003. "From Cannassatego to Outalissi: Making Sense of the Native American in Eighteenth-Century Culture." In *An Economy of Colour: Visual Culture and the Atlantic World, 1660–1830*, edited by Geoff Quilley and Kay Dian Kriz, 60–82. Manchester: Manchester University Press

Poulet, Anne L., with Guilhem Scherf, Ulrike D. Mathias, Christoph Frank, Claude Vandalle, Dean Walker and Monique Barbier. 2003. *Jean-Antoine Houdon: Sculptor of the Enlightenment.* Chicago: University of Chicago Press

Quilley, Geoff. 2003. "Pastoral Plantations: the Slave Trade and the Representation of British Colonial Landscape in the Late Eighteenth Century." In *An Economy of Colour: Visual Culture and the Atlantic World, 1660–1830*, edited by Geoff Quilley and Kay Dian Kriz, 106–128. Manchester: Manchester University Press

Quilley, Geoff. 2011. *Empire to Nation: Art, History and the Visualisation of Maritime Britain 1768–1829.* New Haven and London: Yale University Press

Quilley, Geoff and John Bonehill. 2004. *William Hodges 1744–1797, the Art of Exploration* (exh. cat.). London: National Maritime Museum

Radford, Ron. 2013. "Land and Landscape: The Colonial Encounter 1800–80." In *Australia* (exh. cat.), 90–145. London: Royal Academy of Arts

Rawski, Evelyn S. 2005. "The 'Prosperous Age': China in the Kangxi, Yongzheng and Qianlong Reigns." In *China: The Three Emperors 1662–1795* (exh. cat.), edited by Evelyn S. Rawski and Jessica Rawson, 22–40. London: Royal Academy of Arts

Ray, Romita. 2007. "Storm in a Teacup? Visualising Tea Consumption in the British Empire." In *Art and the British Empire*, edited by Tim Barringer, Geoff Quilley and Douglas Fordham, 205–222. Manchester: Manchester University Press

Retford, Kate. 2006. *The Art of Domestic Life: Family Portraiture in Eighteenth-Century England.* New Haven and London: Yale University Press

Retford, Kate. 2011. "'Peculiarly Happy at Taking Likenesses': Zoffany and British Portraiture." In *Johan Zoffany RA: Society Observed* (exh. cat.), edited by Martin Postle, 100–123. New Haven and London: Yale Centre for British Art and Royal Academy of Arts

Retford, Kate, Gill Perry and Jordan Vibert. 2013. "Introduction: Placing Faces in the Country House." In *Placing Faces: The Portrait and the English Country House in the Long Eighteenth Century*, edited by Gill Perry, Kate Retford and Jordan Vibert, with Hannah Lyons, 1–28. Manchester: Manchester University Press

Reynolds, Joshua. 1968 [1755]. "Reynolds's 'Sitter Book' for 1755." Transcribed and edited by Ellis K. Waterhouse. Journal of the Walpole Society XLI: 112–167

Reynolds, Joshua. 1975 [1797]. *Discourses on Art.* New Haven and London: Yale University Press

Ribeiro, Aileen. 2015. "The Beauty of the Particular: Dress in Liotard's Images of Women." In *Jean-Étienne Liotard 1702–1789* (exh. cat.). London: Royal Academy of Arts

Richardson, Jonathan. 1725 [1715]. Extract from "Essay on the Theory of Painting." In *Art in Theory 1648–1815: An Anthology of Changing Ideas*, 2nd edition, edited by Charles Harrison, Paul Wood and Jason Gaiger, 326–331. Oxford: Blackwell

Riding, Christine. 2006a. "Introducing Hogarth: Past and Present." In *Hogarth* (exh. cat.), by Mark Hallett and Christine Riding, 33–53. London: Tate

Riding, Christine. 2006b. "The Harlot and the Rake." In *Hogarth* (exh. cat.), by Mark Hallett and Christine Riding, 73–93. London: Tate

Riding, Christine. 2006c. "Street Life." In *Hogarth* (exh. cat.), by Mark Hallett and Christine Riding, 119–139. London: Tate

Riding, Christine. 2006d. "Marriage a-la-mode." In *Hogarth* (exh. cat.), by Mark Hellett and Christine Riding, 141–157. London: Tate

Riding, Christine. 2006e. "Crime and Punishment." In *Hogarth* (exh. cat.), by Mark Hallett and Christine Riding, 181–195. London: Tate

Robins, Nick. 2006. *The Corporation that Changed the World: How the East India Company Shaped the Modern Multinational.* London: Pluto Press

Rochebrune, Marie-Laure de. 2000. "Ceramics and Glass in Chardin's Paintings." In *Chardin* (exh. cat.), 37–53. London: Royal Academy Publications

Roland Michel, Marianne. 2003. "Exoticism and Genre Painting in Eighteenth-Century France." In *The Age of Watteau, Chardin and Fragonard: Masterpieces of French Genre Painting* (exh. cat.), edited by Colin Bailey, 106–119. New Haven and London: Yale University Press

Rosenblum, Robert. 1967. *Transformations in Late Eighteenth-Century Art.* Princeton, New Jersey: Princeton University Press

Rosenthal, Angela. 1992. "Kauffman and Portraiture." In *Angelica Kauffman: A Continental Artist in Georgian England*, edited by Wendy Wassyng Roworth, 96–111. London: Reaktion Books.

Rosenthal, Angela. 2008. "Angelica Kauffman." In *The History of British Art 1600–1870*, edited by David Bindman, 82–83. London: Tate Publishing

Rousseau, Jean-Jacques. 1973. *The Social Contract and Discourses*, translated by G.D.H. Cole. London: Everyman's

Saabye, M. 1989. "The Royal Danish Academy of Fine Arts under the Leadership of A.G. Moltke and J.-F.-J. Saly." In *Academies of Art: Between Renaissance and Romanticism*, by W.A. Boschloo *et al.*, 520–532. 's-Gravenhage: SDU Uitgeverij

Said, Edward W. 2003 [1978]. *Orientalism.* London: Penguin Books

Sánchez-Jáuregui Alpañes, María Dolores and Scott Wilcox, eds. 2012. *The English Prize: The Capture of the Westmorland: An Episode of the Grand Tour* (exh. cat.). New Haven and London: Yale University Press

Saumarez Smith, Charles. 2012. *The Company of Artists: The Origins of the Royal Academy of Arts in London*. London: Modern Art Press

Schama, Simon. 1989. *Citizens: A Chronicle of the French Revolution*. London: Penguin

Schieder, Martin. 2003. "'Sorti de son genre': Genre Painting and Boundary Crossing at the End of the Ancien Régime." In *The Age of Watteau, Chardin and Fragonard: Masterpieces of French Genre Painting* (exh. cat.), edited by Colin Bailey, 60–77. New Haven and London: Yale University Press

Schiff, Richard. 2003. "Originality." In *Critical Terms for Art History*, edited by Robert Nelson and Richard Schiff, 145–151. Chicago: University of Chicago Press

Schnapper, Antoine. 2000. "Chardin's Property and Sources of Income." In *Chardin* (exh. cat.), 55–59. London: Royal Academy Publications

Schoneveld-Van Stoltz, H.F. 1989. "Some Notes on the History of the Académie Royale de Peinture et de Sculpture in the Second Half of the Eighteenth Century." In *Academies of Art: Between Renaissance and Romanticism*, by W.A. Boschloo, Elwin J. Hendrike, Laetitia C. Smit and Gert Jan van der Sman, 520–532. 's-Gravenhage: SDU Uitgeverij

Schroder, Anne L. 1997. "Genre Prints in Eighteenth-Century France: Production, Market and Audience." In *Intimate Encounters: Love and Domesticity in Eighteenth-Century France* (exh. cat.), edited by Richard Rand, 69–86. Princeton: Princeton University Press

Schulz, Andrew. 2000. "Satirising the Senses: the Representation of Perception in Goya's *Los Caprichos*. Art History 23(2): 153–181

Scott, Katie. 1989. "Hierarchy, Liberty and Order: Languages of Art and Institutional Conflict in Paris (1766–1776)." Oxford Art Journal 12(2): 59–70

Scott, Katie. 1995. *The Rococo Interior. Decoration and Spaces in Early Eighteenth Century Paris*. New Haven and London: Yale University Press

Scott, Katie. 2000. "Chardin Multiplied." In *Chardin* (exh. cat.), 61–75. London: Royal Academy of Arts

Scott, Katie. 2003. "Child's Play." In *The Age of Watteau, Chardin and Fragonard: Masterpieces of French Genre Painting* (exh. cat.), edited by Colin Bailey, 90–105. New Haven and London: Yale University Press

Selwyn, Pamela E. 2000. *Everyday life in the German Book Trade: Friedrich Nicolai as Bookseller and Publisher in the Age of Enlightenment*. Pennsylvania: Pennsylvania State University Press

Siegfried, Susan. 2007. "Femininity and the Hybridity of Genre Painting." In *French Genre Painting in the Eighteenth Century*, edited by Philip Conisbee, 15–35. New Haven and London: Yale University Press

Simon, Robin. 1987. *The Portrait in Britain and America with a Biographical Dictionary of Portrait Painters 1680–1914*. Oxford: Phaidon

Simon, Robin. 2007. *Hogarth, France and the Rise of the Arts in Eighteenth-Century Britain*. London: Paul Holberton Publishing/Hogarth Arts

Simon, Robin. 2011. "'Strong impressions of their art': Zoffany and the Theatre." In *Johan Zoffany RA: Society Observed* (exh. cat.), edited by Martin Postle, 50–73. New Haven and London: Yale Centre for British Art and Royal Academy of Arts

Smentek, Kristel. 2007. "Sex, Sentiment, and Speculation: The Market for Genre Prints on the Eve of the French Revolution." In *French Genre Painting in the Eighteenth Century*, edited by Philip Conisbee, 221–243. New Haven and London: Yale University Press

Smentek, Kristel. 2014. *Mariette and the Science of the Connoisseur in Eighteenth-Century Europe*. Farnham: Ashgate

Smith, Adam. 1970 [1776]. *The Wealth of Nations Books I–III*. London: Penguin Press

Smith, Bernard. 1985. *European Vision and the South Pacific*. New Haven and London: Yale University Press

Smith, Greg. 2001. "Watercolourists and Watercolours at the Royal Academy, 1780–1836." In *Art on the Line: The Royal Academy Exhibitions at Somerset House 1780–1836*, edited by David H. Solkin, 189–200. New Haven and London: Yale University Press

Solkin, David H. 1993. *Painting for Money: The Visual Arts and the Public Sphere in Eighteenth-Century England*. New Haven and London: Yale University Press

Solkin, David H. 2001. "'This Great Mart of Genius': The Royal Academy Exhibitions at Somerset House, 1780–1836." In *Art on the Line: The Royal Academy Exhibitions at Somerset House 1780–1836*, edited by David H. Solkin, 1–8. New Haven and London: Yale University Press

Solkin, David H. 2007. "'Conquest, Usurpation, Wealth, Luxury, Famine': Mortimer's Banditti and the Anxieties of Empire." In *Art and the British Empire*, edited by Tim Barringer, Geoff Quilley and Douglas Fordham, 120–138. Manchester: Manchester University Press

Stanley-Baker, Joan. 2000. *Japanese Art*, 2nd edition. London: Thames and Hudson

Sunderland, John and David H. Solkin. 2001. "Staging the Spectacle." In *Art on the Line: The Royal Academy Exhibitions at Somerset House 1780–1836*, edited by David H. Solkin, 23–37. New Haven and London: Yale University Press

Susato, Ryu. 2006. "Hume's Nuanced Defense of Luxury." Hume Studies 32(1): 167–186

Tarabra, Daniela. 2006. *European Art of the Eighteenth Century*, translated by Rosanna M. Giammanco. Los Angeles: The J. Paul Getty Museum

Terjanian, Anoush Fraser. 2013. *Commerce and its Discontents in Eighteenth-Century French Political Thought*. Cambridge: Cambridge University Press

Thomas, Chantal. 2001. *The Wicked Queen: The Origins of the Myth of Marie-Antoinette*. New York: Zone Books.

Thygesen, A.L. 1989. "The Early History of the Danish Royal Academy Library." In *Academies of Art: Between Renaissance and Romanticism*, by W.A. Boschloo *et al.*, 511–519. 's-Gravenhage: SDU Uitgeverij

Tinios, Ellis. 2010. *Japanese Prints: Ukiyo-e in Edo*. London: The British Museum Press

Tite, Catherine. 2013a. "Introduction." In *Patronage, Visual Culture, and Courtly Life in Eighteenth-Century Germany and England*, edited by Catherine Tite, 1–12. New York: Cambria Press

Tite, Catherine. 2013b. "'The Idiom of the People of Fashion': Court, City, and Courtly Painters in Eighteenth-Century Kassel". In *Patronage, Visual Culture, and Courtly Life in Eighteenth-Century Germany and England*, edited by Catherine Tite, 35–50. New York: Cambria Press

Tomlinson, Janis. 1994. *Francisco Goya y Lucientes 1746–1828.* London: Phaidon Press

Touati, Anne-Marie Leander and Johan Flemberg [trans. Martin Naylor]. 2013. *Gustav III's Museum of Antiquities.* Stockholm: Nationalmusem

Truettner, William H. 2010. *Painting Indians and Building Empires in North America, c.1710–1840.* Berkeley, Los Angeles and London: University of California Press

Trusted, Marjorie. 2008. *The Return of the Gods: Neoclassical Sculpture in Britain* (exh. cat.). London: Tate Publishing

Tullett, William. 2015. "The Macaroni's 'Ambrosial Essence': Perfume, Identity and Public Space in Eighteenth-Century England." Journal for Eighteenth-Century Studies 38(2): 163–180

Vaughan, William. 2008. "Britain and Europe c.1600-1900." In *The History of British Art 1600–1870*, edited by David Bindman, 54–77. London: Tate Publishing

Victoria and Albert Museum. 1984. *Rococo: Art and Design in Hogarth's England* (exh. cat.). London: Victoria and Albert Museum

Virard, Pierre. 1776. *Essai sur la santé des filles nubiles.* Paris: Monory

Voltaire, François-Marie Arouet de. 1964 [1734]. *Lettres philosophiques ou Lettres anglaises.* Paris: Garnier

Walcot, Clare. 2012. "Hogarth's *The South Sea Scheme* and the Topography of Speculative Finance." Oxford Art Journal 35(3): 413–432

Walczak, Gerrit. 2007. "Low Art, Popular Imagery and Civic Commitment in the French Revolution." Art History 30(2): 247–277

Waley-Cohen, Joanna. 2005. "Diplomats, Jesuits and Foreign Curiosities." In *China: The Three Emperors 1662–1795* (exh. cat.), edited by Evelyn S. Rawski and Jessica Rawson, 178–207. London: Royal Academy of Arts

Walsh, Linda. 1994. "'Arms to be Kissed a Thousand Times': Reservations about Lust in Diderot's Art Criticism." In *Femininity and Masculinity in Eighteenth-Century Art and Culture*, edited by Gill Perry and Michael Rossington, 162–181. Manchester and New York: Manchester University Press

Walsh, Linda. 1996. "The Expressive Face: Manifestations of Sensibility in Eighteenth-Century French Art." Art History 19(4): 523–550

Walsh, Linda. 1998. "Art, History and Politics." In *A103: An Introduction to the Humanities* (Block 3 History, Classicism and Revolution), 155–200. Milton Keynes: The Open University

Walsh, Linda. 1999. "Charles Le Brun, 'art dictator of France.'" In *Academies, Museums and Canons of Art*, edited by Gill Perry and Colin Cunningham, 86–123. New Haven and London: Yale University Press

Walsh, Linda. 2008. "The 'Hard Form' of Sculpture: Marble, Matter and Spirit in European Sculpture from the Enlightenment through Romanticism." Modern Intellectual History 5(3): 455–486

Walsh, Linda. 2012. "Canova, Neo-classicism and the Sculpted Body." In *Art and Visual Culture 1600–1850: Academy to Avant-Garde*, edited by Emma Barker, 219–259. London: Tate Publishing

Walsh, Linda and Antony Lentin. 2004a. "Course Introduction: Enlightenment and the Forces of Change". In *A207 From Enlightenment to Romanticism, c.1780–1830*, Block 1, 5–65. Milton Keynes: The Open University

Walsh, Linda and Antony Lentin. 2004b. "Course Conclusion: An Overview of Romanticism." In *A207 from Enlightenment to Romanticism, c.1780–1830*, Block 1, 109–145. Milton Keynes: The Open University

Walsh, Linda and Robert Wilkinson. 2004. "The Lake District: The Picturesque, the Beautiful and the Sublime." In *Industry and Changing Landscapes*, A207 (*From Enlightenment to Romanticism*) Block 4, 9–50. Milton Keynes: The Open University

Warner, Malcolm. 2004. "Ecce Equus: Stubbs and the Horse of Feeling." In *Stubbs and the Horse*, by Malcolm Warner and Robin Blake, with an essay by Lance Mayor and Gay Myers, 1–17. New Haven and London: Yale University Press

Wassyng Roworth, Wendy. 1992. "Kauffman and the Art of Painting in England." In *Angelica Kauffman: A Continental Artist in Georgian England*, edited by Wendy Wassyng Roworth, 11–95. London: Reaktion Books

Waterhouse, Ellis. 1994 (fifth edition; first published 1953). *Painting in Britain 1530–1790, with an Introduction by Michael Kitson*. New Haven and London: Yale University Press

Weber, Caroline. 2006. *Queen of Fashion: What Marie Antoinette Wore to the Revolution*. London: Aurum Press

Webster, Mary. 1979. *Hogarth*. London: Cassell Ltd

Weichsel, Eric. 2013. "'Most Horribly Done, and So Unfortunately Like': Émigré Artists at the Court of St James." In *Patronage, Visual Culture, and Courtly Life in Eighteenth-Century Germany and England*, edited by Catherine Tite, 51–76. New York: Cambria Press

Weisberg, Gabriel with William S. Talbot. 1979. *Chardin and the Still Life Tradition in France*. Cleveland: Cleveland Museum of Art

West, Shearer. 2008. "Grand Manner Portraiture." In *The History of British Art 1600–1870*, edited by David Bindman, 144–145. London: Tate Publishing

Wettlaufer, Alexander K. 1999. "Absent Fathers, Martyred Mothers: Domestic Drama and (Royal) Family Values in *A Graphic History of Louis XVI*." Eighteenth-Century Life 23(3): 1–37

Wheeler, Roxane. 2003. "Colonial Exchanges: Visualizing Racial Ideology and Labour in Britain and the West Indies." In *An Economy of Colour: Visual*

Culture and the Atlantic World, 1660–1830, edited by Geoff Quilley and Kay Dian Kriz, 36–59. Manchester: Manchester University Press

Whitley, W.T. 1915. *Thomas Gainsborough*. London: Smith, Elder and Co.

Williams, Laurence. 2015. "Anglo-Chinese Caresses: Civility, Friendship and Trade in English Representations of China, 1760–1800." Journal for Eighteenth-Century Studies 38(2): 277–296

Winckelmann, Johann Joachim. 1987 [1755]. *Reflections on the Imitation of Greek Works in Painting and Sculpture*, translated by Elfriede Heyer and Roger C. Norton. La Salle Illinois: Open Court

Wölfflin, Heinrich. 1950 (7th German edition, 1929; first published in German 1915), translated by M.D. Hottinger. *Principles of Art History: The Problem of the Development of Style in Later Art*. New York: Dover Publications Inc.

Wood, Marcus. 2000. *Blind Memory: Visual Representations of Slavery in England and America 1780–1865*. Manchester: Manchester University Press

Wood, Paul. 2012. "The Other Side of the World." In *Art and Visual Culture 1600–1850: Academy to Avant-Garde*, edited by Emma Barker, 261–297. London: Tate Publishing

Wrigley, Richard. 1993. *The Origins of French Art Criticism: From the Ancien Régime to the Restoration*. Oxford: Clarendon Press

Wrigley, Richard. 1998. "The Class of 89? Cultural Aspects of Bourgeois Identity in France in the Aftermath of the French Revolution in France." In *Art in Bourgeois Society 1790–1850*, edited by Andrew Hemingway and William Vaughan, 130–153. Cambridge: Cambridge University Press

Wrigley, Richard. 2007. "Genre Painting with Italy in Mind." In *French Genre Painting in the Eighteenth Century*, edited by Philip Conisbee, 245–273. New Haven and London: Yale University Press

Yarrington, Alison. 2001. "Art in the Dark: Viewing and Exhibiting Sculpture at Somerset House." In *Art on the Line: The Royal Academy Exhibitions at Somerset House 1780–1836*, edited by David H. Solkin, 173–187. New Haven and London: Yale University Press

Index

Note: The page numbers in *italics* denote figures